Gallery Books
Editor: Peter Fallon

TROUBLED THOUGHTS,
MAJESTIC DREAMS

Dennis O'Driscoll

TROUBLED THOUGHTS, MAJESTIC DREAMS

Selected Prose Writings

Gallery Books

Troubled Thoughts, Majestic Dreams
is first published
simultaneously in paperback
and in a clothbound edition
on 17 November 2001.

The Gallery Press
Loughcrew
Oldcastle
County Meath
Ireland

ISBN 1 85235 289 2 (*paperback*)
    1 85235 290 6 (*clothbound*)

A CIP catalogue record for this book
is available from the British Library.

The Gallery Press acknowledges the financial assistance
of An Chomhairle Ealaíon / The Arts Council, Ireland,
and the Arts Council of Northern Ireland.

Contents

for Nuala O'Farrell

Introduction

When, at a literary conference a few years ago, a Swiss poet asked me 'What is your aesthetic as a critic?', I heard myself reply, 'My aesthetic is the belief that there are good poets and bad poets and that one can tell the difference.' This bold declaration notwithstanding, perhaps I am less a fastidious critic than an obsessive reader, someone driven by the need to check out every poetry collection and periodical, someone whose commentaries are informed by primary reading rather than by aesthetics and theories. Indeed, the best justification I can offer for this unscholarly book is the hope that it will direct readers towards primary texts with which they may not yet be acquainted or that it will renew and refresh their interest in already-familiar poets.

Troubled Thoughts, Majestic Dreams is something of a journey through the poetry of our time, a time of world-wide prominence for Irish poetry and a time in which the translated poetry of the world reached Ireland and other English-speaking countries, much of it transported in exotic convoy by A Alvarez in his *Penguin Modern European Poets* volumes. Reviews of poets from Britain (our sometimes overlooked neighbour) and America (always a source of excitement and exasperation), together with a few personal essays, are also included. In making a representative selection from a large output of literary journalism, I have tried to produce the kind of book that provides an option on the casual dip as well as the methodical trawl.

If I tend to shy away from technical or prosodic analysis in my reviews, it is because of my conviction that such analysis bores and stultifies more than it stimulates. As I recalled in a *Poetry Ireland Review* essay (not reprinted here), schoolchildren of my generation studied both Latin and English prosody. Poems were examined by taking them apart, as animals were dissected in biology classes. Slice the rabbit of the poem and name its body parts: the trochee, the caesura, the trimeter, the enjambment . . . What redeemed this education and made for a matchless ground-

11

ing in poetry was the fact that the greatest poems were stockpiled in our memories through learning them by heart. Dissecting the poem taught students to identify the alveoli of its lungs; reciting it permitted them to hear it breathe. A technical analysis of a poem in a scientific era can seem overly eager for the art to be reducible to tangibles and measurables, diagrams and formulas. It is like defining a kiss in terms of the thirty-four muscles and the changes in the brain's amygdala which it involves.

As a reviewer, I am the product of a country which I have never visited: Australia. In 1977, when I was twenty-three, Vincent Buckley — Australian poet, Melbourne University professor, Leavisite critic, honorary Irishman (the phrase, 'we Munstermen', punctuated his conversation like the swing of an auto-hypnotic pendulum) — recommended me to Nuala O'Farrell, literary editor of the Dublin periodical, *Hibernia,* where I became poetry editor and its principal poetry reviewer. If Nuala (an inspirational presence, who was later to be the founding literary editor of the *Sunday Tribune* newspaper) had an aesthetic, it was one which placed a premium on discernment, fearlessness and liveliness in her reviewers — excellent qualities all, though a heady brew when combined with the innate brashness and arrogance of youth; while I like to think that I usually did justice to the books I reviewed, I readily plead guilty to my share of excesses and follies.

Also in 1977, at Seamus Heaney's house one summer Saturday morning, I found myself in the company of a fast-talking and fast-thinking young Australian poet called Les Murray who was acting editor of *Poetry Australia.* This happy encounter (followed by a picnic at Newgrange — Seamus's inaugural sounding of that megalith's chamber music) led to the first publication of my poems and longer critical pieces.

None of my reviews of Les Murray's work seemed to merit reprinting in this volume, although I still harbour hopes of saluting his linguistic inventiveness and formal variousness. Among the many other poets whose absence I regret is Marina Tsvetaeva, whom I elegized in verse and about whose ecstatic and tormented genius I have long intended to write. Indeed, if there are fewer women poets discussed in this collection than I'd wish, it is a result of the vagaries of the reviewing process and not because of any limits to my obsession.

My essays and reviews have been written in the spare half-hours of life. The earliest of them were soberly drafted on a high stool at the formica kitchen counter of the small flat I occupied in Dublin's Marlborough Road, around the corner from the flatland heartland of Ranelagh. Cooking smells would escape from the basement, while — from another flat — a pirate radio station's playlist vibrated through a party wall. But even when I had left the steamy laundrettes and all-night superettes behind, I continued— having little alternative, on account of my crust-earning day-job in the civil service — to work erratically more than systematically towards meeting editorial deadlines. The short review of Tomas Tranströmer was drafted, appropriately enough, in an ice-capped Stockholm where I was attending an EU Customs meeting. I associate my 'Map of Contemporary Irish Poetry' with Seville as much as Dublin; immured in my hotel room overlooking a Moorish wall, I sketched the final pages before joining two colleagues from Dublin (we were attending a course on illicit trafficking in endangered species) at the Irish pub, where they found solace each night of our week-long exile.

Inevitably, however, most of these pieces were written in less scenic circumstances: on steamed-up commuter buses with a pop radio station thumping in the foreground; or at home on an early Saturday morning, the dew still casting its beady eyes on the grass I would mow later in the day; or in the recesses of the night when lights were petering out and the world lapsing into silence. While it is customary to refer to reviewing as 'hack work', a chore performed to appease the rent-collector, my own experience has been different. Leaving aside the fact that, in any event, most magazines can afford to pay little or nothing, I regard the production of literary journalism as a pleasure in itself — an intense form of reading and writing: a stimulus to concentrated reading and a form of writing which offers freedom from anxiety when one's own haphazard poetry faculties are in recession. And, just as some of the most serendipitous dictionary discoveries are made on the way to the word one intended to look up in the first place, the extensive background reading required of the reviewer can lead to some cherished accidental discoveries.

The essential begetters of a book such as this will always be the editors whose cajolings encouraged one to undertake reviews when time did not seem to allow and who stretched the word allocation when space did not seem to permit. I therefore want to thank each of the editors of the publications acknowledged in this volume (including a succession of occupants of *Poetry Ireland Review*'s editorial swivel chair) — not least those editors with whom I have had the most extensive dealings: Mick Imlah (*Poetry Review* and *The Times Literary Supplement*), Peter Forbes (*Poetry Review*) and Stratis Haviaras (*Harvard Review*). In a few cases, such as 'A Map of Contemporary Irish Poetry', some small revision or updating has occurred.

Book publishing is a kind of applied criticism, so I am immensely grateful to Peter Fallon — founder of The Gallery Press and the first poet I saw plain when I came to work in Dublin in 1970 — for offering the most active form of encouragement possible. I also warmly acknowledge the debt of gratitude I owe to Jean Barry of The Gallery Press for her support. Dr Barbara Brown cheerfully undertook the cheerless task of retyping some Tipp-Exed pre-computer urtexts. Tom Guckian was the proof-reader over my shoulder. Finally I want to thank Sinéad Mac Aodha and An Chomhairle Ealaíon / The Arts Council, Ireland: a bursary in 1996 was the goad I needed to begin my excavations for the book which I suspected to be lurking somewhere inside the bulky mounds of old typescripts.

To my fellow-reviewers I am happy to leave the final word.

PART ONE
Autobiographies

Circling the Square: *A Thurles Prospect*

If it is mathematically possible for a square to be the centre of anything, then Liberty Square is the centre of Thurles. It is not, in fact, square-shaped — doubtless, the Christian Brothers' geometry book with its shiny, smelly pages, its spindly drawings and its baffling theorems would have supplied the exact term for it among its heptagons and trapezoids and isosceles triangles. As I passed over the Suir Bridge at the end of the Square, I was often tempted to hurl *pons asinorum* and its fellow theorems into the river. Only the fact that I was required to hand on the book to a younger sibling deterred me.

Apart from Maths and Science, I suffered the curricular subjects — Latin and English in particular — gladly enough. But as the final examinations came to an end, and ecstasy and optimism began to supplant pessimism and dread, the watery grave I had wished for my geometry book was inflicted on some poetry books by my vengeful classmates. Immediately after the English exam, a 'post mortem' took place in which answers were compared; then a noisy funeral service ensued, during which prescribed pamphlets of Milton and Wordsworth were cheered on their final journey over the railings and into Spenser's 'gentle' Suir. I felt like a man at a hanging, afraid to provoke the crowd by admitting to being a friend of the accused.

A town that calls a rectangle a square may be out of line in other respects also. In the matter of saluting friends and acquaintances, things are somewhat backward. The answer precedes the question.

'Well', someone will begin, without the slightest interrogative inflection.

'How ya?', his friend will respond.

And those buses parked each Saturday in the Square — what on earth is a canary yellow bus marked 'Heathrow' or the less flashy one announcing 'Welsh Valley Tours' doing there? Is the town a Bermudan Triangle for buses? Or an unlikely tourist destination? Ask the driver and his French-like Tipperary 'r's will admit that his second-hand bus is destined for nowhere more exotic than Drangan or Drombane. The Welsh Valley bus is crammed with plastic carrier bags rather than holiday suitcases. The Heathrow bus is enjoying a new lease of life among the byroads of Tipperary, paying unconscious tribute to Tony Ryan, the Thurles man who got aviation leasing off the ground.

Thurles has had other aberrations to offer also — the New Cinema, for instance. How could such a building — obviously well into its flaking dotage — be called 'new'? We were perplexed when the teacher posed this challenge to our ten-year-old brains, until I ventured triumphantly, 'Because it was new when it got the name, sir'. Knowing that my grandmother numbered women called Baby and Babs among her friends and coevals helped me to intuit the answer. The films that were shown at the time in Thurles's two cinemas (the Capitol being the alternative venue) weren't exactly new either, and I remember being treated to Sunday matinées of Old Mother Reilly who had stomped straight out of the *Film Fun* comics of my father's generation. I also recall some pathetic film or other being trumpeted on the basis of 'Last Showing in Ireland', which I recognized even then as a pretty desperate advertising strategy.

The house near Thurles where I grew up, with two sisters and three brothers, is called 'Galtee View', though I am by no means sure that the dim scribble of upland to be seen from its bay windows is in fact the Galtees. A Trade Descriptions Act would have a difficult time around Thurles. What was easily identified — if not easily described — was the peculiar smell that every breeze brought us from the sugar factory in the distance. That fermenting odour can never be displaced from the memory of any Thurlesian, nor can the sight of the pale, parsnip-like sugar beets that would tumble from overloaded trucks.

The sugar factory offered work during its 'campaign' to temporary staff. In summer, those in search of casual employment could turn to the bogs a few miles from the town. 'Footing' turf quickly exhausted the townies and most of us had to draw on fictional resources to conjure up the early start, the twittering lark, the blue sky, the implements, the back-breaking labour, the compensatory lunch-bag of wholesome country food, as we struggled to satisfy our teachers' perennial appetite for an essay about 'A Day on the Bog'. Sods of rich brittle turf — barm bracks in which real gold might be found buried — would be dislodged at crossroads and sharp bends; old men would hobble out from town to gather them. How well I can understand why the German artist, Joseph Beuys, smeared some nutritious-looking peat briquettes with butter during an Irish visit and designated them to be works of art.

Work was an awesome concept as one reached the final year at school. A good Leaving Cert would mean a 'call to training' from one of the teacher colleges in Dublin or Limerick or entry as a 'Junior Ex' in the civil service — in short, a 'better' life than bog or sugar factory seemed destined to offer. As I learned the chief industries of Norway or the odes of Keats by heart, I knew that everything in my future depended on my studies. As an added incentive, a tongue-biting teacher would occasionally demonstrate the effects of a thick leather strap on thin pink skin. One of the Christian Brothers admonished us: 'Christian Brothers' boys don't fall in for money or businesses like boys from richer backgrounds. You will have to *work* for a living.'

The Christian Brothers' school which I attended until — barely sixteen-and-a-half — I sat my Leaving Cert exams in 1970, was actually a more mixed school than that Brother seemed to realise. Not 'mixed' in sexual terms — I hadn't encountered a female teacher or pupil within its precincts — but 'mixed' in the socio-economic sense. The sons of doctors and bank managers and 'strong' farmers carved their initials in the old wooden benches alongside those from poorer backgrounds. The name 'Ryan' crossed the class barrier and had to be qualified in some way. 'Which Ryan is he?' an adult would be heard asking. And back would come his verbal identification tag — he would prove to be Ryan Sweep, Ryan Bishop, Ryan Fox, Ryan Linnet or some other Ryan from the litany or menagerie of possibilities.

While the school undoubtedly offered more equality and fraternity (whatever about liberty) than might be found in most city establishments, it would be wrong to pretend that snobbery was unknown. Its nuances were communicated by parents who urged their precious offspring to shun children from mere terraces rather than from individually-named bungalows. A few families sent their sons and daughters to more sophisticated schools in the final year or two, hoping — vainly, in every sense — that boarding school would add a polish to their dull surfaces. During one of our 'religion' classes in a dusty, partitioned, creosote-reeking room at the top of a metal stairs that would barely qualify as a fire-escape, a Brother was dishing out advice:

'Don't even dream of marrying a girl from a better-off background than your own — it'll never work out. A girl from a poorer family will more easily rise to your level.'

Although things became more flexible under the headmastership of Brother Peter Guilfoyle, an inspiring and cultivated man, the commitment to Gaelic games demanded of the school's pupils was enormous. The Gaelic Athletic Association had, after all, been founded at Hayes's Hotel down the street. And we regularly enjoyed half-days from school when Tipperary's hurlers were indomitable and former pupils like Jimmy Doyle held up the All-Ireland trophy like a chalice for our cheers. Most cheered for Jimmy, a few of us for the half-day. I was one of the dissidents who attended national hurling games in the town only to watch the three-card-trick man's dazzling dexterity or to listen to the hawkers ('Ice-cream. Suir Valley Ice-Cream. The last few tubs of ices now') and showmen ('Come on and have a go with your old friend Joe; your mother won't know and I won't tell her').

There was a hurling field, Kickham Park, next to our house. I had been kitted out with studded O'Neill boots and an ash-blond hurley. My elder brother stockpiled back-issues of *Gaelic Weekly*. Past games could be relived in a wallpaper sampler that had become a scrapbook for GAA cuttings in our sitting room. But some genetic freak (for there were hurling fanatics on both sides of the family) rendered me useless and, worse, indifferent when it came to hurling. I would make one or two asthmatic runs after a ball to stay warm during school sports sessions in the railway field. After a few wild swipes at the air with my stick (more Christy Mahon than Christy Ring), cries of 'Keep out of the way, Driscoll' would reach me from a contemptuous full-forward and I'd retreat towards the sideline to my friend John Hickey. John, like a number of students in the school, came from the Kilkenny side of the border and, so, might have seemed less friend than foe to those who viewed the world in hurling terms.

It was with John Hickey that I slipped away from the school crowd as we were being marched to 'games' one afternoon, the way we had marched in pairs to Confession when younger. John and I took our places in the public gallery of the courthouse near the school. We passed an absorbing afternoon watching neighbours accusing each other and witnesses contradicting each other. What we didn't know was that the rain had begun to descend even more copiously than normal and that our drenched classmates had been herded back to the schoolroom. It was then (and only then) that we were missed. In my speech for the defence next morning, I said that I had gone to the court because I was hoping to make a career of the law when I left school. A grudging reprieve was granted and I later fulfilled my undertaking to study Law.

When club games were held in Kickham Park, it was once again the peripheral excitement rather than the sport that would entice me from our back garden. If I wasn't standing behind one of the goalposts acting as a kind of ball boy, I'd be tormenting the man who sold fruit, chocolate and minerals from a van that seemed as ancient as himself: 'Have you any turnips there, Danny?', I'd ask, convinced I was a born comedian. One night after a game, Danny offered a lift to a hurler who was walking the mile or so back to the town. 'No thanks, Danny,' the player answered, charily eyeing the van, 'I'm in a bit of a hurry.'

The teams' supporters would be hoarse with shouting 'Go at 'em like tarriers' or 'Keep the ball on the ground' and rushing about with water bottles and bandages and sections of orange. As the tussle between the teams intensified, the language became less sporting and, at one time, a painted sign stood at the end of the field insisting in large, hand-shaped letters: 'NO CURSING, by Order of the Committee'. I represented the Kickhams' own team in 1966 and actually won a silver medal — not for hurling, needless to say, but for verse-speaking. I declaimed poetry from the back of a truck in Templemore, having reached the final of a festival of sports and culture in honour of Thomas MacDonagh, the Tipperary-born poet and patriot who had been executed fifty years before. My twelve-year-old mug scowled out of a number of newspapers and I was mocked both within and without the family for my sissy accomplishment.

Of the sights to be witnessed on the way home from school, none was more startling than the battery hens to be seen at the front of Danny the van driver's house. As well as hawking at hurling matches, he used to kill and pluck poultry for a fee. He carried out his death sentence slowly — he placed an old car battery on each neck, and, taking a short detour, we would watch the writhing feathers on his lawn. Like wary politicians, we were forever taking detours, afraid to risk the deadening boredom of the same route home two days in a row. Detours to look at the Dinky cars in Kilroy's. Detours to pick out a comic from the dark hardwood display in Russell's newsagents. Detours to check whether the conkers had begun to swell the huge chestnut tree on Ikerrin Road. Detours to view a model tyre in Shanahan's Kickham Street garage or to buy a lucky bag in Muck Gleeson's of Mitchel Street. Like most people, we called Kickham Street and Mitchel Street by their older names, The Pike and The Quarry, chanting

> *Up The Quarry and down The Pike,*
> *That's the way to ride the bike.*

The journey home from school was full of patriotic possibilities, of which streets named after John Mitchel and Charles Kickham were typical. Every taste in heroes was catered for, other streets offering options on Emmet, Parnell, O'Donovan Rossa and Cuchulain. It was the shops, however, and not the names of the streets they stood in which inspired us as children. Sutton's smelled of a nutritious mixture of the grains, seeds, meals and fertilisers that were scooped from open jute sacks. Molloy's and J K Moloney's used a pulley system to transport money from customer to cashier. Harry Cuthbert presided brusquely over his ice-cream machine. The mynah bird in Condon's miniature sweet shop loved the sound of its own voice.

There was a branch of F W Woolworth which we walked round and round during wet lunch hours. The greatest attraction of the place was its stock of exotic, garishly-coloured American comics featuring cartoon characters or outer-space voyagers or heroes of classics and fables. They were fascinatingly different from our usual fare of *Beano* and *Topper*, with ads for pimple removers and trick cushions and prices in dollars and cents. Even the coupons interested me. What was a zip code? Was Tipperary a state? I was reminded of early childhood when I wasn't sure where I lived but conjured up a sleek and ghastly, machine-like vision of the country called 'Ironland' of which my parents often spoke.

The pimples foretold by the American comics surfaced in due course. Pimples and awareness of sex erupted simultaneously and somewhat incompatibly. We began with the vaguest of ideas about sex, ideas embodied by a girl in a blue Ursuline uniform whom we would have ignored or disdained not long before. The clerical students from St Patrick's seminary who came to our school as religious instructors were tolerant, frank and unsensational in the face of provocative interrogation on the subject. They fleshed out our vocabulary and theoretical knowledge but we still had only a shaky perception of what it amounted to in practice. One Thurles friend told me recently that, prior to receiving education on the topic, he thought sex was 'something vaguely like yoga'. While in Buttevant, as a supporter of the school hurling team, he bought a book called 'Techniques of Sex' from a stall. When he perused its contents on the train back to Thurles, he was both educated and alarmed. When a Christian Brother in the carriage asked him what he was reading, real panic set in.

If you were 'going out with' or 'shifting' someone in the town, your attempts to keep the relationship private would be futile. Your first slow march together down the 'watery mall' would scarcely have begun when news of your forwardness would have reached home. Like smoking (shops near the school sold single cigarettes), kissing was one of those activities that never went unobserved. It was the late Sixties and, even if love was not free, hair grew longer, skirts drew shorter, Simon and Garfunkel filled the youth club with the sound of silence, Rolling Stones clones toted guitars at talent competitions and some of the Christian Brothers' liveliest pupils flirted with what passed in Thurles for Maoism (but even the most paranoid adults can hardly have credited that Liberty Square was in any danger of becoming a red square). Though there were 'socials' in the Confraternity Hall, Sunday afternoon 'hops' in Holycross, showbands in the Premier Hall and *céilí* classes in Glenmorgan House, I was content to see life from the standpoint of the Square at lunchtime, the place itself like a dancehall with young males and females congregating separately. One lad, having left school early and found gainful employment clearing the drains at the mushroom plant, was the first of my generation to marry. On his wedding morning, he declared, 'Sure I might as well be a poor man as a poor boy!'

'Free education' was a dividend of the Sixties and with it came the 'free buses' which allowed a good deal more freedom for the sexes to mingle on the way to and from school. The dawn chorus of rattling bicycles on our potholed road came to an abrupt stop. My family lived too close to the town for any of us to qualify for free transport. We spoke of 'townies' with some derision but we weren't quite from the country either. My father was a farmer's son with a foot in the business world and this, too, denied us a clear-cut identity. Mill Road, where we grew up, was one road that lived up to its name, with mills and the remains of mills to prove it. We would watch the paddle-boat mill-wheel at Burns's scooping up the green scummy water. The nearby house, occupied by Paddy Doran — later acclaimed for his skill with greyhounds — was prone to flooding. Virtually every winter, Paddy would have occasion to wade calmly downstairs to a float-ing kitchen.

Farther up the road was Brady's mill, an imposing cut-stone structure. Dan and Josie Brady had retreated to a few habitable rooms in this cavernous building which smelled of mildew, decaying apples, drying clothes, pink paraffin, Churchman's cigarettes. Josie Brady had been a talented musician and still loved to listen to *céilí* music or take part in a sing-song. 'O laws!', she'd exclaim as she reminisced about hours of listening to the Gallowglass Céilí Band at the Fleadh Ceoil or nights of dancing in Borrisoleigh. At dusk, accompanied by Rex the terrier, she would venture out past spicy box hedging and a precarious sculpture of bottles and jam jars to check the water level for some official survey in Dublin. I often posted the cards containing those scrupulously-recorded details of river and mill-race; and I often shopped for Josie as well as my mother after half-ten Mass during the summer holidays. Apart from groceries, I might have to fetch some item of clothing or hardware on 'appro', the shop assistant recording this fact in a ledger until the customer's choice was made and the goods were either bought or returned. Payment for the items could be postponed, as 'tick' was generally granted.

Dan Brady was a sombre man with a quizzical mind. He constructed a loom that produced herringbone tweed and he harnessed the river's current for electricity. When the water level was low on summer evenings, he could rely on an hour or two at most of power: the bulb would flicker, then peter out altogether. The Tilly lamp would be primed for lighting, while my brother Seamus and I sat on the old leather car seat chatting with the Bradys as the day faded out. The principal attraction of Bradys' was television, which my parents refused to sanction at home in case it might interfere with our studies. My first encounter with television, as with so many things (life included — I was born in St Anne's Nursing Home on the Square in 1954) took place on Liberty Square. Telefís Éireann had recently begun its broadcasts and O'Connor's electrical shop was displaying the new device in its window. I joined scores of gloved and hatted viewers outside that window one frosty night to watch — through plumes of breath — an episode of 'Have Gun Will Travel'. We were awe-struck by the invention, the neatness of it, the luxury of it (a cinema at home). A TV Rentals company would soon open farther up the Square.

If you didn't feel inclined to join one of the local clubs and societies in Thurles, there wasn't much to do except talk or take to the high stool. Television aerials began to sprout as suddenly as the mushrooms we used to gather in soft white clumps, their mousy underbellies a pleated marvel. The advent of television did little to affect the level of drinking, since most pubs had acquired a set, but it greatly reduced the incidence of 'visiting' — calling, usually unannounced, on neighbours for a gossipy chat.

Our own entertainments included the Sunday drive — out to Holycross and back by the sugar factory is a route I recall glumly. Or we went 'rambling' with the golden cocker — exploring near-by fields, leaping over ditches of watercress and slime, listening to the narcotic whirrings of summer. Or we picked blackcurrants near a drowsy rose bed in our garden. Or blew bubbles. Or played Post Office. Or laid traps for wasps, counting the corpses in their Kilkenny colours of black and amber. Or on Saturdays we'd watch the traders on the Square peddling glass cutters and pencil torches and second-hand suits. Or on wet Sundays we'd attend a Sale of Work in aid of one of the convents and defer breathing until the Wheel of Fortune had made up its mind where to stop. Or there were Shamrock Bus tours to Glengarriff and The Burren with yarn-spinning drivers and ballad-singing passengers. There were plays: Jackie Andy Ryan directed a cast of seminarians in *Juno and the Paycock* at St Patrick's College, the falsetto rising among the birettas; the annual Muintir na Tíre Drama Festival introduced me to Ibsen, Sheridan, Synge and an even more obscure (and, as yet, pre-Nobel) playwright who provoked me and my schoolfriend Michael Kennedy to outbursts of absurd dialogue after the Guinness Players performed *Waiting for Godot* in the Premier Hall.

And there was the Library where Queenie ruled so benevolently, her voice softened by a lifetime of whispering. She knew everyone's taste and would select a 'doctor and nurse' story for my mother or a military history book for my father if they were too busy or unwell to make a visit themselves. I wouldn't let anyone do my choosing for me, though my choices were predictable enough for years, especially as I had stuck with Enid Blyton the whole way from Noddy to The Famous Five. I dared to interrupt the author's prodigious flow with a fan letter, to which she responded in neat blue biro and characteristically excitable style: 'Thank you for your well-written letter . . . Perhaps one day you will write a book — what a thrill that would be for you — and how proud you would feel when you saw your very own book in the public library! . . .'

In time, Enid Blyton's works were displaced in my canon by Bunter rolling into the quad (no mistaken geometry there), William waging war against civilization and, best and funniest of all, Jennings aghast at seeing his dead-cert plans go awry. The Jennings stories were the first in which I noticed (or was taught to notice by *A Bookful of Jennings*) the contribution that imagery and style could make to the enjoyable telling of a story: 'His glasses were perched athwart his nose like a percentage sign'; 'He tut-tutted like a Geiger counter stuttering over a deposit of uranium.'

I rigged up a large tea-chest, padded with cushions like a sedan chair, and did much of my summer reading within its confines. On other days during holiday periods, I would go cycling with my friend David O'Connor. We would identify an old monastic site from the map, pedalling there past cottages with open doors and plundered Anglia cars, past sleeping sheepdogs and gawking children. We made trips to Kilcooley and Holycross and Hore Abbeys and several to Leigh, a monastery founded in AD 580 — the first recorded fact in Kennedy's *Chronology of Thurles*. We enjoyed the compacted peace within its walls and marvelled at the slim crucifix on one of the tombs. At roof level, a warm breeze ruffling David's Beatle-style haircut, we would look across lush fields and grazing dairy herds and lapping brown oceans of Bórd na Móna bog. I wrote an avant-garde poem about the place when I was in my early teens and I composed the club anthem for the Lone Pine Club, a treasure-hunting, adventure-seeking society based on Malcolm Saville's suspenseful stories. Somehow we failed to achieve the level of excitement attained by our fictional models and, after a few attempts to shadow suspicious-looking characters around the town had proved less than conclusive, we disbanded. Derrynaflan was only eight miles away — well within our cycling range — but it was two non-members with tutting Geiger counters who would later discover the ornate gold treasure hoarded there.

Other summer diversion was provided at Ladyswell by a tame stretch of the river that flowed just beyond Burns's mill. A swimming pool, promised to the town for years, had still not materialized — one of the essays for which I had won a prize in local competitions was called 'Dream Swimming Pool'. Meanwhile, the rough banks of the gravelly river had to suffice on warm days for the children clutching jam jars in which short-lived gudgeons were caught. The grown-ups were swimming in the deeper, dammed part of the river, splashing and showing off or teaching girls how to stay afloat without needing a patched tractor tube to do so.

After the swimmers' short season had dissolved in rain, Ladyswell was abandoned to the fishermen. A cooked trout, the same colour as my distempered bedroom, had landed on my plate a few times after my father had gone fishing. There was a spring at Ladyswell from which neighbouring women carried buckets of water for drinking and cooking. A bucket was hung from each handle of the bicycle which they wheeled back slowly in all weathers, chatting and spilling an occasional asterisk of water on the road. Water for washing purposes was collected from rain barrels linked to drainpipes. Winter mornings began with a breaking of patterned ice.

The weather as the Inter and Leaving Cert examinations loomed always seemed uncharacteristically hot. I remember studying the Mithridatic wars in a bedroom that threatened to curl with the heat. Summer was a rich cacophony of sounds — a pheasant like a squeezed toy, the lingering bark of a fox, the teasing call of a cuckoo, an air force of insects. A ball thuds on hard ground. The conversation of two cyclists rises and falls. Maybe rock 'n' roll music can be heard from a carnival in the town and the imagination takes in chairoplanes and bumpers.

When we were younger, we would have been tucked in bed while all this commotion was occurring beyond the open window. I thought perhaps of these lines from *A Child's Garden of Verses*, the first of many books of poems I borrowed from Thurles library:

> *In winter I get up at night*
> *And dress by yellow candle-light.*
> *In summer, quite the other way,*
> *I have to go to bed by day . . .*

But there would be tomorrow for playing with the Tri-ang trucks in the sandpit. Or for speeding downhill in the 'toboggan' which Seamus and I had built on pram wheels. Or we might exercise the new-found freedom of cycling, by heading up the road past Cawleys' wattle tent. Mary and Johnny Cawley — guarded by their mongrel dogs, Trigger and Flash — were as fierce of demeanour and smoked of skin as any Hollywood Indians but friendly and deferential towards those who had made peace offerings of 'coppers' or food. If we ventured as far as the town, we might discover we had enough money (especially if an uncle has presented us with 'change') for a ripple ice-cream and a bottle of Sinalco at Bertie Connaughton's. The little tailor might be steering his Baby Ford towards Mitchel Street; and there's Johnny Connors, not exactly a giant either, surveying the world from Molloy's corner.

Childhood summers blend into one another for most people. For me, the mowing tractors and sighing cornfields and blooming cowslips belong to no particular summer. The smell of hay was pervasive. The red evenings, flushed with the day's excitement, lingered for a last look before crumbling into a powdery darkness. As the light dimmed, the phosphorescent statue of Our Lady glowed comfortingly in my bedroom. A plaque above my bed showed a child with a candle illuminating the words 'If I die before I wake / I pray the Lord my soul to take.'

The Catholic Church, to which the care of most of the town's souls was entrusted, brought social as well as spiritual comforts to its flock. The half-ten Masses I attended in Thurles cathedral during holidays drew people together for chat as well as prayer. Occasions for prayer seemed infinite — First Fridays, Stations of the Cross, Benediction of the Blessed Sacrament, Our Lady's and Sacred Heart sodalities, Corpus Christi and May processions, Holy Week . . . Retreats brought their own special frisson — the men and women had separate retreats (because they yielded to separate categories of sin perhaps?) as well as separate sodalities and a favoured side of the church. We had a powerful and cathartic sense of spiritual uplift when the visiting preachers had preached, evil habits had been confessed, the Papal Blessing had been administered and the final hymn — 'Faith of Our Fathers' probably — was sung in spirited unison through a haze of holiness and incense.

The Archbishop's palace, the Presentation convent, St Patrick's seminary, the presbytery and the Pallotine Fathers' college extend out at one side of the river. On the other side — like the second wing of the Holy Ghost — are the Christian Brothers' schools and part of the Ursuline girls' school. St Patrick's College is said to have been proposed in 1851 as a suitable location for the planned

Catholic University. Would the sonnets of Gerard Manley Hopkins have been more 'terrible' from a Thurlesian exile? What would the student Joyce have made of the Thurles dialect? The college having in fact become a succesful training centre for priests, an extension was opened in the mid-Sixties reflecting an optimism that was rebuffed by a more secular age: the road to heaven is paved with good intentions. The names of the newly-ordained now take up a very modest space in *The Tipperary Star*.

Like other boys in Thurles, my earliest education was at the hands of nuns, the Presentation Sisters in my case. I remember the teachers at the convent as patient and generous, tending our homesickness with some of the most marvellous toys I had ever seen (a pedal-car fuelled my fantasies for months; a farm set was displayed in a glass case like Sunday china). I had learned to read before I started school at the age of four and I was repeatedly called upon to demonstrate my skill to every visiting nun and inspector. My refusal to drink school milk was looked on in a less indulgent light. I hated the stuff and was more than happy to leave it to its rightful owners, the calves. The formidable Sister Benedict ordered me to stand under a crucifix in her office and gulp down a chalky tumbler of the substance, bearing in mind the sacrifices God had made for mankind. It was the last glass of milk I ever drank.

The sacrifices we made for God included abstaining from sweets for Lent, resulting in gluttonous Easter Sundays. I enlisted in the school branch of the Legion of Mary where my first duty was the delivering of Catholic newspapers with my classmate Michael Donnelly. One Sunday, cutting through the grounds of St Mary's Protestant church on our paper round, we paused to hear the small congregation praying and singing unfamiliar hymns. Out of curiosity and rebelliousness, we longed to enter the plain damp building with jeeps and towbar-fitted cars parked outside. But there was little ecumenical spirit at the time and our under-arm sheaves of *Irish Catholic* and *Catholic Standard* seemed hardly likely to inaugurate it.

As older Legionaries, we visited the Hospital of the Assumption, alias the County Home, originally the workhouse, and chatted with inmates. A number were bedridden; others strolled vacantly around the garden or huddled in the 'smoke house', a structure rather like a public shelter in an English seaside town. The comparison wouldn't have occurred to me at the time, holidays in Curracloe or washed-out day-trips to Clonea or Tramore being all I knew of the sea. We were inland people with accents as flat as the landscape. Thurles was pronounced 'Turrless'. When an English tourist asked me if she was on the right road for Thurles, the perfect tongued-and-grooved 'Th' of her pronunciation and the way she rhymed it with 'hurls' confounded me. Having denied all knowledge of the place, the embarrassing truth dawned on me a couple of minutes after she had disappeared into exhaust smoke and virtually reached her elusive destination.

To grow up in Thurles, whatever one's pronunciation of the name, was to grow up in an anonymous town with no claim on national, let alone international, attention. We regarded Radio Éireann as far too Dublin-centred and, later, too preoccupied with 'The North'. But we survived without attention, self-contained and parochial, old-fashioned in our dark suits and jumpers like photos of Albania. We drank Pomara or County Lemonade and were refreshed by it. We bought solid ice-cream cones in The Milk Bar and were glad of them. We went to Scanlon's or Kennedy's or Killackey's or Hayes's if our bicycles needed fixing. Willie Moroney would sing to us from the organ loft of the cathedral or give us a 'tight' haircut in his barber's shop. We flowed with the consistency of the river up the Square each year in the Corpus Christi procession, the shops replacing brushed-nylon nighties and Guinness toucans with plaster statues and piously embroidered linen cloths. We received Communion hosts at the altar rails and ate local bread — Sweeney's, Coady's, Butler's — around our kitchen tables.

The essential point, of course, is that one can experience immortality anywhere. My childhood intimations in Thurles were as strong as Wordsworth's in Cumbria, the same unshake-able sense of being among eternal things that I would enjoy eternally. It is because such certainties are irrecoverable that places associated with childhood become imbued with a wonder that is more than mere nostalgia. This is no doubt one of the reasons I am always glad when the train eases itself into Thurles station and the water tower can be seen above the town like a parachute. And perhaps it is also why, even so long after my inevitable departure to a civil service job in Dublin, I always feel a bit gloomy when I take my place on the platform to leave behind again all that the town stands for. As I climb into the smoky, beery Sunday evening train, I recall the railway carriage lines from *A Child's Garden of Verses*:

Here is a child who clambers and scrambles,
All by himself and gathering brambles;
Here is a tramp who stands and gazes;
And there is the green for stringing the daisies!
Here is a cart run away in the road
Lumping along with man and load;
And here is a mill, and there is a river:
Each a glimpse and gone for ever!

Thurles: The Cathedral Town, edited
by William Corbett and William Nolan
(Geography Publications, 1989)

At Work

We are a cautious, conscientious bunch on the whole, well-intentioned, middle-of-the-road, always aware there are two sides to every story; family men in anoraks and belted raincoats; night-classing women with sensible shoes; church fund-raisers and sports club secretaries; stalwarts of the pub quiz and the amateur drama circuit.

On a commuter train, you can distinguish us from the business classes, our footwear less shined, our creases less sharp, our cases less chic. On the roads, our tarnished Escorts and Fiestas are never mistaken for company cars. C H Sisson, who once described himself as 'primarily a civil servant — like Chaucer', has summed us up:

> For the most part they are people who find no great diffi-
> culty in keeping regular hours, performing tasks assigned
> to them, sleeping regularly with the same partners. There
> are people who can do none of these things, but our kind of
> fun is not for them. We can rely on one another, we get
> our money regular; we make, one way and another, an
> infuriating phalanx to people who are without these really
> common gifts.

Our index-linked lives may indeed infuriate outsiders; yet it is the ones who got away that I envy. Hugh Leonard, for instance, is sixty-five this year — just the right age to be collecting his pension and his Waterford Glass bowl, after a speech by the Assistant Secretary assuring him of the high esteem in which he was held. Instead, Leonard left his job after fourteen years, ignoring the advice of his boss to 'give up all this playwriting nonsense'.

I live in Dalkey and see enough of Hugh Leonard's sleek Jaguar to suspect that he hasn't had much cause to lament the loss of his Land Commission clerkship. Others, though, were determined to lament on his behalf. In his autobiography, *Out After Dark*, he recalls being taunted by a simpering civil servant with the assurance that, if only he had been smart enough to remain at his desk, 'You could have been an Assistant Principal by now.'

In 1965, Thomas Kinsella stepped down from the celestial heights of an Assistant Principalship to the less secure footing of an American campus. While he was still in the Department of Finance, he told an interviewer that poetry was 'really rather an intense hobby' and added:

> *I'm a civil servant and was actually a civil servant before I wrote any poetry. I never found any clash between the two. In fact, I've found that my mental state when composing a particularly difficult minute is not unlike the process of writing a poem.*

This, to adapt a line of Kinsella's, 'is where I come in'. I was appointed an Assistant Principal when I was twenty-nine and have resisted further promotion. As a member of the Revenue Commissioners' staff, working in the Stamp Duty Office in Dublin Castle, I belong to one of the less popular State institutions ('the lowest form of life', according to one of our 'customers'). My office employs a staff of forty-four and collects vast sums annually from transfers and allotments of shares, sales of property, levies on insurance companies. To ameliorate my image among the literary populace, I can cite the fact that artistic income is tax-free in Ireland, books are not subject to VAT and it is offices such as mine which make the funding of the Arts Council and Aosdána possible.

When publication of my book, *Hidden Extras*, was imminent in 1987, it was announced in *British Book News* as 'a second collection of poems by a tax inspector from Dublin'. I am not, nor have I ever been, party to income tax work. And if I *had* had such a past, publicizing the fact hardly seemed calculated to win poetry sales. Even in an age when poets are tumbling clumsily over each other to find new angles from which to peddle their wares, the Revenue Commissioners angle is a definite non-starter.

Because my job involves interpretation of countless legal minutiae, much of my time is spent dealing with solicitors by letter or phone. Accountants and financial controllers make an appearance sometimes also. And when it comes to escaping the tax net, ex-members of staff — water bailiffs turned poachers — can be the most tenacious anglers for concessions on their clients' behalf. Company amalgamations and reconstructions, *in specie* distributions, site fines and declarations of trust are the stuff my days are made of. I am involved in some drafting of legislation and in preparing appeal cases for the High Court. I have seen Brussels and its Brueghels as a member of a working party on Capital Duty. When the Stamp Duty sections of the Finance Bill are discussed in the Dáil or Seanad, I may find myself in the chamber fleetingly, script in hand, lest the Minister need prompting. At my annual appraisal (a sort of end-of-term report), my superiors give me a higher rating for my 'judgement', 'knowledge of job' and 'performance under pressure' than for 'creativity'.

My being a civil servant at all is due to an accident of birth. If you finish your Leaving Certificate at sixteen, you will find yourself too young for many positions, no matter how respectable your exam results prove to be. Then a stencilled letter comes from the Civil Service Commission offering to accept you as an Executive Officer provided you are 'seventeen years of age on the 1st day of January in the year following entry'. Having been born on New Year's Day, my destiny was sealed. I was presumably — dubious honour — the youngest Executive Officer ever recruited. I opted for the Estate Duty Office, where my starting salary in 1970 was £865 a year and, in due course (a form of words I learned to flaunt in letters), I would be sent to UCD to study Law.

The first challenge in the Estate Duty Office was to find my bearings in a green-covered tome called *Acts and Orders Relating to Death Duties*. Once established at my desk, I became adept at intuiting when the funeral expenses claimed on an Inland Revenue Affidavit (IRA for short) were excessive and at distinguishing a parol trust from a resulting trust. Both work and management were approached with a certain formality: elaborate rituals attached to the 'entries' inscribed on files; older officers were addressed as 'Mister' or 'Miss'. The Misters and Misses danced together each Christmas when desks were stacked away and huge ledgers, embossed with the words 'DEATH INDEX', formed a backdrop to the seasonal gyrations. If a female member of staff married someone from within (a common occurrence) or without the civil service, she was obliged to resign, as though she had somehow disgraced herself.

Death Duties were abolished in 1975. We cheered, of course (Death Duties, you shall die . . .), but we continued to break stone after their reincarnation as Capital Acquisitions Tax. The significance of the abolition for me was its confirmation of the artificiality and aridity of our work. People had spent lifetimes acquiring expertise in particular sections of the Death Duties legislation — families were clothed, fed, reared and educated on the fruits of such evanescent knowledge. Suddenly whole swathes of it were worthless. As a colleague sighed, 'There's no *truth* in tax.'

The poetry and criticism I write is invariably produced after a day's work or on weekends. I leave home at 8.30 and return, deflated, ten hours later. There are still letters to be answered, domestic chores to be performed . . . The idea (and it is amazingly prevalent) that the pace of an office is leisurely enough to allow for some surreptitious composition of poetry is a preposterous one. The telephone shrieks and a solicitor launches into a long hypothetical question. A lachrymose member of staff begs to be transferred to another room or another task. A messenger arrives with *Business and Finance* and *The Weekly Law Reports*. Above all, a pyramid of importunate files is building up. Meanwhile, poems die, ideas are forgotten. As C P Cavafy, a civil servant for thirty years, was well aware, there are penalties to be paid for attempting to serve both Muse and Mammon:

> *How often, in the middle of work, a wonderful idea comes to me, some rare image, sudden verses rising as if fully formed, and I have to put them aside, because the job can't wait. Then, when I go home and have revived somewhat, I try to call them up again — and they're gone. And so it should be. It's as if Art were telling me: I am not some slave, to be dismissed when I come, and to come when it pleases you. I am the supreme Mistress of the world. And if you've turned your back on me — poor wretch and traitor that you are — for this nice little house of yours, and your nice little suit of clothes, for your nice little position in society, then be contented with these things (but how could you be?) and with those few moments when I come and you happen to be ready, waiting to receive me on your doorstep — as you should be, every day.*

Life in an office may be a numbing experience but it is also a representative one — and one which itself can become subject-matter for poetry. To a casual caller, the office is a hushed, mysterious place with magnolia corridors, down which a man in shirt sleeves is walking, file in hand. For those of us who know the reality better, the full gamut of humanity can be identified here — the gamblers, the gossips, the 'characters', the wasters. Suicides, sudden deaths, accidents are visited on staff — not even the most secure job in the most fortified castle is a defence against tragedy. And an office and its hierarchy are the sources of other dramas, in which ambition, jealousy or romance play a part.

Poetry rarely impinges on the lives of my colleagues, although I am enlisted to help with competitions that require quotations to be identified or slogans to be completed. I have composed authentic doggerel for those occasions when a collection is taken up and a massive pink card, graced by a grinning rabbit, is circulated for signature: twenty-firsts, marriages, retirements. The appearance of some lines from Derek Mahon's 'Penhurst Place' on an Irish Life calendar made his work the improbable target of mutterings about the 'chopped-up prose' of modern poetry. Yet, when I publish a book, some of my colleagues are generous enough not only to tolerate this minor eccentricity but to indulge it to the extent of paying for a copy. If poetry has been of limited practical value to me at work, my work has proved invaluable to me in many ways. Both in literary life and family life, my capacity to draft a will and to act as executor has saved money and misery. The discipline acquired in organizing work and in meeting deadlines is of immense benefit also.

My plate glass view of Dublin Castle comes to life in summer when the tourists arrive like pilgrims — the old and infirm by bus, the young and able-bodied on mountain bike or stooped under mountainous rucksacks. They have cameras in common and a tendency to record the sights without actually looking at them. Because of its central location, Dublin Castle is a convenient lunchtime meeting-place and I have welcomed many visiting poets since I took up residence there — Irish poets mainly, though also some non-Irish friends like Miroslav Holub, Jean Valentine and Les Murray. I recorded my *Irish University Review* interview with John Montague there, having first taken time from my annual leave allowance of twenty-nine days (any literary activity during working hours, whether to give a reading or record a radio review, is accounted for in this way).

In July 1987, there was a memorable visit from Joseph Brodsky and Seamus Heaney. 'Is this the Ministry of Justice?', Brodsky inquired hopefully. I should, of course, have replied, 'No, it's the Ministry of Fear!' Predictably, the conversation turned to Auden's poetry which Brodsky reveres so much that he wouldn't allow a sceptical word to be spoken about the later work ('An old man should be able to exhale in his poems') and he even defended the use of 'my dear' in the poems, against which Seamus had confessed a prejudice.

The community life of an office, its rituals, its regularity, its companionship, can be a consolation for the brain-curdling tediousness of the work performed there. To labour alongside pleasant people (as they mainly are) who know nothing about, and care nothing for, the vicissitudes of the poetry world puts one's own trivial successes and failures into acute perspective. When literary disputes are raging or poets' egos are bulging, it is good to have another identity to shelter behind. There are many times when one might feel moved to write, as Wallace Stevens did in a letter to Barbara Church:

> *Our own days are the days of wind and rain, like today.*
> *Yet it is precisely on such days that we give thanks for the*
> *office. Sometimes one realizes what an exceeding help*
> *work is in anyone's life. What a profound grace it is to*
> *have a destiny no matter what it is, even the destiny of the*
> *postman going the rounds and of the bus driver driving*
> *the bus . . .*

If, at indulgent intervals, I allow myself to worry about the effect my job has on my writing, I also wonder how, were I to retire, my writing would cope with having me around the house all day. With a full-time job, I may be treating my poetry too lightly; without a job, I might take it too seriously. I persuade myself that the energy I expend at work is not creative, yet all energy is potentially creative in the final analysis. One may distinguish between a job and a vocation by reference to their respective capacities to confer satisfaction. In a job, it is a relief to get one's duties finished; with a vocation, their completion brings fulfilment.

That I have a job which is not my vocation, that I fantasize about leaving it, that I draft letters of resignation in my mind cannot be denied. Then there are times when I feel inclined to cling to the security of my office until retirement age. If *Waiting for Godot* could bear any further expository weight, I would offer it as a metaphor for the civil service — right down to the final words, 'Yes, let's go', and the final stage direction, *'They do not move.'*

What is certain is that tomorrow morning, at least, I will be back to my filing cabinet and Stamp Duty cases (I moved from Capital Acquisitions to Stamp Duties in 1983). A TD's representations on behalf of a constituent will require attention. I will tease out the phrase 'foregoing provision' in section 31(1)(B)(c) of the Finance Act, 1965, with a solicitor. There will be counsels' opinions to be read and responded to. Or it may be a special day, bringing visitors from the Land Registry or a trip to Pelican House to donate blood.

Just beyond my office lies a manhole cover, like an outsize silver coin, on which '1970' is stamped — the year I began to earn my living in the civil service. If it is removed (as happens during major international meetings at Dublin Castle when the police, for security reasons, leave every manhole open), I catch my pale, indoor face reflected far below. Some say that sewage gushes there, which means I see myself against a background of waste. Others suggest that it is the River Poddle, which flows underground like poetry through the mind. Or could it be a wishing well? And what, I wonder, should I wish for?

Poetry Ireland Review (Winter 1991)

Interview *by Michael Garvey*

How did you come into poetry and how did you come to poetry?

I don't really think you come to poetry; poetry comes to you. I would say that I knew even in early childhood that I wanted to write something or other. Of course, when you are a child, children's books are what you want to write. But, very quickly, I was responding to poetry more than to anything else. In school, when everyone else was furtively opening the textbook underneath the desk, if we were supposed to have learned a poem by heart, I was *hoping* I would be asked to recite. Not because I was some kind of goody-good, but for the pure pleasure of having those wonderful words in my mouth and being able to declaim them.

What I recall from school is a physical reaction to language. The first glimpse of Shakespeare we were offered was:

> *When icicles hang by the wall*
> *And Dick the Shepherd blows his nail,*
> *And Tom bears logs into the hall,*
> *And milk comes frozen home in pail . . .*

I almost fainted as I listened to this. I can also remember a class in which a teacher walked into the room and, without uttering a word, started to chalk on the blackboard:

> *The trees are in their autumn beauty,*
> *The woodland paths are dry . . .*

This — the words, not the chalk! — brought me out in goosebumps and I suppose I gradually wanted to see if I could induce goosebumps of my own making. But I have remained more interested in other people's poems than my own, a fascination which I put to use by writing a lot of criticism.

39

Dennis O'Driscoll

*For most people, words are a currency, a little like money. But, for you,
do the actual tokens have values in themselves?*

What we call inspiration in poetry is usually a visitation of words
and rhythms rather than ideas. I find that if I have the right
phrase in my head, nothing will stop me; but if I don't, nothing
will start me. I have never taken or given a poetry workshop —
poetry, for me, is a private and spontaneous pursuit, not one
which is communal or induced. When I was growing up in
Thurles, where the firemen were part-timers, they would have to
drop whatever they were working at if the fire siren sounded.
Poetry is something like that — if the siren goes off, you have to
interrupt whatever you are doing and respond to the call by
jotting the phrase down. But the alarm can be a false one, the call
may be a hoax. Poets who are anxious about their output see
infernos where there are not even chimney fires. They clutter
poetry publications in the same way that people with minor
ailments are accused of crowding the casualty wards of hospitals.

*How do you draw people to poetry, how do you move people to be open
to it? How do you get people to try it?*

I'm not in the least bit proselytising about the art; I have nothing
of the salesman in me when it comes to poetry. I am particularly
sceptical about the idea of trying to offer people so-called accessible poems as a lure. I don't believe in accessible poems, I only
believe in good poems. I think it was Anne Sexton — a second-
rate American poet — who said that to be second-rate in poetry
was to be nowhere at all.

I would say that poetry for most people is like the Christmas
tree that is kept in the attic and is taken down in its appropriate
season. And I suppose the season for poetry is the season of love
or the season of death — those times when people look to the art
for sustenance. My colleagues at work cultivate all kinds of interests — they may be birdwatchers or soccer fans or chess players;
they don't try to convert me to chess and I don't try to convert
them to poetry. What people want from me at the office is the
answer to crossword clues, help with completing tie-breakers for
competitions ('I love Natural Gas because . . .'), things which are
regarded as turning my alleged word-skills to practical use.

If I were exposing people to poetry, I'd like them to be exposed
to the best poems ever written, even if they can't make sense of

them immediately. The sheer power of a great poem is enough to guarantee that it will ultimately make itself felt if the reader — however uninitiated in the art — is in a receptive mood. But I don't assume — just because I was receptive to poetry at an early age, just because it brought *me* out in goosebumps — that poetry is going to bring everyone out in goosebumps rather than yawns.

You have a full-time day-job, as one would describe it. How do you manage to combine this with your creative work?

I tend to think of poetry as a privileged space one enters from time to time. This may be wishful thinking, but I feel that the more pressured the space, the more intense the response you get when you actually sit down to write there. I have very little time left for writing when the working and commuting and corresponding and lawn-cutting and the rest of it are over. But, much as I would love to be allowed to stay home in the ivory tower, it's probably a healthy thing to be shoved out into the grit and grime of the world. You can expand the scope and the vocabulary of poetry by bringing to it your long-term experience of worlds and words with which poets are rarely acquainted at first-hand.

Like all except the big names, I can lay claim to no more than a marginal poetry constituency. Not enjoying the poetry equivalent of a safe parliamentary seat, I have no option but to earn my living in some alternative way. I won't deny that it can be more than a little disconcerting sometimes to think of others out there having lots of time to sweat over hot poems while you are busily manufacturing lifeless prose to your boss's specifications . . . Still, you do learn from the day-job how to work under pressure and how to organize yourself fairly efficiently, so you are equipped to some degree at least to offset the obvious disadvantages of your situation.

It is only since 'The Bottom Line' that I have been regarded as an office poet and I'm disinclined to fulfil the pigeon-holing expectations which go with this — of writing lots more poetry on the same theme, in particular. 'The Bottom Line' took me completely by surprise, most of it coming in an effortless surge over a very short period. I hadn't deliberately embarked on a long poem about the office world — if anything, I had assumed that I was insufficiently distant from the material for this to be possible.

There is another linguistic level at which my life and my

language intersect, namely the production of the memos and so on that are a fundamental part of my job. Official language sets out to be formal and respectful, but it is old-fashioned to my ear, always at least a generation behind the living language of the time. Editors almost never change a word in the essays or reviews that I write for them. The greatest editorial intervention I experience is in connection with my official work, where my superiors — with whom I get on extremely well, incidentally — re-write memos to ensure that they conform to the standard official mode.

Is this because of their particular needs or because they don't share your discrimination regarding language?

Official language has specific expectations going with it: that it will be couched in a certain tone and will restrict itself to a certain vocabulary. So-called creative language, on the other hand, can be as inventive, as playful, as subversive, as it likes. Wallace Stevens, the great office poet, looked on poetry as 'an unofficial view of being'; if, like me, the poet is a public official at work, then he makes the shift to being a private unofficial at home — a shift which adds considerably to the relish with which one settles down to write poems and reviews.

Mention of Wallace Stevens reminds me to say that there are any number of precedents for poets working in non-academic jobs. Thomas Kinsella and Padraic Fallon were civil servants; outside of Ireland, you find T S Eliot (a banker and publisher), Roy Fuller (a solicitor), R S Thomas (a clergyman), William Carlos Williams (a paediatrician), Philip Larkin (a librarian) and many others . . . . The best English-language poets of the century have, as often as not, been worker-poets — which, alas, is not to say that all worker-poets are good poets!

Can you tell me about the background to 'The Bottom Line'?

'The Bottom Line' is a 550-line poem about the worlds of business, bureaucracy, offices, that kind of thing. From years of working in offices where I came into close contact with the business community — but also through friends in business and from reading the financial press — I became both intrigued and repelled by the language of commerce. That language can be viewed as ugly and transitory but it is inventive and creative too, an Adam capable of naming the contemporary beasts (which now happen to be digital and mechanical). Business is transacted in a world of measurables — output, pre-tax profits, stock exchange indices — whereas poetry likes to think of itself as dealing in immeasurables and infinities.

To speak of 'The Bottom Line' as if it had been planned or premeditated in some way would be dishonest, because — as I said earlier — there was nothing conscious or foreseen about it. Certain phrases were beating about in my head and the more I wrote them down, the more new ones followed on their heels. Because a single 'take' on the business world would not do justice to it, the poem is cubist in construction and written from a multiplicity of perspectives. The obvious poetic response to adopt to business would have been a hostile one or a satirical one. That seemed too easy to me; I also wanted to be sympathetic to this world, to recognize that many of its inhabitants may be unfulfilled, pursuing careers that are not their true calling, grappling with private fears and failures and responsibilities. I hoped to be true to that aspect of it no less than the more critical or satirical side. I didn't want a black and white poem — maybe, in the context, the black and red of credit and debit would be more appropriate colours to choose!

Is there any element of autobiographical material in your poetry?

Rather than being directly autobiographical, I often distance myself from material to which I feel close by writing in an impersonal way or, for that matter, by adopting a persona. There is nothing at all wrong with being autobiographical unless it spills over into confessionalism, in which case readers may confuse sensationalism in the life with merit in the work. Behaving egotistically is something poets are already far too skilled at; they shouldn't be encouraged to capitalize on this through exhibitionist writing.

Can I ask you about the role of the poet in society? Is the poet any way significantly more responsible in this regard than the average citizen?

My belief is that if you look after the language, then the politics will look after itself. If you take the care and trouble to represent things precisely as you perceive them, literally and imaginatively, you will have discharged any obligation to society which you may have. To arrogate to yourself some larger role as seer or clairvoyant is to succumb to a deluded megalomania of a kind which is endemic in the literary world.

Since words are spoken by everyone, the custody of language is a sufficient responsibility in itself for a poet. To inscribe in language some hitherto unexpressed area of experience — to fill in some blank corner of the human canvas — is worthwhile; to speak the small truths that feed into the bigger Truth. Also, the aspiration of poetry is always towards the creation of something permanent in language: in our era of the disposable, the ephemeral, this is counter-cultural — as, indeed, is the fact that genuine poetry transcends the blinkered vision of the journalistic present; it inhabits the present, but it is also very much in dialogue with the inherited forms and the great voices of the past.

What role does subject-matter play in poetry?

Poetry, when it is reviewed, is normally discussed on the basis of its subject-matter, because that is the most tangible part of the work. More important than what is being said is *how* it is being said — including the sub-music of the poem, its undercurrent, its pitch, its tone. These are the intangibles really, rather like the whistle which only a certain species of animal can hear. But poetry teaches you how to hear these sounds and you won't have ventured many lines into a poem before you know whether its author is capable of operating in the multi-level way which mastery of the art demands. However tongue-in-cheek he may have intended to be, I rather agree with the Welsh poet, Duncan Bush, who said that — similar to the manner in which a trained musician can tell, by merely looking at a score, whether it is any good or not — a trained poet can judge a poem's worth by looking at it (even before actually reading it). Texture is always one of the first attributes to reveal itself.

If poems could be tracked by an ECG or a lie detector, you could quickly pick out the dodgy bits, the dishonest bits, the parts where the graph wavers because the poet effectively inserts stage directions such as *Pause for laughter* or *Please applaud* or whatever. I'm all for laughter in poetry, but it should be evoked by something which is intrinsic, organic, to the poem — not something which is tacked on with a view to manipulating an audience reaction. The problem with humour, though, is that people approach poetry with such serious expectations that they may miss the humour on the page if it's not laid on fairly heavily.

Insofar as my poems are humorous, it tends to be in a black or deadpan way; people often won't permit themselves to believe that you could possibly be whimsical about a sombre subject like death unless your intention is conveyed pretty unambiguously at a poetry reading.

Does your fascination with language arise from its sound and structure or with syntax — or a composite of these things?

Poetry is a loyalty to language before it's a loyalty to anything else. If you are a journalist, for instance, you may be expected to sensationalize a story. If you are an advertiser or auctioneer, you may be expected to whip up language in certain ways. There are, of course, poets too who distort the language but they are lesser poets for doing so; indeed, they are not, properly speaking, poets at all.

If you are writing poetry, you are involved in according every word exactly the weight it should have — perhaps the exact weight it was given by the anonymous person whose impulse first brought the word into being. You are honouring the people whose need was great enough to come up with words like 'thirst' and 'trust' and 'pain' and 'yearn'. A true poem would be like a house that never needed to be maintained, in which the paper never peeled and the paint never faded. But that kind of poem — in which every word emits a pristine glow — would be a verbal miracle. Most of the poems we read and write are temporary dwellings, easily demolished because of poor structural engineering or sub-standard materials. One of the most fascinating and alluring aspects of poetry is precisely the fact that a poem is an almost impossible thing to write.

Paradoxically, and despite all I have said about language, poetry — at its heart — is silence. It is an art of words but its deepest power lies in the ability to take you right to the point at which words fail and silence begins — the silence of awe, the silence of the irrational, the silence of the universe . . . You look out for a moment on an infinite horizon to confront the essence of what it's like to be a solitary human being on a strange, infinitesimally small planet in the universe.

Edited version of an interview broadcast
on RTE television's Undercover *(9 April 1998)*
Irish Literary Supplement (Fall 1998)

PART TWO

On Writing

Obiter Poetica: *From a Poetry Sketchbook*

Poetry is hand-crafted language in a mechanized world.

◠

A misprint in my newspaper review of Philip Larkin converts him from anthologist to anthropologist. No wonder the prudish accuse him of having impurified the language of his tribe.

◠

The critic no less than the poet must be a chameleon. Fixed positions are fatal to both.

◠

A review is read before the book, criticism afterwards.

◠

As hard cases make bad law, good causes make bad poetry. The poetry is bad because the response it evokes is one that precedes the poem, that has been earned outside of it.

◠

Love poetry — its subject always different, its object always the same.

◠

Some poets start out as Ministers. Others advance slowly from the backbenches.

❧

A twenty-first-century Coleridge would be subjected to so many distractions that he might not even *start* 'Kubla Khan'.

❧

Poets on radio debating the lack of an audience for poetry remind me of Irish-speakers discussing the prospects for the revival of the language.

❧

No more than you can look at death or the sun can you look directly at a poem which you have just completed.

❧

The angel of 1990s poetry is the fairy of 1890s poetry.

❧

If a man in Ireland tells you he is a full-time poet, you can be sure his wife is a full-time teacher.

❧

For all the talk about the decline with age of the poetic gift, there are certain kinds of poems — poems of broad experience and long perspective — which can only be written by an OAP (old-aged poet).

❧

New Formalist poems like fake Edwardian pubs.

❧

Poetry is the art of yearning.

❧

Hardy's poems combine good writing with bad lighting.

~

A poem's conception should be spontaneous, though labour may be difficult.

~

Writing is defiantly non-cumulative. One poem is not succeeded automatically by a more mature one. Each generation is not more skilled than the one before.

~

The time available to me for poetry after a day at the office is like a tiny profit margin I must work within. Take any of it away and I am at a total loss.

~

Distinctive new poets quickly realize that sanctions are applied against those with the audacity of individuality. If at first you must succeed, try something a little closer to the ruling literary classes.

~

Ireland's standing army of poets may well number 10,000; but there are very few majors in the ranks.

~

Amateur poets write about beggars and street children with the same relish that amateur painters bring to sunsets.

~

The person who insists that poetry must be regular and rhymed is often the type who likes music to be of the 'easy listening' variety.

❧

Reviewers want, if at all possible, to supply happy endings. Like novelists, they may close on a suspenseful note ('It will be interesting to see what this poet does next') or a reconciliatory one ('But, despite my cavils, this is a book which no serious reader can ignore'). Most joyous of all finales are those in which superlatives are popping like champagne corks, and all — reader, reviewer, author, publisher and publicist — live happily ever after.

❧

So many young poets are indulged, so many middle-aged ones ignored. The young poets are assumed to have poet-ential. When they reach middle-age, they are deemed not to have fulfilled it.

❧

Almost all poetry is forgettable. But incisive criticism helps us to remember exactly what was so forgettable about it.

❧

Books of poems are like Parliamentary Bills. The first reading is never sufficient for the Act to be completed.

❧

What hope for the poem of little ironies, the one which provokes nothing more than that snort of recognition by which the cognoscenti make themselves known in the audiences of public readings?

❧

A poem is a textual act, a lust for language.

❧

Inhibited reviewers tend to adopt a neutral tone, to describe rather than criticize. Neutrality is not objectivity.

∼

When we come across a disappointing poem by someone we admire, our initial disappointment is with ourselves — for failing to identify the brilliance we presume to be concealed there.

∼

Poems, like people, should not be judged by their begetters.

∼

Celebratory poetry calls for gifts of an exceptional order. There is something of the fake orgasm about too many poets when they gasp for joy.

∼

Poetry is a juice squeezed from the fruit of experience.

∼

To write a poem, an impulse must take you by surprise. To revise a poem, you must take it by surprise.

∼

A fault in a poem is like a bad smell in a room, something that must be traced as soon as it is detected; otherwise, the poet may grow habituated to the rot.

∼

Mature poets assume they have 'found a voice' when, quite frequently, they have found only a formula.

∼

To get it right in the first draft is the hole-in-one of poetry.

∼

The talent many poets share is that of making the ordinary seem ordinary.

∾

All poetry is experimental; some poetry is 'experimental'. The 'experimental' kind is about nothing except the 'experiment'. It is like the play in which the set is the star, or the opera in which the costumes upstage everything else.

∾

Poetry: the ephemeral in pursuit of the eternal.

∾

I wonder if the rule in competitive walking which requires the athlete to keep one foot touching the ground at all times might have a role in poetry also.

∾

Critics can talk up a friend's bad poem, just as an auctioneer can talk up a client's ramshackle house.

∾

If language was not inherently inadequate as a means of communication, there would be no need for poetry.

∾

A poem is more than its subject-matter because a poem is more than its words.

∾

Poets offer bread to starving language; they will not let it eat cake.

∾

Revisions are like fairy-tale wishes. You make one, then you have to make another to undo the first.

❧

A poet must put an accurate price-tag on life without either borrowing or inflating language.

❧

Today's preference is for poetry that hovers between the oblique and the obscure, that is knowing but not revealing, that hints at significance without doing anything as old-fashioned as delivering any.

❧

Poets with a low inspiration threshold can be very prolific without being talented.

❧

Poetry doesn't move at a speed measurable by journalists. Hence, the media's focus on poems which are political or, better still, 'controversial'.

❧

Poetry is my preferred language. Music is poetry's preferred language.

❧

Poetry is music set to words.

❧

Poetry is a form of alertness; poets, too, must be prepared. They know not the day nor the hour.

Krino (Winter 1993) — expanded

Pen Pals: *Insider Trading in Poetry Futures*

Most poets are not interested in any poetry except their own. Mention all but the celebrity names and they grow vague. They *think* they may know who you mean; the name definitely rings a bell. No, they haven't actually got around to reading any of his books. Didn't he give an Arvon course a couple of years ago? Or was he one of the Forward Prize judges? Wait a minute, did you say Redgrove or Reading?

Insofar as poets deign to notice the work of other poets — staunchest allies and fiercest enemies aside — it tends to be for the purpose of stimulating their own creativity or as a spring-board for discussion at poetry workshops. When poets shortlist friends and faculty colleagues for honours and awards, it is because this is the only contemporary poetry they genuinely care about. Since you can't award the prize to yourself, better to present it to someone who offers camaraderie and perhaps power than to grapple with the aesthetic of a poet whom one hasn't met and who wields no clout. In an age of mass communications, personal communications remain paramount in poetry; the ethos is that of a village: friendships, feuds, gossip, suspicion of out-siders, inflated preoccupation with local matters.

If most poets are not interested in poetry, neither are most non-poets. One of the loneliest places in the world is the poetry section of a bookshop. It resembles the atmosphere, a few minutes after the scheduled starting-time for your reading, when it is clear that no more than two or three souls have gathered at the arts centre in your name. If your bookshop solitude chances to be disturbed, it will in all probability be by an elderly man searching — with much sibilant muttering — for the works of Robert W Service or a student cracking the spine of the Oxford Dryden, from which she furiously proceeds to take notes. The royalty statements — like the bank statements — of the average poet make for sombre private reflection. A typical print-run of 750 or 1,000 will be depleted by complimentary, review and remainder copies as much as by retail sales. Poetry sometimes cannot be given away.

Despite America's population of 250 million and a massive creative writing industry, Herbert Leibowitz, the editor of *Parnassus*, claimed in 1992 that even poets of the stature of John Ashbery or Derek Walcott will generally not sell more than 7,000 copies of a new book. Reflecting on the size of the Poetry Book Society in Britain, Alastair Niven wrote in 1994, 'We are often reading in the papers these days that poetry is the new rock 'n' roll: if so, it must be possible for a poetry book club to have a membership of, say, 5,000 instead of the current 2,000.' Far from being the new rock 'n' roll, poetry sometimes seems like a discordant band of players blowing their own trumpets to an empty auditorium. The top brass will receive support and backing from others; the massed rank-and-file know that you need to be a good solo entertainer in order to catch the neon eye of the media. But the media and poetry are not entirely comfortable in one another's embrace; news stories about poets (on the rare occasions when poetry is news) are written to a then-versus-now formula designed to portray the new-model poet as a regular bloke or babe, the bard next door, who is not going to embarrass you with twee talk about inspiration or mystery: 'Once, versifiers discussed *ars poetica* in cloistered cliques, now they'd rather chat over a pint.' (*Independent on Sunday*); 'Poets used to flake out in foreign parts from an excess of emotion and TB. Not any more — now the complaint might be poetry circuit fatigue.' (*Elle*).

Poetry is an increasingly parthenogenetic art in which poets earn their living by producing new poets. Eliot Weinberger, the translator and critic, believes that poetry is now perceived to be a 'middle-class career': 'American poetry has become a sherry party in a faculty lounge.' If poets suffer from paranoia as miners suffer from silicosis, damaging symptoms peculiar to creative writing syndrome include anxiety about low poem count, leading to constant pressure to prove one's poethood. The most creative thing about these courses — and the secret of their survival — may well be their creation of permanent, pensionable and congenial employment for poets who might otherwise have had to soil their sensitive hands in the outside world. Yet, experience of the wider world will stimulate rather than stifle creativity and can therefore prove to be a beneficial course for poets to follow; tacit recognition of this fact may be gleaned from those anxious jacket notes on American poetry collections which announce that 'Before becoming Emily Whitman Professor of Creative Writing at Pearl S Buck University, the author worked as ski instructor, fast food chef, trapeze artist, lay chaplain, sheep-dip salesman and tug-of-war coach.'

For the young writer who (disregarding the example of some of the greatest modern poets, T S Eliot, Wallace Stevens, Philip Larkin, R S Thomas and many others) is determined to make a living from poetry, the self-interested demands of the white-collar career are in danger of drowning out the disinterested demands of the White Goddess. The word 'Muse' featured on the events list for a recent conference of the Associated Writing Programs in Washington but so, inevitably, did the word 'schmooze'. 'Schmooze It or Lose It: How Professional Relation-ships Affect Our Writing and Teaching' was the frank title of one of the panel discussions. Only by frenetic acts of networking can poets hope to gain their 'rightful' share of grants, awards, fellow-ships, residencies.

Tom Disch contends that 'the workshops . . . encourage indo-lence, incompetence, smugness, and — most perniciously — that sense of victimization and special entitlement that poets have now come to share with other artists who depend on government or institutional patronage to sustain their art, pay their salaries, and provide free vacations'. Ask not what you can do for poetry but what poetry can do for you. Forget the sentimental idea of poetry as a higher calling, a vocation, the obligations of which transcend expectations of recognition or reward. You pat my back and I'll pat yours. You scratch my eye and I'll scratch out yours. Tell me who the judge is and I'll tell you who the winner will be. Faced with ethical standards which poets would be the first to excoriate were they to be revealed in politics or business, it is no wonder that Thom Gunn has been driven to epigrammatic indig-nation:

> *You scratch my back, I like your taste it's true,*
> *But Mister I won't do the same for you,*
> *Though you have asked me twice. I have taste too.*
> ('*To Another Poet*')

Where drunken acrimony might have been one of the besetting hazards of the poetry scene in the past, loving blandness can be an equal if opposite problem nowadays. Harvey Porlock's *Sunday Times* column compared poetry reviews to 'prize-giving in a small, caring primary school: everyone has done terribly well, it's all absolutely marvellous.' Reviews matter more in poetry than in fiction, where publishers — anxious to recoup large advances — try to overrule critical judgements with media interviews and carefully-predigested gossip bites. Objective, informed and lively poetry criticism is a good deal more scarce than it ought to be. Poets often operate on a timid 'Judge not, that ye be not judged' basis, while academics seem more comfortable at elucidation than discrimination. Blake Morrison, in a *Poetry Review* essay, observed:

> *[Britain] is a small island, and the island of poets an even smaller one within it, and inevitably it turns out that poets are soon reviewing poets they have met and may even know well. It can't be helped. But it isn't healthy. Few manage to be plain-spoken or abrasive for long. It is little wonder that poetry reviews become incestuous, impenetrable, or simply dull.*

The smaller poetry magazines might be expected to deliver some of the most challenging criticism, free of the brand loyalty to large publishing houses which operates in national newspapers. But too many of them dissipate their energies in a coterie-inspired cacophony of agony and ecstasy. Either hyper-praise is being doled out like wads of forged bank notes or the reviews are firmly stamped 'No Credit' (in all-too-visible ink). These scarcely merit reading; one hits them in spots simply to confirm that the upbeat muzak in which the genius of friends is celebrated or the military beat with which enemies are laid low has been sustained to the last monotonous note.

Books are not sent out for review; they are sent out for praise. When the enraged poet complains to an editor that a book was not given an 'objective' review, what is meant (except in cases of blatant bias — and these certainly do occur) is that the book should have been given a more favourable one. A balanced book review need not be an 'on-the-one-hand' and 'on-the-other-hand' bore. A wholly negative review can be motivated by the desire to seem clever or to attract attention to the reviewer ('One cannot review a bad book without showing off,' as Auden remarked). At the same time, in Dick Allen's words, 'Appreciations done without real spine actually say to the poet: *I don't take your work seriously enough to tell you when I think it's bad.'*

For examples of consummate spinelessness, one turns to the 'advance praise' caked like cheap make-up on the back covers of American poetry books. Increasingly, such blurbs — mainly solicited from fellow-poets — are to be found defacing British and Irish collections also. Commissioned blurbs are advertising copy masquerading as criticism; the objective is to keep alive the adulatory spirit of the launch-party and to neutralize the sober morning-after headache of the actual reviews. To judge these books by their back covers would, to say the least, be naive. Poets, always ready to pay lip-service to The Truth, adopt a rather relaxed attitude to the truth, 'a disgraceful abdication' from which (to cite Seamus Heaney's view) their blurbs represent. *Esprit de corps* and camaraderie undoubtedly have their place in poetry — and that place is the pub; 'jacketeering', as the *New York Times* calls it, should be left to self-help books of the kind where Harvey K Scheister MD vouches, in snake-oil salesman's tones, for the success of some author's twelve easy steps for putting the zing back into your marriage.

Joseph Parisi, editor of *Poetry* (Chicago) — one of the few magazines where incisive, non-partisan reviews by American critics can still be found — has said of blurbs:

> *Like the reviews in some little magazines nowadays, these capsule commentaries are not only unfailingly complimentary — which is to be expected — but frequently incomprehensible — which is less acceptable. After perusing the hyperbolic and tortured utterances on the bookjackets, the prospective reader may well find the actual contents of the volumes rather anticlimactic.*

Instead of preserving the fabric of language, poets who engage in blurbing (an anagram of 'burbling' as Pico Iyer has noted) bleach it of meaning. Could an immediate worldwide moratorium on commissioned blurbs not be negotiated through International PEN? A blurb non-proliferation treaty would surely come as a relief to the more harassed poets, for whom blurb solicitations are yet another distraction from poetry itself — and one involving even more successive drafts, so as to reach the expected level of passionate intensity.

Pending such a treaty, poets should each be allocated an integrity rating of 100 points, from which 15 points would be deducted for every blurb written and 20 points forfeited every time they review a close friend or colleague or nominate them for an award; a 20 point penalty would also apply to reviews prompted by vengeance, expectation of reciprocal benefit or the desire merely to be controversial. Poets whose ratings fell below 70 would be disqualified from reviewing until they had undergone honesty counselling from a poet-critic such as Lachlan Mackinnon or had learned passages of Randall Jarrell's criticism by heart. Community service, such as tending Geoffrey Grigson's grave or painting Ian Hamilton's fence, would be accepted in partial reparation.

The vast majority of contemporary poems — from the most acclaimed to the most shunned — will have turned to dust before long, as one generation's mediocre output is supplanted by another's. When they are no longer around to promote themselves, today's fresh-faced new poets will be condemned to join their honour-laden elders, whom they disdained and patronized, in the cobwebbed bottom shelves of crepuscular bookshops. A poem is, in a sense, an ideal: a fleeting perfection glimpsed in the poet's imagination but scarcely ever realized on the page. The poet is possessed by the need to flesh out that ghostly ideal in words which, he or she is convinced, were predestined to come together for that purpose. If posterity could speak, it would sound like Randall Jarrell, who — just before his death — remarked in a letter to Adrienne Rich: 'To have written one good poem — *good* used seriously — is an unlikely and marvelous thing that only a couple of hundred writers of English, at the most, have done . . .'

Yet even at its most perfect, poetry is of defiantly minority appeal; in fact, the reactions of audiences at readings suggest that they strongly approve of poets who choose perfection of the performance rather than of the work. William Carlos Williams may have believed that 'men die miserably every day / for lack / of what is found' in poetry. But long experience in a non-literary job has led me to concede that people live contentedly every day without Dr Williams's prescribed texts and indeed seem less miserable than the poets. Perhaps the first steps towards widening the core readership for poetry ought to be taken by poets themselves. Through making the effort to read and come to terms with the best work of all kinds published outside of their own asphyxiating enclaves, poets might even learn to enjoy poetry; less defensive and claustrophobic conditions for the writing, reviewing and judging of verse could also be created. Poetry might come gradually (and without any sacrifice of standards) to seem a more welcoming art — and not a forbiddingly closed shop — in the eyes of the general book-buying public. The present war being waged on poetry by entrenched poets was well-charted by Vernon Shetley in *The Yale Review:*

> *As the poetry world has become more professionalized, our tastes have grown narrower, more sectarian; we like only poets who publish in the journal edited by our friend, or only avant-gardists from our particular block in lower Manhattan, or only the poets who've attended the institution where we received our MFA.*

The standard of poetry written cannot be divorced from the ethical standards of poets, who should adopt their own Hippocratic oath — to use language at all times as an instrument of truth. 'If I were Moses today,' Isaac Bashevis Singer said, 'I'd add to the commandment, not to bear false witness, another one: "Don't praise your neighbor's bad writing."' Ultimately, the point at issue is, as a politician might express it, one of confidence, of trust, of the avoidance of review-rigging. Literary politics far too often leads (as Bruce Bennett's quatrain, 'Frequent Contributor', neatly intimates) to low standards in public places:

> *New issue, and her poems appear again.*
> *Suspicion whispers: is there some connection*
> *between their highly dubious selection*
> *and whom they were submitted to, and when?*

Thumbscrew (Spring 1997)

Enveloped in Poetry

If I belong anywhere, it is among a school of poets about which surprisingly few doctoral theses have been written: The Back of the Envelope School. Members of this school are too busy to engage in literary intrigue and too stubbornly independent to endorse any particular style. To enrol in the school, you must draft your poems on the hoof because you do not enjoy the luxury of a fixed writing regime. Poets who earn a living in busy non-literary occupations are the archetypal Envelopers.

On the hotel bedroom desk at which — away from home on business — I jot down these remarks, there is an array of bonded notepaper bearing the calligraphed words '*In Residence*' under the hotel name. Envelope poets may be literally 'in residence' in an organization, company or even hotel, but they are never 'poets in residence'. Some wrong turning has left them pursuing ways of life which are entirely unconnected with poetry. They seldom, if ever, teach, preach or profess it. Their patrons include Wallace Stevens, who would pause in the middle of dictating insurance letters and scribble down a phrase. Or his fellow-American, Eleanor Ross Taylor, who remarked without bitterness, 'I would write just occasionally, just the poems that demanded it . . . I did keep the house scrubbed and waxed and that sort of thing.' Or, indeed, Philip Larkin who defined work as something you do in order to have spare time.

Back of the Envelopers are not likely to be found in artists' colonies or in writers' workshops because their imaginative antennae would jam with self-consciousness at the very thought of being where one is *expected* to write. They are capable of producing poetry only on a surreptitious basis, when no one else is looking — ideally, when colleagues and neighbours don't remotely suspect them of association with so rarefied an activity.

Ninety-nine per cent inspiration and one per cent perspiration is Envelopers' formula for a poem. It is not that they don't fully appreciate the need for the hard labour of revision — these are people, after all, who (albeit in other contexts) are well used to bringing ideas to fruition. But re-vision is in essence an attempt to realign each successive draft more closely with the vision which seared and soared through the imagination in the first place. The cryptic phrases which they jotted down between a staff appraisal and a client briefing are the chips of rosetta, the scraps of papyrus that speak of an elsewhere and an otherwise. For people driven to distraction by constant demands on their time, consolation lies in the fact that the essential work is already complete when those spontaneous scribblings light upon the back of an envelope or on a sheet of hotel paper. The rest — though it may take weeks, months, years — is a mere tidying up afterwards.

Poetry Book Society Bulletin (Autumn 1999)
Poetry Ireland Review (Summer 2000)

PART THREE

Irishry

A Map of Contemporary Irish Poetry

When visitors to Ireland talk of poetry, they talk of W B Yeats. Irish poets are more likely to change the subject to Patrick Kavanagh or Louis MacNeice. While the Australian poet, Peter Porter, imagines a kind of poetic fitting-closet in which the Irish are 'still lining up to try on Yeats's robes', the reality is that Yeats's lofty rhetoric, like his pince-nez and bow, has come to represent the style of another era. It is not that Yeats is unadmired in his own country but that his poetry belongs to world literature; having towered over the Irish poets of his time, he no longer blocks the light or growth of today's crop.

If Yeats is viewed as a somewhat ambivalent icon by sections of his native audience, it is because questions like 'Did that play of mine send out / Certain men the English shot?' continue to reverberate in Ireland. Yeats's passionate nationalism, his flirtation with fascism, his idealization of the Anglo-Irish 'big house' remain stumbling blocks on the road to appreciation for those who have taken what Denis Donoghue terms 'the political turn in criticism'.

In an *Irish Times* essay published on the fiftieth anniversary of W B Yeats's death, Seamus Heaney urged a redirection of attention to Yeats's 'visionary courage', declaring 'it is time we . . . laid off pressing him too trimly into our own cultural arguments, and even blaming him for our predicaments.' The fact that Heaney, born in the year of Yeats's death, was then at work on *Seeing Things* and ready 'to credit marvels' adds a personal gloss to his conviction that 'Yeats's overall intent was to clear a space in the mind and in the world for the miraculous, for all kinds of rebellion against the tyranny of physical and temporal law.' Limited though Yeats's influence on Irish poetry may now be, Heaney is not the only living poet to have found him an exemplar (the question mark in the title of his 1978 lecture, 'Yeats as an Example?', has by now dropped off like an evolutionary tail). Derek Mahon, as even a superficial visual inspection will confirm, sometimes wields an elaborately orchestrated Yeatsian stanza; Richard Murphy, the last Anglo-Irish poet and a master of form, has 'continually' (his own word) drawn sustenance from Yeats.

What the present eminence of Irish poetry may mask is that Yeats initially appeared to be a once-off manifestation of Irish poetic genius, Ireland's single — and singular — contribution to modern poetry. A few disciples attempted to fill his capacious mantle and disappeared without trace into its lining. The 1930s and 1940s were a stultifying period in neutral Ireland, economically underdeveloped and intellectually constrained. The lack of good indigenous publishers added to the demoralization of poets, while the censorship was, to cite Robert Graves, 'the fiercest . . . this side of the Iron Curtain — and I do not except Spain'. Graves's *King Jesus, I, Claudius* and *Wife to Mr Milton* were banned, as was his translation for Penguin Books of *The Golden Ass* by Apuleius. Austin Clarke's novels and Frank O'Connor's version of a classic Gaelic poem, 'The Midnight Court', were added to the forbidden index. As if to prove that Ireland could match the iron will of Eastern European countries when it came to intolerance, George Orwell's *1984* was banned in July 1949.

John Montague, as late as 1973, asserted that 'The only literary art in which we have not made our presence felt is the one in which we are supposed to excel; this is, poetry. Yeats apart, few Irish poets have been accepted as international figures in the way that Pablo Neruda is, or Octavio Paz, or Ungaretti.' About the same time, Michael Smith began an essay by remarking, 'I think it is true to say that outside Ireland there is little or no interest in contemporary Irish poetry.' Irish poetry may not have enjoyed much prominence in the period following Yeats's death; but Austin Clarke and Padraic Fallon — with scant encouragement — were reshaping the poetry without rejecting the great poet. Patrick Kavanagh, while he acknowledged Yeats's stature, was contemptuous of 'the absurdity and the lie called "the Irish literary movement"', against which he staged something of a one-man counter-revolution. Louis MacNeice is a more complex case; he was — like Samuel Beckett — a deracinated figure, imaginatively bound to Ireland yet belonging nowhere in particular. Asked 'Are you Irish?', he drily replied: 'You might call it that.' His engagement with Yeats was profound (and included authorship of an indispensable introduction to his work) but a natural wariness and solitariness as a poet ensured that he survived the encounter without loss of artistic identity.

MacNeice, Kavanagh, Fallon and Clarke, although minor figures compared to Yeats, are important poets in their own right and not mere trail-blazers for their successors. Patrick Kavanagh is the best-loved by far among general readers (selling, as a Dublin bookseller put it, 'like corn flakes') and he has been eloquently championed by Seamus Heaney, another poet with an unusually broad readership. Kavanagh's curious mix of the earthy and the ethereal touches some plangent chord in the Irish psyche, countering the harpstrung melodies of the national poet, Thomas Moore (whom he ridiculed), with what he called 'a true note on a dead slack string'. If stocks in Patrick Kavanagh and Louis MacNeice have risen steadily in recent decades, Austin Clarke has slipped a little, while serious trading in the absurdly undervalued Padraic Fallon (not published in book form until the year of his death) has scarcely started.

Austin Clarke initially worked so close to the Yeatsian epi-centre that his talent seemed to have suffered permanent damage; his early poems are as second-rate as they are second-hand. Eventually, however, poems concerning the hypocrisies of the newly-independent Irish state and Catholic puritanism aug-mented poems presenting an idealized mediaeval Ireland and analeptic sexuality to create an original, if eccentric and uneven, body of work. Clarke experimented with Irish prosody and one might expect his verbal high jinks and zany rhymes ('doo-da / Neruda', 'Lourdes / uncured') to hold an empathic appeal for Paul Muldoon. However, not one line of Clarke's poetry graces Muldoon's anthology, *The Faber Book of Contemporary Irish Poetry* (1986).

Muldoon's selection, which excludes most of the significant poets from Southern Ireland, depicts the corpus of Irish poetry with a bloated Northern head on a spindly Southern body. The one thing it can be said accurately to reflect is the depth of assur-ance among Ulster writers, editors and critics that their province holds a virtual monopoly of the poetic talent of the island. Oddly enough, Seamus Heaney, who placed Northern Ireland on the map of the known poetry world, tends to be treated less indul-gently than his colleagues; and his great collection, *North*, has been more pounded than expounded by commentators there.

Thomas Kinsella, one of two living poets from Southern Ireland in Muldoon's anthology (Paul Durcan is the other), forges a direct link with Austin Clarke. Kinsella's collection, *From Centre*

City (1994), recalls how 'Again and again, in the Fifties, "we" attended / Austin Clarke' and he has clearly learned from his irascible elder how to launch an effective satirical strike against worldly clergy and unprincipled bureaucrats ('white-cuffed marauders'). As with Clarke, readers may sometimes be baffled by the local detail, but Kinsella's passion and pungency are unmistakable. Another side of Thomas Kinsella's work is the exploration of his family past; he sifts through memory and race memory, uncovering archetypes in the guise of ancestors.

Thomas Kinsella and his near-coeval, Richard Murphy, are scandalously overlooked at present in England and America. Richard Murphy's early books were notable for the energy and agility of their impeccably-designed, solidly-constructed long poems. Ireland is essentially a land of lyrical verse, although Seamus Heaney, John Ennis, Thomas Kinsella, Derek Mahon, Paul Muldoon, Desmond O'Grady, Anthony Cronin and John Montague are among the poets who have written long poems to set beside their more concise works. Whereas Richard Murphy has moved from detached and absorbing narratives to personal and polysemous lyrics, Brendan Kennelly's work has developed in an opposite direction and he now specializes in epic productions which cast figures like the Biblical Judas and the historical Oliver Cromwell in boisterously anachronistic roles.

The epic ambitions of John Montague sometimes squeeze his tender lyrics into submission, though like trodden wildflowers they are capable of springy resilience. Montague has affinities with American poetry (William Carlos Williams is a master he shares with Thomas Kinsella) and was an inspiring mentor for student-poets when he taught at University College in Cork. Montague, the love poet and devotee of the White Goddess, influenced Theo Dorgan; the overlap of the personal and political in Thomas McCarthy's verse owes something to *The Rough Field*; the oriental, Gary Snyderesque touches of Montague left their mark on Seán Dunne.

Paul Durcan (who studied History and Archaeology at UCC) enjoys, as does Brendan Kennelly, a huge popular following and is noted for his mesmeric public performances. Durcan's work divides critics, some praising it as visionary, comical, satirical, others finding it baggy and verbose, the work of a jester to the middle-classes. When two discordant views of his work appeared in the critical magazine, *Graph*, the single point of harmony between the critics related to Durcan's oral qualities ('undoubtedly better heard than read'). Durcan took from Patrick Kavanagh — as Thomas Kinsella did from Austin Clarke — a sense of the sufficiency and validity of the local, drawing unapologetically on Irish names, places and controversies.

Far from exhibiting symptoms of cultural cringe, of post-colonial deference to London, a poet like Paul Muldoon not only uses peculiarly Irish references (even breaking into the Irish language occasionally) but piles on the arcana — Irish and non-Irish — to the point where the burdened newspaper reviewer (actually an Oxford academic, John Carey, in this instance) accuses the poems of standing around 'smugly, knowing that academic annotators will come running'. Some of Ciaran Carson's verse, much of Paul Muldoon's and most of Medbh McGuckian's has proved to be less limpid and accessible than that of their elders in Northern Ireland, Seamus Heaney, Derek Mahon, Michael Longley and James Simmons. Perhaps this is a byproduct of the need to carve out an identity which is distinctly separate from such a celebrated generation. Criticism of Medbh McGuckian's verse is inclined to over-emphazise its obscurity, adopting too literal an approach to a poet whose work demands the total surrender of the reader to its sensuous stream of un-consciousness. Ciaran Carson raises tall tales to the level of art and makes his own nimble-footed border ballads:

> *I lay bound in iron chains, alone, my* aisling *gone,*
> *my sentence passed.*
> *Grey Belfast dawn illuminated me, on board the prison*
> *ship* Belfast.

Enormously inventive and immensely influential (not least for his technical virtuosity), Paul Muldoon is ultimately more a poet's poet than an academic's. Many of his followers drew the line at *Madoc*, however, especially when that line offered no greater sustenance than 'De dum, de dum, de dum, de dum, de dum'. or 'O spirochete. O spirochete. O spirochete'. The relief as well as acclamation which subsequently greeted 'Incantata', his potent and poignant lament for the artist Mary Farl Powers, suggested that a whimsical poet (Muldoon wears motley even on the blackest occasions) is not exempt from expectations of substance. Michael Longley's elegant poems are reticent but not obscure, picking their way delicately through dark times (he remained in Belfast throughout the Troubles) towards the illuminations of love and landscape. Derek Mahon's ironic, urbane, sceptical outlook points to a kinship with Louis MacNeice (a sustaining father-figure for Northern Irish poets), although the visionary, eschatological nature of poems like 'The Banished Gods', 'The Apotheosis of Tins' and 'A Disused Shed in Co. Wexford' is without Irish precedent. Both Mahon and Longley have had intervals of silence in mid-career, whereas MacNeice's middle period was marred by his persistence in publishing poems which relied on sophisticated metrical strategies to disguise their imaginative inertness. The visionary side of Seamus Heaney's talent is very different from Derek Mahon's and, in *Seeing Things*, he hovers on winged feet where he had stepped with clodded feet in his intensely evocative and physical early poems. 'Gleaning the unsaid off the palpable,' his language is so radiantly distinctive as to amount virtually to a personal dialect.

From the soaring achievements of Seamus Heaney to the average volume of Irish poetry can be a dizzy drop. Ireland must be one of the least difficult places in the world in which to have a book of poems published. Collections appear which even a vanity press might blanch at — and they are not only printed but publicized and praised as well. A national reputation is not all that hard to achieve when the nation is a small one; indeed, a modest international reputation may prove possible if the poet comes to the attention of those students and academics for whom Irish Studies represents an attractively compact alternative to courses on cultures of a more intimidating size and complexity. As a result, the unexamined poem may seem not worth writing and the approbation of American academics is feverishly sought.

The ventriloquial manipulation by Irish poets of their own reputations occurs at home as well as abroad because there is a surprising dearth of little magazines in Ireland and not nearly as much critical debate as one would expect from so literary a culture. Critical judgements are more often muttered into Guinness glasses in the après-reading bar than uttered in the journals and book pages. Between the blandest reviews (which generate a kind of advertising copy) and the most aggressive (which take the primitive form of defending territory), a handful of poet-critics — including Peter Sirr and Gerald Dawe — redeem an otherwise dismal situation with informed and independent judgements. These are very much the exception: many poets are as cautious about committing themselves to critical prose as they are timorous in their approach to the actual writing of poetry. Irish poetry, like Australian, has had an anti-Modernist bias, as if it had been chastened by Ern Malley rather than energized by James Joyce and Samuel Beckett. And — here the news is more mixed — there is little or no rap, sound, concrete or L-A-N-G-U-A-G-E poetry; no manifestos, no schools, no slams and none of the fragmented constituencies into which poetry has split elsewhere.

Much is made of the Modernist strain introduced by the Thirties' poets, Denis Devlin and Brian Coffey, who spent a large portion of their lives away from Ireland and are commended for their awareness of European poetry (especially French) — an awareness which is literally written all over their work. Later poets, including Seamus Heaney, Derek Mahon, Nuala Ní Dhomhnaill and Michael Hartnett, have assimilated European influences without fanfare, while Peter Sirr, Harry Clifton and Michael O'Loughlin have produced an intelligent, urbane poetry of love, exile and alienation which connects them with the English poets, Michael Hofmann and Stephen Romer.

There are poems by Devlin and Coffey without which Irish poetry would be the poorer and narrower; and they helped to pave the way for poets like Gerard Smyth and Paul Murray whom Michael Smith recruited to his adventurous New Writers' Press (and for more recent Modernists who have sought reputations outside Ireland: Billy Mills, Randolph Healy, Catherine Walsh and Maurice Scully). Yet, its sophisticated surface sheen notwithstanding, Coffey's telegraphically concise style can harbour a certain banality of utterance. Denis Devlin, although the better poet, is frequently stilted, displaying a disconcerting lack of ease with his idiom — perhaps even with his medium — and appearing both to find and borrow a voice within the confines of a single poem.

The Dedalus Press, which has collected the poems of Coffey and Devlin, has also published Hugh Maxton, who seems uniquely at ease with high Modernist experiment and caustic social satire. The publisher of the Dedalus Press, John F Deane, who shares with Devlin the themes of love and spirituality, was one of the poets whom John Devitt named in the *Irish Literary Supplement* as victims of 'the premature rigidification of the canon' in Ireland. All kinds of unclassifiable figures (from Jo Slade to Joe Sheerin, Gerard Fanning to Gerry Murphy, Patrick Galvin to Macdara Woods, Tom Mac Intyre to James J McAuley) are unaccounted for when critical roll calls are taken. Before poets are divided into the damned and the saved, one would expect them at least to be judged. And it is not just over-reliance on hearsay evidence which prejudices their chances of a fair trial. Canonical questions are further complicated by the fact that the Irish poets living in England (Bernard O'Donoghue, Fergus Allen, Peter McDonald, Matthew Sweeney, Maurice Riordan, Robert Johnstone, Tom Paulin) and America (James Liddy, Aidan Rooney-Céspedes, Sara Berkeley, Seamus Deane, Eamon Grennan, Greg Delanty, Gerard Donovan, Eamonn Wall) move in discrete publishing, reviewing and reading circles which rarely overlap.

One public challenge to critical orthodoxies concerned the under-representation of women in the three-volume *Field Day Anthology of Irish Writing*. 'Never has there been an anthology which has caused so much anger among women,' Eavan Boland (whose poems were included) declared; the protest resulted in the preparation of a fourth, all-women, volume — which both remedies an injustice and creates an undesirable shift towards the ghettoizing of writers who have shown scant interest in literary segregation. Indeed, Eavan Boland — authoritative as poet, critic and role model — opposes separatism of all kinds, not just between male and female poetry ('I think that separatism in a small country like Ireland would be another form of censorship') but also between Northern and Southern Irish poetry, where a Czech and Slovak-style secession always seems on the cards ('We are not Northern poets or Southern poets. We are poets first, and then Irish poets. To cash in on labels, to make division a marketable commodity, dishonours the nature and tradition of our poetry.')

Medbh McGuckian has frankly stated: 'I *do* feel very close to the other Northern poets . . . I don't feel close to people in the South, except for Nuala Ní Dhomhnaill and maybe Eiléan Ní Chuilleanáin.' One common characteristic of these women is what Ní Chuilleanáin has identified as 'a lot of folklore themes in the background', deployed in a manner which owes little or nothing to Yeats; Eavan Boland, too, is very conscious of the importance of

> *the oral song*
> *avid as superstition,*
> *layered like an amber in*
> *the wreck of language*

and the remnants of a nation.

Rita Ann Higgins writes a very down-to-earth poetry which is oral insofar as it draws on colloquial means for satirical ends. Her poems are outspoken and urban while those of another talented Galway-based poet, Moya Cannon, are understated and depopulated. The strong oral strain in Paula Meehan's work is rooted in a Dublin idiom which is not incompatible with a piercing and rhythmic lyricism. Eiléan Ní Chuilleanáin's subtle poems, rich in atmosphere and telling detail, succeed through implication and suggestion more than assertion.

Having long earned recognition in fiction and visual art, it is only in recent years that Irish women have begun to publish poetry in abundance. A short list would include Mary O'Donnell, Roz Cowman, Sheila O'Hagan, Leland Bardwell, Joan Newmann and Mary O'Malley (most of them published by Salmon Press). Nuala Ní Dhomhnaill has transformed the image of Irish poetry and the Irish language from something compulsorily taught, joylessly learned, associated with all that is puritanical and pious and dreary, to something lively, vibrant, even sexy ('Is there a word for sex in Irish, indeed! Is there an Eskimo word for snow?') Despite the insistence by one of the major twentieth-century Irish-language poets, Seán Ó Ríordáin, that 'Ní file ach filíocht í an bhean' ('Woman is not poet but poetry'), the gifted Ní Dhomhnaill is not the only modern woman poet in Irish. 'An Chéim Bhriste' by Áine Ní Ghlinn is a justly-celebrated poem and Ní Dhomhnaill herself derived comfort from the presence among her predecessors of Caitlín Maude and Máire Mhac an tSaoi. Biddy Jenkinson's wry and pungent poems are less well-known than they should be because their author has a private persona (the name she uses is in fact a pseudonym) rather than a public one (through readings or the media). Such things ought to be irrelevant, of course; but, in Ireland, where it was once proclaimed that 'A country without a language is a country without a soul', it might now be claimed that a poet without publicity is a poet without a name . . .

Nuala Ní Dhomhnaill, Máire Mhac an tSaoi and Biddy Jenkinson have all written remarkably incisive and provocative essays in English ('I can write prose in English no bother, and even jingles and verse', Nuala Ní Dhomhnaill admits, 'but *never* poetry.') As essayist, Biddy Jenkinson assumes a defiant stance: 'I prefer not to be translated into English in Ireland. It is a small rude gesture to those who think that everything can be harvested and stored without loss in an English-speaking Ireland.' At a time when bilingual anthologies and collections have sold unexpectedly well and drawn increased notice to the work of poets like Nuala Ní Dhomhnaill, Michael Davitt, Gabriel Rosenstock, Liam Ó Muirthile and Cathal Ó Searcaigh, the gesture may be larger than it seems. For those of us who can read Irish, yet who welcome assistance with recondite words and usages, such publications are more than a convenience; they are an incentive. There are obvious risks which apply to all minority languages: poets writing with translation in mind; 'translatable' poems being regarded as superior to 'untranslatable' ones; 'creative' English versions which give misleading impressions of the originals. Despite these concerns, and while not denying the danger — identified not alone by Biddy Jenkinson but also by other significant poets such as Gréagóir Ó Dúill and Louis de Paor — that (in de Paor's words) 'the English side of the page would swallow up the original', I am inclined to regard dual-language texts as a contribution to slowing the ebb, if not turning the tide, for Irish:

> *The tide gone out for good,*
> *Thirty-one words for seaweed*
> *Whiten on the foreshore.*
> ('The Death of Irish', Aidan Carl Mathews)

Thomas Kinsella's critical study, *The Dual Tradition* (1995), dates the earliest surviving Irish poetry 'from a time of adjustment to the new Christianity in Ireland, in the fifth or sixth century' and the origins of a recognizable Anglo-Irish literature from the era of Jonathan Swift (1667-1745). Kinsella, who has himself translated many of the most crucial Irish-language texts, observed in his *New Oxford Book of Irish Verse* that 'the Irish tradition is a matter of two linguistic entities in dynamic interaction, of two major bodies of poetry asking to be understood together as functions of a shared and painful history. To limit a response to one aspect only . . . is to miss a rare opportunity: that of responding to a notable and venerable literary tradition, the oldest vernacular literature in Western Europe, as it survives a change of vernacular.'

The fact that, almost everywhere in the country, English has supplanted Irish as the vernacular presents a serious predicament for Irish-language poets because they lack what Máire Mhac an tSaoi calls a 'spoken linguistic hinterland to draw on' and must represent the hi-tech contemporary world in a language which is rooted in pre-industrial rural society. Yet, notwithstanding a commissioned report intimating that as few as 8,751 people may remain in Irish-speaking communities, the work of Nuala Ní Dhomhnaill attracts a far greater following than that of the vast majority of English-language poets. Her generation — several of whom, as students in University College, Cork, were associated with the mould-breaking magazine, *Innti* — has found ways of adapting Irish-language poetry to an urban age, if only to react against the city (as Cathal Ó Searcaigh's more alienated poems do) or to bring together the worlds of folklore and deep-freezes (as Ní Dhomhnaill herself so adroitly manages). Gabriel Rosenstock's poems seem at once oriental and occidental, ironical and mystical. Michael Davitt finds his language as capable of responding to a middle-east massacre on television as to the demands of love or satire. And the satirist in Liam Ó Muirthile savages the kind of ossified and introverted Gaelic culture which is served up to tourists and with which the Irish language becomes tainted by association.

If the house of Irish-language poetry has many mansions, from Cathal Ó Searcaigh's cottage in rural Donegal (an area celebrated in his poems) to Nuala Ní Dhomhnaill's home in a Dublin suburb, some poets inhabit Irish on a kind of time-share basis. Bilingual writers who have published in English and Irish include Micheal O'Siadhail, Michael Hartnett, Críostóir Ó Floinn, Rita Kelly, Eithne Strong and Pearse Hutchinson. Micheal O'Siadhail had won acclaim as a poet in Irish before writing exclusively in English; Michael Hartnett, on the other hand, resolved in 1975 to divorce himself from his English Muse and 'court the language of my people'. Ten years later, Hartnett's 'English dam' burst and his subsequent outpourings of lyrics, long poems and translations veered with great distinction between the two languages; more than two languages, actually: he brought Ferenc Juhász and John of the Cross into Irish. Gabriel Rosenstock, incidentally, has not only translated Francisco X Alarcón, Willem M Roggerman and Peter Huchel into Irish but Seamus Heaney and W B Yeats also (a decidedly Irish take on Theodore Roethke's 'I take this cadence from a man named Yeats; / I take it, and I give it back again.')

The considerable number of poets, born in the 1960s and 1970s, who have been enlisted by Irish and British publishers include Katie Donovan, Siobhán Campbell, John Hughes, Rosita Boland,

Dennis O'Driscoll

Caitríona O'Reilly, Sinéad Morrissey, Vona Groarke, Conor O'Callaghan, Colm Breathnach, Martin Mooney, Colette Bryce, James McCabe, Enda Wyley, Alan Moore — and Pat Boran, found at his moving best in 'Children':

> *Children in ill-fitting uniforms*
> *drive adults to school, and children*
> *argue the cost of tobacco*
> *in the Newsagent's nearby . . .*
>
> *And who is it who makes love in the dark*
> *or in the light, who haunts*
> *and who does all our dying for us,*
> *if not children?*

Among the newest names, a few — notably, the English-based David Wheatley and John Redmond and the Czech-based Justin Quinn — have been active as cosmopolitan editors and critics as well as poets; Wheatley and Quinn co-edit the internationally-minded *Metre*, while Redmond is associated with the iconoclastic English journal, *Thumbscrew*. At the other end of the age scale, an often-overlooked trio from Ulster, born in the 1920s, Padraic Fiacc, Robert Greacen and Roy McFadden, is itself ripe for critical reappraisal in the light of substantial editions of their work from Belfast publishers, the long-established Blackstaff Press and the enterprising Lagan Press. As well as having discovered poets as different as Eamon Grennan, Michael Coady, Eiléan Ní Chuilleanáin, Kerry Hardie, Aidan Rooney-Céspedes and Peter Sirr, The Gallery Press has repatriated other important writers (Derek Mahon, Richard Murphy, Medbh McGuckian, John Montague) from British imprints. Gallery is edited by Peter Fallon from his rural fastness in County Meath, a setting made vividly familiar to his readers through the supple and sympathetic way he incorporates the voices and visions of his community into conversational yet highly-crafted poems.

Trace elements of the respect, tinged with fear, which traditionally surrounded the poet in Ireland have trickled down the centuries and, albeit in heavily-diluted form, permeate the contemporary period. Summarizing the customary attitude of people in Gaelic society to someone with the status of poet, Máire Mhac an tSaoi wrote: 'Cross him at your peril! He can bring you out in blisters or, more ambiguously, put horns on you, and, unless you treat him with munificence and consideration, your cattle will sicken and your crops rot in the ground. But, if he is favourably disposed towards you, your memory and that of your people will live for ever . . .'

The present situation of Irish poetry need not be romanticized. Much of what is published scarcely deserves to be termed poetic, let alone prophetic, and is more likely to dull brains than to rot crops. Yet, it is fair to say that poets are taken seriously in Ireland to a degree that is exceptional among Western countries. Thomas McCarthy, not without a certain exasperation, confirms this: 'If English poets suffer from indifference, Irish poets suffer from too much public expectation.' And Eiléan Ní Chuilleanáin has written of the yearning among the public for landmark events in Irish society to find a response in poetry. Beyond Yeats's 'Great hatred, little room', such great expectations provide the best grounds for hoping that poetry will continue to play a vital role in 'Ireland in the Coming Times'.

Poetry (October/November, 1995) — expanded

Foreign Relations: *Irish and International Poetry*

Much Irish poetry criticism (if it is not outright exaggeration to speak of there being *much* Irish criticism) places a chosen few Irish poets (Beckett, Devlin, Coffey) in an international context, leaving the rest to be considered largely in domestic terms. There is a tendency to regard the internationalism of the former as an achievement in itself, regardless of the actual quality of the work, while the latter are measured by local rather than global standards. A bizarre situation arises when hyperbolic claims made for the strength and vitality of Irish poetry are accompanied by a reluctance to criticize flagrantly defective work, as if the family tree — despite its alleged sturdiness — would come crashing down in the first breath of fresh critical air.

The undiscriminating tolerance of second-rate poetry, witnessed outside no less than inside the country, may stem in part from a romantic view that Ireland is awash with inspired and instinctive poets whom even the gentlest of critical tools would wound. Poetry remains a cottage, rather than university, industry in Ireland. The *sui generis* bravura of talents like Rita Ann Higgins and Joe Sheerin points to the merits of a poetry which owes its existence to private enterprise. But, for all its freedom from the tyranny of 'schools of poetry' (in both senses), Irish poetry is surprisingly conservative for the most part.

A good deal of the verse written since Yeats is by no means 'well-made' and gives priority to subject-matter over craft. Northern Ireland, perhaps because of the Anglo-Irish mediation of MacNeice and a closer contact with English exemplars, has produced a higher proportion of well-crafted poetry than the South. The poetry to be found in Irish collections and magazines may lack polish on the one hand and experimental edge on the other. Such 'experiment' as one finds consists of the usual typographical realignments hooked together with ampersands.

Concrete poetry, sound poetry, L-A-N-G-U-A-G-E poetry and other styles reflecting shifts in linguistic, literary or philosophical sensibility have barely infiltrated Ireland. Even dialect poetry and demotic poetry — mastered by Tom Leonard and Liz Lochhead in nearby Scotland — are foreign to Irish poets.

Irish poetry is not only largely non-experimental but non-Modernist also. Attempts are made from time to time to legitimize a new line of descent — or dissent — that runs through Joyce and Beckett to Devlin and Coffey but they have met with limited success. Devlin and Coffey have their enthusiastic adherents: younger poets tracing Modernist forebears are more likely, however, to look to the founding fathers in English — two expatriate American poets — than to two minor expatriate Irish poets who emulated them. When Samuel Beckett championed Devlin and Coffey in the 1930s, he found himself, like many commentators since, supplying the predictable genealogy: '. . . they have submitted themselves to the influences of Corbière, Rimbaud, Laforgue, the *surréalistes* and Mr Eliot, perhaps also to those of Mr Pound . . .' Devlin's willingness, notwithstanding his cosmopolitanism, to tackle Irish Catholic subject-matter was welcome, even if he has been overshadowed in this regard by the more linguistically engaging work of other writers from Joyce to Heaney.

As far as English poetry is concerned, Ted Hughes and maybe Tony Harrison or Carol Ann Duffy are the only contemporaries for whom one could claim a following (albeit a very limited one) in Ireland. Michael Longley, James Simmons, Richard Murphy, Thomas Kinsella and Seamus Heaney have all come under the sway of English poetry; yet one would now be hard-pressed to find any young Irish poet on whom the impact of English poetry was equivalent to that of Auden on Kinsella or Hughes on Heaney. The question of influence is one which can be pursued to the point of utter absurdity, a poem being treated as no more than the speculative sum of its manifest influences. There are plenty of plagiarizing poets, of course (and not always enough percipient critics to identify them). Some poets are, in fact, comparable with those painters who can reproduce a scene perfectly from a picture postcard but who are stumped when faced with the challenge of an original scene. On the other hand, the openness of major poets like Heaney and Mahon to different poets and poetries stimulates growth without jeopardizing individuality of voice or outlook. Heaney, one concludes, *needs* to write under the tutelary spirit of writers whose works or lives are exemplary. His use of language is so distinctive and his imaginative procedures are so confident that he has been able to submit to the guardianship of Hughes (in the early books), Lowell (in *Field Work*), Dante (in *Station Island*) and Milosz (in *The Haw Lantern*) and, in the process, to develop where a lesser talent would seem merely parasitic.

The attainments of modern Irish poets — not least, Heaney himself — have given contemporary practitioners a self-confidence and self-assurance that borders on the self-deceptive. A blind belief in the superiority of the local produce has supplanted the longing gaze towards London. While this represents a healthy move from what Patrick Kavanagh termed provincialism to parochialism, the practical consequences can sometimes be equally stifling.

What Kavanagh does is to make the parish an acceptable unit of literary currency with an international exchange rate. Actually, he over-values it as, like so many poet/critics, he sets about converting his own practice into theory:

> *The parochial mentality . . . is never in any doubt about the social and artistic validity of his parish. All great civilizations are based on parochialism — Greek, Israelite, English. In Ireland we are inclined to be provincial not parochial, for it requires a great deal of courage to be parochial. When we do attempt having the courage of our parish we are inclined to go false and to play up to the larger parish on the other side of the Irish sea.*

Even if we are confident enough to have stopped looking over our shoulders, few of us are now sufficiently rooted to find Kavanagh's parochialism attainable — though Richard Murphy's Connemara, Peter Fallon's Meath, Thomas Kinsella's Liberties, Michael Coady's Carrick-on-Suir, Francis Harvey's Donegal and Rita Ann Higgins's Galway all display elements of parochial autonomy.

Kavanagh's own poem, 'Epic', is a paean to parochialism. Its passing reference to 'the Munich bother' does not diminish our hunger for a vision capable of grappling with the consequences for humanity of that 'bother'. On its own terms, however, 'Epic' is a fine poem written in an easygoing manner appropriate to its subject-matter. We know we are a long way from the creative writing class when we note the careless juxtaposition of 'I *made* the Iliad . . .' with 'Gods *make* . . .' Again, in one of Kavanagh's canal bank sonnets, we find 'light looks' too close for critical comfort to 'And look!'. Spontaneity is everything in poetry of this kind, the sonnet form operating as a lock gate through which the words flow and tumble. It is surprising how often Irish poets — even those whose Muses speak less fervently than Kavanagh's — will show a similarly scant concern about word-repetitions, line-endings and other stylistic matters.

An instance of a poet who combines strong parochial loyalties with an urbane outlook is Michael Hartnett. He brings equal zest to haiku set in Dublin and a ballad for local consumption about the small town of Newcastle West ('a poet's not a poet until the day he / can write a few songs for his people'). So well has he integrated his influences that local references and international styles blend flawlessly. Indeed, one can never be sure whether the ascetic, pared-down language of certain poems is Western or Eastern in origin, whether it is post-war or pre-Christian:

> Black frost, pike locked
> below the ice,
> the winter season.
> I give thanks for life
> among these dead,
> the bony men of trees
> and the leaves along
> the road, like the webbed
> feet of dead
> waterfowl:
> the winter season,
> the pike locked
> below the ice.

Hartnett's cross-fertilization has borne copious fruit as he moves freely among poetries, translating Ferenc Juhász into Irish and Lorca, Heine, Catullus, Haicéad and Ó Rathaille into English, and learning from Pasternak no less than Ó Bruadair.

Despite his deep roots in Munster, Hartnett has transcended the limitations of 'regionalism', as conceived by John Hewitt, in which a poet shrinks back from the greater world and sets out consciously to choose 'materials and subjects' which are 'presented by his native environment'. Whatever its chances of inhabiting Kavanagh's parish, a book like *Ulysses* could not have been constructed from native materials alone; and Hewitt's regionalism — based on 'loyalty to our own place, rooted in honest history, in familiar folkways and knowledge, phrased in our own dialect' — seems too self-limiting to produce anything but minor literature. John Montague has said that Ulster regionalism 'usually meant writing about your cottage in the country or, indeed, only people East of the Bann. So the whole doctrine seemed to me spurious, F R Higginsy'. He is surely right in his observation that

> The real position for a poet is to be a global-regionalist. He is born into allegiances to particular areas or places and people, which he loves, sometimes against his will. But then he also happens to belong to an increasingly accessible world . . . So the position is actually local and international.

This attitude is alert to the political, economic and environmental upheavals which uproot people and force them into new imaginative relationships with their native places. The universal informs the particular as well as vice versa. The global village casts light on the deserted village. The path to Montague's own *Rough Field* was smoothed by the examples both of Irish poets (Goldsmith, Kavanagh) and American poets (Pound, Olson, Duncan, Snyder).

If Michael Hartnett finds literary England blocking his view of Europe ('For years, we have been up against the great bulwark of England between us and Europe'), John Montague is confident of circumnavigating it: 'In ways that are difficult to define . . . an Irish writer has a better chance of being a European than an Englishman'. Montague was thinking principally of Denis Devlin who, as a career diplomat, had professional as well as literary contact with Europe. His fellow civil servant, Padraic Fallon, was posted no farther away than Wexford, as a Customs and Excise official. Fallon's bluff, conversational cadences are unmistakably Irish but there are other aspects of the poems — their philosophical insights, the ease with which they incorporate the mythical — that reveal the presence of a cultivated poet who carries his intellectual baggage far more lightly than Devlin. One does not have to travel beyond the Customs desk to discover foreign poetry, of course, and he translated Baudelaire and Rimbaud, was familiar with Rilke, and admired newcomers such as Larkin and Hughes.

Tempting though it is to assume that his interests ran counter to the putative intellectual stagnancy of the 1940s and 1950s in Ireland, his son, Brian Fallon, argues otherwise:

> *I suspect that Dublin literary life at the time was livelier and better informed, more sophisticated and cosmopolitan in the real sense, than it is today. The recent generation has — perhaps largely unconsciously — denigrated it so that its own avant-garde, liberalising role should shine all the brighter by contrast.*

Another poet — again a civil servant and diplomat — who cannot be ignored in any consideration of Ireland's foreign relations in literature is Valentin Iremonger, who has said:

> *Writing about poetry in* The Bell *and* The Irish Times *in the '40s, I was trying to bring the attention of anyone in Ireland who might be thinking of writing, to the contemporary English and American poets so that they would learn that there was a side of writing different to that we had become accustomed to in the first forty years of the [twentieth] century with the influence of Yeats; and I think I was the first person who tried writing in the modern idiom.*

Iremonger's *Reservations* (1950), appearing from a small imprint (Envoy) in a small edition, was a solid if modest landmark in the sterile publishing landscape in which it took its distinguished place. It was an object lesson in how to avoid the dazzle of Yeats by looking in an alternative direction; and that lesson was not lost on Kinsella and Montague who, in a sense, fulfilled Iremonger's promise. Although Iremonger never developed as a poet, his achievement is still considerable, not least his introduction into Irish poetry of a colloquial, sceptical, disillusioned contemporary tone that now seems a pre-echo of the Movement poets in England.

What Thomas Kinsella brought to his early work above all else was the Audenesque note, struck so authentically in 'A Lady of Quality'. Despite his mastery of form, and a musicality admired by Auden himself, Kinsella later chose to take aboard his craft some of the techniques of Pound and Williams. The idea of closure gradually disappears as the work becomes, almost paradoxically, more precise and more fragmentary. The pressure of an intensely-experienced life cracked through the orderly façade of the poems and he sought 'a form which ought to be felt as a whole, rather than in, e.g., stanzaic expectations'. His shifting literary loyalties might suggest that Kinsella was one of Kavanagh's fashion-following provincials, altering when he alteration finds. That would be absolutely wrong. Not only did Kinsella change course when he was, in fact, at the height of his metropolitan reputation — when his name was synonymous with Irish poetry in England and America — but he pursued a personal vision with a relentlessness which can hardly have been calculated to court popularity. Foreign readers expect Irish poets to 'sing' and Kinsella's new style, which became (in every sense) serial, was not universally applauded.

There is, actually, an Irish music in Kinsella's later work — not only in those poems which elegize the composer, Seán Ó Riada, but also when he incorporates portions of the oldest Irish literature into 'Notes from the Land of the Dead', 'Finistère' and other poems. Given his intimate knowledge, as translator, of Old Irish texts and of the fragmentary state in which many of them have survived, it is clear that the direction ultimately taken by Kinsella's work has not been prompted by the Modernist model alone. At crucial moments in its post-Yeatsian evolution, Irish poetry in English reveals Gaelic roots — one thinks of Clarke's technical experiments with assonance; of Valentin Iremonger's wry admission, 'What John Montague refers to as the loose colloquial line that I use in fact derives from Gaelic poetry'; or of Paul Muldoon's 'Immram', where the tone is Chandleresque but the narcotic imagery is not without traces of the ancient *Immram Curaig Maíle Dúin*.

Celtic quill and steel nib fuse in Seamus Heaney's work also — notably in the final section of *Station Island*, where the spare style of *Buile Suibhne* and the utilitarian bareness of East European poetry converge. Heaney is a persuasive proselytizer for the cause of East European writing in *The Government of the Tongue*. His disenchantment with aspects of the American poetry scene intensified his eastward gaze towards the lands of Holub and Herbert, Milosz and Mandelstam; and he speaks disdainfully of America's 'grant-aided pluralism of fashions and schools, a highly amplified language of praise which becomes the language of promotion and marketing'; of 'a disgraceful abdication from truth in the words that are wrapped around books'; of 'a blurb-induced sleep of the critical faculties [which] has tended to produce not monsters but molehills'. Molehill poetry is now the norm in those countries (contemporary Germany, according to Hans Magnus Enzensberger, as well as America) that enjoy the prosperity to promote the art and the leisure to dabble in it *en masse* but where kindness kills creative tension. Whatever Heaney's impetus, there remains something dramatic and unprecedented about a major Irish poet looking to the poets of Eastern Europe for a new sense of moral integrity, for a lower rate of verbal inflation. His collection, *The Haw Lantern*, casts more light than any essay on his anxious search for a language appropriate to that 'Republic of Conscience' which he aspires to represent.

Derek Mahon, like Seamus Heaney, had the verbal poise and prosodic virtuosity to operate successfully within the mainstream English tradition. However, he too cast his sights more widely, eschewing England 'with its love of light verse and nostalgia for poets in uniform' in favour of Cavafy, Brecht and French poetry. Mahon's unique outlook — that of mystic, sceptic, 'open-minded existentialist' — has protected him from domination not only by English poetry but also by those powerful poets with whom he has grappled as translator. One needs only to compare the closing lines of his translation of *Les Chimères* by Gérard de Nerval:

> *Note, in the wall, a fierce interrogation.*
> *Dumb matter is the word made flesh, therefore*
> *Subject it to no base manipulation.*
>
> *Even now a God hides among bricks and bones —*
> *And, like an eye closed in the womb, a pure*
> *Spirit evolves beneath the glaze of stones!*

with his own imaginative acceleration of them in 'The Mute Phenomena':

> *An ordinary common-or-garden brick wall, the kind*
> *For talking to or banging your head on,*
> *Resents your politics and bad draughtsmanship.*
> *God is alive and lives under a stone.*
> *Already in a lost hub-cap is conceived*
> *The ideal society which will replace our own.*

Mahon, also a notable translator of Philippe Jaccottet, is not alone in this activity. His generation has contributed the Sorescu and Tranströmer of John F Deane, the Lorca and Juhász of Michael Hartnett, the Machado and Hernández of Michael Smith, the Nemes Nagy of Hugh Maxton and the Celan of Brian Lynch and Peter Jankowsky. Apart from the conclusive evidence which translation itself supplies, hearsay evidence from conversations and interviews deepens one's conviction that an eclectic range of foreign poetry has begun to engage Ireland's poets. At the risk of indulging in nothing more than a bout of literary matchmaking, I would point to Matthew Sweeney's admiration for Charles Simic, Peter Fallon's for Wendell Berry, Ciaran Carson's for C K Williams, Medbh McGuckian's for Osip Mandelstam, Paula Meehan's for Anna Akhmatova, Gerald Dawe's for Joseph Brodsky, Eavan Boland's for Adrienne Rich, Gerard Smyth's for János Pilinszky, Peter Sirr's for Fernando Pessoa, Mary O'Donnell's for Ingeborg Bachmann, Thomas McCarthy's for George Seferis, Richard Murphy's for C P Cavafy and the internationalism of a great many of the Irish-language poets . . . It would be possible to go on and on but the point is clear: all poets compile personal anthologies and those of Irish poets now extend far beyond the exclusively French and Classical repertoire which once seemed to represent the limits of the known poetry world.

As teachers, too, Irish poets roam the globe, especially to the US: Eavan Boland, Thomas Kinsella, Seamus Heaney, Eamon Grennan, James Liddy, John Montague, James J McAuley, Paul Muldoon, Greg Delanty and Seamus Deane . . . The impact of America on the output of these poets has been far from uniform — scarcely discernible in the case of Heaney (apart from his brief Lowell period), liberating in the work of Liddy, while Muldoon's verse (thanks to Chandler, Frost and the cinema) had discovered America long before its author had gone there to live. Padraic Colum, W R Rodgers and Joseph Campbell were the pioneering settlers; and emigration to the US — where poets can make a living as poets — has become an Irish literary tradition. Vincent Buckley, in his book *Memory Ireland*, points to some curious aspects of the Irish poet's relationship to America, in particular his or her need to remain recognizably Irish:

> *Irish poets in general are like ambitious youngsters trying to escape from the working class. America is the upper-middle class. Their vertu, however, the source of their*

energy and appeal, is in the Irishness which they are trying to escape; they have therefore to emphasize this or some version of it. Their destiny, their complex fate, is not to become Americans, but to be Irish in relation to America.

The development of Irish Studies Programs on North American campuses is a welcome one, establishing what one hopes will be discriminating rather than indulgent centres of awareness. One hopes, too, that those Irish poets who choose to stay in Ireland will not be considered less Irish or less interesting because they are less visible in America.

If, as Seamus Heaney contends, 'English poetry has become aware of the insular and eccentric nature of English experience', what is one to say of Irish experience? Our 'local row' in Ulster has profoundly affected the consciousness of many poets and, naturally, those from Northern Ireland in particular. Yet the Northern Troubles, for all their appalling atrocities, have not engendered the kind of fundamental reappraisal of human nature necessitated by the Jewish Holocaust, nor have they raised doubts remotely akin to those of Adorno regarding the possibility of poetry being written after Auschwitz. In Europe, the horrors perpetrated during World War Two led to a tentative, unadorned 'anti-poetry' style — exemplified by the poems of Brecht and his followers as well as those of central European poets like Celan, Pilinszky, Popa and Różewicz. It is notable that the one Irish writer to have assumed a central position in European literature after the war and to have radically revamped its forms is Samuel Beckett, an active participant in the French Resistance and recipient of the Croix de Guerre.

Derek Mahon is sceptical enough ('And all the time I have my doubts / About this verse-making') to evince certain anti-poetry tendencies in his minimalist moods. And Seamus Heaney, as mentioned earlier, has been drawn to those East European voices who were forced to question the relevance of art and who bore witness to the most unpalatable truths. Clearly, revulsion at the betrayal of language by poets and publishers in America is not the only impulse fuelling his East European predilection:

I keep returning to them because there is something in their situation that makes them attractive to a reader whose formative experience has been largely Irish. There

> *is an unsettled aspect to the different worlds they inhabit,*
> *and one of the challenges they face is to survive amphibi-*
> *ously, in the realm of 'the times' and the realm of their*
> *moral and artistic self-respect, a challenge immediately*
> *recognizable to anyone who has lived with the awful and*
> *demeaning facts of Northern Ireland's history over the*
> *last couple of decades.*

For Southern Ireland, the war was an 'Emergency', a time when tea and silk stockings and petrol were in short supply. Isherwood's *Goodbye to Berlin* had been banned three months before the fighting began and Proust and Freud would be suppressed by the Censorship Board while Hitler was blazing an ashen trail through the books and cities of Europe. Irish experience was neither relevant nor representative as far as the rest of Europe was concerned and our literature was marginalized. Austin Clarke, the poet best equipped to have been the conscience of the 'Emergency' period, produced no collection of poems between 1938 and 1955. Of the poets born in the mid-1920s, Maurice Harmon has observed that 'Born into and shaped by a chaotic and apathetic Ireland, they found no satisfying vision of life within their own country'. Searching for a post-war identity, they saw in the disillusionment of their contemporaries abroad an analogue for their own peculiar disillusionment at (and with) home. But Derek Mahon suggests that it is the upheaval in the North that has enabled Ireland to recover some of the common ground lost during the war:

> *Like Louis MacNeice and others, I always believed that*
> *Ireland should have been in the war. I understand the*
> *arguments against but I think in the last analysis Ireland*
> *should have been in there. Not having been in the war*
> *shunted Ireland to the sidelines, and I think she's been*
> *forced back into the twentieth century by events in the*
> *North, by the forgotten North.*

As it happens, the notion of the periphery holding the centre is a critical commonplace now. The names generally cited are Les Murray, Derek Walcott, Seamus Heaney and, by dint of exile and of his writings in English, Joseph Brodsky — four poets who grew up far from the major literary capitals of London or New York. They bring to poetry previously invisible lives and landscapes, hitherto inaudible words and cadences, a commit-ment to form (including rhyme) and a lack of any post-war inhibition about giving vent to full-throated melody. Peter Forbes, the editor of *Poetry Review*, has categorized these poets (along with Czeslaw Milosz) as constituting potentially the most important movement since the Auden generation and 'the first school since 1920s' Modernism not to be closely tied to the culture of any one nation'. Kavanagh's 'parochialism' may be unattainable now and Hewitt's 'regionalism' is in certain respects undesirable; but Montague's 'global regionalism' is proving itself to be versed in the needs of a contemporary readership.

No country is self-sufficient and Ireland, like other countries, is an importer as well as exporter of poetry. Irish verse has profited from its exposure to writing from abroad and all of our major figures have, at one time or another, succumbed to foreign liter-ary powers — sometimes to the extent of temporarily losing their own accents. On the whole, though, it must be said that the curiosity of most Irish poets and readers is severely limited, so that outside developments are discovered late and only those foreign poets who have made unignorably large reputations become known here. Now that so many poets live and work around the world (making 'notes / towards a poetry of exile', as Peter Sirr wrote from Holland), or have done so for extended periods in the past, like Pearse Hutchinson, Desmond O'Grady, Mary O'Malley or Richard Murphy (who has polished the reflec-tions he found on the 'mirror wall' in Sri Lanka), this matters a great deal less; challenging new ideas are being picked up at first-hand. The prospect of native, let alone nationalist, subject-matter ever again becoming prescriptive is inconceivable. The original sin imprinted by one's birthplace is not easily shriven, however, as the poets in exile confess: Joe Sheerin reveals his true colours to the English in 'Green Experiences', Michael O'Loughlin finds 'The plastic sun of Finglas / Squatting on every horizon', while Harry Clifton, having lived in several continents, concludes that 'Where we live no longer matters / If it ever did . . . / . . . There are powers / No border can contain'.

Irish poetry has travelled a long way without ever losing touch with home.

Poetry in Contemporary Irish Literature,
edited by Michael Kenneally (Colin Smythe, 1995)

Troubled Thoughts: *Poetry Politics in Contemporary Ireland*

Like any small indigenous industry, *Irish Poetry Inc* looks abroad for growth. Poets born into this country, with its limited literary infrastructure and its marginal domestic market, try to export their produce to America and spend time marketing it there. Becoming a poet in Ireland is a matter not so much of apprenticeship as audition. Successful poets need to be seen and heard; and (as it is claimed of beauty pageants) 'personality' counts for a great deal if you are to win the star prizes: transatlantic trips, prominence at literary conferences, triumphal entry into the canon of Irish Studies.

More and more Irish poets have critical spokespersons at home or abroad whose role is pitched somewhere between that of a political aide and a public relations consultant. The poet effectively becomes the client of the critic who — in return for privileged access — will dictate to the public how that poet's work should be read and interpreted. Elucidation takes precedence over evaluation and protectionism is the favoured economic tool. Ireland's critical vacuum, which quickly fills with the hot air of special pleading, has one obvious source: the extreme difficulty of publishing honest (and, inevitably therefore, tough) judgements in a country where the reviewer is liable to bump into his subject on the journey to mail the review. Honest, informed critics will not often enough have cause to be the bearers of good news about Irish poetry (all the hype about our national genius for the art notwithstanding) and anyone who dares to challenge the cosily-agreed hierarchy will be resented.

The only option left to a battle-scarred Irish reviewer may be to cross over to neutral territory, reviewing foreign poetry for foreign periodicals. One does not need to be starry-eyed about London or New York to rebel against the complacencies and conflicts of the domestic literary scene. When the Northern Irish poet and regionalist, John Hewitt, is quoted on the dangers of becoming an 'airy internationalist', it is the air that tempts me rather than the internationalism — air to breathe in the stifling bell-jar of Irish literary life, where rivalries and resentments are experienced with a scalding edge and intimacy. Things become distorted at close range; and, as Denis Donoghue has written, 'Like everything else in Ireland, poetry is contentious. There is always an occasion of outrage.' Belfast versus Dublin. Ireland versus England. Paul Muldoon's Faber anthology (with its pro-Northern bias) versus Thomas Kinsella's Oxford anthology (which dismisses the 'Northern Irish Renaissance' as 'largely a journalistic entity'). Women versus the Field Day Anthology (in which female writers were under-represented) . . .

In its more permissive moods, *Irish Poetry Inc* is an equal opportunity employer, with some publishers and editors not noticeably discriminating on grounds of merit or talent. No wonder Irish poets are taken at their own valuation by the media; the one who shouts loudest is the 'best', for whom magazine pages will open, studio microphones redden, festival audiences foregather. It is cheerful but awful.

Every so often, a 'poetry boom' is declared. While the optimists 'talk up' poetry, the print-runs and sales of all but a small minority of poets remain very modest. Nonetheless, something of the traditional respect for poetry does linger and it creates a receptive environment in which verse may be written in English and Irish. Literary visitors to Ireland are struck by the fact that poetry is not regarded by the Irish as an abnormal activity. Richard Tillinghast has remarked:

> With so much negative discussion of poetry in the United States, where it is periodically suggested that there are too many poets, that 'no one reads poetry anymore,' it has been a tonic to live in a country where poetry enjoys a vital, secure place in the national culture. While at home I am likely to introduce myself to strangers as a writer or a professor, simply to avoid the tiresome conversations triggered by announcing that I am a poet, here people are comfortable with poets and poetry. In Ireland, where the leaders of the 1916 Easter Rebellion were poets, where Yeats's picture appears on the twenty-pound note, where the mayor of Galway is a poet, one begins to recognize that the alienation and isolation many poets feel in the

Dennis O'Driscoll

> US are inherent not in the art itself but in the commer-
> cialized, television-dominated culture in which we live.

One practical indication of the standing of poets in Ireland is
the fact that about forty belong to Aosdána, an affiliation of artists
(including composers and visual artists as well as writers) who
have 'made an outstanding contribution to the arts in Ireland'.
Members who are resident in Ireland are eligible to receive an
annuity from the State, the implications of which have given rise
to remarkably little public debate; most of the poets avail of the
largesse. Aosdána ('poets of the tribe') is administered by the Arts
Council in Dublin; new members are elected by the existing
membership — a factor which must exert its own subtle
constraints on Irish artistic life, both in the personal and critical
spheres. Aosdána has made it easier for writers to settle permanently at home. But, because reputations are increasingly beamed
home through America, the poet who remains in Ireland is in
danger of not being regarded as a truly Irish poet at all. As Alfred
Corn has observed:

> No one can say that America has been inhospitable to the
> Irish poets. On the contrary, we apparently prefer them to
> our own domestic product, greeting them with praise and
> university employment as soon as they present them-
> selves. That has something to do with America's probably
> ineradicable cultural inferiority complex before the
> achievement of Europe . . . but also with specific virtues
> the Irish bring with them — humanity, verbal fluency,
> and a convincing pastoralism.

Northern Irish poets as well as Southern Irish ones are entitled
to apply for Aosdána. The two Arts Councils, North and South,
jointly fund a number of projects and publications. Nevertheless,
relations between Northern and Southern Irish poetry are not
invariably cordial, so that neighbourly tension sometimes spills
over into acrimony. Southern Irish poets tend to believe that
Northern Irish poets command an unfair monopoly of attention.
In a restrained summary of this position, Seán Dunne (introducing his *Poets of Munster* anthology) remarked:

> Not one poet from the Irish Republic is included in The
> Oxford Book of Contemporary Verse, *to cite just one*

94

example, and this is a situation which recurs so often that one can only conclude that the editors of such books have simply not bothered to seek out the work of poets whose names are not heard within the pale of conventional taste. There is no sense of Southern Ireland as a spawning-ground for poetry.

Northern Irish poets and critics allege sloppiness and ineptness in much Southern Irish writing. John Hughes, expressing himself with less than restraint, wrote in 1993: 'Contemporary Irish poetry is in a bad state. Most of it — particularly in the South — is self-indulgent, lifeless, lazy, turgid, sentimental and unimaginative.' Having read newspaper accounts of the exchange visits which take place between Northern and Southern schoolchildren, to foster better mutual understanding, I am tempted to recommend similar schemes for poets.

Instead of re-staging the battles of the books which have been fought in Ireland, insofar as poetry anthologies in particular are concerned, I would like to focus on one anthology, *A Rage for Order* (Blackstaff Press, 1992), edited by the poet Frank Ormsby. In that way, rather than analyzing what have been earnest and arid controversies on the whole, attention can be concentrated on an issue of profound literary relevance: the response of poets to violence and community conflict. *A Rage for Order*, according to its editor, 'celebrates . . . the values of art in times of violence. In particular, though not exclusively, it celebrates the poetry written during the phase of Northern Ireland's Troubles which began in 1968.'

A Rage for Order is not without precedent. An earlier Troubles anthology, *The Wearing of the Black*, edited by Padraic Fiacc, appeared from the same publisher twenty years earlier. Although premature, and still more uneven in quality than Ormsby's book, it remains of relevance as an early act of Ulster stocktaking. In his unsatisfactorily brief introduction, Fiacc states that the structure of his anthology is 'symphonic in form'. At 350 pages — twice the length of *The Wearing of the Black* — Ormsby's valuable but over-conscientious anthology is a Mahlerian 'symphony of a thousand'.

The Northern Irish Troubles precipitated an upsurge of interest in the poetry of that province where, to quote from Derek Mahon's 'Derry Morning', each incident was 'a measurable / Tremor on the Richter Scale / Of world events, each vibrant scene /

Translated to the drizzling screen'. *Newsweek*'s 1986 article, headed 'A Literary Flowering in Ulster', bore the caption, 'Amid turmoil, a new breed of writer thrives'. In a knowing journalistic style, owing nothing to Heaney's own melodic prose, the article went on to remark that 'The most exportable of the lot has been "Famous" Seamus Heaney'; and it is true that Heaney's eloquence and charisma as well as his towering talent have crucially contributed to the high standing of Ulster poetry. Heaney's first collection of poetry, written before the Ulster violence, had already established him as an exceptionally gifted poet whose reputation would have flourished independently of political or journalistic factors. So, while Heaney and other outstanding poets of his generation — especially Derek Mahon and Michael Longley — attracted notice as a result of the Troubles, their individual voice prints had already signalled the beginning of a new phase in Irish poetry.

Faced with a tragic, complex and violent situation, the Ulster poets became war poets only reluctantly. Michael Longley has written:

> *I would insist that poetry is a normal human activity, its proper concern all of the things that happen to people. Though the poet's first duty must be to his imagination, he has other obligations — and not just as a citizen. He would be inhuman if he did not respond to tragic events in his own community, and a poor artist if he did not seek to endorse that response imaginatively.*

Where public events are concerned, the response of the poet will be a matter not merely of talent but also of imaginative affinity. Medbh McGuckian's exclusion from *A Rage for Order* is presumably to be explained on the grounds that her work had not, until very recently at least, dealt specifically with the Troubles. However, having lived all of her life in Ulster (Heaney, Mahon, Muldoon, Gerald Dawe, Tom Paulin and Seamus Deane moved elsewhere) and having worked with prisoners there, the Troubles are sure to have influenced the vocabulary and imagery of certain poems and heightened the intensity with which love, family and home are invoked in others. Her own position on the matter was stated succinctly in an interview published in 1990:

Poetry is not a servant of politics. The Troubles affect my life and enter my poetry that way, but I avoid them as a subject as I avoid taking arms against a sea. The crisis informs my work, naturally, but I can't confront it there; it is too complex. What other writers do is not for me to lay down. If they live in England and America, outspokenness is easier because safer. I have touched on the subject implicitly in poems like 'Dovecote', written at the time of the hunger strikes, or 'The Blue She Brings With Her', for a mother whose son was destroyed. But one could argue that I don't deal with or solve anything; I just suggest an attitude of compassion in what is part of a universal tragedy.

This 'attitude of compassion' applies to other Northern Irish poets also; their poetry could never be mistaken for propaganda. In Michael Longley's words, 'The revolutionary poem in Ulster now tends to be an elegy. It resists any notions of selective mourning.' When the dead are mourned, as in two of Longley's best-known poems, 'Wounds' and 'Wreaths', his regret at wasted lives transcends the limitations of conventional protest poetry.

In a lecture, 'Feeling Into Words', Seamus Heaney spoke of his search, as the Ulster conflict developed, for 'a field of force in which, without abandoning fidelity to the processes and experience of poetry . . . it would be possible to encompass the perspectives of a humane reason and at the same time to grant the religious intensity of the violence its deplorable authenticity and complexity.' The poet must be faithful to the art of poetry as well as to the facts of the situation. A 'balanced' poetry would be bland and a protest poetry would be unbalanced. For guidance, Heaney found himself looking to 'Mandelstam and other poets from Eastern bloc countries'.

Heaney's Mandelstam 'stands for the efficacy of song itself'; he is a model of integrity, courage and truth. Mandelstam also appears as an iconic figure in poems by Seamus Deane ('Son of Petropolis, tell us, / Tell us how to turn into the flash') and Tom Paulin ('The Other Voice'). Clearly, some cross-fertilization exists between the poetry of Northern Ireland and Eastern Europe. A Polish poet and translator, Piotr Sommer (born in 1948), has testified to having learned from the careful weighting of the personal and the political to be found in Ulster poetry. It would, nonetheless, be an absurdity to make any direct comparison between post-1969 Northern Ireland and pre-1989 Eastern Europe. Over 3,000 people died in the Ulster Troubles and many more lives have been blighted by the conflict. However, the deplorable repressions and discriminations endured by Northern Irish Catholics were never on a scale remotely comparable with those suffered by people under various Communist dictators. Punning on the red of Ulster rather than of Communism (the red hand is the emblem of the province), James Simmons offered this Protestant confession:

> *One Protestant Ulsterman*
> *wants to confess this:*
> *we frightened you Catholics, we gerrymandered,*
> *we applied injustice.*
>
> *However, we weren't Nazis or Yanks,*
> *so measure your fuss*
> *who never suffered like Jews or Blacks,*
> *not here, not with us;*
>
> *but, since we didn't reform ourselves,*
> *since we had to be caught*
> *red-handed, justice is something*
> *we have to be taught.*

Far from being suppressed or censored, the work of the best contemporary Northern Irish poets has been a much-celebrated aspect of Ulster culture, officially supported by the Arts Council in Belfast (where Michael Longley and Ciaran Carson, in turn, have directed the literary programme). It is difficult to see, therefore, why a poem like Tom Paulin's 'Where Art is Midwife', should have been selected for *A Rage for Order*. There is a certain affectation about the inclusion of a poem in which East European censors 'on day-release' are being taught to recognize the significance of some — not exactly taxing — metaphors ('This poem about a bear / Is not a poem about a bear'). But, even if Ulster poets were spared the pressure to speak in the coded Aesopian language of East Europe, they naturally (like poets anywhere) sought out metaphors which would enable them to bring reality into sharper imaginative focus. In Heaney's 'bog poems', iron-age victims of ritual murder are revived with a powerful contemporary charge; Derek Mahon finds an Ulster resonance in Basho's

Japan, as Michael Longley does in Homer's Greece.

Occasionally, these poets feel compelled to speak with absolute directness — Heaney recalling how a friend's 'candid forehead stopped / A pointblank teatime bullet' or Longley elegizing a civil servant:

> *He was preparing an Ulster fry for breakfast*
> *When someone walked into the kitchen and shot him:*
> *A bullet entered his mouth and pierced his skull,*
> *The books he had read, the music he could play . . .*

Padraic Fiacc's style can be so plain as to make other poets seem artful even at their most direct: 'They pump six bullets into you.' A front-line bard, he reports from the scene of the crime. His poems have a jagged immediacy, although — like a damp match — they often splutter out unsatisfactorily. An important presence for younger Ulster poets, Fiacc is at his best when recording the out-takes of the Ulster conflict, as when — dumping leaves — he startles a young British Army soldier: 'We are that close to each other, I / Can nearly hear his heart beating.'

Ciaran Carson, too, has mapped Troubles Belfast with its security checks, drinking shebeens, punishment shootings and narrow escapes. While capable of vividly direct language, he has also made a specialty of indirection — 'Hamlet' illustrates his freely-associating colloquial mode, rich in unravellings and inter-weavings, and his shorter poems are those of a nuts-and-bolts poet who can put war into words:

> *Suddenly as the riot squad moved in, it was raining*
> *   exclamation marks,*
> *Nuts, bolts, nails, car-keys. A fount of broken type.*
> *   And the explosion*
> *Itself — an asterisk on the map. This hyphenated line,*
> *   a burst of rapid fire . . .*

'In the area of politics', Stanislaw Barańczak has written, 'there are two things in which the poet is an expert. Human suffering and human dialogue.' Inevitably, however, all but the most opportunistic poets will have doubts about the relevance and efficacy of poetry in the face of political conflict. Seamus Heaney is aware that a poet seen through watchtower binoculars will seem 'not worth bothering about . . . not about to set times wrong or right'. Tony Harrison, sharing a plane journey between Belfast and Newcastle with British soldiers, knows that his fellow-passengers will not read what he writes. The young Ulster writer, Martin Mooney, in 'Radio Free Nowhere', seems to allow for the possibility of something valuable, if 'almost unnoticeable', being lodged in the ears of those who hear 'a poem or a manifesto / sandwiched between records'.

W H Auden (whose overworked 'poetry makes nothing happen' should now be escorted into well-earned retirement) has claimed that, in cases of social or political injustice, only two things are effective: 'political action and straight journalistic reportage of the facts'; he added that 'A poet, *qua* poet, has only one political duty, namely, in his own writing to set an example of the correct use of his mother tongue which is always being corrupted.' Paul Muldoon's '7, Middagh Street' accommodates some of Auden's doubts, while alluding to Yeats's 'The Man and the Echo' ('Did that play of mine send out / Certain men the English shot?'):

> *If Yeats had saved his pencil-lead*
> *would certain men have stayed in bed?*

> *For history's a twisted root*
> *with art its small, translucent fruit*

> *and never the other way round . . .*

The entwined roots of poetry and politics cannot so readily be disentangled and it may be in recognition of this that Muldoon, later in the same polyphonic poem, puts antithetical words in Louis MacNeice's mouth: 'For poetry *can* make things happen — / not only can, but *must*'.

What causes genuine poets to proceed warily in the presence of politics is not only the fear of writing ineffectual poetry on the one hand, or propagandist poetry on the other, but also the concern that they might mar their work with misjudgements. Not every poet brings to politics the wisdom of Czeslaw Milosz; the delusions of Ezra Pound, Pablo Neruda and Hugh MacDiarmid suggest that scepticism rather than genius may be the best protection against political naivety. There is also a question of proportion; the anger of Austin Clarke in some of his brave satires can now seem disproportionate to its occasion. Sam Burnside's poem,

'In and Out of Derry', offers a distant prospect of the Troubles: 'In a hundred years it will warrant a paragraph / In some history book . . . and they'll not know / Or not reckon the fear in pubs, in shops . . .'

As politician and bishop rendered language numb with their routine condemnations, the poets of the Troubles — through their sense of individual life and individual loss and common humanity — tried to restore its power of feeling and to model new, less stereotyped ways of thinking. At this point, a further danger (one not unknown to Ulster poetry) surfaced. It was well-defined by Jerzy Jarniewicz:

> *The urge to produce work which is, above all, technically impeccable, combined with the poets' highly literary preoccupations, results in the tendency to aestheticise. However powerful and controversial the subject may be, it becomes innocuous when overwhelmed by the formal execution and wit of the poem.*

Jarniewicz does not exclude Heaney from the charge of aestheticization, although Heaney is himself amply vigilant in this regard, allowing his cousin (commemorated in 'The Strand at Lough Beg') to return later and haunt him with just such an accusation:

> *'You confused evasion and artistic tact.*
> *The Protestant who shot me through the head*
> *I accuse directly, but indirectly, you*
> *who now atone perhaps upon this bed*
> *for the way you whitewashed ugliness and drew*
> *the lovely blinds of the* Purgatorio
> *and saccharined my death with morning dew.'*

Elsewhere, though, Heaney has made a strong defence of the 'achieved poem' tradition to which Ulster poets adhere ('style, formal finish, linguistic relish'). Against the charges of 'evasion' and 'whitewash', he pleads that the concern 'with poetry itself' of his fellow-poets 'wears well when we place it beside the protest poetry of the Sixties'. This is an Irish version of the 'cooked' versus 'raw' debate; both Heaney and his cousin (who, ironically, addresses the poet in high style) have a point, and I can see no reason why a poet of stark informality should be any less capable of rising to the Ulster challenge than an equally-endowed poet of polished formality.

The issue of 'taking sides' in the conflict is toyed with playfully in the work of Paul Muldoon and Rita Ann Higgins, painfully in a poem by Paul Durcan:

> *In a public house, darkly-lit, a patriotic (sic)*
> *Versifier whines into my face: 'You must take one side*
> *Or the other, or you're but a fucking romantic.' . . .*

The most dramatic instance of a poet outside of Eastern Europe being coerced to adopt a party line is recorded in Seamus Heaney's poem, 'The Flight Path'. Home from America and exulting 'at being back', he is suddenly joined on his train journey by a 'grimfaced' senior republican who 'sits down / Opposite' and attacks 'head on':

> *'When, for fuck's sake, are you going to write*
> *Something for us?' 'If I do write something,*
> *Whatever it is, I'll be writing for myself.'*

Speaking for himself is the only way in which a poet can speak for others, a point Heaney had made in 1975 when he wrote:

> *During the last few years there has been considerable*
> *expectation that poets from Northern Ireland should 'say'*
> *something about 'the situation', but in the end they will*
> *only be worth listening to if they are saying something*
> *about and to themselves. The truest poetry may be the*
> *most feigning but there are contexts, and Northern*
> *Ireland is one of them, where to feign a passion is as repre-*
> *hensible as to feign its absence.*

Heaney's scrupulous approach towards language, probing words for their etymology and placenames for their history, together with his strongly-developed sense of conscience (he is scrupulous in this sense too) have made him an exemplary practitioner of poetry in a time of conflict. Although he was — and is — essentially a poet of 'pre-reflective experience', he felt a duty to bear witness (albeit entirely on his own terms) to the Troubles. As Jan Patocka remarked to Vaclav Havel, 'The real test of a man is not how well he plays the role he has invented for himself, but how well he plays the role that destiny assigned to him.'

The poems in *A Rage for Order* are literary rather than popular — tribal songs, triumphal ballads and newspaper verse are omitted — and its contents will have made more impact in university campuses than among the peacemakers and warmongers of Ulster. When Senator Gordon Wilson (whose daughter's tragic death in the Remembrance Day bombing of 1987 is commemorated in Ormsby's anthology) spoke at the time of the 1994 IRA ceasefire announcement, it was for lines by John Greenleaf Whittier that this great conciliator reached in order to give expression to his hopes. A member of the Irish government, on the same occasion, quoted John F Kennedy, Amelia Earhart and a snatch of rhyme by an author whose name he could not recall.

Whatever bitterness Southern Irish poets may feel at their relative neglect, the residence in the South of John Montague, Seamus Heaney, Gerald Dawe, Derek Mahon and Seamus Deane will undoubtedly have contributed to cross-border understanding. John Montague's epic, *The Rough Field*, in which his story and history chime, has been influential but its poetry gets lost in anthologization. Gerald Dawe, who opposes any partitioning of Irish poetry, has — through his work as editor, critic and poet — proved a tireless mediator between the Northern and Southern literary communities. He looks forward to an era when 'writers will no longer get attention because they come from a certain part of the country. The sooner the Troubles are out of Irish writing, the better.' Two Southern poets deserving of particular mention are Richard Murphy and John Ennis. Murphy, in his long poem, *The Battle of Aughrim*, struck a balance between the Anglo and Irish parts of himself and traced their legacy into the present. 'Amazement', about the Maze prison hunger-strikers, employs the anaphoric language of the beatitudes (with their glorification of peace and mercy) to examine the paradoxical world of those whom 'a word imprisoned and a word could save'.

John Ennis's 'Londonderry' is a remarkable poem — a Southern Catholic is writing from the viewpoint of the Northern Protestants besieged by James II in 1689, two years before the Battle of Aughrim. It recognizes that nobody has a monopoly on Irishness:

> *If we look to London, why do you rage?*
> *'Irish', were you so planted from Adam?*
> *Intruders, we both sailed west to furze-lit hills,*

Dennis O'Driscoll

like you, we dug dykes, sowed corn, threw up roofs . . .

The generosity of Ennis's vision finds its Northern correlative in
the work of John Hewitt (1907-87). Notwithstanding what
Patricia Craig terms an 'instinctive aversion from Catholicism (a
matter of temperament, not bigotry)', his poems are notable for
their spirit of tolerance and reconciliation. The section of Hewitt's
long poem, 'Freehold', which is excerpted by Ormsby, finds the
poet inspecting — and meticulously describing — a Catholic
church interior. Having come, out of boredom, to stare, he later
feels that he should have stayed to understand:

> *I had gone there a vacant hour to pass,*
> *to see the sculpture and admire the glass,*
> *but left as I had come, a protestant . . .*
> *The years since then have proved I should have stayed*
> *and mercy might have touched me till I prayed.*

Despite an overheated final stanza, 'The Coasters' is one of
Hewitt's best poems; satirical and scathing, it addresses itself to
the smug and thriving middle-classes who felt virtuous and
liberal because they 'had a friend or two of the other sort', but
who ignored, or remained dangerously ambivalent towards, the
growing threat of community violence. Hewitt himself was no
'coaster'. From the 1940s, alongside his topographical lyrics
about the Ulster countryside, he was tracing the title to that
countryside of those who had been 'planted' there from 'the ripe
England of the moulded downs'. Standing his ground and
staking the claim of his people to permanent residence in Ireland
by virtue of hard work and long tenure, his stance was forthright
and firm but never aggressive:

> *So I, because of all the buried men*
> *in Ulster clay, because of rock and glen*
> *and mist and cloud and quality of air*
> *as native in my thought as any here . . .*

Nearly thirty years later, in the light of the many premature
burials in Ulster clay, Hewitt published a rare example of a
persuasive public poem about the Ulster violence. 'Neither an
Elegy Nor a Manifesto', addressed to 'the people of my province
and the rest of Ireland', reflects a belief in poetry as a force for good:

The careful words of my injunction
are unrhetorical, as neutral
and unaligned as any I know:
they propose no more than thoughtful response;
they do not pound with drum-beats
of patriotism, loyalty, martyrdom.

So I say only: Bear in mind
those men and lads killed in the streets;
but do not differentiate between
those deliberately gunned down
and those caught by unaddressed bullets:
such distinctions are not relevant . . .

Seamus Heaney, a prophet who has been received somewhat carpingly in his own province, adopts a convincing public voice in the vatic middle section of 'Triptych' and in parts of 'The Cure at Troy' ('hope for a great sea-change / On the far side of revenge'). Two rather public pieces, certainly among the best-known poems of the Troubles — Heaney's 'Whatever You Say Say Nothing' and Thomas Kinsella's 'Butcher's Dozen' — are excluded without explanation from *A Rage for Order*. Neither represents its author at full strength, though both have far more relevance than, say, Derek Mahon's very fine but scarcely pertinent poem in memory of Louis MacNeice. The Heaney poem ('Manoeuverings to find out name and school, / Subtle discrimination by addresses') and the Kinsella ('The shame is theirs, in word and deed, / Who prate of Justice, practice greed') may be too explicit for Ormsby's liking but, by excluding them, he risks an anthology with too much order and too little rage.

Dannie Abse has pointed out that British poets (so ready, it seems, to write of crises in Bosnia and Kuwait) scarcely ever attend to their own Northern Irish backyard. The British visitors to *A Rage for Order* come on as 'special guest appearances' rather than as participants in an ongoing dialogue between one part of the United Kingdom and another. A superb poem with an English setting, 'Sunday in Great Tew', was actually written by an Ulster poet who lives and teaches in England, Peter McDonald. His leisurely outing to 'this model village / a half-hour's drive from Oxford' coincides with the horror of the Remembrance Day bombing in Enniskillen. Brushing lightly past words like 'loyalist', 'victory' and 'memorial', the sense of horror is conveyed all the more potently for being filtered through 'the subtle fog' of a chocolate-box village where the pub is named the Falkland Arms and the conversation jumps 'from one silence to another / in ripe Oxonian vowels'.

Skilfully evoking the peace of Great Tew while simultaneously adumbrating 'far-off acts of war', McDonald's suspicion of moving too far from the realm of given experience and everyday language is typical of the best Troubles poetry and of what has saved it from becoming parasitic on violence. Few, if any, of the Northern Irish poets engage in active politics and they would undoubtedly agree with Czeslaw Milosz about the importance of moving forward 'to experiences that are shared by other human beings and not be constantly turning around in the circle of our experiences of the time of war'.

John Hewitt was active in left-wing politics from his youth. The airy internationalism which — in a 1945 essay — he denounced in literature was far more malign in politics, not least when it took the pro-Soviet form espoused at the time by Hewitt himself. How ironic therefore that one of the finest and most humane poems in *A Rage for Order*, Hewitt's 'The Colony', should call to mind the allegorical style forced on East Europe's dissident poets by Communist censorship. And, while again stressing the vast gulf which separated the Northern Irish experience from the East European one, Hewitt's poem, which tells neither the Unionist ('make amends') nor the nationalist ('this is our country also') what they will have wanted to hear, must have taken courage to publish in 1953. Frank Ormsby writes that '"The Colony", in which the speaker is a Roman colonist, may have served as a model for younger poets of how to address the Troubles obliquely with a dynamic balance of involvement and restraint'. Decades after its composition, with the Northern violence in full spate, 'The Colony' was being quoted in an *Irish Times* editorial, in the writings of clergy and the orations of politicians. The Taoiseach of the time, Jack Lynch, cited it in a speech in Philadelphia on St Patrick's Day 1971. The poet as prophet comes too early and the poet as elegist comes too late. In the words of Franco Fortini, 'Poetry changes nothing. Nothing is certain. But write.'

The Southern Review (Summer 1995)

·

Valentin Iremonger

Sandymount, Dublin

The June 1944 issue of *The Bell* finds a civil servant cutting James Joyce down to size. The twentysix-year-old Valentin Iremonger arrives at the considered conclusion that 'neither *Ulysses* nor *Finnegans Wake* repays the effort required to read them through again: once read, they are for the casual quarter-hour, the night-cap'. Elsewhere in the same issue, Iremonger lays down some laws about his chosen art: 'Poetry has little to do with Truth, Sincerity or what-have-you, and ultimate truths . . . are out of place in poetry which only establishes the conditions within which truth exists.' The brash tone is that of a young man on the make, intent on sweeping all before him. The future would surely be his.

This selection of poems displays a cover photograph of the martello tower in Iremonger's birthplace, Sandymount, as if to throw out a further challenge to that other martello tower a little distance down the coast in Sandycove. It is hardly an equal contest. Iremonger's output proved less than Joycean in original-ity and quality, though he would later claim to have been the first poet in Ireland 'who tried to write in the modern idiom'. What-ever the legitimacy of this claim, it is true that many of his best poems adopt a colloquial, breezy idiom which anticipated some of the characteristics of the Movement poets.

A Larkinesque melancholy pervades his first — and only — full-length collection of new poems, *Reservations* (published, appropriately for a future diplomat, by *Envoy* magazine). *Reservations* (1945) preceded Philip Larkin's *The Less Deceived* by five years. To have reservations is to be less deceived and Iremonger writes of Swift as unable to 'make himself believe / Happiness as other than being well-deceived'. The title poem of *Reservations* had appeared in that same June 1944 issue of *The Bell* accompanied by at least one sentiment which brings us close to the broody side of Iremonger's temperament that is encountered

more in his poetry than his criticism: 'It is the struggle against . . .
"the soul's incurable loneliness", against the fact that he must
account to himself for his deeds, that makes a man a poet.'

Throughout *Reservations* he struggles against 'the soul's incurable loneliness' and adumbrates a sense of profound hurt and
dread. A dark night of the soul suffuses 'Dark Way', one of the
two poems from *Reservations* (the other being 'The Toy Horse')
which I particularly miss from *Sandymount, Dublin*. With 'no
artificial daylight for the mind', darkness brings

> *the shapes of our wicked fancies*
> *That, baulked in the daytime, gather round at night*
> *With their terrible accusations and their gross demands . . .*

The very titles of other poems, 'Alone by Night' and 'Night,
Again Night' (also excluded from the present selection), speak
from a similarly sombre recess of the psyche, while 'July Evening
— Storm Coming Up' ends: 'Now for the decisions of the night,
the heart's undoing: / The time where reason and emotions meet.'

Much of Iremonger's poetry is concerned with (and about) the
passing of time. He counts the minutes and looks forward — but
with fearful rather than cheerful anticipation. Now that spring is
here can winter be far behind? His 'minutes move on to a fate
they cannot retard'. In the final stanza of 'A Marriage Has Been
Arranged', it is as if a MacNeice theme had been matched to a
Larkin tone:

> *The problem, of course, is to hold this minute Now*
> *In perpetuo while growing ourselves to ripeness; how*
> *To have Time held up by some blunt traffic cop*
> *So letting us, the unfortunate pedestrians, across.*
> *It can't be done, I suppose; so I wish her, my dear,*
> *As much happiness as she can conveniently bear.*

A drama of lost love, lost time, lost opportunity is repeatedly
rehearsed, and poems like 'Elegy for the Commencement of
Winter', 'From New Ross' and 'Clear View of Summer' tend to
blur into one another. 'There are bad times coming / When you and
I will look with envy on old photographs', the latter warns, while
another jeremiad laments a 'winter already in our numbed
hands'. He must forgo 'summer consolation' and 'spring
expectancy'; 'spring and winter are the same to me / Whose seed

is stunted with the year's advance'. So many of these rueful, elegiac, wartime poems adopt seasonal disguises that it comes as little surprise that, when the tension underlying the work is apparently resolved through love, the occasion is celebrated with a 'Poem in the Depths of Summer'. *Reservations*, which opened with a 'Backward Look', closed with this poem in which he was able to look forward with favour and without fear. He has divined a deep 'reserve of love':

> *. . . And, though winter, perhaps,*
> *Invest us, here we have sustenance, over and above*
> *Our possible needs — till like trees we blossom*
> *Again, our lives' leaves tossing.*

So *Reservations* ended and with it, to all intents and purposes, the poetical career. Like William Empson, he had lost his subject-matter due to his new personal circumstances. And, also like Empson, he would write a good poem ('The Invocation') about not writing. The rest of his meagre output consisted mostly of wilful efforts to revive his old afflatus. Iremonger, who made his own selection for *Sandymount, Dublin* did well to exclude some of these, even if he brings to the front of the volume two 'new' poems in Irish which are of curiosity value only. By the time the final, platitudinous poem is reached (home thoughts from New Delhi in 1969), the reader's reservations are beginning to out-number the author's.

But, whatever one's misgivings, early Iremonger is well worth attending to and deserves a secure, if minor, place in the roll-call of Irish poets after Kavanagh for poems like 'Icarus', 'Soldier from the Wars' and 'The Dog'. 'This Houre Her Vigill', Iremonger's finest poem, is maddeningly denied perfection by the redundant and tin-eared word, 'rebelliously', in the penulti-mate line. Many of his love-torn, time-worn, decay-haunted poems are memorable also, hovering between cynicism and romanticism and redolent of certain adolescent moods and youthful despondencies. His career as a poet was brief and flawed; yet there is enough substance in this book to earn it a modest space on the bookshelf, to be taken down — at the very least — 'for the casual quarter-hour, the nightcap'.

Irish Literary Supplement (Spring 1989)

Thomas Kinsella

1 *His Struggle*

'But for real pleasure there is nothing to equal / sitting down to a
serious read', as Thomas Kinsella's 'A Technical Supplement'
declares. He himself is a serious poet whose work gives real
pleasure. The pleasure derives, not least, from following
Kinsella's imagination to the points where myth and memory,
anecdote and archetype converge. The seriousness can lead to an
overly solemn tone, but is frequently modified by caustic wit. In
his interview with Peter Orr in 1962, Kinsella stated that he was
'striving continually for greater clarity and directness and regular
pace — fitting the pace to the poem and making it an immediately comprehensible whole as far as possible'. The later work
seldom qualifies as 'immediately comprehensible' and exploratory
poems like 'Songs of the Psyche' and the *Out of Ireland* sequence
take us to a depth where reading light shines only faintly. His
heuristic and open-ended approach to writing does not,
however, preclude it from still satisfying his own criterion of
being as comprehensible 'as possible' — though readers might
wish him to be more forthcoming with the annotation of certain
poems.

Kinsella's meanings are wrenched from the struggle — his
'good fight' — to find a language which will do justice to the full
range of human experience. His conviction that talent 'persisted
in without change / grows ridiculous' has informed his own
practice. The 'eliciting of order from significant experience' represents one of his most enduring aspirations. In his earliest poems,
written in strict Audenesque and Yeatsian forms, he tended to
impose order rather than elicit it. At that stage, he was countering
time and chaos with symmetry and grace; the result, at its
weakest, was a poetry that could be artificial as well as deriva-
tive. His early style won Kinsella wide notice; and it is a measure
of his commitment as an artist that he was prepared to move

away from the ready-made forms of which he was an applauded master towards more risk-taking and improvisatory ones:

> *Take, for example, this work in hand.*
> *Out of its waste matter*
> *it should emerge solid and light.*
> *One idea, grown with the thing itself,*
> *should drive it searching inward*
> *with a sort of life, due to the mirror effect.*
> *Often, the more I simplify*
> *the more a few simplicities*
> *go burrowing in their own depths*
> *until the guardian structure is aroused.*

His reading of nineteenth-century poetry, above all else, had taught Kinsella how much misspent effort could be expended on 'an imposed plan'. In a 1968 lecture, he noted that 'the temptation to impose order or purpose is always great, and if yielded to the price is great'. The nearest that Kinsella has come to 'an imposed plan' in later years is the numerological system, beginning with zero, which first surfaced in 'Notes from the Land of the Dead' and which is essentially his own private game-plan or poem-plan. It is a relief to find this 'system' operating, in practice, as a guiding principle rather than a slavish programme. Some of his finest poems ('A Technical Supplement' and 'Tao and Unfitness at Inistiogue on the River Nore', for example) elude schematic subjugation altogether.

Despite the fragmentary nature of individual poems and sequences, Kinsella's output has come to seem exceptionally unified. Echoes of earlier poems — together with notions of horror, process and change, faith in the healing power of love and a host of recurring images (sidereal harmony, 'fall' etc) — occur in the later books. Of particular interest is the way he has twinned his Gaelic literary inheritance with his Modernist literary aesthetic. Excavating his family past, Kinsella found it merging into a tribal past; the excitement and apprehension entailed in the discovery of Ireland itself become analogues for the poet's own voyage of self-discovery. Overcoming the discontinuity of Irish literature (which he lamented in his lectures, 'The Irish Writer' and 'The Divided Mind'), Kinsella has salvaged and recycled passages and images from *Lebor Gabála* and other sources in poems like 'Ancestor', 'Survivor', 'Finistère' and 'The Oldest

Dennis O'Driscoll

Place'. The result might well have been a hideous hybrid of the prehistoric and the Poundian; in Kinsella's hands, however, the cross-fertilization has produced work which requires acclimatization on the part of new readers but which rewards as much as it demands.

Tracks 7 (1987)

2 *His Wit*

The very idea of Thomas Kinsella as a witty poet — 'witty' in the contemporary colloquial sense, with strong connotations of pleasurable humour — would be enough to raise a laugh in some critical quarters. 'I have devoted / my life, my entire career, / to the avoidance of affectation, / the way of entertainment . . . ', the protagonist of his poem, 'At the Head Table', reminds himself with more than a little pride and defiance. If — as seems reasonable — Kinsella's readers assume that the inner voice in the poem speaks for the poet himself, they will find nothing to surprise them in its sentiments. 'Entertaining' may be a description which certain contemporary publishers like to pin — along with their hopes — on new poets but Thomas Kinsella (who has stated that 'the notion of . . . poetry as linguistic entertainment seems to me a trivial exercise') recoils from the word.

If 'entertaining' is not a praise-word in Kinsella's austere critical vocabulary, the word most commonly applied to his work by critics is 'brooding'. Patrick Kavanagh may be characterised as earthy or W B Yeats as airy or Austin Clarke as contrary; but Kinsella is forever brooding. Peter Sirr — one of Kinsella's most sympathetic critics — speaks of his 'darkly brooding art' and his 'brooding unity of tone', while Edna Longley — one of his severest critics — allows that he is 'a brooding, challenging presence on the poetic scene'. Calvin Bedient, whose response to Kinsella's unfolding work gradually became more severe than sympathetic, claimed that Kinsella had 'brooded himself to pieces' in *Notes from the Land of the Dead* (1973).

By the 1990s, when 'At the Head Table' was published, the idea of poetry as entertainment was well-established in the English-speaking world: not just the rapid reaction rap artist or the slickly professional performance poet but the mainstream poet who could be relied upon to serve 'accessible' poetry to the beer-drinkers at village arts festivals. Long before then, however, Thomas Kinsella had established a reputation as a writer who was singularly sceptical about popular movements like the Beats ('Poetry and Allen Ginsberg do not occupy the same space'), someone whose readers were greeted at the entrance to one of his books with a blurb of uncompromising — not to mention uncommercial — honesty, stating that 'His subject in general . . . is a developing view of life as ordeal. These poems are concerned with the human process as it endures disorder and erosion and death.'

Kinsella's image as a poet with an 'ordeal-cup', rather than a pint, in his hand is reinforced by the pronouncements of reviewers and critics who find him — as his well-disposed *Irish Times* interviewer put it — to be 'serious' and 'unironic'. 'Sombre', 'sour', 'stern', 'grim', 'gloomy' and 'portentous' are words found — not without partial justification — in critiques of Kinsella's work. Reviewing *Collected Poems 1956–1994* (1996), John Montague wrote:

> With the Morrigan, or Celtic Scaldcrow of death, on the front cover, and Kinsella's horn-rimmed and bearded gob peering obliquely at us from a back panel, we know we are in for a serious time. I wonder if this can be traced back to an early identification with the best but most sombre of our 19th Century poets . . . Clarence Mangan?

Montague recalled the 'appreciative and wide audience' which Kinsella's 'positively charming' early books, *Another September* (1958) and *Downstream* (1962), had won him. It is a sad irony that Kinsella's readership declined in size as his work increased in power. One fundamental reason why early Kinsella is inferior to middle and late Kinsella is because the early poems, impressively crafted though they are, achieve fluency without personality; too much in the acclaimed first collection speaks in a false accent — suggestive of false sentiments — and betrays an almost foppish fastidiousness about the handling of everyday language. In the tender 'A Lady of Quality', one of the poems where the depth of underlying feeling *is* unmistakable, it is the more lively and down-to-earth lines ('country ladies who could wind / A nation's love-affair with mind / Around their little fingers') which help the poem to survive grandiloquence of the 'a train to Southward, hark!' variety.

Dennis O'Driscoll

Kinsella's revisions and excisions over the years have left some
of these poems — including 'A Lady of Quality' — 'hacked clean
for better bearing', like the trees in 'Mirror in February'; but there
are surviving lines even in the best of the early poems, such as
'Baggot Street Deserta' ('We fly into our risk, the spurious'),
which typify the work of a poet who has found a literary voice
but not a personal one. Indeed, like many young poets, he seems
to have discovered everyone's voice except his own; 'he do' the
poets — Eliot, Auden, Yeats and others — 'in different voices'.
One suspects earnestness more than irony behind the capitalization or personification of words like 'Youth' and 'Sorrow' — it is
difficult for a contemporary poet to be playful in language which
raises the word 'Art' to capital status ('the old mistakes / And
discords in a work of Art'). As he told John Haffenden in an interview, 'at the beginning my poems were influenced by literature
more than by fact. I would regard the direct dealing with matter
as something that requires great sophistication and equipment.'

It could be argued that the poems in *Another September* were
damaged not only by their lack of originality but by their lack of
wit. One feels that several of these poems could have benefited
from a modicum of parody in their use of anachronistic language,
some hairline crack in the formal mask, less stiffness in the
footwork of the words which partner the graceful metric. After
all, Patrick Kavanagh could take the capitalization of words like
'Eternity', 'Woman' and 'Spirit' in his stride. But Kavanagh's
comic stance and his philosophy of 'not caring' for orthodoxy —
which allowed him to recreate the sonnet in his own image and
likeness — developed only gradually. Similarly, the forging of an
intensely personal vision, indifferent to the expectations of literary fashion, has become the lonely hallmark of Thomas Kinsella's
work in the evolutionary years following *Another September*.

That younger British poet-anthologists like Simon Armitage
and Robert Crawford in their *Penguin Book of Poetry from Britain
and Ireland since 1945* and Sean O'Brien in another post-1945
anthology, *The Firebox*, would consider Thomas Kinsella adequately
represented by a single poem in each volume is a measure of how
far his star has fallen in England from the days when he was
looked on as potentially the best Irish poet after Yeats and was
routinely honoured by the Poetry Book Society. Harry Clifton
reminded readers of *Poetry Review* in 1997, 'Not twenty-five years
ago, Lyman Andrews in a *Sunday Times* review praised Thomas
Kinsella, whose *New Poems 1973* had just appeared, as one of half-

114

a-dozen significant poets then at work in the language'. A perceptive review of the same Kinsella collection in *The Listener* was
headed 'Poetry Moves to Ireland'.

Having been featured in the second of the *New Lines* anthologies (1963), closely associated with the Movement in England,
Kinsella might have become an Irish outrider of that group which
included Philip Larkin, Kingsley Amis and John Wain. Although,
in the event, he was to defect to the arch-enemy camp of Ezra
Pound and Modernism, Kinsella's condemnations of contemporary poetry ('It's not one of the lucky times. There's a lot of bad
poetry, bad poets, bad critics and bad readers'), and his unleash-
ing of merciless and witty broadsides against public and private
targets, are in keeping with the spirit — and, as it were, the letters
also — of Larkin and Amis. But, while Larkin's image among the
reading public accords him his humour as well as his gloom,
Sean O'Brien's comments in *The Firebox* suggest that Kinsella is
now regarded as abstruse and dour: 'Kinsella's work is at times
heavily allusive, even cryptic . . . his poems are often studied and
strenuous, with lyricism and drama in thrall to a larger seriousness which is also shadowed by W B Yeats.'

A poet can survive a reputation for complexity, as the recent
rise to prominence of Anne Carson proves; but, since poetry
connotes language operating at its most vital pitch, any hint of
dullness is as fatal to a reputation as a hint of absent-mindedness
would be to a cardiac surgeon. Kinsella's readers must, ideally,
learn to grapple with a formidable range of esoteric material from
Old Irish literature to Jungian archetypes — allusions which a
general audience will pursue only if persuaded that their efforts
will be amply rewarded by a poetry which reveals itself to be far
from dull. More annotation by Kinsella would clarify what, to
borrow his own remarks about Austin Clarke, might be termed
'poems of such economical means . . . that the essential facts, on
whose basis the poem communicates, need to be extracted with
Holmesian care'. It would certainly assist perplexed readers of
goodwill like Elizabeth Gaffney who, in a *New York Times* review
of *From Centre City* (1994), complained of a withholding of 'information that might have better oriented the reader within the
poet's private terrain'.

Readers can, to some extent, 'orient' themselves by attending
closely to Kinsella's nuanced and subtle linguistic registers; in the
words of Ezra Pound's 'Canto VII', they must 'drink . . . the tone
of things'. Indeed, his least-appreciated and least-recognized

tonal quality — his wit — holds the potential to win him a far wider audience than the 'fit . . . though few' on whom he can count at present. Recalling the shock caused to guests at Robert Frost's eighty-fifth birthday party when the writer (hitherto synonymous with apple-pie pieties and wholesome rustic rituals) was publicly pronounced by Lionel Trilling to be 'a terrifying poet', one can imagine readers who value ascetic austerity as an end in itself proving equally resistant to the notion that his wit is crucial to the success of some of Kinsella's best poetry. To emphasize his wit is to deepen, not diminish, Kinsella's portrayal of life's 'terrible actualities' (another phrase of Trilling's). Any poet who can write of 'The irreducible / malice and greed of the species' or who posits 'culpable ignorance' as our 'distinguishing' feature is not in denial about the darker human truths and is all the more rare and necessary a presence for that reason. Yet, Kinsella's tenebrous visions are no more monochrome than Samuel Beckett's.

An eighteenth-century master of the light touch, Oliver Goldsmith — the central figure in Kinsella's *Citizen of the World* (2000) — observed that 'The solemnity worn by many of our modern writers is, I fear, often the mask of dullness'. Thomas Kinsella — anxious lest humour be mistaken for frivolity — becomes overly solemn in tone or too abstract in language on occasion. But many of his best poems can draw on his full armoury of wit, from rapier-sharp sardonicism to wry observation; in doing so, they not only eschew dullness but also embrace a salutary ambivalence, refusing the polar simplicities of black or white and recognizing the contrary forces at work — indeed at war — in the human spirit. Commenting on Bakhtin's remarks concerning Rabelais, Felicity Rosslyn summarizes the critic's view that 'Laughter takes account of our human condition, which makes us ambivalent, and in which the wise poet will always leave room for his poetry to say more than he himself intends'. Her quotation from Bakhtin asserts that laughter can be the way of truth as well as the 'way of entertainment'; that, indeed, an earnest poem is an incomplete one:

> *True ambivalent and universal laughter does not deny seriousness but purifies and completes it. Laughter purifies from dogmatism, from the intolerant and the petrified; it liberates from fanaticism and pedantry, from fear and intimidation, from didacticism, naiveté and*

illusion, from the single meaning, the single level, from
sentimentality. Laughter does not permit seriousness to
atrophy and to be torn away from the one being, forever
incomplete. It restores this ambivalent wholeness.

A loosening and lightening of tone first becomes a marked feature of Kinsella's work in the jaunty couplets — as Audenesque as they are Augustan — which open *Downstream* (1962). The poem is set in italic type, as someone once suggested (ironically, of course) that perhaps all ironic utterances ought to be presented, so as not to confuse the credulous:

I wonder whether one expects
Flowing tie or expert sex
Or even absent-mindedness
Of poets any longer. Less
Candour than the average,
Less confidence, a ready rage,
Alertness when it comes to beer,
An affectation that their ear
For music is a little weak,
These are the attributes we seek;
But surely not the morning train,
The office lunch, the look of pain
Down the blotched suburban grass,
Not the weekly trance at Mass . . .
Drawing on my sober dress
These, alas, I must confess.

Kinsella's lines are an overture without an opera in that they bear minimal relationship in style or content to the *Downstream* poems which follow. If anything, they seem like a rehearsal for the disaffected suburban visions in the first movement of his symphonic 'Nightwalker'. The breezy tone and the predominantly octosyllabic couplets show Kinsella in thrall to a poem like W H Auden's 'New Year Letter'. 'A Country Walk', from the same collection, takes bold steps in the direction of everyday speech, through unadorned talk of 'a gombeen jungle' and an atmospheric, if determinedly downbeat, invocation of 'A lamp switched on above the urinal' and a 'silent handball alley'.

W H Auden, as a light verse virtuoso and editor of the classic *Oxford Book of Light Verse*, never disdained 'the way of entertainment' — indeed, Kinsella described Auden and MacNeice as having been 'inclined toward intellectual entertainment'. Nonetheless, Auden — the seminal early influence — remains a mentor whom Kinsella honours in poems ('Memory of W H Auden') and interviews ('his capacity to emerge throughout his career, whatever the pressure, with a poem of grace, beauty, charm, seductive rhythm') although he would 'later . . . find much more satisfaction in the forms of Ezra Pound's *Cantos*'. In the 'Warning' pasted at the beginning of his *ABC of Reading* (one longs to see it super-glued to the 'fly-leaf' of the *Cantos* also, rebuking its rambling and hectoring passages), Ezra Pound observes that 'Gloom and solemnity are entirely out of place in even the most rigorous study of an art originally intended to make glad the heart of man' and he adds, for good measure, this definition from Lawrence Sterne: 'Gravity, a mysterious carriage of the body to conceal the defects of the mind.' One can imagine how avidly the lightly-tripping poet and 'sober' civil servant of the *Downstream* prologue would have responded to an early Pound poem like 'Further Instructions':

> Come, my songs, let us express our baser passions,
> Let us express our envy of the man with a steady job
>   and no worry about the future.
> You are very idle, my songs.
> I fear you will come to a bad end.
> You stand about in the streets,
> You loiter at the corners and bus-stops,
> You do next to nothing at all . . .

Within Kinsella's larger structures — with their recurrent motifs, reprise of images, resistance of closure — individual lyric poems do separate themselves. In this sense he could be said to combine the traditions of both Auden and Pound (his early and late masters), while refusing the conventional trajectory of the former and the imperious obfuscation of the latter. *Downstream* contains more Auden than Pound, the balance tilting towards Pound after *Nightwalker and Other Poems* (1968). While many of the *Nightwalker* poems were too solemn for their own good, it was evident that the poet had a great deal of real-life tribulation with which to struggle practically as well as imaginatively: he drives 'from worry to worry' and is driven through 'ordeal after ordeal'. The 'peaks of stress' are his vantage point for viewing the fallen world. But, just as the couple in 'Remembering Old Wars' can rise 'each dawn . . . (to) renew each other with a savage smile', the poet of the title poem, 'Nightwalker', can smile 'in antipathy' at modern Ireland.

The incisions scored by 'Nightwalker' owe some of their depth to the authority of Kinsella's first-hand experience as a fortuitously well-placed civil servant. His civil service career included a period as private secretary to T K Whitaker, the administrative head of the Department of Finance. Whitaker is credited with pioneering modern economic planning in Ireland, including measures for the encouragement of greater foreign investment in the country. Gifted and committed though Kinsella the civil servant undoubtedly was, he would afterwards exercise his liberty (complete with a satirical allusion to the inscription on the Statue of Liberty) to take a poet's sounding on national developments:

> *Robed in spattered iron she stands*
> *At the harbour mouth, Productive Investment,*
> *And beckons the nations through our gold half-door:*
> *Lend me your wealth, your cunning and your drive,*
> *Your arrogant refuse. Let my people serve them*
> *Holy water in our new hotels,*
> *While native businessmen and managers*
> *Drift with them chatting over to the window*
> *To show them our growing city, give them a feeling*
> *Of what is possible; our labour pool,*
> *The tax concessions to foreign capital,*
> *How to get a nice estate through German.*
> *Even collect some of our better young artists.*

Throughout 'Nightwalker', whether presciently lampooning Charles Haughey 'on his big white harse' or — in another instance of word play (this time punning on the word 'state') — depicting a Catholic education system which ensures that there will be no 'lack (of) civil servants in a state of grace', Kinsella's mordant wit is in step with his scorn. The businessmen in 'Nightwalker', looking down on the city through profit-tinted glass, will be followed in later books by Dublin's city fathers gazing with 'visages of rapine' from another window ('Night Conference, Wood Quay') and the church-city conspirators of 'Social Work':

> *A pair of furious Corporation officials*
> *had stepped across to one of the high windows*
>
> *with the social workers — the very Catholic doctor,*
> *the house agent at his elbow, silver-haired —*
> *and the parish priest, present as an observer.*
>
> *The latter had chatted pleasantly before the meeting*
> *but was otherwise quiet. He was speaking now*
> *at the centre of the group, the others nodding.*

The devastatingly detached tone of 'Social Work' replaces the 'full-throated outcry' of 'Nightwalker' with no loss of withering wit. These later poems, in which authority figures are scrutinized and found gravely wanting, dispense with editorializing elaboration and let the facts speak for themselves. Early Irish poetry, which he has translated into plain direct English, may have exerted its stylistic influence here. It is just about arguable, too, that — like small-scale Voyage poems — Kinsella's wanderings in 'Nightwalker', 'A Country Walk', even 'Tao and Unfitness at Inistiogue on the River Nore' follow the Gaelic precedent of the *immrama*, though the 'Wandering Rocks' section of *Ulysses* is never to be discounted as an influence on his Dublin poems in particular.

The fact that the tower in 'Nightwalker' is James Joyce's in Sandycove rather than W B Yeats's in Ballylee signifies more than a transition from a rural, peasant-centred poetry to an urban, commuter-belt poetry. Joyce is important to Kinsella as a full-blooded Modernist who also happens to be a fellow-Dubliner; not only is Kinsella, like Joyce, a narrator of Dublin's streets and a chronicler of its characters, but he also learns to let the city speak in its own ironic accents as Joyce does most memorably in the 'Cyclops' section of *Ulysses*. Employing little in the way of imagistic embellishment, Kinsella's poems owe their success surprisingly often to their capacity to reproduce the wry, deflating, semi-sardonic timbre of Dublinspeak. For readers of Thomas Kinsella, an address like Phoenix Street elicits something of the totemic affection which readers of *Ulysses* feel for Eccles Street. Although identified most closely with the Inchicore, Kilmainham and Liberties areas of his childhood (Thomas Street, Bow Lane, Basin Lane, Irwin Street, The High Road, The Liffey Hill, the Model School), his books provide access to other Dublins also:

Phoenix Park, Westland Row, Ely Place and locations where he worked (like Merrion Street) or lived (Baggot Street and Percy Place) as an adult.

In 'One Fond Embrace', Kinsella — long before Ireland's tribunals on planning and political corruption had been convened — condemned the appallingly inappropriate planning decisions made in modern Dublin. Dublin Corporation's readiness in the late 1970s and early 1980s to bury the Viking hatchet, the very origins of their own city, under the asphalt surface of a car park is blasted with a cloacal curse. The writing fairly crackles with scathing wit and scalding satire; for the resonance of its place-names, I quote from the version published in *From Centre City* (1994):

> *Invisible speculators, urinal architects,*
> *and the Corporation flourishing their documents*
> *in potent compliant dance*
>
> *— planners of the wiped slate*
> *labouring painstaking over a bungled city*
> *to turn it into a zoo:*
>
> *Southward from Fatima Mansions*
> *into the foothills,*
> *to where the transplanted can trudge*
>
> *from Bridget's Terrace and Kennedy's Villas*
> *via Woodbine Crescent and Cherryfield Heights*
> *to Shangri-La for a bottle of milk;*
>
> *Northward past our twinned*
> *experimental concrete piss-towers*
> *for the underprivileged;*
>
> *and at the heart, where the river runs*
> *through Viking ghosts at every tide*
> *by a set of shadow structures*
>
> *that our city fathers, fumbling in their shadow budget,*
> *beheld in vision for a while,*
> *pulverising until the cash failed,*

Dennis O'Driscoll

> *laying flat an enduring monument to themselves,*
> *an office car park sunk deep in history.*
> *May their sewers blast under them!*

At the conclusion of 'One Fond Embrace' itself, Kinsella — like a Shakespearean actor addressing an epilogue to his audience — steps forward and quoting Diderot declares, 'Enough. / That there is more spleen / than good sense in all of this, I admit . . . ' Yet, even at this most splenetic, Kinsella can be as amusing as he is outraged. A critic and anthologist of the 'dual tradition', insisting that the Gaelic and Anglo-Irish literatures are in 'dynamic interaction' and must be considered in tandem, he is capable as a satirist of fusing the invective of the seventeenth–century Dáibhí Ó Bruadair (whom he has translated) and the 'savage indignation' of Jonathan Swift (whose *A Modest Proposal* is comically invoked in 'One Fond Embrace'). It is notable that in the introduction to his critical essay, *The Dual Tradition* (1995), Kinsella remarks of Gaelic poetry that 'the formal bardic satires were not merely random criticism or the release of bad temper, but the identification and castigation of princely failings'; this is doubtless how he sees his own moral crusade against the corrupt modern princes of city and state.

Vivian Mercier in his study, *The Irish Comic Tradition* (1962), identifies the lampoon as 'by far the commonest kind of Gaelic satire'. Just how comfortably this tradition accommodates Kinsella's spiky work is evident not only from his force as a lampoonist but also when one considers the numerous other categories and sub-categories of satire once found in Irish. Though many of the satirical sub-species are no longer fully understood, one can imagine an Irish-language Kinsella cutting the sharpest of swathes through the three 'basic' types ('declaration, insult, incantation') at the very least. Further literary categories which Mercier locates in Ireland's comic tradition include triads and riddles. Indeed, the two genres are interrelated; as Mercier observes, 'Every saying in *Trecheng Breth Féni (The Triads of Ireland)* implies a riddle, although the form in which we now have these pieces of gnomic wisdom suppresses the question.' With an appropriate symmetry, Thomas Kinsella's translations from the Irish include *Thirty Three Triads*:

> *THREE smiles that are worse than griefs:*
> *the smile of snow melting, the smile of your wife when*

> *another*
> *man has been with her, the smile of a mastiff about to*
> *spring.*

> *THREE scarcities that are better than abundance:*
> *a scarcity of fancy talk, a scarcity of cows in a small*
> *pasture,*
> *a scarcity of friends around the beer.*

Kinsella's poem, 'Anniversaries', recalling his marriage in 1955 (and perhaps the fact that this was also the year of publication of *Thirty Three Triads*), offers an engaging triad of his own: 'The three qualities that are necessary / She has, namely: patience, / deliberation, / and skill with the instruments'. A more musical trio — 'a major triad of strings' — is heard in *Her Vertical Smile* (1985).

Kinsella's 'skill' with the riddle has surfaced in a number of ways. Most explicitly, it is demonstrated in the poem, 'Dream', which follows the rumbustious title poem of *Open Court* (1991); the latter is a literary satire set, not in the Celtic Twilight, but in the twilight zone of McDaid's during its heyday as a Dublin literary pub. The title hints at a judgemental stance (critical and personal), while nodding towards another 'court' also, Brian Merriman's comic *Midnight Court*. In its original Peppercanister Press publication, 'Dream' was sub-titled 'a puzzle'. Derval Tubridy reveals that 'A Riddle' was among the titles Kinsella had originally considered for the poem:

> *The elements of this riddle or puzzle are two creatures,*
> *one a monopod, situated in 'a stony desert, baked and*
> *still', who come into contact with two successive groups*
> *of 'human figures'. Taken in conjunction with 'Open*
> *Court', 'Dream' can be read as the allegory of the Irish*
> *cultural scene . . . around the mid-[twentieth] century.*

Perhaps in deference to the jurisdictions of legal and literary courts alike, Kinsella in the caustic and entertaining 'Open Court' itself (as in the finger-pointing 'You' sections of 'One Fond Embrace') leaves his characters tantalisingly, riddlingly unidentified. But, like any riddle, there would be little pleasure without some possibility of at least guessing the answers:

> *. . . a ruined Arnold turns his face*

> *snarling into empty space,*
> *flecks of black about his lips.*
> *Next, a ruined Auden slips*
> *lower on the leather seat,*
> *his tonsure sunken in defeat* . . .

Returning to its ancient roots, the riddle, too, animates the final sections of one of Kinsella's most majestic poems, 'Finistère', a poem which borrows the voice of Amergin, the ur-Irish poet of *The Book of Invasions*:

> *Who*
> *is the bull with seven scars*
> *the hawk on the cliff*
> *the salmon sunk in his pool*
> *the pool sunk in her soil*
> *the animal's fury*
> *the flower's fibre*
> *a teardrop in the sun?*

At one point in the 'Finistère' voyage of discovery, the parallels between inner and outer exploration, between the pagan past and the Christian future, are among the many intimations neatly encapsulated in the exclamation 'Our Father' which one of the voyagers blurts out ('there was a little laughter'). In the Gaelic tradition — as in all languages presumably — the pun is a favourite species of verbal wit. A few of Kinsella's funniest puns occur in 'Hen Woman', a poem appearing at a critical juncture in his work: near the beginning of 'Notes from the Land of the Dead'. 'Hen Woman' evokes in sensuous slow-motion a climacteric moment when an egg emerges from the bird, only to be 'smashed against the grating'. For all the symbolic importance of this 'egg of being' for the major phase of his work on which Kinsella was then embarking, his treatment of the incident is light and playful — even the critics' favourite epithet provides an opportunity to pun when he refers to the 'brooding' silence. Every rift in 'Hen Woman' is loaded with wit:

> *I feed upon it still, as you see;*
> *there is no end to that which,*
> *not understood, may yet be noted*
> *and hoarded in the imagination,*

in the yolk of one's being, so to speak . . .

Kinsella chose to end the version of 'Hen Woman' in his *Collected Poems* with the woman's good-humoured shrug of acceptance: ' . . . she laughed / and let the bird flap away. / It's all the one. / There's plenty more where that came from!' The *New Poems 1973* text closed with a two-line valediction ('Hen to pan! / It was a simple world.') which has been shown by scholars like Carolyn Rosenberg, who have gone to work on this particular egg, to contain more than meets what Kinsella calls 'the yolk and white' of the eye. As Brian John succinctly states, 'The Greek for "one in all," *"Hen tō pan"* is the ancient alchemical formula, as Kinsella would have learned from Jung.' Deadpan humour indeed!

The woman's exclamation — 'It's all the one' — therefore proves to contain more than a dash of proverbial wisdom, echoing what another scholar, Thomas H Jackson, calls 'Kinsella's now characteristic rejection of the boundary between the psychic or imaginative and the physical'. Other poems in 'Notes from the Land of the Dead', such as 'A Hand of Solo', can bear scrutiny as dramatically vivid recreations of childhood scenes or as more allegorical and archetypal vignettes in which a humorous colloquial phrase like 'You'd think I had three heads!' (with its Hecate associations) or the eating of a pomegranate (shades of Persephone) allow the poem to resonate without making heavy weather of the symbolism. Kinsella himself has admitted to having been 'electrified and thrilled that, after putting so much weight of memory on the pomegranate, it also responded mythologically'.

Kinsella is a low-key but very touching chronicler of domestic life and love, permitting the occasional exultant sentiment to escape ('I . . . embraced all / this hearth and home'); and he can surprise readers with his delicacy, observing a clump of reeds 'nestling a lark's eggs in a hoof-print' or portraying his childhood self as a 'dark little / blackvelvet-eyed jew-child'. On the other hand, the ferocity of his invective, outrage, even hate, can be startling. In *A Technical Supplement* (1976), originally published with a cover illustration from Denis Diderot's *Encyclopédie* implying that the pen may be as mighty as the penknife, are we to take lines like 'There isn't a day passes but I thank God / some others I know . . . / didn't "fulfil their promise"' at face value or, turning the other cheek, treat them as ironic? Quoting Yeats ('Out of Ireland have we come. / Great hatred, little room, / Maimed us at the start'), Joseph M Hassett has written:

Dennis O'Driscoll

> *The common bond that linked Yeats, Swift and 'the nation*
> *itself' was hate. 'No people,' said Yeats, 'hate as we do in*
> *whom that past [of English persecution recounted by*
> *Lecky] is always alive.'*

Kinsella, having like Yeats and Swift been 'hurt' into poetry, firmly belongs in the *saeva indignatio* lineage. 'I went with Anger at my heel', *Butcher's Dozen* (1972) begins; the *Collected Poems* ends with lines in which 'On a fragrant slope descending into the fog / over our foul ascending city / I turned away in refusal'. There is much turning away in refusal, revulsion and contempt in the work, some of it simultaneously amusing and fearsome. The child in *The Messenger* (1978), led by his father in protest from the church 'in the middle of Mass past everybody', grew up with the uninhibited courage to speak his mind satirically, scornfully and truthfully about public and private matters. And, while I would tend to agree with Brian John that Kinsella's 'strengths have always been more clearly evident when anatomizing the self', I would still emphasize the exemplary importance for contemporary Irish writing of an unfettered poet who remains fiercely and stubbornly independent of the establishment — resisting all of its honours and institutions, works and pomps, and prepared to expose its hypocrisies fearlessly and comprehensively. He is a true dissident: obstinate, inconvenient, discomfiting, essential.

The Kinsella nose is as sharp as his tongue — nobody in Irish poetry has a keener sense of smell, whether for sniffing out public scandals or detecting more homely 'odours of apron and cabbage-water and whitewashed damp'. In tense situations relating to his extended family, some droll scene-setting and speech-transcription can introduce a note of comic counterpoint. 'Dura Mater', an emotionally-charged family poem, begins not untypically with an olfactory evocation: 'A potato smell came out from the kitchen door, / and a saucepan smell, with a piece of meat boiling'. The description of the mother figure which follows is interlaced with undercurrents of speech; as so often in Kinsella's work, the frustrations which attend all human relationships are painfully but ironically apprehended:

> *She came along the passage in her slippers*
> *with a fuzz of navy hair, and her long nails*
> *held out wet out of the washing water.*

Come here to me. Come here to me, my own son.

Stiff necked, she put up her pursed mouth
at her grown young — whatever idea she had of it
in there behind the ill temper in her eyes.

Will you look at him. How do you stick him at all . . .

Everyday Dublin phrases are woven equally wittily and authentically into many later poems — works of almost miraculous transparency and economy, which serve (like the comparable Dublin comedy of the 'Cyclops' section of *Ulysses*) as a perfect entry point for new readers. Kinsella's rhythmical gifts, impressive from the start, never deserted him; but the later rhythms are those of heard speech more than received metrics. Despite their apparent simplicity — seeing and hearing their world through a child's sharply-focused eyes and finely-tuned ears — poems like the prefatory panel of 'Settings' in *Songs of the Psyche* (1985) adumbrate themes which are accorded their due adult weight and complexity elsewhere in Kinsella's poetry.

Childhood speech and vision are allowed their purest — almost unmediated — distillation in *St Catherine's Clock* (1987). Having added witty Brueghel-like glosses to an eighteenth-century print of Thomas Street by James Malton ('a couple of mongrels / worrying the genitals out of each other'; 'a hag / toils across the street / on her battered business, / a drained backside / turned toward St Catherine'), the poem moves from Ireland's historical past — including the execution of Robert Emmet in Thomas Street — to the more recent past of Kinsella's own family, a family intimately connected with the Thomas Street area. As in 'Dura Mater', the sequence entitled '1938' includes some cruelly objective but credible and funny descriptions, sketched in the most perspicuous language:

Aunty Gertie shuffled
across the scullery. She had
big slippers and a slow bum.

Little Uncle Ned was always in and out
grinning at her. (Uncle Larry said
she could stick him in her pocket.)

> *She could let a long belch*
> *up her neck, like a noise*
> *coming up out of a jug.*

As well as cruel humour, '1938' contains instances of tender humour — one winning example, in which the child has internalized a demotic version of some cardinal sins, is particularly rich in the unrevised Peppercanister version:

> *Sometimes it sounded like she was giving out*
> *but she was really minding us.*
>
> *I know I was not bold*
> *even if I did terrible things.*
>
> *I was not a barefaced liar*
> *or a thick-ah or a go-boy, or a pup.*
>
> *I never went with the gets next door*
> *or that cur down the street . . .*

Kinsella's wit can spring at the most unlikely moments, as happens in the 'coda' to 'Her Vertical Smile'. The main spotlight of this poem is on Gustav Mahler, 'arms uplifted on the podium'; and Kinsella clearly identifies with 'the force of will / we find everywhere / in his strange work: / the readiness to embrace risk'. Order and chaos are explored, along with art and death, creation and fall (in a diverting transcription of the Sistine Chapel ceiling, 'our first parent' is 'propped on an elbow, / a languid and burly young man / with everything limply on show, / and a little out of condition', while God the Father is depicted 'with the nub of the matter displaced / in a fold of His purple shift'). After elevated, agonized and eloquent ruminations on the demands of great art ('Is there anything quite like / getting to the root?'), the finale — or fall — is unexpectedly comic: 'Nine are the enabling elements / in the higher crafts / and the greatest of these is Luck. / I lift my / baton and my / trousers fall.'

'Her Vertical Smile' revisits Kinsella's friendship with the composer Seán Ó Riada. In fact, it opens with a short extract from a prose memoir written to accompany the re-publication in book form of his Peppercanister elegies for Ó Riada, *A Selected Life* (1972) and *Vertical Man* (1973). This often hilarious memoir, enlivened by bravura pen-portraits ('a wide-cheeked lipless face like a cobra, and black slit eyes shaded under his cap'), shows the young Kinsella and Ó Riada to have shared a mischievous sense of fun:

> *The first drunken evening I recall was spent with some journalists in a pub called* The Kind Ladies, *a dreary den in a street of warehouses somewhere behind Amiens Street. We were a pair of simple and lonely seamen from the Baltic, and were made welcome as such. We made monosyllabic attempts at communication with the inhabitants, in soft expletives, and there was a lot of laughter.*

Even the companionable Ó Riada, however, does not escape without a word-lash from the sober elder Kinsella for having succumbed to 'the way of entertainment' by becoming 'in the final phase . . . an entertainer / among the lesser gentry'. Notwithstanding his scolding attitude towards anything that smacks of entertainment (in *The Dual Tradition*, scant interest is shown in the comic sides of Swift, Goldsmith, Kavanagh and Beckett), Kinsella has never in fact banished or renounced his comic and satiric gifts; flashes of wit can light up his darkest poems — just as humour and demotic speech mingle with, indeed help to unify, the esoteric, mythic and personal elements in one of Kinsella's favourite poems, 'The Waste Land'.

It would be highly misleading to play down Kinsella's opacity, to pretend that 'all's / A fiction that is heard of . . . difficulty' in his poems. Nonetheless, while humour may not be high in his hierarchy of literary values, he is far too good an artist and much too driven a satirist to forgo the virtues and pleasures of a wit which attaches itself so naturally to his voice rhythms. The visual material chosen for some of his Peppercanister publications, especially *The Messenger* and *A Technical Supplement*, is itself illustrative of a wryly ironic sense of humour.

Striking a different note from most contemporary Irish poets, Kinsella refuses to restrict the scope of poetry by subscribing to the commonly-held view that one of its prime functions is to celebrate. He proves the art equal to many other tasks also and does not attempt to endow his poems with the happy 'closure' which is denied to most human lives. But the disenchanted severity of his vision does not diminish his master-artist's sensitivity to the dangers of the monotone and the monotonous ('I can see I am

growing tedious') and wit is one of the means he employs —
whether unwittingly or consciously — to alter moods and shift
perspectives. In 'The Route of the *Táin*', the mood of the group
'who had set out / so cheerfully to celebrate' Kinsella's translation of the great Irish epic passes through 'irritation' and back to
cheerfulness before the poem's final darkness closes in. The poem
is a study hovering between constancy and mortality, light and
shade, sobriety and wit:

> *The morning sunlight pouring on us all*
> *as we scattered over the mounds*
> *disputing over useless old books,*
> *assembled in cheerful speculation*
> *around a prone block,* Miosgán Medba
> *— Queen Medb's* turd . . . ? *And rattled our maps,*
> *joking together in growing illness*
> *or age or fat. Before us*
> *the route of the* Táin, *over men's dust,*
> *toward these hills that seemed to grow*
> *darker as we drove nearer.*

The first of Kinsella's *Thirty Three Triads* provides a preliminary
summary of his manifold virtues as a poet:

> *THREE excellent qualities in narration:*
> *a good flow, depth of thought, conciseness.*

And, his own work reminds us, a fourth 'excellent quality' is wit.
As recently as *The Pen Shop* (1997), where his curses 'pursue' the
Dublin bus which threatens him with 'a broadside of . . .
windows against my face', or *The Familiar* (1999), with its triad of
virtues — tonal ('going in together / with our animal thoughts'),
olfactory ('Her things on the floor / a sigh of disorder / box of
her body / in an oxtail odour') and demotic ('"You are very good.
/ You always made it nice"') — Kinsella has again demonstrated
that his wit is an inextricable part of his profoundly serious art.

Irish University Review (Spring/Summer 2001)

Padraic Fallon

Collected Poems, edited by Brian Fallon

The American painter, Eric Fischl, has spoken of his disillusionment in art college at finding his paintings relentlessly combed for influence. When his teachers 'discovered' fifty painters in a single example of his work, he knew it was time to leave. Padraic Fallon's poetry could be approached in a similarly sleuthing manner. A feather from Leda's 'Kingbird', a Baudelairean perfume, a rag of Raftery's: the clues pile up. And yet, for all the effort involved, the evidence points to an awareness of other poets' work more than to any decisive influence. The identity paraded is Fallon's own.

If Patrick Kavanagh was 'never much considered by the English critics', Padraic Fallon was not much considered by the Irish ones either. You will not find a single reference to him in the indexes of otherwise indispensable books like Seamus Deane's *Celtic Revivals* or the essay compilation edited by Terence Brown and Nicholas Grene, *Tradition and Influence in Anglo-Irish Poetry*. Edna Longley greeted his substantial first book, *Poems,* as 'largely a non-event'. The critical strategy — when there is any — is to attack Fallon as a minor acolyte of Yeats and leave him for dead. It is as if the ranking of his generation had been finalized and it is too late for further entrants to be considered. Fallon published reluctantly and developed slowly (only eight of the inclusions in the *Collected Poems* had been written by the age of forty). Although a collection was planned by The Orwell Press thirty years before, it took until 1974 — the year of his death — for *Poems* to appear. By then, literary expectations had greatly altered and it was easy to dismiss Fallon as belonging to a different world, where the landscape was still wild and western and the twilight still Celtic. The dominant collection of the period was entitled *North*, not *West*.

In fact, some of Fallon's distinctive qualities stem from his seeming at once ancient and modern. Steeped in Irish balladry and classical mythology, he also had a comprehensive knowledge of modern poetry from the youthful Rimbaud to the youthful Muldoon. Padraic Fallon was born in Athenry, County Galway, in 1905. Brian Fallon speaks of him as 'a countryman by background and ancestry who grew up in a world where the tramp-poet Raftery was still a fairly recent memory, and Gaelic folk-song was a living tradition and not an archive culture'. In the ironic 'For Paddy Mac' (a poem addressed to his poet-friend, Patrick MacDonogh), Padraic Fallon distances himself from any assumption that, by virtue of his background, he enjoys automatic access to some kind of authentic peasant poetry:

> No poets I knew of; or they mouthed each other's words;
> Such low powered gods
> They died, as they were born, in byres.
> Oh, maybe some rags and tatters did sing.
> But poetry, for all your talk, is never that simple . . .

Despite these caveats — so deftly spun — Eavan Boland is surely right in her suspicion that 'the classical references, freedom from Jansenism, regional colour and raw power in Padraic Fallon's poetry were a surprising but authentic survival of the eighteenth-century spirit of Irish poetry'.

Fallon spent much of his life as a Customs official — he is allotted a page in the 'Personalities' chapter of Réamonn's *History of the Revenue Commissioners*. His first posting was in Dublin ('I sat there in the Custom House window over / The salt harbour, a young man'). Early encouragement as a poet came from 'AE' and later Dublin friends included 'Seumas O'Sullivan' and Austin Clarke. From 1939 to 1963, he lived in Wexford where by all accounts the title he laboured under ('Customs and Excise Officer, Registrar of Shipping, Mercantile Superintendent and Receiver of Wreck') was the most onerous part of his job. There was time to be a husband and father, to sail, to farm twenty acres and to write. His output included poetry, stories, essays, a journal, stage plays and seventeen radio plays. While he tended to write directly on to the typewriter, he often tested out alternative drafts in ink; the inspired last lines of 'Yesterday's Man' (' . . . a quayside memory, the Frau / Of the Dutch Captain's hanging out her wash, / So young, so young, transfiguring me') can be found sketched on a driving licence form.

In the early Fifties, in his 'Journal' in *The Bell*, he had commented: 'There is more to life than despair of life. There is this body-joy in its own energies, the thing that makes trees grow and men marry . . . Let despair come later. Having lived his joys, he will cope with that, too.' All of Fallon's poems are, in a sense, 'later' poems and he was over fifty when his best work was written. To the end, his poems kept their undespairing composure and an inner equilibrium (qualities captured well in Conor Fallon's bust of his father). Eavan Boland recalled him in his final years — at a time when the despairing poetry of Plath and Berryman was at the height of its influence — 'speaking with a truly unusual sort of peace and strength about the poetic process itself'.

Fallon's mastery of speech rhythms in poetry is one of his major achievements. While not wishing Irish poets to be confined to Irish themes, he was conscious of the fact that 'Behind us, a powerful ghost, engaging our rhythms to some hereditary and ancient wheel, is the Irish language'. He forged a synthesis of demotic with poetic, dialect with dialectic; and a play like *Steeple Jerkin* has all the vividness and viciousness of a small world whose street battles are fought in words. The poems are musical, leisurely, droll, moving from the mundane to the numinous with barely a change of register. His casual tone can, admittedly, lead to a certain bagginess in the writing — and to vagueness, as if he had begun talking to himself for a moment, the voice disappearing into a fog. At their best, however, the conversational poems have depth, charm and some of the digressive tendencies for which Ciaran Carson is now admired:

> *And I remember*
> *Trooping to the top of the stone just*
> *Such a galaxy. Or do I? My God,*
> *I've sat there in patched shorts,*
> *In the very weather of the thing, and must*
> *Scratch my head to remember . . .*

It would be absurd to deny that Padraic Fallon was influenced by Yeats, but equally absurd to contend that he was unable to cope with that influence. As he wrote of Eliot and Yeats, 'You have read them, you have absorbed them, they are part of your blood stream. Go thou and do not likewise.' It is arguable, in fact, that some of the best things in Fallon's poetry, as in Kavanagh's, sprang from that resolve to 'do not likewise'. To be one of the first literary sons of a new state, working in the shadow of so huge a father figure, was not an easy fate and some rebellion was inevitable. Fallon's unpredictability, so attractive an aspect of his work, may have originated from such a rebellious impulse. Peter Sirr has written: 'I value the work for its openendedness, its riskiness, its preparedness to be led by metaphor and tone.' There are times when the unpredictability becomes a kind of uncertainty, the poet appearing to improvise as he loses his place in the script. In general, though, by following the undulations of his imagination, even the bumpiest ride will end at an impressive distance from its starting line — as evidenced by 'River Lane', 'Boyne Valley', 'Totem'. This serendipitous quality ('I never know what I think about anything until I come to write about it') carried an enormous appeal for Fallon, not least because of its contrast with Yeats who 'never discovered himself through a poem. He had made his mind up before he wrote it down'.

An even more original device of Fallon's for surviving Yeats was to make him a character in his poems, to mythologize the great myth-maker and his circle. Lady Gregory, for instance, becomes a Penelope who 'pulls home / Rogue-lord, artist, world-wanderer, / Simply by sitting in a house . . .' The fact that the setting is Fallon's own countryside ('The very road I took this morning / In the downpour') lends an added frisson to these poems. 'Yeats's Tower at Ballylee', the earliest of them, finds him inhabiting Yeats's spirit and speech as well as his structure. It is a risky, remarkable, triumphant performance. Fallon sees the tower as a manifestation of Yeats's boyish dreams; but, through its loneliness and desolation, 'he became a man'. Fallon's identification with Yeats leads him to the point where he begins to 'know the terror' of the older poet at first hand. Identification gives way to self-identity; and out of the struggle with the visionary Yeats comes a personal poetry and a personal vision: 'Around me now from this great height / Is a vision I did not seek. I have avoided it . . .'

The most engaging of these poems (in which Fallon conducts what Donald Davie has called 'his direct and unabashed dialogue with that overbearing predecessor') is the cleverly-titled 'Yeats at Athenry Perhaps'. Although it concerns a non-event, a non-meeting between Fallon as a boy and the poet changing trains for Gort, its dramatic possibilities are fully exploited. The peasant-idealizing poet wouldn't deign to 'muddy a feathered foot' among ragged real-life peasants; but he is imagined, nonetheless, exploring the town ('We had our towers too'), with its unmythical women ('Ours kept the house and answered the chapel bell') and its gossips ('every peeling window was an eye'). Like the railway tracks, the worlds of Athenry and Coole would never actually converge:

> *No, he'd have sat down by the line and waited*
> *Melting his bits of ore or watched the sky*
> *Jolt from the saltmills of the Atlantic over*
> *A town that died so often of the rain . . .*

The country town with its Norman keep and rain-drenched chapel always stirs something profound in Fallon's imagination. He guides us over the bridge, through the square, down the back lanes. We see a 'fawnstoned ballalley', 'paintwashed shops', 'the hag's head / Curing slowly on / The smoking half door, like ham' and the 'knobbly young / Hairslick with the fag end on his tongue'. Artificial colouring is never added and the atmosphere of the place is evoked no less by suggestion than by description. As Peter Sirr puts it, 'Fallon looks less *at* his world than *through* it, in search of the lost worlds the visible one echoes'.

Those lost worlds acquire an epic dimension when Fallon is prompted to seek out the Troy in every town, the Alp in every hill, the God in every man, the Athens in Athenry. The full gamut of human experience and emotion occurs in microcosm in small places, the stifling limitations and the limitless potential existing in defiance of each other. We are shown people living in 'decent anonymity' who have no wish to be 'tugged forth' into a poem — among them (in 'A Visit West') the poet's Uncle Ben. The setting is again Athenry:

> *Between yawns life goes on*
> *With some cunning to*
> *Accomplish itself.*
> *Children are born,*
> *To up and vanish like me,*
> *Mostly . . .*

Uncle Ben is described by Fallon as a 'feckless double'; and seeing doubles — even conquering them — becomes something of a leitmotif in his work. Yeats is, to an extent, a double or *alter ego* in the poems already mentioned. Death is 'the twin of Life'. The beautiful and mystical 'Brother Twin' (with echoes of 'AE') trades the visions of a Connacht shepherd with those of a twin from 'The empty begging bowl of the East'. And there are the double exposures of the poet himself — the young and the old — in 'To the Boy' and 'Yesterday's Man' ('here, confronting me / With an air of great doings, is an old familiar'). Among his 'versions' of classical poetry, he is drawn to the story of Heracles and his twin.

Doubles and doppelgängers surface in a number of Fallon's radio plays also, one character often representing the darker side of the other. In *Two Men With a Face* (broadcast as *Mister Janus*), one protagonist eventually absorbs his fellow. John Coan ('The Judgeen') is 'feckless, lazy, lethargic', vices which his employer, Mr Keane, 'extirpated' from himself. What Keane is unable to shake off is a total obsession with Coan, on whose every move he stands in judgement ('You need the Judgeen as a visible symbol of your own triumph over self and circumstances'). In a startling denouement, judge and judgeen, employer and employee, Keane and Coan become one.

Diarmuid and Gráinne, another of the radio plays, presents the struggle between darkness and light, good and evil, in these terms: 'It is in our knowledge that every one who is born into the light has a double that is born into the dark. And the deeds of the one are the shadowy deeds of the other, and though they work in different substances they are of equal strength and of equal fame in their separate worlds.' Further pursuit of the double (complete with a Shakespearean confusion of roles) occurs in the powerful and eventful play, *The Hags of Clough* ('Twins. In all / The tales one kills the other'), and in the nightmarish (and sometimes Nighttownish) *The Five Stations* where the father accuses the son of having 'two selves': 'One of them I'll welcome home. / The good one. Bury the other in good deeds.' Mary, eloping with Toby in *At the Bridge Inn*, is ominously aware that she shares a name, a face and a voice with her repulsive mother and seems doomed to harden into her ways.

Laborcham the priestess tells Conor, in the radio play *Deirdre*, 'Little king, man is both male and female, incomplete till they wear faces for one another'. Of all potential twinnings, it is that of man with woman which most excites a poetical response from Fallon, who is 'the haunted man on the main of love', writing not so much love poetry as poetry about love. That man/main chime is a characteristic instance of wordplay — a tendency Fallon shares with Austin Clarke (whose poems are more lumbered with guilt). Fallon is uninhibited in his celebration of the 'bright otherworld habits' of women — and the use of 'otherworld' is significant in this context. The erotic glosses must have seemed particularly daring in the Ireland of their day (lending added irony to the rumour that, at one time, his Customs responsibilities included some censorship work). We are shown woman in a Munch-like triptych of 'Goddess, kitchenwoman, whore' and in the guises of Eve, Venus, Lakshmi, Helen, Athene and Mary. Although 'the mythic properties are hard to bear', it is only through myth that he can distance himself sufficiently from the object of his fascination to unravel the archetypes and probe the mystery. Yet he is aware — to the point of self-rebuke — of the danger he runs:

> *Dangerous, dangerous*
> *This mythology. The doctors know it*
> *And reason of it now like any poet.*
> *Lover, go back no farther than your birth:*
> *A woman is a woman, not the earth . . .*

Irrespective of what formula he uses — that of Raftery wooing Mary Hynes or a meditation on a Hindu goddess — imbalance in the representation of woman (crowned and placed on a Gravesian pedestal or 'most royal on her back') remains a danger, though Fallon's search for the truth of the matter is honest ('The River Walk'), humane ('Evening Off') and wittily self-mocking ('Poet Passing').

The mystery and awe of life and love on a human scale captivate Fallon and, for all his use of myth, he is content to find 'a theme in what occurs'. He likes 'things as they are, / World as it is, the wonder just round the corner'. In 'Brigid Her Eve', his prayer is for

> *. . . just something*
> *To show you've been around and the day holy*
> *Like Sunday or lucky like*
> *The day when a poet is lucky enough to say*
> *Something of importance to himself*
> *That must*
> *Acknowledge and ignore you, the miracle*
> *Taken for granted, being natural . . .*

Dennis O'Driscoll

Having addressed his father as Jahwah (*sic*) and Helios, he interjects, 'not / That I'd like you in big translations / Who were rich enough / As your own man'. Mythology in some of his poems is simply an ironic device. In others, the allusions trip in and out of his stanzas as nonchalantly as 'Greek verbs and Latin nouns' off the tongue of Padraic Colum's 'Poor Scholar of the Forties'; and a more direct use is made of myth than in the shadow plots of *Ulysses* or *The Waste Land*.

'Brigid Her Eve' is one of several poems in which the visual and imagistic elements are strong — qualities which Brian Fallon in his helpful 'Afterword' to the *Collected Poems* associates with the influence of Rilke who, in turn, was influenced by Rodin. 'The Christmas Vigil' visualizes 'the trees / With aboriginal arms still making / Yesterday's rain / From the day's soft grey substance' and the equally vivid 'Bullocks in a horned frieze staring / Egyptian from the roughmasoned gateways'. A pointillist image is formed from 'A peopled sea, the hulls in a haze of morse'. 'A Flask of Brandy', about a childhood errand run for a 'Lionwoman', is full of colour and wonder, its lines as bright as a circus tent's stripes. 'The Dwelling' is delightfully cubist, while only quotation can do justice to the lovely ease with which the watercolour images flow in 'Weir Bridge':

> *Whole gravels are in rut.*
> *The ocean has come home to melt away*
> *The salt, to lie under*
> *A maybush and almost tenderly*
> *Suck from the lazy heavens a blue-green fly.*

There is a painterly quality about some of Padraic Fallon's translations also. Though I find his 'versions' of poems to be the most resistible part of his oeuvre, a few (such as the anarchic and energetic 'To Pan' and the stately 'Solvitur Acris Hiems') represent classical scenes transformed by a modern master. The original authorship of the 'Homeric Hymns' may be a mystery but the brushstrokes with which Fallon reproduces them are characteristic of his own original work:

> *They lay*
> *On the coarse mountain twitch that turned*
> *Into sweet cowlick under*
> *Another shape . . .*

The radio plays include many 'versions' of early Irish sagas, from *Diarmuid and Gráinne* (first broadcast in 1950) to *Deirdre* (dated February 1956), with *The Vision of MacConglinne* and *The Wooing of Étaín* in between. While the subject matter was scarcely novel, his treatment of it certainly was. For instance, the MacConglinne play makes far more elaborate use of the source material than Austin Clarke did in his sprightly but short play, *The Son of Learning*. The lack of a contemporary following for radio drama deprives Fallon of a hearing in a medium in which he excelled and which, according to Peter Sirr, he regarded as 'a kind of roomy alternative to the long poem, a form he disliked'. It may be that the audience for *The Vision of MacConglinne* — if such existed — would now expect its satire to be directed against hunger for power rather than against the church; but, as it is, the play transmits a timeless exuberance.

At one point, the impertinent MacConglinne is so starved that talk of women fills him with an unnatural desire: 'At this moment I would eat a woman if she were boiled, broiled, boned or on the fillet; if she were baked, brawned, browned, underdone, overdone, or a mere juice in the black bottom of a country skillet; and I would eat her family after and then begin upon her family tree.' Any son or daughter of learning who is preparing a thesis on women in Padraic Fallon's writings should not ignore the more serious — even feminist — utterances of this play. When Ligach, the Queen, has been outraged by her husband's behaviour, she claims 'these my rights': 'freedom from the demands of a husband unless I will it otherwise; freedom in travel, indulgence of fancies, equal rights of sovereignty; separate establishments in the same establishment.'

The feminist theme is developed in *Deirdre*, a play very different in emphasis from the less dramatic Yeats work of the same title. Padraic Fallon's output generally evinces an intuitive sense of the importance of female influence to the wellbeing of the world, of Eve to Adam, of Mary to Christ ('The least erotic of the gods'). It is implied in *Deirdre* that there was a native Irish tradition of respecting 'the delicate balance between the sexes' to which the macho King Conor (reared in Scandinavia) does violence. In Conor's view, a woman is only 'another necessary tool' and he clings to his destructive belief that by exalting 'the male above the female . . . I but follow the order of natural things'. Poet and priestess warn him against his hubristic ways: 'Degrade her, who is the lover and the mother, and there will be the rut of animals, season without sequence, empty bodies and the mortal no longer on speaking terms with the major emotions on which it travels into deity.'

Diarmuid and Gráinne, the first of his radio plays and (according to Brian Fallon) 'a landmark in his literary career', is written with a spare elegance, hammered out like a gold Celtic lunula. Much of the dialogue is swift and lean, almost incantatory, a style appropriate to a play about a couple on the run; a brisk, nervous dialogue is also the hallmark of the eloping lovers of *At the Bridge Inn*. The characters in Fallon's plays convince both as individuals and archetypes. The language tends towards a heightened prose, the words drawing attention to themselves as verse only when a lyrical note is struck or when the 'commentator' (who acts as a kind of chorus) counterpoints or ironizes a dramatic situation in verse. Fallon's charge against Austin Clarke is not one which could be levelled against his own work: 'He mistakes a play for a lyric. We can ponder a lyric but we listen to a play. And the mysteries of assonance and dissonance bypass us. Rhythmic writing is enough.'

In *Diarmuid and Gráinne*, the lyrical passages show Fallon's command of the bare line of early Gaelic poetry:

> *I hear Fionn,*
> *He is the sweet bell sound of evening,*
> *He is dusk dropping, he is the dew.*
> *He is the warm hush of flocks moving.*
> *A sweet comrade is Fionn.*
> *He is sleepy stalls. The byres are full.*
> *Corn is hived; and over the empty pastures*
> *Comes the cooking smoke from houses, a rich warm smell,*
> *Fionn is here.*

Fallon at his most simple can be at his most supple, avoiding his more tiresome excursions into overwrought and circuitous writing. There is beauty in the weather eye beholding Cornwall at the end of the poem, 'Painting of My Father', and in 'The Head' as it relaxes into 'fat uddered / Cow-lawns by river houses, woods that spoke in oak'. And there are an island's simple pleasures

> *Of everyday affairs, a neighbour's voice,*
> *A woman at the churn,*

A child in wonder at the half door,
The split pollock drying in the sun . . .

As I suggested at the start, it is Fallon's defects rather than his strengths which critics — anxious perhaps to be relieved of the burden of re-arranging the pantheon to accommodate a latecomer — emphasize. If we are determined to highlight warts at the expense of face, then Kavanagh and Clarke will emerge even more blemished than Fallon. Anyway, there are not so many good Irish poets that we can write off a figure of Padraic Fallon's stature like some kind of bad debt, no longer worth pursuing. He is a poet who conveys, in a peculiarly Irish context, the universal struggle to live, love and find our bearings ('that journey / From nothing to identity'). Our gratitude in his presence invariably runs well ahead of our doubts. And it is with a similar ratio of gratitude to doubt that he himself views poetry:

> *. . . things work into the word*
> *Only to be imprisoned, or kennelled like a dog . . .*
> *The monologue intrudes, my words let me*
> *Into a poem, not into the poetry.*
> *And yet a man must walk*
> *Out of his mystery, if he's to meet it*
> *Face to face, in talk,*
> *And guess from words omitted the major and delicate*
> *Evasions of his ghost*
> *Who is the host*
> *To every massive feeling and must live it.*
> *Create me, says the poet, I am a body*
> *For every word, the large word that was lost*
> *And the word you'd throw a dog;*
> *Transform me who travel towards infinity*
> *In a makeshift monologue.*

Poetry Ireland Review (Summer 1990)

Seamus Heaney: 'The Biretta'

One has to doff one's hat to a poet so richly gifted that he can afford to exclude a poem as good as 'The Biretta' from his super-Selected or semi-Collected. The absence from Seamus Heaney's *Opened Ground: Poems 1966-1996* of this poem, hailed as 'a master-piece' by John Bayley when he reviewed *Seeing Things* (1991), is one of the few serious sins of omission in a volume which confirms the poet to be a stern and sound critic of his own work.

Heaney is so well known for his downward glance towards spongy bog and squelching mud, and for his increasingly upward gaze towards the dazzling and visionary, that his readers might neglect to notice what is happening in between. Although 'The Biretta' evokes an item of priestly head-dress, it is not one of those poems in which an artefact seen at eye level is also envisioned at spirit level. Here, Heaney is seeing *things* as they are without raising them — upon the blue guitar or church organ of his imagination — to other, loftier planes. As with 'A Sofa in the Forties', the clerical hat — despite being 'potentially heaven-bound' — is 'earthbound for sure'; it never promises to lift off into outer space like 'The Pitchfork', another of the objects in *Seeing Things* whose physical appearance and spiritual essence are conveyed.

Typically, Heaney exalts the humble, remarking of the pitch-fork that it 'came near to an imagined perfection'. The more exalted biretta is, however, humbled: far from conferring an aureole of sanctity on its wearer, it merely 'left a dark red line on the priest's brow', rather like the 'line of . . . pressure' etched by the policeman's cap in 'A Constable Calls'. Long-term acquain-tance with birettas during his schooling has demystified them for Heaney. Yet, the poem is not just about the headwear but about all of the associations which he conjures out of the hat: memories of Latin classes, of Masses in the diocesan college where he was educated, of fiery preachers, of fidgeting as an altar boy with a tassel which 'the backs of my fingers remember well', of poems and paintings and objects he has loved.

In his object poems, Heaney does not so much defamiliarize the ordinary as refamiliarize it, recovering it afresh by finding words that are fresh enough to make these objects amenable once more to evocation and imagination: 'whatever is given / Can always be reimagined', as he remarks in 'The Settle Bed', refusing to settle for the standard responses. Heaney's etymological intimacy with language enables him to intuit the names by which things recognize themselves and to which they answer with alacrity. Robert Graves counselled poets to avoid 'stand-in' words, assuring them that, with persistence, the 'real' words can always be identified. Think of how long it took the English language (a language glorying in the works of a former bricklayer, Ben Jonson) to divulge the perfect words for something as basic and everyday as bricklaying — or for the word 'slur' to have its good name restored:

> *Over and over, the slur, the scrape and mix*
> *As he trowelled and retrowelled and laid down*
> *Courses of glum mortar. Then the bricks*
> *Jiggled and settled, tocked and tapped in line . . .*

Heaney's 'guttural muse' periodically impurifies the language of the tribe as a way of revitalizing it. Like Czeslaw Milosz, he accepts that there are times when what a poem requires most of all is to be 'roughened up'. Not only will such a poem gain in immediacy but what Heaney has called the 'nicely held tension between poetry's need to be true to the impurities of life and its need to remember that it intends to be pure language' can be explored and exploited. In 'The Biretta', as so often in Heaney, narcotically regular metre is deliberately eschewed. His breach-more-than-observance approach to strict metre allows for a kind of flexibility within form; and rhymes vary from masculine (tall / hall) and feminine (crises / rises) to what might best be categorized as neuter (resist / Mass).

Heaney's way of seeing things is not a way of seeing through them. Philip Larkinesque disillusion and scepticism are not his style; he prefers to 'credit' (a favourite word) things rather than discredit them. When, in *Seeing Things*, he meditates on 'The Pitchfork' and 'The Settle Bed', it is the adjectives that are laid on rather than the irony. The settle bed is 'Trunk-hasped, cart-heavy, painted an ignorant brown. / And pew-strait, bin-deep, standing four-square as an ark . . . / Upright, rudimentary, unshiftably planked'. The pitchfork is 'Sweat-cured, sharpened, balanced, tested, fitted', shaped from 'tapering, dark-flecked ash / Grown satiny from its own natural polish'. 'The Biretta' too is launched on a sea of adjectives, defying the conventional (not to mention conformist) wisdom of the writing workshops that adjectives are to poems as icebergs to *Titanics*. Another Heaney trait (in this case, admittedly, a less compelling one) is the tolerance of repetitions of words; where most poets would raid the thesaurus for alternative usages, Heaney — again engaging in a form of 'roughening up' perhaps — positively revels in the practice.

W B Yeats used repetition to good rhetorical effect:

> *. . . Public opinion ripening for so long*
> *We thought it would outlive all future days.*
> *O what fine thought we had because we thought*
> *That the worst rogues and rascals had died out.*

In 'Coole Park and Ballylee, 1931', when he writes movingly of the dying Lady Gregory, 'Sound of a stick upon the floor, a sound / From somebody that toils from chair to chair', we catch a characteristic Yeatsian sound. On the other hand, the dazzle of a swan 'So arrogantly pure, a child might think / It can be murdered with a spot of ink' is diminished by Yeats's blind spot in not noticing the unfortunate repetition of 'spot' nine lines later in 'A spot whereon the founders lived and died'. Heaney's permissiveness towards repetition comes perilously close to blotting his own swans in one of his very best poems, the sublime 'Postscript', when he records ' . . . Their feathers roughed and ruffling, white on white, / Their fully grown headstrong-looking heads'. If Heaney's poetic laws are sanctioned by precedent, Yeats is not his only authority. 'The Biretta''s risky double deployment of 'in' ('out and in / *In the name of the Father*') takes comfort — and counsel — from the colloquial Frost of 'Mowing' ('What was it it whispered?') and his starker 'Desert Places' ('The woods around it have it — it is theirs').

The graphic accuracy (indeed the 'grace of accuracy') of Heaney's language is evinced by the biretta's 'triple-finned black serge'; the hat's innards are not skimped either — the lining is not mere satin but, more precisely, 'crimped satin'. And the poem listens as well as looks, hearing the priest's mannered delivery of the words which accompany his 'fastidious' sign of the cross : '*In*

the name of the Father and of the Son AND / Of the Holy Ghost . . .'
What impresses even more than the poem's local detail is its
rapid turnover of associations, effortlessly marshalled without
clutter or loss of clarity — rather like the Domenico Scarlatti of
Basil Bunting's poem, 'Briggflatts', who 'condensed so much
music into so few bars / with never a crabbed turn or congested
cadence, / never a boast or a see-here'. The poem's opening — its
triple-take, its hat-trick image ('Like Gaul, the biretta was divided
/ Into three parts') — draws on memories of St Columb's College
where Heaney learned Latin from priests whose God, like Gaul
and the biretta, was divided into three: Father, Son and Holy
Ghost.

The 'triple-finned . . . shipshape' biretta which 'seemed to
batten down' transmutes into various ship shapes later in the
poem, culminating in a boat in which a priest is rowed to admin-
ister the last rites to a dying man. Heaney's flotilla of funerary
vessels had previously included D H Lawrence's 'The Ship of
Death' ('one of my favourite poems'), the death ship in *Beowulf*
(his excerpt from which first appeared in *The Haw Lantern*) and a
passage of Mandelstam's prose in which poetry is compared to
an Egyptian ship of the dead: 'Everything needed for life is stored
in this ship, and nothing is forgotten'; Heaney ended a talk at the
1979 MLA convention with this quotation. From start (Aeneas
setting out 'to sail the Stygian lake') to finish (the 'raging and
bawling' Charon of *The Inferno* ferrying the damned), precarious
voyages are negotiated and choppy waters navigated in *Seeing
Things*. The best-known twelve-liner of the 'Squarings' sequence
— the one about the ship docking in the air above the praying
monks of Clonmacnoise — is followed by an even better poem
(shore-bound in this instance) which begins, 'A boat that did not
rock or wobble once / Sat in long grass . . .' The title poem,
'Seeing Things' — itself divided into three parts — commences
with a voyage undertaken by Heaney and his family to
Inishbofin (off the Galway coast) in the 1970s. The final section of
the poem is a childhood recollection of a near-drowning incident
that left the poet's father 'strange' without his customary hat,
which the river had claimed.

It is the church father's headgear which, turned on its head,
prompts the various boating analogies in 'The Biretta' ('Now I
turn it upside down and it is a boat'). At first, the poem informs
us, the upturned biretta 'is . . . a paper boat'. *Seeing Things* is a
collection very much written in the name of the father; 'The

Biretta' too is touched by the death of Heaney's father in 1986, five years before the book was published. To make the connection between the paper boat and the poet's father more explicit, one must look to the subsequent collection, *The Spirit Level*; there, Heaney's father is found fashioning paper boats ('A dove rose in my breast / Every time my father's hands came clean / With a paper boat between them, ark in air'). In the wake of the paper boat, 'The Biretta' turns to a boat on paper — 'the one that wafts into / The first lines of the *Purgatorio*'. Next — with its oars of ore — comes 'that small boat out of the bronze age / Where the oars are needles and the worked gold frail'. Like the paper boat and the *Purgatorio* (Dante, of course, being one of his long-standing mentors), the gold craft has personal associations for Heaney and has not been selected arbitrarily; he is referring to the 'frail' gold boat, with cruciform mast, which was among a hoard of precious objects discovered at Broighter, in County Derry. Now in the National Museum of Ireland, the boat is part of Heaney's ancestral inheritance as a Derryman and therefore significant in a poem pervaded by memory — a poem in which it is the poet's recollections of things seen, said, read, cherished and experienced that hold together what might otherwise have been a diffuse and disjointed work.

On initially learning that 'The Biretta' had been Heaney's contribution to *Art is My Life* (1991), a book assembled by Brian P Kennedy as a tribute to James White (Director of the National Gallery of Ireland for many years), I mistakenly assumed that the El Greco reference in the fifth stanza was intended as a salute to White and a nod of recognition towards his El Greco-owning museum. But that stanza seems, in fact, to have been added during Heaney's final revisions for *Seeing Things* and proves surprisingly absent from the earlier version of 'The Biretta' published in *Art is My Life* (and also in the *TLS*). Since I speculated wrongly about El Greco, I might therefore be equally wrong in surmising that the poem's final craft — a painted boat upon a painted river — was intended as a gesture towards James White. The painting in question, Matthew J Lawless's 'The Sick Call' (in the National Gallery of Ireland), was reproduced opposite the text of 'The Biretta' in *Art is My Life*. This painting too is stored in Heaney's memory vault — it has long been a favourite of his; what makes its presence in the poem audacious and unexpected, however, is the fact that the portrayed priest answers the sick call in a wide-brimmed black hat rather than a biretta (which would have brought the poem neatly full-circle). Or, as Heaney himself writes of the sombre boat traversing the reedy water:

> *But in the end it's as likely to be the one*
> *In Matthew Lawless's painting,* The Sick Call,
> *Where the scene is out on a river and it's all*
> *Solid, pathetic and Irish Victorian.*
>
> *In which case, however, his reverence wears a hat.*
> *Undaunting, half domestic, loved in crises,*
> *He sits listening as each long oar dips and rises,*
> *Sad for his worthy life and fit for it.*

The kinds of 'test-outs and pull-backs, re-envisagings' which, technically and imaginatively, the drift from biretta to boat to broad-brimmed hat demands are not unfamiliar in Heaney's poetry. 'A Basket of Chestnuts' (which immediately precedes 'The Biretta' in *Seeing Things*) also alludes to an Irish painter — in this case, Edward McGuire (Maguire in Heaney's poem), whose portrait of Seamus Heaney as a young poetic acolyte at an altar-like table was reproduced on the back cover of *North* and hangs in the Ulster Museum. The poem mentions that portrait before shifting focus to what 'he did not paint when he painted me' and what 'wasn't in the picture and is not'.

Heaney's emphasis on the potency of what is absent, his capacity to walk 'round and round a space / Utterly empty, utterly a source', is connected with his sense of loss at the deaths of his parents. For all the tassel-light playfulness of language and the resistance of religious pieties in a poem about a religious object, there is something sorrowing at the heart of 'The Biretta'. Whether or not the allusion to 'The Sick Call' was influenced by the fact that 'The Biretta' was being published in honour of James White, the choice of that painting is striking in a book which opens with Aeneas' plea to be allowed to sail to the underworld 'for one look, one face-to-face meeting with my dear father'. 'Clearances', *The Haw Lantern*'s sonnet sequence commemorating Heaney's mother, recalled the parish priest who had responded to the sick call and was going 'hammer and tongs at the prayers for the dying'. As well as drawing a visual pun from the painting's title, a sickle glimpsed in the corner of Matthew Lawless's boat suggests not just the grim reaper but the scythe-swinging mower in 'Man and Boy' (another *Seeing Things* poem). The mower, who tells Heaney's father that he has mown the field 'as clean as a new sixpence', could double as an image of death and redemption:

> He has mown himself to the centre of the field
> And stands in a final perfect ring
> Of sunlit stubble.

Matthew James Lawless (1837-1864), painter of 'The Sick Call', died of consumption and not one other painting by him can be traced. The Scripture-citing full title of the work is 'The Sick Call: Is any man sick among you? Let him bring in the priest of the Church, and let them pray over him, anointing him with oil in the name of the Lord (James 5:14)'. According to Brian P Kennedy's *Irish Painting* (1993), Lawless was described by one of his contemporaries as 'a rattling good Catholic' and his picture 'may have been prompted by the experience of receiving the Catholic sacrament of Extreme Unction'. The model for the priest — his prayerfully-downcast eyes shadowed by his glum hat — is thought to have been Lawless's physician ('Physician, heal thyself'), a touch as deft as one of Heaney's own.

Among the seven souls crowding Lawless's raven-black rowing boat, as it hastens to the house of the dying man, are three altar boys who — like Heaney — have no doubt 'received' birettas into their hands when Masses were said. It is noteworthy that the biretta is 'received', not held or taken — 'received' as one receives a sacrament, or is received into a religious faith. The most casual words and phrases in 'The Biretta' ripple beyond their primary meanings in the way that a great painter will neglect no part of the canvas, however peripheral. Only the line 'It was antique as armour in a hall' lacks wider resonance. The 'pillbox' shape of the biretta in the first stanza is answered by the sickness at the end of the poem. And, if the biretta 'put the wind up me and my generation', this colloquialism is not out of place in a poem through which various boats (albeit not under sail) are floated.

The 'call' of 'The Sick Call' is extended to the priest's personal calling, his vocation. Heaney's strongly-defined sense of poetry as a vocation — as something 'in the realm of the sacred' — finds affirmation in his translation of Virgil's lines from the *Aeneid* ('The Golden Bough') in *Seeing Things*: 'If fate has called you, / The bough will come away easily, of its own accord'. 'His reverence' in 'The Sick Call' is said by Heaney to be 'sad for his worthy life and fit for it' — an allusion perhaps to Matthew's Gospel (8:8) where the centurion says to Jesus, 'Lord, I am not worthy that thou shouldest come under my roof: but speak the word only, and my servant shall be healed'. In 'The Biretta', Seamus Heaney applies words with a healing scrupulousness appropriate to a poem of memory and mourning; the final phrase, 'fit for it', also plays with the proverbial wisdom concerning a calling, 'If the cap fits, wear it'. 'The Biretta' is a perfect fit.

Harvard Review (Fall 1999)

Derek Mahon

Selected Poems (1990)

Derek Mahon's poems are among the most lyrically graceful of our time. What distinguishes them, however, is not the fact that they keep faith with formal writing in a free verse age but the manner in which they undercut and transmute that tradition. On first acquaintance, Mahon's poems seem to display all of the qualities required to ensure them a place in the mainstream English canon — a mastery of technique, a lyrical poise, a range of conventional imagery. That his best work eludes the pitfalls of such writing (vacuous virtuosity, thudding closure . . .) is due to a number of singular attributes: a heightened sense of doom, an ironic and sceptical wit, a visionary — almost mystical — imagination.

Mahon's visionary gifts are particularly notable. It is his capacity to imagine the lives of objects and to empathize with them that lends a poem like 'The Mute Phenomena' its power ('God is alive and lives under a stone. / Already in a lost hub-cap is conceived / The ideal society which will replace our own.') The final line of his celebrated poem, 'A Disused Shed in Co. Wexford', may echo the close of David Gascoyne's 'Ecce Homo' ('That man's long journey through the night / May not have been in vain'); yet the subtle admixture of the ironic and transcendent in this and other poems is entirely Mahon's own.

Oddly enough, it is the visionary side of his talent that Mahon himself seems to distrust or, at least, undervalue. No alternative explanation can account for the exclusion from this book of some of his best work, even as he insists to interviewers that *Selected Poems* contains 'the ones that matter, you can forget all the rest'. 'The Apotheosis of Tins' and 'The Banished Gods' — two of the ten Mahon poems rightly included in *The Penguin Book of Contemporary British Poetry* — are absent, as are equally indispensable poems such as 'The Mayo Tao', 'Matthew V. 29-30' and

'Poem Beginning with a Line by Cavafy'. The result is that readers new to Mahon acquire a more bland and tame impression than is either accurate or necessary.

Selections from the early volumes have been curtailed to make room for some less urgent poems of Mahon's middle period ('An Old Lady' and 'Soles', for instance). The new sections appended to the 'Light Music' sequence add little in the way of illumination. And 'Light Music' is not the only poem to gain nothing by revision — some poems actually lose as a result. 'Consolations of Philosophy' (here in its third published version), which once ended

> *Oh, then a few will remember with affection*
> *Dry bread, mousetrap cheese, and the satisfaction*
> *Of picking long butts from a wet gutter*
> *Like daisies from a clover field in summer*

now closes with

> *There will be time to live through in the mind*
> *The lives we might have lived, and get them right;*
> *To lie in silence listening to the wind*
> *Mourn for the living through the livelong night.*

This latest version not only lifts a key phrase from his own poem, 'Leaves', but in asking a single stanza to bear the weight of 'live', 'lives', 'lived', 'living', 'livelong' is fatally impoverishing what had been a richly resonant quatrain. A number of other poems, such as 'Girls on the Bridge' (which originally came to a halt with an appropriately Munchian screech), seem tampered with rather than improved. It is because his readers have come to associate his best work with a kind of perfection that Derek Mahon's shortcomings as a poet always grate. His explorations of existential bleakness, loneliness and doom lend his poems a unique aura and edge. He is to be found measuring light against darkness, beauty against its loss, celebration against alienation. The result is an elegiac poetry of great poignancy.

Mahon is haunted by 'the lives we might have lived' had personal or evolutionary circumstances so dictated. This theme is pursued through several fine poems — 'Leaves', 'Lives', 'Deaths', 'Ecclesiastes', 'Afterlives 2'. He takes his exploration further in a series of monologues spoken by Ovid, Van Gogh, Hamsun and the forger Van Meegeren among others. Unlike many 'persona' poems, no effort is made to capture the individual timbre or language of the speakers — the interest is psychological not semantic. Other poems derived from the lives and works of artists blend the autobiographical with the biographical ('Death and the Sun'), offer versions of translated work ('Brecht in Svendborg') or, far more convincingly, sketch period portraits ('A Kensington Notebook'). Artists are not the only outsiders within reach of his sympathies — there are poems about islanders, gypsies and hermits.

Mahon's own speaking voice is heard most clearly in his somewhat Audenesque verse-letters, which are discursive, clever and syntactically daring. The verse-letters, together with 'The Attic', 'Dawn at St. Patrick's', 'The Old Snaps', 'The Woods' and 'Craigvara House', add up to an honest and touching, if reticent, self-portrait. 'Craigvara House' is the finest of his later poems, reassuring evidence that Mahon can still rise to exquisite lyrics with exquisite rhymes (' . . . a first thrush / practising on a thorn bush / a new air picked up in Marrakesh'). Other poems in the later pages of the *Selected Poems* which deserve to be preserved alongside the best of the early work include 'One of These Nights', 'The Terminal Bar' and — a successful experiment with Irish rhythms — 'Achill'. Despite his Modernist sympathies as a critic, Derek Mahon has become more formally conservative over the years, abandoning occasional ventures into concrete poetry and prose poetry for neat stanzas and clear, uncluttered lines.

Although he grew up in Belfast, where he was born in 1941, Mahon allows the Northern Irish Troubles only an oblique role in his verse. 'The Last of the Fire Kings' is determined to be 'through with history' and is frustrated by his inability to gain release from 'the barbarous cycle' of violence. 'The Snow Party', in the poem of that title, might be a political party, cold and silent in the face of atrocities committed 'In the service / Of barbarous kings'. At the very least, it portrays the poet (represented by Basho) in a passive, even escapist, role — out of touch with, and unable to touch, the world of action. It is typical of Mahon's imaginative sweep that the perspective should be as broad as possible in time and place and that the poem's implications should be universal, not provincial.

Light is a healing element in this book and painters are recurring figures; in fact, poems devoted to paintings, painters and writers account for about a quarter of its pages. Philosophical and literary allusions and quotations are common also. Mahon is, to this very limited degree, a Poundian poet. Like Pound, he delights in making free translations or 'versions' of foreign texts, gorgeously conveying the sly eroticism of Ovid ('Aroused, I grabbed and roughly tore / until your gown squirmed on the floor') and the anarchic energy of Rimbaud's 'The Drunken Boat'.

Derek Mahon's *Selected Poems* is the product of a gifted poet, whose best work is tinged with an atmosphere of transience and foreboding. While the book does not altogether do justice to the full range and depth of his very considerable talent, it contains many moving and impeccably crafted poems. From a darkness of outlook and a lightness of technique he has drawn — like master-pieces of chiaroscuro — some of the glories of contemporary verse.

Quadrant (June 1993)

The Light Touch: *Light Verse and Quotations*

There is no *Oxford Book of Irish Light Verse*. Australian? Yeah.
American? Yup. And, of course, there is W H Auden's pioneering
anthology of 1938, followed forty years later by Kingsley Amis's
tidier and tamer *New Oxford Book of Light Verse*. Ireland's poets
have certainly had their lighter moments across the centuries and
those who would be automatic choices for an anthology of light
verse include not only the obvious Jonathan Swift, Oliver
Goldsmith, Thomas Moore and anonymous balladeers but countless masters of wordplay and witticism in the Irish language. An
eighth-century poem about a monk called Cú Chuimne was
translated by John V Kelleher:

> *Cú Chuimne in youth*
> *Read his way through half the Truth.*
> *He let the other half lie*
> *While he gave women a try.*
>
> *Well for him in old age.*
> *He became a holy sage.*
> *He gave women the laugh.*
> *He read the other half.*

On the whole, Irish poets have proved themselves to be more
adept at satire and song than at parody and *vers de société*. One
would not need to delve very deeply into Ireland's history from
the seventeenth century onwards to strike the jagged rocks on
which *vers de société* would have quickly perished in a society
which was linguistically, culturally and socially fissured. The
introduction to *An Duanaire* (the anthology of 'Poems of the
Dispossessed' edited by Seán Ó Tuama, with translations from
the Irish by Thomas Kinsella) observes that 'a great deal' of the
Gaelic poetry from the seventeenth to the nineteenth century is
'political poetry or a response to social — and linguistic — injus-

tice. The purely personal lyric voice is rarely heard, except in folk poetry, but there is no mistaking the strong personal feeling that attaches itself to public issues.' The tone of these poets can be light even when the sentiments are heavy-hearted, as in a poem by Dáibhí Ó Bruadair (1625–1698) which laments the neglect by the native Irish of their own traditions. This is a gritty antecedent of Wordsworth's 'The World is Too Much With Us', directed at the inhabitants of white-washed mud and smoke-stained thatch:

> *The once-proud men of this land have swapped*
> *giving for gaining, culture for crap:*
> *no tunes on the pipes, no music on harps —*
> *we* ourselves *have buried the summer at last.*

Michael Hartnett, who translated those lines — and who, from a young age, strongly identified with Ó Bruadair — has written both in English and in Irish. Even his poems in English are sometimes as redolent of the work of the great Gaelic satirists as a plucked harp-string might be of mead halls and spinning wheels. The stealing of his cat occasioned nine stanzas of invective (one, presumably, for each of the animal's lives) which rained down a scalding shower of curses on the thief and his loved ones:

> *May rats and mice them ever hound,*
> *may half of them be of mind unsound,*
> *may their house burn down to the ground*
>   *and no insurance;*
> *may drugs and thugs their lives surround*
>   *beyond endurance!*

> *May God forgive the heartless thief*
> *who caused our household so much grief;*
> *if you think I'm harsh, sigh with relief —*
>   *I haven't even started.*
> *I can do worse. I am, in brief,*
>   *yours truly, Michael Hartnett.*

Faced with the prospect of a retaliatory strike of such vehemence, it is little wonder that wariness of the toxin-tipped armoury of the bard should survive even in the Ireland of mobile phones and offshore trusts. As recently as January 1998, *The Tipperary Star* newspaper was reminding its rural readers — not altogether tongue-in-cheek — that 'There is and always has been agreement on the fact that for good or ill the bard is no man or woman to be snubbed under any circumstances, and he or she who would even contemplate doing so is putting himself or herself severely at risk.'

Despite their occasional forays into satire, virtuoso wordplay and epigrammatic comedy, contemporary poets in Ireland produce little that could take its place in the mainstream light verse tradition — marked by deftness of means, sharpness of wit and strictness of metre — which was represented in England by poets such as John Betjeman and Philip Larkin and which flourishes there today at the skilled hands of Wendy Cope, John Whitworth, Sophie Hannah, Kit Wright, James Fenton and John Fuller. University wits who prefer their poetry — like their brandy — neat, novelists who dabble on the side in bawdy quatrains, aristocratic types with a flair for the diamond-sparkle of a neatly-turned rhyme, bedridden maiden aunts whose secret indulgence is nonsense verse — none of these roles is filled by Ireland's rather uniform cast of poets. The one verse form which has no embarrassment threshold, the limerick, may take its name from an Irish city; but even the burly members of Limerick's famous rugby clubs have failed to sport any examples — however coarse — of this most amenable of literary genres.

If anything, Irish poets seem rather guarded about their few excursions into light verse, as though verse were a vice. A leaden poem by Tom Paulin directs a sneer at 'a culture of bungalows / And light verse'. Derek Mahon, the least heavy-handed of poets, has used 'light verse' as an accusation against the English (though his own later clerihews and river rhymes in *The Hudson Letter* suggest that the practice is no longer indictable). Even Seamus Heaney will more readily collect an off-form 'serious' poem than his scintillating 'Verses for a Fordham Commencement', which must therefore circulate in limited editions. Like Hartnett's curse, Heaney's blessing is administered through Burns metre:

> *So now, together,* gaudeamus,
> *Because, as sure as my name's Seamus*
> > *To-day's the day*
> *For* homo ludens' *revelry*
> Ad majorem gloriam dei.
> *Rejoice then, and as jazzmen say,*

Take it away

Onwards towards the sasparilla,
Jack Daniels, Bushmills, Schlitz and Miller,
The dry martini —
And if the drier types demur
Or if your dates object, declare
You were prescribed whiskey galore
By Doctor *Heaney.*

Another Ulster poet, James Simmons, has at times come close to the style of light verse — textually formal and sexually free — espoused by the dextrous English light-versifier, Gavin Ewart. Surprisingly, though, given his reputation for weighty allusions, some of the best light verse in Ireland flows from one side of Paul Muldoon's manifold talent — his pen flashes different nibs the way a Swiss Army Knife brandishes blades. Critics who were dismissive of his allegedly Ogden Nashian rhymes may yet concede dazzlement at the nimble ingenuity of 'Hopewell Haiku' and the nerve and verve of 'Long Finish', a poem which celebrates his tenth wedding anniversary. Tin may be the metal traditionally associated with that anniversary; but — as the punning poet might himself put it — tinn-itus is not a problem for Muldoon's perfectly-tuned ear:

The wonder is that we somehow have withstood
the soars and slumps in the Dow
of ten years of marriage and parenthood,
its summits and its sloughs —
that we've somehow
managed to withstand an almond-blossomy
five years of bitter rapture, five of blissful rows . . .

∼

One poet with an Irish surname, who is readily associated with distinguished light verse, is X J Kennedy. As it happens, XJK is as American as JFK and may be as outright gifted where pithily quotable commentary is concerned. Among the X J Kennedyisms I transcribed for my quotations column (entitled 'Pickings & Choosings') in *Poetry Ireland Review* was one regarding light verse: 'Trying to print light verse in this country nowadays is like trying to peddle mink coats at a convention of militant ecologists.'

Much of what is said and written about poetry floats into the stratosphere or merges with the dust which smothers the back issues of small-circulation magazines. Using a fine-mesh prospector's pan, one can chance upon glittering nuggets of broadcast and printed wisdom as well as tawdry chunks of fool's gold (with apophthegms as with poems, the William McGonagalls outnumber the Lord Byrons). *Hamlet* may have been dismissed by a disillusioned woman as a play full of quotations; but the major publishing houses recycle their material so lazily that their books of quotations resemble anthologies of clichés. As far as poetry is concerned, the time has surely come to update our stock of definitions, to wind our minds around something a little less timeworn than 'What oft was thought but ne'er so well expressed', 'the best words in the best order' or 'emotion recollected in tranquility'.

Over-familiar though they may have grown, these aperçus of Pope, Coleridge and Wordsworth served poetry well as succinct encapsulations of the art. And it is not inappropriate that the most famous utterances about poetry should be epigrammatic; after all, good epigrams and lyric poems have much in common: they are concise, precise and memorable. Ted Berrigan's jest about poems being stories with the boring bits left out could be extended to claim that aphorisms are essays with the boring parts omitted. Besides, some of the best modern poet-critics have had epigrammatic turns of mind: W H Auden, Ezra Pound, Wallace Stevens, Marianne Moore, Seamus Heaney, Philip Larkin and Randall Jarrell (or Randall Farrell — another Irish-sounding American — as he is listed in my edition of the *Oxford Dictionary of Literary Quotations*).

Among over two thousand uncollected remarks which I garnered for my magazine column, I was glad to find some which complemented my favourite quotations from the not-too-distant past. One of the growls of that great epigrammist, Cyril Connolly ('Poets arguing about modern poetry: jackals snarling over a dried-up well'), meets its match in a comparison made by Sean O'Brien between quarrelsome poets and 'ferrets fighting for mastery of a septic tank'. I was reminded of a droll observation of John Ashbery's ('There is a view that poetry should improve your life. I think people confuse it with the Salvation Army') when I spotted an equally agnostic Michael Donaghy decrying the 'socially self-conscious poets and very right-on, PC poets, who talk about bringing poetry to the people as if it was some sacred mission, like converting the natives to Christianity'. Karl Kraus's jaundiced view that 'A poem is good until one knows who wrote it' is corroborated by Charles Baxter's equally colourful — and, no doubt, verifiable — gibe that 'The one thing that can get a poet irritated and upset is the thought of another poet's poems.'

Oscar Wilde, the most quoted of all Irish authors, remarked that 'a poet can survive anything but a misprint' (a point obviously lost on publishers of quotations — in one book I consulted, the word 'anything' is replaced by 'everything', leaving me wavering between versions like a scholar of the Dead Sea Scrolls . . .) And was it misprints, mishearing, misunderstanding or mere misspelling that led to the misnomers in the magazine, *Writers' Monthly*, where it was reported that the spellbinding poet, Carol Ann Duffy — who has been known to keep a volume or two by Les Murray, Paul Durcan and Eavan Boland on her shelves — was in fact 'knee deep at the moment in the poems of Lez Murray, Paul Dacre and Ivan Boland'? A telephone poll conducted by the BBC a few years ago, to find Britain's 'favourite poem', left the exasperated telephonists not only knee deep, but drowning, in a flood of calls. According to a London newspaper, the nominations (or, at any rate, those listed by staff) included 'Not Wading but Drowning', 'Allergy in a Country Churchyard' and 'The Rhubarb of O'Mark I am'.

I collected more quotes of many colours than Tony Curtis — the Irish poet, who assembled a selection of them — could reasonably (or, at any rate, legibly) squeeze into a 100-page book. Some of them confirmed that brevity and wit go together like boiled eggs and soldiers; other quotations were impressive for their insights, their metaphors, their sheer eloquence. The poet Wendy Cope, author of some of the best contemporary light verse, proved to be one of the shrewdest and sharpest analysts of poetry and the poetry scene — though, frustratingly, I discovered too late for my column her barb impugning the high motives of the Modernist male: 'The reason modern poetry is difficult is so that the poet's wife can't understand it.' One way of getting round Christopher Logue's conviction that 'Poetry cannot be defined, only experienced' is for the definition itself to be a poem. The most swoon-inducing, hair-bristling quotation I recorded came from an interview with Seamus Heaney (the line breaks and stanzas are mine!):

Dennis O'Driscoll

What I want from poetry
is the preciousness and foundedness
of wise feeling become eternally
posthumous in perfect cadence . . .

You want it to touch you
at the melting point
below the breast-bone
and the beginning of the solar plexus.

You want something sweetening
and at the same time something unexpected,
something that has come
through constraint into felicity.

My becoming a hunter-gatherer of quotations was perhaps a predictable destiny; as part of my schooling, I was obliged — like most of my generation — to memorize countless proverbs in Irish at school. Having learned to sound wise beyond my schoolboy years, ('There's no hearth like your own hearth'; 'It's a long road that has no turning'; 'Praise the young and they will flourish'), I then put this wiseacre tone into practice when writing essays in Irish which became a kind of join-the-dots of proverbs. English-language essays and school debates were also expected to showcase the student's command of the cliché and the quotation. Marks would be deducted for originality. Weaker students got their lines crossed and their metaphors mixed, resulting in surreal hybrids worthy of Paul Muldoon's poem, 'Symposium' (in which 'One good turn deserves a bird in the hand' and 'There's no smoke after the horse is gone'). Fluid examples from Tipperary — where I grew up — include 'You can take a horse to the water, but you can't make him lay an egg' and 'It went in one ear and out the other, like water off a duck's back'. Wasn't it that master of the one-liner, Ambrose Bierce, who defined quoting as 'The act of repeating erroneously the words of another'? Memory is the mother of the Muses, but there are definitely times when absentmindedness amuses.

Harvard Review (Spring 1998)

PART FOUR

US and UK

The Best American Poetry 1997

Edited by James Tate

Dividing America's published poets into camps — cooked and raw, neat and beat — is a largely redundant activity by now. One is tempted, cynically perhaps, to classify all of them as realists, albeit realists of a peculiarly modern kind. They are more likely to be found drafting applications for tenure-track teaching posts than drawing up manifestos. If they experience Bohemia, it will be as a country — visited on a grant or fellowship — from whose bourn the traveller returns with an album of exotic poems, ideal ballast for his or her next blurb-encrusted, award-bestrewn collection.

Far from being the unworldly loners of the popular image, poets strut through American campuses with titles of the 'Distinguished Visiting Professor' type, which bespeak a poorly-developed sense of irony, self-mockery or hubris. Substantial incomes can be topped up — where alimony or social mobility requires — by positions as 'core faculty' at Summer Writing Programs in off-season skiing towns. On the picturesque farms which serve as the private retreats of the more affluent, tie-beam barns will have been converted into studio space decorated with Navajo wall-hangings. There, the high productivity required to maintain high visibility in the little world of poetry is word-processed into existence — loose, runny slabs of narrative verse or tight, costive, self-conscious formal verse.

Poetry can take root anywhere and there are some poets who flourish in a university environment. Charles Wright, one of the most impressive contributors to *The Best American Poetry 1997* (his long poem, 'Disjecta Membra', seems poised between Li Po and Pound), is a university professor who described himself in his *Paris Review* interview as 'almost a 100 percent product of the writing workshop system', adding that 'it was not only good for me, but necessary as well'. Although Wright serves as conclusive proof that workshops can work, he too has reservations about the current graduate programs, likening them to 'feedlots or holding pens'. Some of the most vibrant poetry in English is being written by teachers of creative writing; yet the notion of poetry originating almost exclusively in a university environment is no more palatable — and no less dangerous — than the over-dependency of farmers on one or two strains of high-yield wheat for the grain harvests of the Great Plains. It would be a disaster for poetry if its weedier cousins — rap and slam — were to be the only organic alternatives to the workshopped crop.

While the teaching of poetry is now an activity capable of providing secure employment and a career structure for many of America's poets, the poets themselves are not altogether happy. One thinks of Stevie Smith's pug:

> *O Pug, obstinate old nervous breakdown,*
> *In the midst of so much love,*
> *And such comfort,*
> *Still to feel unsafe and be afraid . . .*

Their unhappiness stems from the fact that the audience for their books (sumptuous two-tone hardbacks with tooled initials like family Bibles) is mainly limited to the enclosed orders of university poets, and students intent on picking up the tricks of the trade. They see themselves not as denizens of academia but as denim-clad free spirits; their dream is to be read and revered rather than hired to indulge the callow confessions of fledgling poetic talents.

Introducing the 1998 *Forward Book of Poetry*, John Fuller sagely remarked: 'Most poetry eventually joins the vast shelves of the unread and most readers of poetry follow a beaten track. Time, which is said to be the mother of truth, can all too easily confirm habit and lay its slow dust on the unclamorous.' 'Time' will have to work overtime, wading through the voluminous floodwaters of modern American poetry, to see how much remains that is living, breathing and deserving of rescue. 'Unclamorousness', however, is not an accusation one would level against the more horn-tooting contributors to *The Best American Poetry 1997*, guest-edited by James Tate (who supplies a first-rate introduction). As you struggle through their triumphal commentaries on their own poems (published at the back of the book like answers to brain-teasers), you begin to feel glad to be facing these authors across a page rather than from the front row of a poetry reading.

David Lehman's informative and elegant forewords, as series

editor of *The Best American Poetry* volumes, are a State of the Poetry Union address. Also generally useful are the detailed notes on contributors which are included. These are a boon if you want to track down further work by the poets in the anthology who really *are* the 'best' — poets of the calibre of Robert Hass ('Interrupted Meditation' is the anthology's masterpiece) and Albert Goldbarth — as well as less-established writers like Catherine Bowman and Beth Lisick whose lively prose-poems make you wonder whether their other work is equally enjoyable. Unfortunately, Catherine Bowman is one of the poets whose patience-fraying explanatory note at the back of the book tempts you to reconsider your favourable judgement of her poem at the front ('I'll start out by saying that I do not believe that all of society is murderous . . .'); Lisick, on the other hand, is witty and snappy, summarizing her poem in a single streaming sentence which stifles one's unworthy bias against her membership of a poetry slam team, performing in places like the Lollapalooza Festival: 'It was written for parents who retire to gated communities of steel-framed homes and former television stars who drink nightcaps in their pajamas while gardenias bloom in the desert.'

Given the earnestness and self-importance of so many of the contributors to this anthology, both the MFA Boomers and their elders ('When I gave him the poem, he said, "I wasn't expecting anything this good"', goes one double-edged example), I began to wonder if the poetry slammers might not be needed, after all, to challenge the complacencies of the contemporary academy, just as the Beat poets — for all their superficiality — famously did in the Fifties. One minor task I have in mind for the slammers is to shoo away some of the unnecessary angels, who are so common in American writing as to have become the pigeons of the poetry world. Intended to bestow instant spirit-cred — spirituality and solemnity, mystery and profundity — on poems, they represent one of the nervous flutters of millennial verse. In *The Best American Poetry 1997* alone, you will find at least eight poems (one or two, admittedly, quite good) in which angels make a flying visit or swoop down to earth for a refuelling stop. It is high time their wings were clipped.

Poetry Review (Spring 1998)

The Irish Ashbery

The writ of John Ashbery scarcely runs in Ireland. His writings are known from reputation rather than from reading — and his reputation here does little to encourage readers. As long ago as 1981, in a review of *As We Know*, I lamented the fact that 'it is the more somnific aspects of his work which seem to have gained notoriety in this part of the world'. Later that year, Ashbery gave his first poetry recital in Ireland, an event which took place not in Dublin but in a hall (not quite a disused shed) in Gorey, County Wexford. That reading was organised by James Liddy who has brought to his own poetry some of the New York School spirit of risk, adventure and wit. And if Ashbery's American pre-eminence leaves most Irish readers of poetry cold, Ashbery himself is equally sceptical about Ireland's poetry hierarchy, declaring James Liddy to be 'one of the most original among living Irish poets, perhaps the most' and adding 'His work has not received the attention accorded his more famous contemporaries, Seamus Heaney and Thomas Kinsella, for example, but I am convinced of its superiority.'

Seamus Heaney's 1985 response to Ashbery's work emerged in a published conversation with Joseph Brodsky where he remarked that the poetry 'is a centrally heated daydream. And it's also sorrowful, it knows that it's inadequate'. Thomas Kinsella, whose later work has deep Modernist roots, might be expected to be more enthusiastic. However, while — like Heaney — he enjoys Frank O'Hara, he has stated plainly: 'I cannot appreciate Ashbery.' If, despite these rebuffs, the Irish Ashbery trail were to be pursued further, it might well lead to Medbh McGuckian whose name was, from the beginning, linked by reviewers with his semi-surreal obliquities. Interviewing her for RTE radio after *The Flower Master* first appeared, I therefore posed the obvious question, only to be told that she had never read Ashbery. Even *Self-Portrait in a Convex Mirror*, the acceptable face of Ashbery in many readers' eyes, was unacceptable to Edna

Longley, a sympathetic critic of McGuckian's poetry. Reviewing the book in *The Honest Ulsterman*, she portrayed its author as someone guilty of 'transatlantic garrulity' and 'awesome inanity', concluding that 'The title of this book sums up its complete failure to reflect anything but its author's self-infatuated face.'

Notwithstanding the hostility and indifference with which Ashbery has been regarded in Ireland, one of his most persuasive international interpreters is in fact an Irish critic, Denis Donoghue. Donoghue has written lucidly of Ashbery in the *New York Review of Books* and has broadcast a shrewd and searching interview with him on BBC Radio 3. Nearer home, in *The Irish Times*, Eavan Boland too has been an astute interviewer and reviewer of Ashbery. Neither Eavan Boland nor Denis Donoghue tries to play down the difficulties which Ashbery's work presents. Boland argues that 'Only his marvellous cadences, his uncanny stylization of ordinary talk, save the reader from absolute confusion. And then not always.' Donoghue is equally candid when he states, 'The difficulties are not in local meaning, but in knowing or even sensing how one such meaning bears upon the text.'

Personally speaking, I find Ashbery's drive towards experiment refreshing if not invariably rewarding. The great value of his work is in its spirit as much as its letter and he has the courage to risk losing readers in the pursuit of an altered sensibility and a fresh purchase on experience. The danger of such writing is that it can make a fetish of novelty, becoming a trivial TV-age poetry in which the screen continually changes as the writer's attention span proves shorter than the reader's. At its most concentrated, though, the pleasures of Ashbery are less those of the sharp eye and keen ear than of the lively imagination. He seems to be engaged not so much in a transformation of tangible reality as an escape from it — the creation of a parallel mode of apprehension, drawing on the unconscious, the oneiric, the random, in which everything is grist to his imaginative mill:

> . . . *In the next town there's a grist mill and a blacksmith,*
> *or was that part of a dream, or did it really exist in a past*
> *one can focus on, extracting its kernel until, like a ship,*
>   *the shell turns round,*
> *advances on us and speculation is undone for today.*

In general, the longer the Ashbery poem the better, insofar as this affords the reader time to adapt to its environment, to adjust to its imaginative weather; indeed, the best poems both enact and stimulate such an adjustment. The result is language on a different plane, like mathematics in a different base, a poetry which is peculiarly rich in angles, tones, perspectives.

Like most Ashbery readers, I have a special affection for 'Self-Portrait in a Convex Mirror', which introduced to his poetry the virtues of modesty and clarity which come across so strongly in his art criticism and interviews. Criticism of Ashbery's own work, whether supportive or not, is rarely helpful when we return to read the poems; his poetry attracts academic elucidation but also proves resistant to it. Irvin Ehrenpreis aptly observed, in a review of *Self-Portrait*, 'Among the muddles of our critics is the assumption that if an author has persuasive theoretical grounds for his literary practice, the reader ought to be satisfied that what the man writes is good.' However silly and untenable many of the theoretical claims made for Ashbery may be, he has achieved enough in practice to have earned the respect and interest of readers — not least in cautious Ireland.

PN Review (September/October 1994)

John Berryman and W B Yeats:
Majestic Dreams

He was born John Allyn Smith, Jr, in Oklahoma on 25 October 1914. And he became John Berryman, taking his stepfather's name after his father's apparent suicide in 1926. And he in turn became the writer, part-Irish in ancestry, who joked that he would publish as O'Berryman. Given his obsession with Yeats, William Butler Berryman might have been a more suitable name; Robert Lowell, having read the Dublin 'Dream Songs', called him 'the best Irish poet since Yeats'.

It is impossible to think of Berryman's poetic development without thinking of Yeats, whom he said he 'didn't so much wish to resemble as to *be*'. For all the Audenesque echoes of the early poems, it is Yeats who was his supreme exemplar in poetry. 'I began work in verse-making as a burning, trivial disciple of the great Irish poet William Butler Yeats,' he wrote in 1965, 'and I hope I have moved off from there.' Yet, only one year later, he was moving back towards Yeats, using a Guggenheim Fellowship to live in Ireland with his family from September 1966 until the following June:

> *I have moved to Dublin to have it out with you,*
> *majestic Shade, You whom I read so well*
> *so many years ago,*
> *did I read your lesson right? did I see through*
> *your phases to the real? your heaven, your hell*
> *did I enquire properly into?*

As a student at Clare College, Cambridge, in 1936, Berryman kept a photograph of Yeats over his desk 'where I can see it always, looking up, or across from my big chair or the lounge'. In his 1965 commentary, Berryman spoke of Yeats as someone who had saved him, during his literary apprenticeship, from succumbing to 'the then-crushing influences of Ezra Pound and T S Eliot'. It was Yeats too who gave him the idea of attempting plays and other dramatic writings as a 'mask for my life': a good grounding for the future author of so many poems using masks, dialogue and speech rhythms. The mask initially tended to obscure the man and Randall Jarrell, writing in 1948, spoke of Berryman's early poems having been 'possessed by a slavishly Yeatsish grandiloquence which at its best resulted in a sort of posed, planetary melodrama, and at its worst resulted in monumental bathos'.

Yeats may have been reduced to a 'Shade' by the time of Berryman's visit to Ireland in 1966. However, even while still alive, he appeared in an appropriately visionary guise to Berryman at Cambridge. A letter to his mother, dated February 14 1937, is quite matter-of-fact about the visitation:

> *Wednesday evening while I was reading here, suddenly my attention wandered, as if forcibly; I shut my eyes and an image rose before them, not clear but strong: I saw that it was the figure of Yeats, white-haired and tall, strug-gling laboriously to lift something dark which was on his right side and below the level on which he stood; as it came into my view, he lifting it with difficulty, I saw that it was a great piece of coal, irregular, black. He raised it high above his head, hair flying and with a set expression, brilliant eyes, dashed it to the ground at his feet, a polished ground that might have been a floor: the pieces rolled away silver.*

The apparition had made itself visible to Berryman on the eve of his Yeats lecture to Clare College's literary society on 11 February 1937 ('The Dilettante Society here in Clare / asked me to lecture to them on Yeats / & misspelt his name on the invitations'). It was after that lecture that he first met the Irish composer, Brian Boydell, whom he was to remember affectionately over thirty years afterwards:

> *Friendless in Clare, except Brian Boydell*
> *a Dubliner with no hair*
> *an expressive tenor speaking voice*
> *who introduced me to the music of Peter Warlock*

who had just knocked himself off, fearing the return
of his other personality, Philip Heseltine.
Brian used to play The Curlew *with the lights out,*
voice of a lost soul moving . . .

Part of the fascination of *The Curlew* for Berryman was no doubt
the fact that it consisted of settings of Yeats's poems. A 'religious
ritual' was how Brian Boydell described to me the habit he and
Berryman developed of listening to this melancholy music in the
dark, followed by 'about ten minutes' of absolute silence. The
success of his Yeats lecture gave Berryman the confidence to think
in terms of a biography of the poet. He planned to cycle through
Ireland, gathering material on Yeats and arriving at a critical
evaluation of 'his achievement in the drama, in various kinds of
prose, in moral philosophy, and in poetry'.

A few months before this, Berryman had written to his mother
enclosing a 28-line verse homage to Yeats which seems to have
been later revised to a 14-line poem, the second stanza of which
reads:

> *An aged man there is in Ireland now*
> *Alone who is the honour of that praise:*
> *Craftsman intense and disciplined, a man*
> *Who set apart luxuriance and ran,*
> *A creature of bone and heart and formal brow,*
> *With swifter sun the passionate long race*
> *And won, that lonely man.*

Berryman sent his imitative encomium to the great man, together
with a letter of 'prose praise' and a postscript declaring his wish
'to see him when I got to Ireland if that was possible'. Yeats's brief
reply, in 'a quite illegible and characterless scrawl — in fact the
worst I've ever seen' was deciphered as approving of 'the poems
you select for praise' and adding his thanks 'for the eloquent
compliment of your verse'. This letter from Yeats's Rathfarnham
home drove its recipient into a frenzy of impatient anticipation:
'If only I can see him and talk with him and see the tower and the
winding stair and Coole Park, my joy will be complete. I read him
constantly and have dozens of the poems by heart, which is good
because I needn't have a book to be able to say them anywhere,
on the bicycle or in bed.'

After a sleepless and uncomfortable overnight sailing from

Liverpool to Dublin in April 1937, Berryman found that the object of his journey and the subject of his projected book was actually in England. Making the best of his visit, he informed his mother by a letter addressed 25 Harcourt Street, Dublin, that he was now determined to meet Yeats's daughter: 'I own a passionate desire to see her — my God what lines he wrote for her and she in the cradle!' Passion, that quintessentially Yeatsian emotion, abated when he and Anne were introduced: 'Having imagined her as a dazzling beauty, I saw myself as Yeats' son-in-law. I was crushed to find she was quite plain.'

Berryman, who had informed his mother that 'If I don't soon see Yeats, I shall be consumed', was saved by an invitation to afternoon tea at the Athenaeum on April 16. Despite Dylan Thomas's best efforts to ensure that Berryman was drunk and disorderly for the occasion ('He found my Cantabrigian sherry-sipping "effete"'), it proved very memorable. Yeats ('rather wonderful looking in a sort of a blunt, patrician kind of way') spoke to his admirer of 'Many things: Swift, Indian thought and what he calls "artistic pessimism", Spengler, "Demon and Beast", the dance plays and a new one he has written, Parnell, music and poetry, various aspects of his philosophy . . . The statement I recall most vividly is this: "I never revise now except in the interests of a more passionate syntax, a more natural."'

What might seem a trivial aspect of the meeting became a focus for recounting it in verse. As he told Peter Stitt in his *Paris Review* interview:

> At a certain point, I had a cigarette, and I asked him if he would like one. To my great surprise he said yes. So I gave him a Craven-A and then lit it for him, and I thought, 'Immortality is mine! From now on it's just a question of reaping the fruits of my effort.'

The first fruits of the long-desired rendezvous can be found in the fifth of the *Sonnets to Chris* in which the love for the master threatens, momentarily at least, to rival the love for the eponymous mistress:

> The poet hunched, so, whom the worlds admire,
> Rising as I came in; greeted me mildly . . .
> I lit his cigarette . . . once I lit Yeats' as he
> Muttered before an Athenaeum fire

> *The day Dylan had tried to slow me drunk*
> *Down to the great man's club . . .*

As though it were a handing on of a torch, a perpetual flame, the proffered Craven-A remained the pivotal image of the encounter, its cynosure. An uncollected 'Dream Song' from about 1958 is a further example:

> *Yes, yes, I offered him a cigarette, —*
> *to my amazed awe he accepted it,*
> *and waited for a light.*
> *A light! I did that too, with one of those stub*
> *infallible Swan Vestas, the world's best,*
> *while the famous club's fire roared . . .*

Among the collected 'Dream Songs', the cigarette flares brightly also. Number 215 tells the tale with economy as well as pride:

> *Took Henry tea down at the Athenaeum with Yeats*
> *and offered the master a fag, the which he took,*
> *accepting too a light*
> *to Henry's lasting honour. Time abates.*
> *Humourless, grand, by the great fire for a look*
> *he set out his death in twilight . . .*

Before *The Dream Songs*, however, came *Homage to Mistress Bradstreet*, a late (if, ironically, ventriloqual) discovery of his own voice at the age of thirty-nine. Even here, Yeats played a role. Of the form of the poem, Berryman remarked: 'The eight-line stanza I invented here after a lifetime's study, especially of Yeats's, and in particular the one he adopted from Abraham Cowley for his elegy "In Memory of Major Robert Gregory".'

The *persona* of Anne Bradstreet is itself one of those antithetical masks of which Yeats would have approved. But, as with *The Waste Land*, the poem is increasingly read against the background of its author's personal circumstances at the time of its composition. The result is that an early critic, even one as perceptive as John Frederick Nims in his 1958 essay, a 'Homage in Measure to Mr. Berryman', may now seem over-anxious to make historical sense of the poem. John Haffenden, who — as Berryman's punctilious biographer — is well-placed to establish the connection, sees the poem as 'both a lament for a doomed marriage —

John and Eileen Berryman split up later that year — and a homage to a figure uniting mistress and wife'.

For some readers, *Homage* remains the high point of Berryman's career; and, though not sharing this assessment, I would certainly regard it as his most flawless poem. It is the first fully achieved example of Berryman's ability to deploy a pliant language which combines a formal, even rhetorical, quality with an informal, even conversational, one. The sinewy syntax-driven style is notable for its compact, compressed stanzas and the supple transitions between poet and poetess, past and present. Reading it, we are witnesses to a high-wire balancing act along the tautest of ropes:

> *Bitter sister, victim! I miss you.*
> *— I miss you, Anne,*
> *day or night weak as a child,*
> *tender & empty, doomed, quick to no tryst.*
> *— I hear you. Be kind, you who leaguer*
> *my image in the mist.*
> *— Be kind you, to one unchained eager far & wild . . .*

While readily acknowledging the role Yeats had played in influencing the stanzaic shape of *Homage*, Berryman was reluctant to concede any debt to Hopkins's 'The Wreck of the Deutschland', claiming to have read only the first stanza. It is, nonetheless, impossible to imagine that the rhythmical risks run by this poem (or the earlier *Sonnets to Chris*) could have been taken without the precedent of Hopkins. Paul Mariani — another biographer — reports that, when Rosalie Moore juxtaposed lines of *Homage* with lines of Hopkins, Berryman was 'astonished' by the similarities.

Although Hopkins was not forgotten by Berryman during his second and more extended stay in Dublin ('Father Hopkins, teaching elementary Greek / whilst his mind climbed the clouds, also died here'), it was Yeats, needless to say, to whom his thoughts most frequently turned. As with *Homage*, Yeats was credited with the stanza form that had evolved for *The Dream Songs*: 'That I got from Yeats — three six-line stanzas. His songs don't really resemble mine, but I did get that from him.'

Speaking of *The Dream Songs* to the *Harvard Advocate*, Berryman said, 'I wrote about a hundred in Dublin . . . I killed a lot of songs in Ireland, too'; and to *The Paris Review* he remarked that 'obviously if I hadn't got a Guggenheim and decided to spend it in Dublin, most of Book VII wouldn't exist'. 'In Dublin', as John Haffenden observed, 'every event became the occasion for a poem.' Dropping a cigarette in Grangegorman hospital, a friend's intercession on his behalf with a bank, his tenant's arrears — everything was convertible into song. If he sought a theme, he certainly did not seek for it in vain: the regret expressed by Philip Larkin (once a devoted Yeatsian himself), that subjects such as having 'passed my driving test first go' do not make for poetry, would have struck Berryman as sheer defeatism.

The Dream Songs become clearer with every additional insight into what Berryman said, did, read; without notes, too many of them leave the reader knocking for entry — taunted, snubbed, frustrated. Their mode of address can be so personal and intimate that the reader becomes for Berryman a kind of confidant, an insider who is presumed to understand exactly what he is talking about. But this taking of the reader into his confidence is also part of Berryman's appeal — and, when combined with his wit, charm and ingenious handling of linguistic registers, one is in a mood to agree with his own boast: 'I have a style now pared straight to the bone and can make the reader's nerves jump by moving my little finger.' And yet the jagged, buttonholing quality of *The Dream Songs* works in a somewhat hit-and-miss way, the poet risking everything to accurately plot the experience-curve of a life. When habit overwhelms judgement, 'Dream Songs' get cobbled together from whatever scraps happen to be at hand (Number 307 among the Irish Songs is a perfect instance) so that they seem haphazard rather than serendipitous.

A phrase used in Berryman's elegy for Sylvia Plath, 'the geography of grief', describes one of the most impressive aspects of *The Dream Songs*: their powerful cartography of the psychological and physical features of grief and loss. The elegiac Songs for Delmore Schwartz are among the most searing and touching things he has written ('Ten Songs, one solid block of agony'). And his virtuosic elegy for Wallace Stevens veers between the playful and mournful, without sacrificing the critical:

> He lifted up, among the actuaries,
> a grandee crow. Ah ha & he crowed good.
> That funny money-man.
> Mutter we all must as well as we can.
> He mutter spiffy. He make wonder Henry's

Dennis O'Driscoll

wits, though, with a odd

*... something ... something ... not there in his flourishing
    art.
O veteran of death, you will not mind
a counter-mutter.
What was it missing, then, at the man's heart
so that he does not wound? ...*

In coming by sea to Ireland in 1966, Berryman, the master
elegist, felt that he was 'Leaving behind the country of the dead'.
This, of course, was impossible; death could not be thrown
overboard so wilfully and he continued to be haunted by death
and possessed by a death wish. Ironically, Cobh (where he disem-
barked from the *Carmania* on September 1), being part of
Munster, would have been regarded in Celtic mythology — to
quote Maurice Harmon — as 'paradoxically ... both the land of
the dead and the place of origins'. By the time we reach 'Song
344', an 'exquisite October Sunday' in Herbert Park, Dublin is
darkened by the long shadow of Delmore Schwartz's death. Ten
Songs previously, in another death-tinged bulletin from 'startling
Ballsbridge, / our sedate suburb, the capital of What Is', he finds
himself at odds with Yeats, though even here a sneaking admiration survives:

*Yeats knew nothing about life: it was all symbols
& Wordsworthian egotism: Yeats on Cemetery Ridge
would not have been scared, like you & me,
he would have been, before   the bullet that was his,
studying the movements of the birds,
said disappointed & amazed Henry.*

On arrival in Dublin, the Berrymans — John, his third wife,
Kate (an Irish-American, about twenty-five years his junior),
together with their four-year-old daughter, Martha — lodged in
the Majestic Hotel in Baggot Street. A week later, they took
possession of rooms without a view: a drab end-of-terrace corporation house at 55 Lansdowne Park, Ballsbridge, all too convenient to The Beggars Bush pub (where he is fondly remembered as
a friendly, well-behaved regular and where a photograph taken
of him with Jack Ryan, then the owner, still hangs on the wall).
The rent was $140 a month and this 'trim suburban villa', as

176

Berryman glorified it, was to be their home for the remainder of their Irish stay. A next-door neighbour told me that the Berrymans tended to keep to themselves, though John's stentorian voice occasionally penetrated the walls. In a letter from Ballsbridge on 15 December 1966, Berryman claims to have finished *The Dream Songs* and adds:

> *I still have the terrible editorial & administrative labour of making Bks V & VI of the 300 but I — can't write any more, at least until I am thro' w. the second volume & open the great yellow folder I brought fr. Mpls, w. fragments, better than many of the finisht songs. But I feel remote & lost without my poem, & gave hell to an editor of* The Irish Times *the other evening, why I don't know.*

In fact, Berryman, who was supposed to be in Ireland precisely in order to complete that editorial work, was unable to stop writing; even when he felt he 'could write no more', he made a Song about it. He *did* prepare the sonnets (which had been secretly composed twenty years before) for publication and the prefatory note to the book is from 'Ballsbridge, Dublin, October 8th, 1966'. On the exact date of that preface, he confessed to his publisher that he was engaged in 'incessant production' of new 'Dream Songs' and that he had written 'some 40 in the last month alone'. Berryman, by then, had created a poetic organism capable of digesting any experience and turning it into poetry; the poet in him had been set free but the critic had been muzzled.

There is both a gain in clarity and a loss of density in the later 'Dream Songs'. Berryman himself accepted that 'it takes about three Songs in Books 5 and 6 and 7 to get done what I was doing in one in the first volume.' In 'Song 303', for instance, which dates from May 1967, we are treated to what might be the diary entry for a not particularly eventful day: 'Brought Jerry with me home last night, Kate got cross . . .' On the other hand, he still writes superbly in parts of Book VII; and, having assured a reporter that 'of course' his inspiration would now be Irish, he does tragic justice to Jonathan Swift and is able to comment shrewdly, comically, poignantly (if sometimes superficially) on Irish life. Indeed, familiarity breeds contempt as well as affection: 'Some of my travel & Irish songs are beauties . . . and some take it out on the Irish — I'll teach these bloody islanders. But we've met excellent people too.' A letter to his mother, dated 2 January 1967, effectively concedes that when a man is *not* tired of Dublin, he is tired of life: 'I'm tired of Dublin; no genius here . . . It's very hard, older, to make friends.' The black mood of that letter was no doubt coloured by a painful fall the previous night, which he blamed on the side-effects of Thorazine ('one of my drugs').

If Berryman had hoped to snatch inspiration from the Dublin literary air, the fact that Yeats — not to mention Swift, Joyce and Hopkins — were all in the land of the dead left him in colloquy with ghosts: 'The whole place is ghostly: no wonder Yeats believed in fairies . . .' He seems to have been fairly isolated, lonely ('friends now to be telephoned / only when drunk and at enormous cost') and alcoholic (spending a week at Grange-gorman hospital for treatment). Some of Terence Spencer's 1,200 or so photographs, taken in Dublin to accompany a *Life* article by Jane Howard, reveal him with — but not entirely of — the bemused drinking fraternity in public houses. He can also be seen at home, adrift in an ocean of papers, a bottle of whiskey bobbing nearby. Cigarette smoke wraps itself around him like sea fog. Excursions outside Dublin — among them, a few days in Achill and Sligo by hired car — were rare and brief. Spencer shows him — quite evidently, a willing photographic subject — in Tara and other ancient sites as well as in numerous city settings (St Patrick's Cathedral, Joyce's Tower, the National Gallery, Herbert Park, Kingsbridge).

'Whiskey and Ink', the article by Jane Howard, painted a *Life*-size portrait of Berryman, loud, garrulous, exasperating, entertaining:

> *When Berryman's marriage-broker instincts get the better of him, anyone is fair game: friends, cab drivers, waitresses, stewardesses, students, former students, receptionists in offices, guys who pick up litter in parks. When he comes on some stranger, he says: 'And what might your name be, sir or miss? And are you married; Ah! You're not? Why not? And how are your prospects? And what's wrong with that man or girl right over there across the room? Up you get! Get to it!' . . .*
>
> *Then there is his voice. If there's anything he isn't it's a mumbler. Waiters in restaurants, clerks in stores and sextons in historic churches he visits are always coming up to ask him please to quiet down, because when*

Berryman is emotionally moved (which is most of the time), HE LOSES CONTROL OF THE VOLUME OF HIS VOICE AND SHOUTS AND ROARS . . .

Apart from the attentions of *Life* magazine, Berryman was also in the public eye as a result of a BBC television interview, recorded in Dublin and broadcast in March 1967; it took three days to winkle a half-hour of lucidity from the drunken poet. A $5,000 award from the Academy of American Poets occasioned a return, in May, to New York where he gave a poetry reading at the Guggenheim Museum. He was so patently unwell from the effects of alcohol that friends arranged for him to enter the French Hospital for treatment. He is still at work on drafts of 'Dream Song 380', entitled 'From the French Hospital in New York, 901', in a number of Terence Spencer's photographs.

The BBC interview, conducted by A Alvarez, caught Berryman's intensity and exuberance as he read 'Dream Songs' in a spiky, modulated way, leaving phrases momentarily dangling in suspense, pausing, shouting — a performance at once playful and soulful, ironical and rhetorical. At one stage of the interview — echoing something he had written about Stephen Crane, years before — he remarked that certain things are so ghastly 'you cannot respond to them directly' and he pointed to the role of Henry's friend in *The Dream Songs* ('Mr Bones', with whom he has some very amusing dialogues) in 'relieving the tension, the hopeless solitude of Henry'. Alvarez later described the Berryman he interviewed as a poet whose 'fierce and flushed' face was 'shrouded by a wild beard that hung down his chest like a bib': 'He looked like St Jerome in the desert, emaciated, unsteady, a man at the end of his tether.'

The BBC interview and *Life* magazine feature were for foreign consumption. Berryman's one public event in Dublin was a reading shortly before his departure, an advertisement for which was included in *The Irish Times*:

Graduates Club
76 Fitzwilliam Lane, Dublin 2
Monday 19 June
at 8.30 p.m.
JOHN BERRYMAN
Pulitzer prize winning American Poet
presented by Poetry Ireland and

Dennis O'Driscoll

Lantern Theatre. Tickets 3/- from
Brown Thomas or at door.

John Montague, who organised it with the help of Basil Payne
and Liam Miller (whose Dolmen Press had printed announce-
ments incorporating 'Dream Song 312'), recalled this as 'one of
the strangest readings I have ever attended'. On the eve of the
reading, during drinks at the Lansdowne Park house with
Montague and the painter Barrie Cooke, Berryman brooded over
a tattered *New York Review of Books* cutting — the hurtful review
which the first volume of *The Dream Songs* had received from his
friend and arch-rival, Robert Lowell, a couple of years before.

The American editor and critic, David Krause, was at the
reading among 'a rowdy, half appreciative and half skeptical
crowd of assorted Dublin literati and stray visitors':

> *The reading was slow in getting under way because most
> of the audience, as well as Berryman himself, arrived late
> and somewhat cheerfully well-oiled from the pubs. Then,
> when things were about to begin, the unpredictable
> Patrick Kavanagh, who had announced in advance to all
> who would listen that he was in reluctant attendance,
> emitted one of his loud harrumping coughs and stomped
> out, followed by his entourage of grumbling cronies.
> Kavanagh felt insulted, it turned out, because during the
> introductory remarks the name of Austin Clarke, who was
> not in attendance, had been mentioned — Clarke, his
> hated rival poet whose mere name Kavanagh had
> absolutely forbidden anyone to mention in his presence.*
>
> *After Kavanagh's gauche departure the reading finally
> got well under way, though accompanied from time to
> time by shouts that sounded like praise or dubious throat-
> clearings, and intermittent rumbles of obscure argument,
> interrupted now and then by hurrahs of approval from
> John Jordan. At one point when the crowd noise threat-
> ened to upstage Berryman, the formidable Ronnie Drew,
> rising in defense of poetry and his new American drink-
> ing companion, shouted menacingly for order in the hall,
> and he got it, temporarily.*

John Montague's own account of the reading he arranged (in
which, incidentally, the name which offended Kavanagh's sensi-

tive ears is said to have been that of Liam Miller) concludes that 'It was a great success, though a nerve-wracking one, the apotheosis of his Dublin stay'.

'And how will his last day in Dublin be, / Away so many labours?' By the time Berryman left Dublin with his family, later in June 1967, the labour of 'The Dream Songs' was largely behind him, though the final sifting would still take time. Kate — handwashing clothes, typing 'Dream Songs' and enduring her husband's constant drinking — was doubtless relieved to see the last of Ireland. To Berryman, Dublin was 'crawling with delicious people', even if they failed to reach the hoped-for level of brilliance. Free of distractions, he had written feverishly, especially during the first few months of his stay; and it must puzzle some readers of Berryman's very American poem (a twentieth-century 'Song of Myself') to chance suddenly upon Songs depicting Irish ankles ('the thickest in the world') and Irish rain ('the wettest place on earth') and the country as a whole, contrasted favourably with 'detestable' Iowa:

> *Adorable country, in its countryside*
> *& persons, & its habits, & its past,*
> *martyrs & heroes,*
> *its noble monks, its wild men of high pride*
> *& poets long ago, Synge, Joyce & Yeats,*
> *and the ranks from which they rose.*

That list of martyrs, heroes and monks, and the similar catalogue of 'ruined abbeys, / discredited Saints & brainless senators, / roofless castles' in 'Song 321', show Berryman's Irish imagination working on a somewhat touristic level when it moves from the personal to the general.

Readers of *The Dream Songs* will think of Whitman and Pound as influences on Berryman before they will think of Yeats. It is greatly to Berryman's credit that his veneration of Yeats did not destroy his own stylistic independence, as happened to many poets in Ireland and elsewhere, and that he survived his thraldom to become such a highly original and individual (if notoriously uneven) writer. I think that, for Berryman, the ultimate importance of Yeats was as a lifelong touchstone for poetry: a higher court of appeal — beyond jealousy — to which even someone beset by rivalry and insecurity could always look for guidance and standards. He complained to David Krause that the

Irish were 'afraid of their giant, they envy their Olympian. He's too big for them. I loved him and he was too big for me for a long time, but I've come to Ireland now to make up with him'.

It was the living Yeats who drew Berryman to Dublin for the first time; and it was to communicate with his 'Shade' that he returned for the second time. There was not to be a third time:

> *Fresh toils the lightning over the Liffey, wild*
> *and the avenues, like Paris's, are rain*
> *and Henry is here for a while*
> *of many months, along with the squalls of a child,*
> *thirty years later. I will not come again*
> *or not come with this style.*

London Magazine (June/July 1995)

Robert Hass: *Beyond Words*

Robert Hass is a poet of sunlight and sadness, of yearning and celebration. His world brims with beauty but is rimmed with loss. He knows the miracle of earthly bread and wine ('Sourdough french bread and pinot chardonnay') but also how lives are blighted by too little bread ('hunger, helpless terror') or too much wine ('empurpled Irish winos'). There is something hedonistic about his work, rooted no doubt in the culture of California — where he was born in 1941 — yet something inconsolable too, rooted perhaps in his childhood with a mother who was an alcoholic: 'parents / quarreling, somebody / drunk'.

Poets who are determined to celebrate life sometimes do so with sanctimonious fervour, as if a downbeat tone were necessarily less honourable, let alone less true. In reality, celebratory poetry is exceedingly difficult to write if it is not to seem complacent or sentimental, spilling through the clenched teeth of a false smile. Robert Hass, whose second collection (published in 1979) was called *Praise*, can strike and hold the affirmative note very convincingly, never allowing it to outlive its moment. He is a poet in whom thought and feeling seem inseparable — his grasp of history is almost sensuous. Few poets can balance truth and beauty with such poise:

> Bird cries and the unembittered sun,
> wings and the white bodies of the birds,
> it is morning. Citizens are rising
> to murder in their moral dreams.

While Hass is well aware of the unbearable heaviness of being ('The refuse of my life / surrounds me and the sense of waste', he puns in a poem about garbage), his poetry can be like light and air, difficult to grasp but real and redemptive and beautiful. In an essay by Robert Wells, I came across a quotation from Cesare Pavese's diary which immediately brought to mind the transcendent, almost religious, quality which Hass's poems achieve when they 'give off light': 'There has been so much talk, so much description, so much alarm about our life, our world and our culture, that seeing the sun and the clouds, going out into the street and finding grass, stones, dogs, moves us like grace itself, like a gift from God, like a dream, yet a real dream, which lasts, which is there.'

The range of Hass's poetry, both in subject-matter and style, is considerable and the range within each poem even more so. Spry modulations of tone sweep his poems along as they cascade down the page, hurling images and ideas from line to line. That quick turnover of things observed and absorbed works superbly in the poignant 'Old Dominion' and the dazzling 'Natural Theology', though one's bearings can be lost in the dense verbal growth of certain poems. Yet a degree of density is necessary to sustain Hass's more synoptic visions and one misses it in a few of the looser, linear poems included in his otherwise compelling third collection, *Human Wishes* (1989).

As well as dense Hass and loose Hass, there is fragmentary Hass. A successful example of this style is 'Maps', one of the first poems in his first book, *Field Guide* (1973). But the 'Cuttings' sequence is slight and, while individual sections of 'The Beginning of September' delight, making them cohere is another matter. Even when not at his very best, Hass tends to be doing or trying something of interest. Like Czeslaw Milosz, whom he has extensively translated, he is a relentlessly experimental poet, with none of the cheerless antisepticism which deadens so much avant-garde verse. *Human Wishes* contains eclogues, prose poems and prose blossoming into verse as well as a kind of verse journal ('Santa Barbara Road'). In the prose poems, simplicity is occasionally achieved at the cost of subtlety, but 'Novella', 'A Story About the Body' and the astonishing 'Paschal Lamb' (where Hass returns to an earlier preoccupation, the Vietnam War) prove the immersion in condensed prose to have refreshed his art.

Hass's luxuriant lines — whether long and loping or short and springy — are always rhythmically satisfying. He is a poet of body language, for whom 'Some days . . . / the quick pulse of blood / through living flesh / is all there is'. And the Oriental tang pervading his work is not unexpected from someone who has written with authority about Issa, Buson and Basho in his sumptuous gathering of essays, *Twentieth Century Pleasures*; all three poets appear in *Field Guide* also. One characteristic of Japanese haiku which Hass has mastered is the use of delicious juxtapositions and contrasts. When he quotes Buson's 'Night deepens — / sleep in the villages / and the sound of falling water', he is not so far from the glorious twinnings and triplings to be found — like hidden haiku — in his own poems: 'a scent of lemon and a drift of song', 'Cold water, hot sun, the whole of an afternoon' or the porcelain delicacy of:

> *On the oak table*
> *filets of sole*
> *stewing in the juice of tangerines,*
> *slices of green pepper*
> *on a bone-white dish.*

Robert Hass uses a rich vocabulary and his poems are hypnotic with the names of plants and places and creatures. In an early poem, Wittgenstein is mocked ironically, the poet's words transporting the reader beyond words: ' . . . when I said, "The limits of my language / are the limits of my world," you laughed. / We spoke all night in tongues, / in fingertips, in teeth.' Two magnificent poems, 'Meditation at Lagunitas' and 'Picking Blackberries with a Friend Who Has Been Reading Jacques Lacan', challenge the modish notion that language is merely self-referential, that 'because there is in this world no one thing / to which the bramble of *blackberry* corresponds, / a word is elegy to what it signifies'. Hass has the true poet's capacity — never more needed than now — to show how words can break the language barrier and answer for themselves in the world outside:

> *Charlie,*
> *laughing wonderfully,*
> *beard stained purple*
> *by the word* juice,
> *goes to get a bigger pot.*

Poetry Ireland Review (Autumn/Winter 1994)

Charles Simic

Looking for Trouble: Selected Early and More Recent Poems

To judge by his prolific output, Charles Simic is one of the light sleepers of American poetry. Since *Hotel Insomnia* in 1992, he has published two collections of poetry and two volumes of prose. Even when he does snatch some sleep, his dreams are converted into verse. There is something unmistakably dream-like about the unexplained paradoxes and transitions which occur in his poems. If the earliest work was surreal (ants in Quakers' hats, smoke on crutches, a self-doubting bedbug), the ominous atmosphere of the later poems is less amenable to categorization.

Simic's early books are rather under-represented in *Looking for Trouble*, while his two latest volumes are definitely over-represented. He generally absents himself from his own creations and would clearly like his poetry to live upon images alone. When his poems succeed — as those from *Charon's Cosmology* (1977), *Classic Ballroom Dances* (1980) and *Austerities* (1982) triumphantly do — it is because the images arise out of imperatives which his later output is inclined merely to simulate. The excellent 'Baby Pictures of Famous Dictators' belongs in the same album as Wislawa Szymborska's 'Hitler's First Photograph':

> *Lovable little mugs smiling faintly toward*
> *The new century. Innocent. Why not?*
> *All of them like ragdolls of the period*
> *With those chubby porcelain heads*
> *That shut their long eyelashes as you lay them*

> *down . . .*

Simic's strongest work is not only powerful and unsettling in its imagery but also written against the American grain. Born in Belgrade in 1938, he was sixteen before he emigrated with his family to America in a windowless cabin of the *Queen Mary*, having learned English in Paris from the World Church Service. Much of his work seems European rather than American in style, as if the translation process had been bypassed and the poems had gone straight into neutral English. Like those of his fellow-countryman, Vasko Popa, Simic's poems resemble the songs of a composer behind which folk melodies may be detected. He writes free-verse ballads and versified fairy tales. His short, spare, stark lyrics could slip unnoticed into the company of fellow-Serbians, like Novica Tadić and Aleksandar Ristović, whose poems he has translated. As he wrote in 'Empire of Dreams':

> *On the first page of my dreambook*
> *It's always evening*
> *In an occupied country.*
> *Hour before the curfew.*
> *A small provincial city.*
> *The houses all dark.*
> *The store-fronts gutted . . .*

Introducing his anthology of Serbian verse in English translation, *The Horse Has Six Legs* (1992), Simic remarked that, in translating these poets, he was returning to his 'psychic roots' with 'English words in my mouth'. What sets Simic's work apart from that of his American counterparts — and what tempted me to place it among the East Europeans rather than the Americans — is not only its brevity, intensity, impersonality, humour and understatement but the fact that it is written in what the poet, William Corbett, calls 'a voice with history in it'. For Simic, the past is literally a foreign country — his birthplace — and one in which wartime horrors were perpetrated during his childhood ('Blackouts, arrests, hostages taken and shot, hunger . . .') Hardly surprisingly, therefore, Simic's pivotal sequence, 'White' (at 236 lines, a marathon in comparison with his usual sprint), is an expedition to the outer realms of the expressible, a samphire-gathering raid at the very edge of articulacy:

> *Out of poverty*
> *To begin again*
>
> *With the taste of silence*
> *On my tongue*

Dennis O'Driscoll

> *Say a word,*
> *Then listen to it fray . . .*

However blank the reader's initial response to 'White' may be, the poem is tantalizing enough to stimulate re-reading (just as it has provoked Simic himself to so much re-writing that the current version seems less a makeover than a transplant). Through a blizzard of images — snow, frost, the Arctic Circle, a white city, a wedding dress — we glimpse the poet breaking the ice to release the wellsprings of memory, inspiration and, ultimately therefore, poetry ('Because I'm nothing you can name, / I knew you long before you knew me').

Almost thirty years after the first version of 'White', Simic continues to write impressive, arresting work. But a certain predictability of lighting, casting and scripting has reduced the dramatic appeal of his poems and they make a far greater impact as single spies in magazines than as book-length battalions. Having grabbed attention with buttonholing beginnings, they often fail to sustain the interest, struggling lamely to the finishing line. *Looking for Trouble* contains some truly riveting poems. Yet, to be repeatedly surprised in the same way is scarcely to be surprised at all and Simic is a poet who is overdue a change of direction.

Times Literary Supplement (13 February 1998)

James Schuyler

Selected Poems

We know exactly where we stand with James Schuyler — and when. His poems are specific about dates, settings and weather. He shadows the movements of the sun so closely that one imagines him measuring the time with a sundial. We learn what he has for breakfast ('oatmeal, orange juice and coffee'), his Blue Cross / Blue Shield number (11223677 Ho8), the contents of his shopping list ('Little apples / Paper napkins? / Guerlain Impériale / Steak . . . '). His addictions, his illnesses, his homosexual longings are revealed in a casual, conversational, confidential style. We are on first-name terms with his friends (who include distinguished poets and painters): Frank and Darragh, Trevor and Joe, Kenward and John. If the writing must be interrupted by a belch, telephone ring or the call of nature, his readers will be kept fully informed.

James Schuyler's poems tend to be live performances. At their worst, as in *A Few Days* (1985), they can resemble faux-naïf doodles, casualness lapsing into inconsequentiality. By contrast, *The Morning of the Poem* (1980) contains outstanding examples of how he blends art with life in a poetry of small talk, asides and running commentaries. With his neuroses, confessions, slang words and brand names, Schuyler cuts a figure which may be too American for European tastes. Yet, bizarre though it might at first seem, it is not altogether fanciful to make a comparison between Schuyler and the quintessentially English poet, Roy Fuller — even if the diffidence and decorum of Fuller are in marked contrast to the Whitmanesque sprawl of Schuyler's longer songs of himself.

Apart from their obsession with music, Schuyler and Fuller share a gift for creating poetry from whatever happens to occur in the course of an ordinary day; in Fuller's words, they try 'with poetry to match / Everyday's marvellous and varied prose'.

Masters of the offhand tone; celebrators of the mundane; urban naturalists: both poets are exceptionally inclusive. Schuyler can write about 'dishwater detergent' or 'trash burning in an old oil drum', while Fuller's 'old man's daily doings' include an adventure with 'washing-up water' and 'a journey to the bin'.

If Fuller's formality is that of the building society lawyer, Schuyler's visual gifts are those of an art curator (he worked for the Museum of Modern Art in New York). He is New York's nature poet; or perhaps the term should be 'weather poet': weather is nature in the city. Sometimes the weather poems are thin-lined and crisp, like tracks in snow; or they unroll like scrolls of oriental verse. Among the long and long-lined poems, 'Hymn to Life' is one of those in which Schuyler thinks and talks aloud, a freewheeling display that keeps its balance for as long as it keeps moving (for thirteen pages, to be precise). March is portrayed there as a month 'of fits and starts, winds, / Rain, spring hints and wintry arrears', while in 'The Crystal Lithium' each of the months is conferred with an identity:

> . . . *April, goofy and under-dressed with a loud laugh, and*
> *May*
> *Who will of course be voted Miss Best Liked (she expects*
> *it),*
> *And June, with a toothpaste smile . . .*

Of the longer works, 'The Morning of the Poem' (forty-nine pages) is Schuyler's masterpiece. The title poem of a collection which won a Pulitzer Prize, it records a summer spent with his mother at her house in western New York State ('Two people obstinate as mules, who love each other'). Mixing memory and desire, pathos and humour, one idea or observation or recollection borrows and undercuts another. Against all expectation, a combination of lyrical intensity and diary-entry casualness succeeds in holding the reader's unflagging attention. Its language is direct but luminous, its authority that of accuracy.

The kind of poetry which James Schuyler favours is extremely literal and therefore extremely risky — a poetry of the given world, of the view through the 'miraculous contrivance' of the window, a poetry as concrete as the street he observes outside. A Hopper-like shadow on an incinerator shaft or a photo-realist perspective on 'back-lighted / buildings through the slits / between vertical strips of blinds' suffices as raw material —

neither big issues nor spectacular experiences are required. His preference is for things 'of no / real use and yet / essential as a button / box, or maps, green / morning skies, islands and / canals in oatmeal, the steam / off oyster stew'. Often embarrassing as a love poet, and over-inclined towards what Edmund White termed the 'gee-wizzy mannerisms' of the New York School, he is nonetheless light in touch, limpid in language and frequently moving.

Schuyler's descriptive and evocative powers are fundamental to his achievement. Never lost for words with which to describe snow, he imagines it 'compiling / a white and wordless / dictionary'. Buildings acquire a lyrical, fluid quality under his responsive gaze: the UN (like a 'green wave'), the Chrysler ('silver, soluble'), the Empire State ('its pearly height') and 'junky' structures on Elizabeth Street ('carious, and the colour of weak gums'). His debut as a poet was a late one — his first collection did not appear until 1969, by which time he was forty-six and his younger friend, Frank O'Hara, was dead. Among the New York School poets, Schuyler — who assimilates into poetry those aspects of daily life which are usually relegated to prose — is closer to O'Hara than to Ashbery. Indebted to both, he is more gifted than either, transforming what seem like spontaneous jottings into affectingly transparent poems and using witty interjections and inspired fade-outs to save his work from flatness. Here is a discovery waiting to be made.

Poetry Review (Spring 1991)

Allen Ginsberg and Adrienne Rich

Death & Fame: Poems 1993-1997 and *Midnight Salvage: Poems 1995-1998*

He was born in 1926. She was born in 1929. Allen Ginsberg's Jewish father was a teacher who also published poetry. Adrienne Rich's Jewish father was a scientist and 'amateur poet'. Both Ginsberg and Rich began as formalists. Both were strongly influenced by many of the same poets, from William Blake to William Carlos Williams. Both protested vehemently against the Vietnam War and were tireless campaigners for social justice. Both championed sexual emancipation — he as libertarian and male homosexual, she as feminist and lesbian. The 1974 National Book Award was shared between them.

Ginsberg's rhetoric may be louder than Rich's; yet, by giving voice to voiceless women, she lays claim to an even more far-reaching agenda than his. In a 1980 interview, she commented that 'It would interest me if I saw men . . . really being able to take the risks that women are taking, have taken, not just on our own behalf but on behalf of every movement against oppression, through all history.' The 'Please Do *Not* Disturb' sign, famously suspended by Ginsberg from his penis at a party, flashed exactly the opposite message to what feminists like Rich had in mind. While Ginsberg gave credit to Bill Clinton (when he was President) for raising the question of gay membership of the US armed forces, Rich contended that the 'very institution of the military itself' was the real issue.

Allen Ginsberg's career as a poet ended in the early hours of March 30th 1997, a week before his death, when he penned the regrets list entitled 'Things I'll Not Do (Nostalgias)', the final poem in *Death & Fame*. His list begins with Albania and Bulgaria — among the few places on the globe where he had failed, in seventy hectic years of life, to leave his sandal prints. For a man who proclaimed that 'Fossil Fuels retard the planet', he did more than his share — abetted by Volkswagen campers and international airlines — to accelerate its retardation. As befitted an inveterate *New York Times* reader, Ginsberg reacted spontaneously in verse to day-to-day events and sometimes merely sounded like a cranky correspondent to the Letters page. The evils of the World Bank, the plight of the homeless, the duplicity of Senator Jesse Helms — 'the Moralist King' — all receive attention in his farewell collection.

The validity of Ginsberg's viewpoint is rarely in doubt (always allowing for rhetorical hyperbole, especially where the woes of America are concerned); but when the poetical response is as predictable as the polemical one, his repeated outrage achieves nothing more productive than tedium. A poem like 'Newt Gingrich Declares War on "McGovernik Counterculture"' already looks as dated and faded as a 1995 newspaper cutting. It is sad to find Ginsberg in the year of his death squandering his dwindling time and considerable talent on 'Virtual Impunity Blues', a protest poem aimed at the old reliables (President, Pope, FBI, CIA) which is effective neither as protest nor as poetry. There is much in *Death & Fame* which would amuse and entertain in performance — and Ginsberg was a feisty, charismatic, rousing performer. On the less mesmerizing page, however, his 'First thought, best thought' approach to writing can evoke a 'First reading, last reading' reproach from his readership. A number of the poems are proof that fame — with the fawning indulgence it attracts — can spell death for the self-critical faculty. Some poems in *Death & Fame* are platitudes masquerading as prophecies; others would bring a rash of blushes even to the cheeks of a McGonagall:

> *I'll be leaving for retreat,*
> *Where they make me salt-free meat*
> *along with Gelek Rinpoche*
> *Who's got ailments same as me,*
> *in Michigan Camp Copneconic*
> *Where I'll room with Mr Harmonic . . .*

Ginsberg's exuberance and humour are more winning in 'C'mon Pigs of Western Civilization Eat More Grease' where he lards his high calorie descriptions of fatty foods until laughter and disgust are simultaneously provoked. Finally — a true disciple of Blake — he sees a world in a grain of fat:

> . . . *Western cuisine rich in protein*
> *cancer heart attack hypertension sweat*
> *bloated liver & spleen megaly*
> *Diabetes & stroke — monuments to carnivorous*
> *civilizations*
> *presently murdering Belfast*
> *Bosnia Cypress* (sic) *Ngorno Karabach Georgia* . . .

Quieter successes in *Death & Fame* include the elegies for youth ('"You know what I'm saying?"', 'Popular Tunes'). Old enough to qualify for senior citizen discount at Alfalfa's Healthfoods, Ginsberg touchingly recalls the songs of his boyhood 'echoing thru Time's skull as my beard's / turned white'; or he meets, fifty years later at a school reunion ('retired, wife on his arm'), somebody whose beauty once left him 'dumbstruck'. The drugs Ginsberg takes are no longer illicit or hallucinogenic but rather prescription medicines for high blood pressure and heart complaints. With the explicitness of a poet who eagerly adopted Whitman's 'suggestions for candor, spontaneity, openness, frankness', Ginsberg spares the reader no detail of his bodily functions and this collection displays marked coprophiliac tendencies. He brings to the 'watery tureen' of the toilet bowl the kind of loving attention that Keats bestowed on his Grecian urn. In place of 'Beauty is truth', though, we are offered the rather less elevated insight that 'Shit's a glimpse of Truth'.

Patrick Kavanagh (who, incidentally, admired Ginsberg for his lack of 'ponderosity') might have spoken for Adrienne Rich when he wrote, 'Surely my God is feminine'; her truths are cast in a resolutely female light. While she has written no single poem of the calibre of Ginsberg's 'Kaddish' — a desolate portrait of a disturbed mother — several of the outstanding post-war collections have had Rich's name attached to them. Her work is more literary, less populist, than Ginsberg's; in the realm of politics, however, she too can overindulge the expectations of her audience. Poetry and politics co-exist in a delicate symbiosis; it takes only a minute chemical imbalance in the ratio of ideology to imagination for the wellsprings to become tainted and the poem to be rendered unfit for general consumption. What has saved Rich's surest poems from succumbing to the temptations of triumphalism and the rhetoric of the quarrel with others is her finely-tuned ear; her sensuous, yearning music transcends ephemeral argument and the divisive limitations of language itself. It is a classic case of the poem knowing more than the poet. She has written tellingly in her essay, 'Blood, Bread, and Poetry', that 'any poet who mixes the poetry of the actual world with the poetry of sound interests and excites me more than I am able to say.'

Adrienne Rich is not exactly a poet of hilarity and high jinks in the Ginsberg mode, nor does one sense that — like Ginsberg — she accepts that (for all the importance of ideological concerns) the poem as fibreglass pleasure craft is no less valid than the poem as steel-hulled container ship. There is a leaden quality about some of the freight in *Midnight Salvage*, an uncharacteristic absence of buoyancy:

> *Had never expected hope would form itself*
> *completely in my time :: was never so sanguine*
> *as to believe old injuries could transmute easily*
> *through any singular event or idea :: never*
> *so feckless as to ignore the managed contagion*
> *of ignorance the contrived discontinuities . . .*

Rich follows in the 'footprints of light' of the photographer Tina Modotti and, more rewardingly, keeps 'vigil' with the poet, René Char, during the French Resistance. Individual lines can be memorable ('art is a register of light'; 'memory shooting its handheld frames') and the scene-setting is occasionally evocative — though the promise of the atmospheric openings is not fulfilled in the later sections of poems like 'Midnight Salvage' and '"The Night Has a Thousand Eyes"'. What quickens certain poems into life is memory — the memory of the childhood game 'getting wilder as the lights come on' in 'A Long Conversation' (an over-long and over-loose mosaic of testimonies and quotations ranging across considerations of love, economics, language, torture, art, 'struggles for justice' and much else) or the memory of a date with a 'paraplegic GI' in 'Seven Skins', a vulnerable poem which is also a vivid snapshot of the Fifties:

> *Shall I drop you, he says, or shall*
> *we go back to the room for a drink?*
> *It's the usual question*
> *a man has to ask it*
> *a woman has to answer*
> *you don't even think.*

Dennis O'Driscoll

Rich still laudably insists on the subversive potential of language ('That the books are for personal use / only — could I swear it? / That not a word of them / is contraband — how could I prove it?'). But in affluent, unfazed America, assimilation continually neutralizes subversion. Both the countercultural Ginsberg and the radical feminist Rich acquired lucrative university Professorships, are published by prestigious mainstream houses, have been showered with adulation and honours (twelve lines worth of major prizes are listed on the dust jacket of Rich's gold-embossed hardback). Allen Ginsberg's work is done; he has become his admirers. Adrienne Rich still has work to do; resisting the expectations of her admirers will be an important part of it.

Poetry Review (Winter 1999/2000)

Stephen Dobyns

Velocities: New & Selected Poems

Give or take an Adrienne Rich or a Frank O'Hara, British and Irish enthusiasm for modern American poetry is still largely centred on those poets who meet their readers halfway across the Atlantic: Berryman, Lowell, Bishop, Roethke, Hecht, Wilbur and Plath. Although he has written admiringly of Rilke, Ritsos, Mandelstam and Zbigniew Herbert, Stephen Dobyns's influences are more obviously American (North and South) than European. The very appearance on the page (and the overall page-count here is a voluminous three-hundred) of a good many of the poems in *Velocities* will induce resistance in readers who assume that poetry served up in slabs of long-lined free verse — rather than in manageable stanza-sized bites — is bound to be indigestible.

Just how deceptive appearances can be in Dobyns's case becomes clear on closer examination of his poems. Granted, his weaker work can seem casual, if not careless, in its use of language, with little rhythmical or syntactical interest. But, as Dobyns's painstaking essays in his critical volume, *Best Words, Best Order* (1996), indicate, he is far from indifferent to — let alone ignorant of — the craft of poetry. It is precisely because of the facility with which he shapes, paces and plots a poem that he succeeds so well at a style of narrative poetry which would otherwise collapse under the tonnage of its words. An early sequence of crisp, sententious poems, 'Grimoire' (more than half of which is reprinted in *Velocities*), provides a tantalizing glimpse of the poet Dobyns might have become had he chosen to trim his poetic sails. The broader canvas allowed by a more sprawling style draws on his practice as a novelist with no less than fifteen fiction titles to his name (including the Charlie Bradshaw detective series). Instead of writing a poetical prose, Dobyns frequently resorts to a prosaic poetry; the result, contrary to expectation, is fresh and inventive, as if his prose — reversing the Molière role — had been surprised into the discovery that it had been speaking poetry without knowing it.

Dobyns, performing a crime writer's autopsy on lifeless poetry, has written that 'A failure in much writing, especially poetry, is that the writer has not created sufficient tension, has not done enough to make us want to know. If the writer takes the reader's interest for granted, then he or she will fail.' A gifted storyteller, even the surrealist touches in his poems are at times equivalent to the embellishments in a lively yarn. Yet he is as distant from cloying populism as he is from pretentious post-modernism; and his impressively versatile talent is equally capable of revivifying ancient myths ('Orpheus', 'Theseus Within the Labyrinth') or broaching contentious contemporary issues ('Desire'):

> *Why have men been taught to feel ashamed*
> *of their desire, as if each were a criminal*
> *out on parole, a desperado with a long record*
> *of muggings, rapes, such conduct as excludes*
>
> *each one from all but the worst company,*
> *and never to be trusted, no never to be trusted?*
> *Why must men pretend to be indifferent as if each*
> *were a happy eunuch engaged in spiritual thoughts?*

Dobyns is the laureate of loneliness and longing, of dashed hopes and frustrated expectations. 'Syracuse Nights' depicts someone 'rushing full tilt toward (his) personal zero'. The disaffected man in 'It's Like This' feels constantly on the threshold of some revelation which will enable him to transcend everyday banalities. 'How to Like It', Dobyns's finest poem — and one of the finest and most poignant of contemporary poems — is typical of his work in its detached, deadpan tone, its sudden shifts of focus, its blend of individual observation and general speculation, its realism undercut by a dab of surrealism. In this instance, the surrealism comes in the shape of a dog whose promptings and goadings are really the inner voice of the 'unsettled' man who longs to escape from his humdrum existence, 'to get in a car and just keep driving'. This is a *Waiting for Godot* of suburban America, its protagonist eager for something to happen, anxious to make something happen, resigned to the fact that nothing will happen:

But the dog says, Let's just go back inside.
Let's not do anything tonight. So they
walk back up the sidewalk to the front steps.
How is it possible to want so many things
and still want nothing . . .

Dogs stray all over Dobyns's work — grey and brown, leaping and licking, spaniels and setters. Taking his cue from the painter, Balthus — the self-styled 'King of Cats' — Dobyns might well label himself 'King of Dogs'. Although it is the menace of Eric Fischl and the moodiness of Edward Hopper that are often suggested by his poems, the painters on whom he lavishes sustained attention are Cézanne (portraits of the artist in sonnet form) and the cat-loving Balthus (an entire collection, *The Balthus Poems* (1982)). In so painterly a writer, whose acknowledged exemplars include Stanley Spencer and George Grosz, it is not surprising to find — despite the author's disclaimer ('they were not intended to interpret the paintings or explain the intentions of the artist') — that many of the Balthus poems start out with a paraphrase of a particular painting, before going on to take liberties which widen its frame of reference. *The Balthus Poems* never reach the heights of Dobyns's best work, which dates from *Black Dog, Red Dog* (1984) onwards, although they helped to hone his skill at burrowing imaginatively into other lives. It is regrettable that the selection made for *Velocities* excludes the risk-taking 'Nude in Profile' and 'Dream', which are truly Balthusian in spirit, in favour of what are sometimes more bland, even evasive, poems.

In fairness, it must be added that a tendency to blandness is among the last accusations one would level at Stephen Dobyns's poetry as a whole. Over the seven collections from which *Velocities* is compiled, he has written poems which are audacious and original, their vision at once dark and humane. His selection is not sufficiently selective, however, and there is much in the early work which one perseveres with only because it is by the author of the later work. The number of his outstanding poems is fairly small; nevertheless, they are numerous enough — and their standard high enough — to support the conviction that he is one of the most admirable and enjoyable poets now writing in English.

Times Literary Supplement (29 November 1996)

Mark Halliday

Selfwolf

Mark Halliday cuts a modish figure in his poetry — street-wise, wary of rhetoric, citing pop songs as holy writ. What you see on the front cover of his third collection, *Selfwolf*, is what you get: the poet as regular guy, his crumpled Levi's and two-tone trainers suggesting a cool and casual style, the telephone (he is photographed using a payphone) preparing us for a language that is intimate to the point of sometimes addressing the reader directly ('I was realizing that if I wanted to I could use the telephone instead of writing the poem', as Frank O'Hara — one of Halliday's influences — put it) but which is also rather prosy (wordiness and flatness are among the principal risks he runs).

Like Thom Gunn, the 'sniff of the real' is what Halliday (born in Michigan in 1949) is after; he wants a poetry which is capable of evoking lost youth, of recording an average life, of giving expression to the consumerist cacophony of America with all its securities and insecurities. Since the fall of the Berlin Wall and the intermittent successes of the Ulster 'peace process', questions concerning the relationship of poetry to oppression and violence have arisen with fresh urgency ('What was the connection between East European poetry and censorship?', 'Were the Ulster poets a product of the violence?') For all his laid-back air, Halliday makes a serious contribution to this debate, implying that poetry must be tested against inexperience as well as experience; that art cannot live on extremity alone:

> *Did he once survive tornado,*
> *earthquake, flood? Absolutely not. And he sure as hell*
> *never crouched in a fucking jungle ditch while fucking*
> *AK-47 bullets sprayed mud on his fucking helmet.*
> *How does he think he can talk about fear?*

> *He was never tortured by the police of Paraguay*
> *or even arrested in Turkey. He has never spent a single*
> *   night*
> *in jail . . .*

Up-to-the-minute though his poems are, Halliday keeps faith with old-fashioned ideals of truth and beauty. As someone who confessed (in the course of his published dialogues — 200 pages of them — with his former teacher, Allen Grossman) to 'ignorance of trees, bushes, rocks, birds, and rivers and what they do all day', his notion of beauty is predominately human — female and young, preferably — with some inbuilt self-chastisement in deference to the feminist age. His pacy first collection, *Little Star* (1987), presents male lust in all its nakedness, however disapprovingly it may be regarded: 'I wonder if any intelligent feminists / will ever read this poem. / I hope so; though the prospect makes me tense. / I wonder how much I have damned myself.' In *Selfwolf*, he remembers his poem about a woman with 'long bare legs':

> *Embarrassed now*
> *I imagine a female editor*
> *who received 'The Woman across the Shaft'*
> *as a submission to her magazine — the distaste she felt —*
> *perhaps disgust she felt — I imagine her*
> *grimacing slightly as she considers writing 'Pathetic'*
> *on the rejection slip . . .*

For Halliday, poetry is the ultimate preservative. To find words equal to the challenge of documenting and perpetuating ordinary experience continues to be the task he sets himself. He frequently draws on his memory bank and one is struck by the elegiac air which can attach even to his more celebratory moments. He was a prodigy of poignancy, feeling the pain of lost youth when that youth was in its full Sixties swing: 'Richard played both sides of *The Early Beatles* at least twice, / and we all got the point: the point was that at twenty / we could already be nostalgic for vanished youth.' Halliday has written poems which — to paraphrase Alfred Corn — will make his readers nostalgic for the American youth they never had: the student dorms, the hitch-hiking and foreign travel, the night drives at speed to the beat of Derek & the Dominos. *Little Star* was a book with a pulsing soundtrack ('Bell Bottom Blues', 'Key to the Highway', 'Hello Goodbye'); though the volume has been lowered, music still vibrates through some of the later poems also. And if Halliday's soundtracks are cinematic, so too are the tracking shots which they accompany. Someone steps 'out of Sax's Steak Sandwiches / with a large Coke to go, / straw stuck thru plastic lid'. A paperboy walks 'a forgettable side street back of the hardware store / down from the brick Methodist church'. A layered reality is Halliday's speciality: a snatch of song, a chance remark, a recollection, an observation occur spontaneously and simultaneously; his poems reach for understanding through evocation.

Halliday's memories — of little significance in themselves — are elevated above banality and triviality by pathos, a pathos derived from his overpowering sense of evanescence. If 'nothing gold can stay', what hope for the less gilded moment when 'A truck bearing the name of a potato chip company / makes an assertive turn and clunks out of sight in the rain'? Whereas, in *Tasker Street* (1992), Halliday had agonized over 'loss loss loss of what we feel and think', memory overload is the problem in the more recent 'Removal Service Request', a poem in which his possessions have tales to tell that are not of the bedtime kind:

> *It is 2:45 A.M. I can't sleep. The apartment is too noisy.*
> *It's totally quiet. It's filled with the noise of the past.*
> *How does anyone sleep after the age of thirty-five? Things*
> *gather in your apartment and stay, each thing learns*
> *to emit its own signal, its own night-noise . . .*

'Removal Service Request' is a good poem which falters towards the end. It is followed by 'Tonette', a poem which lurches from weak start to abysmal finish, Halliday's prose mimicking poetry not unlike the way he describes having mimicked a musical performance at school. His poems can be risky edifices — daring, sprawling, tentative, improvised — and they require the strong cement of his speech rhythms to stave off disintegration.

Alan Bennett has wryly commented that 'Cars abandoned by the road nowadays often bear a notice saying "Police Aware". Maybe one could slap "Poet Aware" on a beauty spot or even on some particularly touching vagrant.' Mark Halliday's awareness level is extremely high; and, instead of settling for poetic clichés of the landscape or bleeding heart variety, his books offer a wide windscreen vision on the richly representative experiences which

Mark Halliday

he captures with comic yet rueful brilliance. His own ironic self-awareness is part of the picture, because the doubts, dilemmas and delusions that surface in his work are themselves so characteristically contemporary. True to the rituals and mores of its time, *Selfwolf* is a *Beowulf* for an unheroic age:

> *Last night when I washed the dishes every move I made*
> *had a heroic kind of distinction. Do these two forks at*
> *   once,*
> *rinse them swiftly, drop them in the drainer deftly*
> *producing that satisfactory clatter, now do the plates,*
> *washing the bottoms as well as the tops, my left hand*
> *so acrobatic in its connubial cooperation with my right —*
> *where is Martin Scorsese, doesn't he want to get this*
> *on film?*

Poetry Review (Summer 2000)

Marianne Moore

The Selected Letters of Marianne Moore, edited by Bonnie Costello, Celeste Goodridge and Cristanne Miller

Marianne Moore's longest poem is called 'Marriage'; and, on the cover of her *Selected Letters*, she looks like the twinkle-eyed grandmother of the bride: wide-brimmed hat, white cotton gloves, sparkling brooch, braided woollen jacket and pearl-buttoned pleated blouse. In reality, though, she never became a grandmother or, even, bride. A passing reference to '7 suitors' notwithstanding, there is only one serious hint in these 550 pages of letters that marriage was a possibility; this occurs, not in correspondence with an intimate friend, but in a business letter to a monumental mason. Paying a deposit on the cost of her mother's Vermont marble headstone, she tells the mason that — despite the fact that she does not 'expect to marry' (she was sixty at the time) — 'it would be best to have my name engraved . . . below my mother's as planned, but to leave space for a line beneath it (*above my date of birth*) were a line ever to be inserted there, designating marriage'. How the mason, Mr Meals, reacted to this convoluted instruction is not divulged; readers of her poems will, however, recall her depiction of marriage as 'this amalgamation which can never be more / than an interesting impossibility'.

One consideration which would have made marriage problematic for Marianne Moore was her single-minded devotion to her mother, Mary, who was eighty-five when Mr Meals's monumental efforts were called for. Her family circle, or rather triangle (Moore never met her father), also included her brother, Warner, with whom she corresponded so regularly and at such length that her later letters to him had to be destroyed in order to assuage his wife's jealousy. The introduction to this book notes that 'The Rosenbach Museum and Library, which houses the correspondence between members of the Moore family, lists over

13,500 leaves (often written in small hand on both sides)' between the years 1905 — when Moore entered Bryn Mawr College — and 1947. Nothing in Marianne Moore's life was complete until relatives had been informed. Warner, the worshipped brother, is addressed as 'Bible' in certain letters; but, like Mary (variously called 'Bunny', 'Mole', 'Mouse', 'Bear' and 'Fawn'), Warner is assigned animal names too — canine ones, like 'Biter', as well as 'Toad', 'Turtle' and 'Badger'. A letter from Marianne to fifty-seven-year-old Warner begins 'Dearest Elephant-Ears, Your brother is back from Bryn Mawr'. The 'brother' alluded to here is none other than Marianne, who sometimes referred to herself in the third person and the masculine gender; even the assiduous editors of this volume cannot quite make sense of the opening remarks about herself ('Willow') which she makes in another letter to Warner: 'Willow has exhibited his coon at two drug stores for 50 cents in each case and was only induced by his Uncle Snapper to liberate it . . .' No wonder Marianne Moore was so expert at avoiding self-exposure in her poetry.

Moore's student correspondence is atwitter with news of her crushes at the all-female Bryn Mawr; there are intense friendships ('terribly fond'), special relationships ('I've just been out walking with Frances (B). She is "it" for me'), fallings-out and makings-up. But — given the limited evidence — it would be idle to speculate too much about Moore's sexuality; it would be intrusive also: one of the most attractive aspects of her work is — to use a phrase of her own — its 'reticent candor', the ability to be individual without being personal, to adumbrate but not to confess. Rifling through her correspondence might in itself constitute behaviour unbecoming were it not for the fact that her letters clearly meant a great deal to their author. Even as a student, she was evaluating their literary merits ('My letters are better than my stories . . .') She later expressed herself 'most impatient to read Flaubert's correspondence' and her review of a selection of Emily Dickinson's letters praised the book for enabling one 'to forget the ruses and dust-obscured emulations of ambitious biography'.

A biographer in search of character traits would find Moore's letters extremely revealing — not in content, but as confirmation of their author's tireless professionalism and conscientiousness. It is clear that she responded promptly and comprehensively to all letters — whether from friends, fellow-poets or the readers and autograph-hunters whose 'tons of irrelevant mail' necessitated up to fifty or sixty replies a day in the last decades of her life; as she declares in her poem, 'Bowls', 'he who gives quickly gives twice / in nothing so much as in a letter'. T S Eliot, H D, Ezra Pound and William Carlos Williams were among Moore's earliest literary correspondents; indeed, it is astonishing how soon after graduation from Bryn Mawr — where she was advised 'not to major in Eng. if I want to be sure of my degree' — she was publishing poems in magazines like *Poetry* (Chicago) and *The Egotist* and edging close to the centre of influential literary and artistic circles. Moore, born in 1887, had grown up in Missouri and Pennsylvania; an ambitious and determined perfectionist, her move with her mother to New York City in 1918 provided what her beloved Henry James called — in a phrase she cited at the end of her poem, 'New York' — 'accessibility to experience'.

By 1925, 'Fangs' (another of Moore's pet names) was top dog at *The Dial*, one of the best literary magazines of the time. During her four-year editorship (the journal closed for financial reasons in 1929), she wrote no poems but published terse, densely-argued, quotation-laden criticism and 'comment'; and there were innumerable business and editorial letters (she took critical secateurs to any over-luxuriant work submitted). D H Lawrence was one of the more revered contributors with whom she corresponded. While Marianne, whose family sobriquets also included 'Weaz', 'Rat', 'Gator' and 'Basilisk', was an animal-lover by nature as well as name and could be counted on to savour some of Lawrence's poetry ('Snake' was a special favourite), one wonders how she overcame her puritanical instincts to do business directly with the author of *Lady Chatterley's Lover*.

Moore was an original, with an eye for originals. She had a confidence in her judgement derived from her Bryn Mawr 'literary apprenticeship' and the unconditional approval she enjoyed from her family; yet, the puritanical side surfaced sometimes. 'Prudery and conventionality' were among the accusations levelled against her by contributors unhappy with the narrowness of her *Dial* code of conduct. She loved *Dubliners* and *Chamber Music* but was out of sympathy with *Ulysses* and *Finnegans Wake*. Even the use by Elizabeth Bishop of 'water-closet', in the poem 'Roosters', was too much for Moore to stomach; she remarked to her fellow-poet: 'If I tell Mother there is a feather on her dress and she says, "On my back?" I am likely to say, "No. On your rump," alluding to Cowper's hare that "swung his rump around". But in my work, I daren't risk saying, "My mother had a feather on her rump."'

The plot of Marianne Moore's friendship with Elizabeth Bishop has been too often rehearsed to need a repeat performance here. But the publication of Moore's letters within a few years of Bishop's (*One Art*, 1994) means that, in some cases, both sides of the story can now be heard at first-hand. The fact that Bishop's correspondence was published within fifteen years of her death, whereas Moore's has had to wait twenty-five years, accurately reflects the current state of their respective reputations. Bishop is now praised beyond the limits of her undoubtedly genuine and important achievement, whereas Moore's present reputation is no match for her exquisite talent. If Bishop is a bishop, then Moore — *il miglior fabbro* — is a cardinal.

Though busily observing and describing, Moore's verse is marked by poise and sangfroid. It is not that she has tamed the world but that she has ordered it, sometimes grappling with tricky syllabics and knotty rhyme schemes in the struggle to do so. With her devastating eye, moral mind and inscrutable countenance, she might be America's Wislawa Szymborska. Michael Hamburger associates Moore with the 'anti-poets' of Eastern Europe; for all her social orthodoxy and decorum, she was a nonconformist — even revolutionary — poet. If part of the pleasure of Moore's poetry lies in seeing the rules broken with metre-defying panache, the fact that the rule-breaker is a law-abiding, God-fearing woman who cannot reconcile herself to the use of the phrase 'water-closet' adds to the diverting improbability of the spectacle.

What the best of Moore's letters share with her poems is a refusal to accept a drably functional world — against which she deploys her dazzling descriptive powers. She reconciles us to the world by presenting incontrovertible evidence of its marvels, drawing up an inventory of its assets like some unimaginably articulate estate agent. We may smile in recognition at the ostrich 'whose comic duckling head on its / great neck revolves with compass-needle nervousness / when he stands guard', but with less familiar animals (such as the jerboa) the more exact the description the more fascinatingly incredible the creature that answers to it: 'It hops like the fawn-breast, but has / chipmunk contours . . . Its leaps should be set / to the flageolet; / pillar body erect / on a three-cornered smooth-working Chippendale / claw'.

Moore's descriptive gifts do not desert her in her letters; indeed, many of the early letters are like sketchpads for poems.

No detail escapes her: visiting a critic's 'quarters', she notes for Warner that the cushions were 'panne velvet and African brown taffeta with ruffles'; on another occasion, she tells him of seeing at the zoo 'a blue bird of paradise from New Guinea — with a jet black head and breast like sealskin — black shoe button eyes with a dazzling white line above and below each eye, two long limber black tail feathers, a haze of cinnamon brown feathers back of each leg and a similar smoketree of bright blue under the tail'. As time passes, one senses that the best lyrical observation is being conserved to meet the incessant demand for poems and articles, though the letters never entirely lose their descriptive bite — as when she excitedly thanks Elizabeth Bishop for a package containing 'the snake-fangs, the rattle, the alligator-teeth, and the shells': 'The rattle in nine or ten ways is a mechanism of inexhaustible interest. I foolishly used to imagine that it was a series of pockets with little "nasturtium-seeds" in them, and am amazed to see this nesting of a chained membrane in another membrane. Also the varied tones of the brown when the rattle is held up to the light, suggest a great many things.'

Moore's knowledge of the natural world is very much a city dweller's, gleaned from magazines like *National Geographic* and visits to zoos, circuses, and museums. One likes to think that, had she lived to see the growth of the modern ecology movement, she would have supported it as energetically as she supported baseball. It is, however, surprising to find no reference to Rachel Carson or *Silent Spring* in this book or in her *Complete Prose*. Having been radical when young (socialist and suffragettist), she became conservative when older ('a staunch Republican' who preferred Hoover to Roosevelt); while firmly distancing herself from anti-Semitic sentiments, she lapsed into the hectoring phonetics of Ezra Pound-speak when writing to the old ranter: 'I hated George Meany till he said he was agoing to get to Washington to tell Nayroo to his face that he is a Russian Agent.' Overall, the style of these letters ranges from the simple ('Shakespeare is certainly hard to beat', addressed to Warner) to the mixture of mannered and good-mannered which — addressing to impress — she resorted to in correspondence with figures like T S Eliot: 'I received a few days ago your play, *Murder in the Cathedral*, and you are truly to be thanked; also to be envied, because the triumph of living is to influence others; sorry as one is that there should be knowledge that would make the writing of some parts of it possible.'

This book of eloquent and engaging letters will not hold much appeal for non-specialist readers. Far less entertaining than Larkin's, far less gossipy than Plath's, the correspondence can be stiff and stilted and self-consciously Jamesian in places — Moore rarely unbraids her hair outside of the family; letting it down would be to let herself down . . . Nonetheless, there is some wonderful writing in this volume and devotees of Moore's ingenious poems will hang on to every word, paragraph and PS. Discreetly and efficiently edited though it is, for the most part, the book does contain blemishes at the level of annotation, indexing and dating. Why, to give just one example, is a question mark needed in dating a letter (to Louise Crane) 'February 14 [1940?]', when internal information in the letter — readily verifiable against Bishop's *One Art* — leaves no doubt whatsoever as to the year in question?

Feisty, fussy, funny, prim, punctilious, lovable and exasperating — one misses hearing from Miss Moore when her cape and tricorn hat disappear into the void. Actually, because of illness, the flow of letters ceases some years before her death in 1972: the last post is dated 3 January 1969 — 'I still want to paint', she tells Elizabeth Bishop and her companion in that final letter, '— all the fur on my bushy best paintbrush-brush eaten up by a moth.' Marianne Moore was a collage artist more than painter, incorporating newspaper cuttings and magazine images into her poems — poems which remain mothproof and timeproof.

Metre (Autumn/Winter 1998)

Sylvia Plath

Bitter Fame: A Life of Sylvia Plath by Anne Stevenson

Reviewing Linda Wagner-Martin's biography of Sylvia Plath, Anne Stevenson remarked that 'It is probably too soon to ask for a fully-documented, historically objective biography of Sylvia Plath. The principal members of her family are still alive and vulnerable. Another generation will have to assume responsibility where this one, in the nature of the undertaking, cannot'. We have had fair warning, therefore, not to expect *Bitter Fame*, Stevenson's own biography of Plath, to be the last word on the subject. Her book is welcome and timely, nonetheless: welcome because its author is not only a distinguished poet and independent-minded critic but also an exact contemporary of Plath who experienced similar transplantation from America to England; timely, because she records first-hand impressions by Ted Hughes's circle before death imposes its own form of belatedness.

Entry to the Plath Estate is not gained without supervision and Anne Stevenson alerts us to the cramped conditions under which she operated by describing the book as 'almost a work of dual authorship' with Olwyn Hughes — Plath's redoubtable sister-in-law, for many years the guard dog of the estate. The Olwyn Hughes interventions can be petty and defensive; but despite the discretions she was obliged to observe (and it is difficult to quibble with those which were genuinely motivated by a need to protect the privacy of the living), Anne Stevenson has written a biography which illuminates Plath's years in England, where her best work was written. The hostility with which this biography was greeted by many reviewers is an indication of the extent to which people identify with Plath. Because they will have read her intensely personal poems and made free with her letters, journals and autobiographical prose, her readers come to feel that they know her better than the first-hand witnesses to her life and are, therefore, stakeholders with an obligation to ensure that she is 'properly' depicted. Anne Stevenson applies a powerful dose of facts to the more Plathological tendencies of the poet's followers. A myth can, however, be as addictive as a drug and the withdrawal symptoms just as painful.

The mercurial Plath sketched by Anne Stevenson, given to extremes of emotion, is recognizably the force behind the *Ariel* poems. It is the protean nature of the poet that her admirers tend to overlook. There is no single all-purpose Plath; instead, there are countless Plath lookalikes: imperious and defenceless, charming and offensive, resolute and despondent. Her letters and journals find her frequently attempting to define herself, only to slip the moorings of each definition and drift off again between lonely headlands of fantasy and despair. Plath's fears and rages, letdowns and longings are, however, only heightened versions of our own. She gives a local habitation and a name to feelings of alienation and isolation which most people experience, even in a somewhat lower key. Women in particular, Stevenson observes, 'discovered in her work a shocking revelation of extremist elements in their own psyches'.

There was an astonishing thriftiness and thoroughness about Plath's methods. Not only did she recycle her life into language — her poems are flesh made word — but she converted it into the language of prose as well as poetry. Her brief encounters with the Devon beekeepers, for instance, resulted not only in some of her best poems but in at least one letter and some startlingly vivid journal entries. The personal nature of her work is such that biographical insights yield literary insights. Her relationship with Ted Hughes — a true marriage of minds — can be relevant to the poetical progeny in a way that Wallace Stevens's curious coalition with his wife, Elsie Moll, is not. Contrasting the literary styles of Hughes and Plath, Anne Stevenson states: 'Throughout their writing partnership, husband and wife explored a common theme in their poetry: both were interested in anthropology, primitive myth, and religion. But Ted Hughes's work turned outward to the natural world beyond the self as Sylvia Plath's never could. Her entire development as a writer had consisted of steps, in a halting progress that often made it difficult for her to live, toward the revelation of the elusive vision at the core of her being.' Plath confessed to identifying her husband 'with my father at certain times', a father whom she had lost at the age of eight, vowing never to speak to God again. When threatened with the loss of her husband to another woman, her vulnerability level reached new heights; she ripped the telephone, on which Hughes's mistress had just called, from the wall. Her anger was channelled into devastating creative energy in poems that were less polished but far more dazzling than her earlier work:

> *The black telephone's off at the root,*
> *The voices just can't worm through.*
> *If I've killed one man, I've killed two . . .*
> *Daddy, daddy, you bastard, I'm through . . .*

The triumphant 'I'm through' means not only that she has exorcised her father figures but also that her call — her cry — is getting through: she is finally able to communicate her inside self to the outside world.

Despite occasional flashes of Hughes-tinted glasses ('Ted had shown himself to be a loving father and the most domestically centred of fathers'), Anne Stevenson's overall detachment adds much to the authority and conviction of the biography; she leaves room for compassion but lets us supply our own tears. Her uncluttered writing contrasts with that of Dido Merwin, whose crudely vengeful memoir is one of three extended testimonies appended to the book. While there is no reason to doubt the faithfulness of this account, it is surprising that the recollections have not been refracted through more forgiving and understanding impulses after thirty years. Or, perhaps, the permanence of the scars inflicted on Merwin's memory tells us something of the searing side of Plath's personality. Anne Stevenson identifies Plath's limitations ('a set of intricate, obsessive variations on a few themes') while recognizing her stature ('astonishing literary genius'). One of her chapters is headed with that prescient letter to Plath from her patron, Olive Higgins Prouty, which exhorted her to 'Sometime write me a little poem that isn't intense. A lamp turned too high might shatter its chimney. Please just *glow* sometimes . . . ' The globe — the bell jar — surrounding Plath's lamp shattered violently in the end; but the sulphurous smell remains and the brilliant, ethereal afterglow.

Poetry Ireland Review (Spring 1990)

Philip Larkin and Work: *Toad Hull*

Philip Larkin 1922 — 1985, Writer is carved on the white unlovely gravestone. By day, he worked as a librarian; he manned the night shift as a writer. If the writer lives on through his books, the Brynmor Jones Library which houses the books of Hull University is a memorial to the professional zeal and vision of Philip Larkin as librarian. 'A librarian of national stature and a poet of international renown' was how his colleague, Maeve Brennan, summarized his standing; and Edwin A Dawes (who, as Chairman of the Library Committee at Hull, worked closely with Larkin) remarked that the 'scant regard' paid by obituarists to Larkin's 'eminence' as a university librarian was 'a source of sorrow to his staff and colleagues who knew well the skill and dedication he brought to bear on his daily round'.

The young Larkin turned to librarianship, having failed interviews for the Civil Service and Foreign Office ('I must obviously show that I don't give a zebra's turd for any kind of job'). Apart from preferring to stay at home and struggle at being a novelist, there was another good reason why librarianship would not have been Larkin's first choice of profession. As David M Baker has pointed out, 'the general perception of librarianship' at the time 'was one biased toward the clerical and the routine':

> *When Larkin first went into library work, librarianship was indeed a lowly profession. It was wartime, and most professions were simply marking time until hostilities ceased. Immediately prior to this, librarianship had suffered from the economic depression of the 1930s.*

With the Ministry of Labour closing in on him, he quickly took a job as a librarian employed by the urban district council of Wellington in Shropshire. The hours were long, the stock outdated, the town dull, the work (which included stoking the boiler) not exactly enthralling. Adopting a characteristic voice,

pitched between irony and arrogance, he told his friend Jim
Sutton that he spent 'most of my time handing out tripey novels
to morons. I feel it is not at all a suitable occupation for a man of
acute sensibility and genius'. Yet even in the fusty, frustrating
environment of wartime Wellington, Larkin showed real flair for
the job, doubling the stock of books and, with it, the library's
register of borrowers during his two-and-three-quarter years
there.

When Larkin left Wellington in September 1946, it was to take
up another library post — as an assistant librarian at Leicester,
the first of three universities which would share the remainder of
his working life. Larkin was the only adult male member of staff
at Leicester; and, of a photograph taken at Hull (where Larkin
was appointed Librarian in 1955, having by then worked in
Belfast as well as Leicester), Alan Bennett wrote: ' . . . there is not
a man in sight. Surrounded by his beaming middle-aged assis-
tants — with two at least he was having or would have an affair
— he looks like a walrus with his herd of contented cows'. The
hysterical horror of some Larkin commentators notwithstanding,
it is hardly unusual for a working life to condition a love life —
even if Larkin was, in a manner of speaking, married to the job to
a polygamous degree. From a schoolgirl borrower at Wellington
to his middle-aged secretary at Hull, and from the wife of a
university colleague at Belfast to his lifelong companion, Monica
Jones (a lecturer at Leicester), his roll-call of lovers is intimately
connected with his work.

Larkin's letters are not exactly glowing testimonials to his job
satisfaction. 'Twenny-fivve yeares ago, my little bro: in Xt, I took
up my present position STARING DOWN THE LAVATORY
BOWL', was his 1980 progress report for Kingsley Amis. And in
1956 (just one year after his initial descent into Hull) he was
characterizing his routine as one of 'work and letters and work
and social sodding engagements and work and going home to
see my mother and sodding *work* . . .'. There are also philippics
against work as a 'vile thing' and as 'something you do in order
to have spare time'.

It is, I am sure, obvious to all except the most jaundiced critics
that his letters are not always to be taken at face-value; often
written with the entertainment of their recipients in mind, hyperbole, scurrility and self-mockery were the order of his daily mail.
When T S Eliot wrote to Ezra Pound in 1922 that 'Of course I want
to leave the Bank, and of course the prospect of staying there for

the rest of my life is abominable to me', he meant exactly what he said; and he acted accordingly when, at the age of thirty-seven, he took very early retirement from Lloyds Bank and joined Faber as an editor. Only towards the end of his career — and his life — did Larkin's interest in his job wane and retirement seem a serious option. He remarked to Barbara Everett in a 1981 letter:

> 'Work' is more then ever a refuge from reality; at least when I say work I mean my office and telephone and dictaphone: all the work is done by my staff, and especially my deputy. I am reminded of a remark (about someone else) that 'he had long ago delegated all responsibilities except that of drawing his salary'.

A bitter constituent of Larkin's disillusionment was the fact that financial cutbacks by his beloved Mrs Thatcher had begun to haunt Hull with the spectre of terminal decline: 'I began my library career singlehanded, and it looks as if I shall end it that way, sitting at the turnstiles of a vast bat-haunted cobwebbed building beside one flickering candle stuck in a bottle.'

As long as the library was well-funded and well-stocked, Larkin's devotion was impressive. Criticizing the biographer, Andrew Motion, for allowing himself 'to be overwhelmed by his discoveries of Larkin's private life', John Saville ('a colleague of Philip Larkin for thirty years, from the day he arrived in Hull until he died in 1985 . . . an open and committed socialist within the Marxist tradition'), in a letter to the *London Review of Books* wrote:

> Larkin was a professional librarian. He spent more of his waking hours for thirty years on Library affairs than on any other work . . . Over the years Larkin assembled a highly competent staff who almost without exception both liked him and respected him. As did his academic colleagues outside the Library. The record of libraries in British universities in the post-war decades is by no means a story of successful endeavour or of strenuous academic pressure to improve facilities. At the University of Hull Larkin developed a much superior library than was to be found in most institutions of comparable size, and it was a considerable achievement.

Dennis O'Driscoll

Although one might assume that he had better things to do with his time and talents than attending such bodies as the Library Users' Sub-Committee, Larkin's sense of duty made him an inveterate committee man: Chairman of the Poetry Book Society, the National Manuscript Collection of Contemporary Writers and the 1977 Booker Prize Committee, member of the Literature Panel of the Arts Council and the advisory committee of the Queen's Gold Medal for Poetry, not to mention a range of library activities that makes his life seem like one long committee meeting. A committee set up to deal with parking led to suggestions, according to Andrew Motion, that it owed its existence to the Librarian's determination 'to park his car where he wanted: by the back door to the library'. B C Bloomfield, Larkin's bibliographer, compiled the following list for *Larkin at Sixty*:

> *A member of the Standing Conference of National and University Libraries (SCONUL) representing his University, he has served on the Training and Education, Buildings, Publications and Inter-Library Loans Sub-Committees; and I still remember with delight the informal oral reports of the Sub-Committee on Statistics which consisted of Philip Larkin and Geoffrey Woledge, then Librarian of the London School of Economics. Philip has also served on the Joint Committee with the former Association of British Orientalists and as alternate Chairman of the South East Asia Library Group . . .*

Only Roy Fuller, the solicitor-poet, who had also served as Chairman of the Poetry Book Society — along with his Chairmanship of the Arts Council's Literature Panel and of the Building Societies Association's legal advisory panel, his directorship of the Woolwich Building Society and membership of the Library Advisory Council, the Law Society's Working Party on Conveyancing and the BBC's Board of Governors — could equal Larkin at dispelling the notion of poets as impractical or unworldly people. One thinks, say, of the unfortunate Marina Tsvetaeva, who was both impractical and unworldly. 'Even the knowledge that her children depended on her for food did not prevent Marina from walking out after a single morning' from a card-indexing job, according to Elaine Feinstein:

> What shall I do, by nature and trade
> a singing creature (like a wire — sunburn! Siberia!)
> as I go over the bridge of my enchanted
> visions, that cannot be weighed, in a
> world that deals only in weights and measures?

The extent to which, over the years, Larkin had been willing to serve in various library-related capacities outside as well as inside his own institution does not suggest an overriding concern to conserve his energies for poetry. Vernon Watkins, who 'deeply impressed' Larkin as a student, was a bank clerk who — rather than jeopardize his freedom to write — always refused promotion although (in his own words) 'I've seen manager after manager saying to himself, I'll make a cashier out of Watkins! But it never worked.' To Larkin, he seemed exemplary because of his total devotion to poetry and because 'Plainly he had not the slightest intention of "living by writing" . . . and found banking much more acceptable than pot-boiling.' Larkin's emulation did not extend to refusing promotion, however, and he climbed the library pay-scale concurrently with his elevation on the literary scale.

Larkin, in fact, derived evident (if not invariably acknowledged) fulfilment from being at the top of the library ladder. Battling for funds, craning over building plans with hard-headed and hard-hatted architects and engineers, amassing archives of manuscripts, pamphlets and photographs — Larkin was in a position to ensure that the library (in an apposite phrase of Andrew Motion's) 'was stamped everywhere with his personality'. Maeve Brennan has given a sense of the frenetic activity at the library in the Sixties and early Seventies:

> These were halcyon years of expansion for the Library, during which the staff increased from 20 to 91, the book stock more than trebled to 474,500 volumes, and the grant increased six-fold to £180,500. Many new departments were formed and new subjects introduced, all needing library provision. Growth was so rapid that the planning of a major extension, known as Stage II, began in 1962. Building was completed in 1969 . . .

With, no doubt, a certain justifiable pride in putting his own achievements on the record, Larkin published *The Brynmor Jones*

Dennis O'Driscoll

Library 1929 — 1979: a short account in 1979. This discreet booklet gives some flavour of the formidable skills — technical and diplomatic — which were needed to oversee the developments described by Maeve Brennan. In its impersonal, official voice, the booklet speaks of the architect's 'differences of opinion with the Librarian on such questions as floor loading, stanchion grids and load-bearing walls'. Dry though the style of the history may be, Larkin's characteristically deadpan (virtually bedpan in this case) humour is not entirely absent: 'In 1931 the Library had become a repository for manorial records, and in 1951 a lavatory in mid-site was converted to hold them.' Larkin's history finds him engaged in a professional separation of his admiration for Mrs Thatcher from his anger at her government's policies on university funding ('in those days [the 1960s] a good library meant a well-stocked library: government-inspired denigration of the ideal of self-sufficiency had not yet begun'). There is also an unexpected welcome for the library's major holding of material on labour history, including the books of the Fabian Society and papers relating to 'individuals whose lives had been spent either in trade unionism, the parliamentary labour movement or in the advocacy of pacifism or similar aims'.

It would not presumably have taken so long for Larkin's literary eminence to be recognized — nor for his first major collection, *The Less Deceived*, to be published — had he lived in the thick of literary London rather than in red-brick peripheries like Belfast and Hull. Because of his stammer and his palm-drenched nervousness about public speaking, he was never destined for the reading circuit, joking in a letter to Richard Murphy that 'the reputation I could make by appearing publicly is nothing compared to the one I make by remaining hidden'. As for a life of literary journalism, Larkin — a disciple of Cyril Connolly — would surely have been attentive to his strictures on the subject in *Enemies of Promise*. Larkin's library job allowed him to produce literary journalism at his own pace and on his own terms. He told A N Wilson in a radio interview: 'I write *very, very* slowly and with great pains; and I think to make a living by journalism or any other subsidiary literary activity, you have to be a quick reactor.'

During the same interview with Wilson, Larkin acknowledged the more personal, social side of the workplace: 'Being in touch with people, arguing with them, agreeing with them, discussing with them, that's what my job brings me and that's the part I enjoy.' Office life offers a poet endless opportunities for contact with non-literary people, people whose outside lives are centred around greyhound-breeding, whist-driving, rock-gardening, people for whom 'Books are a load of crap' is a truism (or, as Wallace Stevens inscribed a copy of *Harmonium* for a colleague in the bond-claims department: 'To my good friend. When you read this, you won't know what the hell it's all about.') Work — in both its practical and social aspects — saves writers from excessive bookishness, not to mention the academic delusion that all the world's a page. It is likely that the extravagant imaginative flights of Wallace Stevens owe much to his need to transcend the straitlaced language and ambience of surety bonds, to which they represent a colourful, almost escapist, counterbalance.

For men like Wallace Stevens and Philip Larkin who were not gregarious by nature, the daily contact with colleagues provided a social life which did not cut across the nocturnal poetry life. Stevens would be found at the Canoe Club on Wednesdays, enjoying cold-beef luncheon with Hartford Accident colleagues. And if the Hermit of Hartford could be bibulously high-spirited enough to kick a tray of hors d'oeuvres from the hands of a Canoe Club waitress, we should not be surprised to catch a glimpse of the Hermit of Hull as he emerged from the bookstacks 'behind the leader of a conga in which everyone had joined' at the library's Christmas party.

Further sightings of the smiling private man are found in Maeve Brennan's recollections: presiding wittily over retirement parties, mimicking acquaintances and mocking menus, hosting Hallowe'en celebrations at home with mulled wine and model witches. Larkin, without his work colleagues, could easily have succumbed to drink and depression, being prone to excesses of both. His most convivial period at Hull was in the first years after his arrival there (Sunday cycles with library friends would be followed by toasted crumpets spread with Gentleman's Relish); but Leicester and Belfast had brought a mixture of work and play also. Twenty-five years after leaving Leicester, he still treasured memories of the social life that had flourished there — 'tennis on the long-vanished courts, dances and theatricals', the repartee over staff lunches, the 'almost familial' atmosphere. The five years from 1950, during which Larkin worked in Belfast as a sub-librarian at Queen's 'perfect little paradise of a library', brought him the 'best writing conditions' he ever had:

Dennis O'Driscoll

> *I wrote between eight and ten in the evenings, then went*
> *to the University bar till eleven, then played cards or*
> *talked with friends till one or two. The first part of the*
> *evening had the second part to look forward to, and I*
> *could enjoy the second part with a clear conscience*
> *because I'd done my two hours.*

Larkin, who lived more often than not in the upper rooms of
university-owned buildings, was sometimes as equivocal about
his job as he was about life itself; giving it up would be unthink-
able, holding on to it could be unbearable. This is the territory
traversed in his two most notable poems about work, 'Toads'
(1954) and 'Toads Revisited' (1962). 'Toads' lends its ear to that
inner voice which taunts the frustrated office worker to the point
of exasperation, if not resignation:

> *Why should I let the toad* work
>   *Squat on my life?*
> *Can't I use my wit as a pitchfork*
>   *And drive the brute off? . . .*
>
> *Ah, were I courageous enough*
>   *To shout* Stuff *your pension!*
> *But I know, all too well, that's the stuff*
>   *That dreams are made on:*
>
> *For something sufficiently toad-like*
>   *Squats in me, too;*
> *Its hunkers are heavy as hard luck,*
>   *And cold as snow,*
>
> *And will never allow me to blarney*
>   *My way to getting*
> *The fame and the girl and the money*
>   *All at one sitting.*
>
> *I don't say, one bodies the other*
>   *One's spiritual truth;*
> *But I do say it's hard to lose either,*
>   *When you have both.*

A poem which seemed perfectly clear in direction becomes

derailed in the confusion of the final stanza of 'Toads' — largely because the dilemma it professes to face is a non-existent one. It is not, as the poem pretends, courage which the poet lacks but will. As in his letters, there is a certain amount of posturing afoot, exaggeration in the service of amusement. Instead of imagining himself (an unmarried man with limited financial responsibilities, after all) enjoying independence and fulfilment as a freelance writer — a scenario too dull to sustain his poem — Larkin invokes a caricature alternative life nourished on windfalls and tinned sardines, his freedom shared with whippet-thin wives and barefoot nippers. His list of situations vacant for the retiree to choose from is not quite an occupational therapist's dream; other than alliteratively, it is difficult to associate Larkin with 'lecturers, lispers, / Losels, loblolly-men, louts'. 'Toads' is really a witty blast against the inevitability of having to work to earn a living. His pretence that options are being weighed up leaves Larkin unable to arrive at a convincing — and therefore a clear — summing-up at the end.

'Toads Revisited' could be said to be a witty blast against *not* working. Again, caricature abounds ('Palsied old step-takers, / Hare-eyed clerks with the jitters') but, on this occasion, those 'dodging the toad work' do not 'seem to like it'. The poet permits himself more openly, and therefore more convincingly, the comfort of believing that the choices he has made are the correct ones. 'Toads' and 'Toads Revisited' are both, finally, poems of wry self-consolation, poems which shy from self-confrontation and self-challenge. Timidly but engagingly, he concludes that there are worse fates than earning one's bread with the help of one's 'loaf-haired secretary':

> . . . *give me my in-tray,*
> *My loaf-haired secretary,*
> *My shall-I-keep-the-call-in-Sir:*
> *What else can I answer,*

> *When the lights come on at four*
> *At the end of another year?*
> *Give me your arm, old toad;*
> *Help me down Cemetery Road.*

With his waistcoats, watch chains and gleaming size 12 shoes, the Larkin who settled down to work behind his 8' x 4' desk might have seemed like T S Eliot (or indeed Wallace Stevens) one of Virginia Woolf's men in a 'four-piece suit'. However, especially in his younger days, there were concessions to a certain artistic flamboyance — bow ties, bright shirts, vermilion, orange or petunia socks. On a table in his office, he displayed a framed photograph — not of mother or lover, but of Guy the Gorilla, with whose incarceration he claimed to empathize. The tortoise-shell spy-glass on the windowsill equipped him for closer scrutiny of 'honies', svelte students sweeping below his net-curtained first-floor window (he had a low opinion of his own looks, finding in some of Fay Godwin's photographs 'my sagging face, an egg sculpted in lard, with goggles on'). Larkin enjoyed the tolerance, trust and camaraderie of old colleagues — he felt at home in the library; the secretary, who typed his private correspondence and knew the whereabouts of his porn-ography cupboard, described herself as 'really a sort of wife to him'.

Absorbing though library work could be ('just the right blend of academic interest and administration that seems to match my particular talents, such as they are'), Larkin can scarcely have considered it quite on a par with poetry in his life. Even beneath the stale crust of middle-aged cynicism, there still survived something of the twenty-one-year-old enthusiast who could remark in a letter to his friend, Norman Iles:

> You see, my trouble is that I simply can't understand anybody doing anything but write, paint, compose music — I can understand their doing things as a means to these ends, but I can't see what a man is up to who is satisfied to follow a profession in the normal way. If I hadn't the continual knowledge that 'when all this bloody work is through for today I can start work again' or 'this half-hour is simply ghastly, but one day it will have been digested sufficiently to be written about' — if I didn't think that, I don't know what I should do. And all the people who don't think it, what do they do? What are they striving for?

After having published two early books of witness, Primo Levi was content to believe (albeit mistakenly) that his life as a writer was over: 'I was a chemist, I had a profession which gave me a living and wholly absorbed me, I did not feel the need to write anything else.' For Larkin, on the other hand, there was, in later years, the desire without the performance: 'I haven't given poetry up; but I rather think poetry has given *me* up, which is a great sorrow to me — but not an enormous crushing sorrow. It's a bit like going bald: you can't do anything about it.' 'Aubade', his last great poem, was published in 1977 and for the remaining eight years of his life he was largely blocked as a poet, unable to contemplate a successor to *High Windows*. Jean Hartley, a friend since her Marvell Press days, recalls asking him 'if he had a new book ready': 'Well, you know how I usually have half a dozen substantial ones and eighteen or so fillers? I've got the fillers . . .'

Larkin's output, even prior to this, was small. *The Whitsun Weddings* and *High Windows* (each about ten years in the making) contain a mere seventy-two pages between them and one wonders how much his job may have contributed to such exiguity. It is arguable that the consistently high standard of the poems is attributable to the fact that, being independent of the literary world, he could literally afford to publish irregularly and only when under intense imaginative pressure. Alternatively, it may be surmised that Larkin, who mused about what would happen if 'I sat down after breakfast with my faculties fresh', could have produced an even more distinguished oeuvre had it not been for the demands and distractions of the library. Surveying the same period (1946 to late 1983) as the core work in the *Collected Poems*, Philip Gardener calculates that

> *his annual average was only about four [poems], with years like 1950, 1953 and 1954, in which he completed 21, 14, and 16 poems respectively, being massively outweighed by years in which he managed to write only three or less: after 1954, in fact, his yearly output (to judge from Thwaite's inclusions) was never more than eight, and after 1971 never more than four.*

Office work has become less meaningful as the roles assigned to people within large corporations and institutions have grown increasingly fragmented. Nothing is individually completed by many workers, except perhaps the daily crossword (and the fanatical devotion to crosswords within offices may itself significantly reflect the 'solving emptiness / That lies just under all we do'). By contrast, Larkin, as he brought his building and other library projects to fruition, had an outlet for creative energy and one which may have reduced the pressure to write poetry. As Les Murray might say, the Brynmor Jones Library *was* a Larkin poem.

Larkin's long-standing premonition that death would claim him, as it had his father, at the age of sixty-three proved grimly accurate. His intense dread of death, his years of gazing into its hollow eye-sockets, had prepared him only too well for a cycle of 'x-rays, barium this-and-thats, liver scans, blood tests and plenty of sleepless nights'. His cancer was beyond the reach of surgery as the poet himself was beyond the reach of consolation, having written himself past illusion: 'The trouble is,' he told Andrew Motion, 'I've written scenes like this so many times there's nothing to surprise me.'

Always careful of money and fearful of being without it, Larkin by a cruel irony did not live to collect his pension. When he had considered opting for early retirement in 1980, he felt that 'the loneliness would be dreadful'. Like Roy Fuller and Wallace Stevens, he would surely have been incapable of severing the link with his former workplace even after retirement age (*'Stuff your pension!'* indeed!), continuing to serve on committees and advisory bodies.

'Whatever keeps you from doing your work has become your work', according to a proverb. The solitary word 'writer' on Philip Larkin's headstone in Cottingham tells only half his story. And we have the writer's own word for this:

> *The daily things we do*
> *For money or for fun*
> *Can disappear like dew*
> *Or harden and live on.*
> *Strange reciprocity:*
> *The circumstance we cause*
> *In time gives rise to us,*
> *Becomes our memory.*

London Magazine (June/July 1996)

George Mackay Brown

For the Islands I Sing: An Autobiography
Selected Poems 1954-1992

George Mackay Brown was a warm, welcoming man; but there was something remote and unreachable about him also. He cut a lonely figure, whether glimpsed on the green bench at Mayburn Court, near his bachelor flat in Orkney, or self-portrayed at the kitchen table where — with a Bic ballpoint and Basildon pad for tools — he communed with John Gow, the pirate, or Magnus Erlendson, the martyred Earl of Orkney. 'Thank God not to be fashionable!', he remarked cheerfully to me once. The antithesis of today's attention-craving poets, he wrote in 1983: 'Booker prize — Nobel prize — what a song and dance about such baubles! What does it matter, the opinion of a few contemporary judges, compared to the near-infallible verdict that time sends down its long corridors?'

Travel 'bored' Mackay Brown and neither of his two brief journeys beyond Orkney and the Scottish mainland inspires him to anecdote in *For the Islands I Sing*. This autobiography was written in 1985 and a six-page appendix added in 1993; it was then put aside for posthumous publication. His one visit to England — the highlight of which was a centenary Mass for his poetical and religious exemplar, Gerard Manley Hopkins — occurred in 1989. Twenty-one years previously, an award from the Society of Authors to assist foreign travel had taken him no farther than Ireland, a trip which began gloriously but then stalled because of car troubles.

For the Islands I Sing — the title is derived from the first line of Mackay Brown's turbulent maiden voyage as a poet, *The Storm* (1954) — is revealing about some matters, not least about the state of inebriated indolence in which he lived for many years; however, it could scarcely be classified as confessional. It must be virtually unique among autobiographies in biting the hand that writes it: 'Over the past four centuries there has been too much emphasis on the life and personality of authors — great streams of reminiscence, biography and autobiography.' He begins with Orkney's story rather than his own; his natural reticence made the birth of this book a laboured one. After some initial foot-shuffling and throat-clearing, he finally blurts out: 'I was born in the town of Stromness, on the main island of Orkney, in October 1921.'

With a broad brush, two contrasting portraits of Mackay Brown may be painted, each at once faithful and incomplete. Together, they approximate to the full picture. From one perspective, he seems reclusive and romantic, his imagination dominated by ancient lore and legend; a *Country Living* contributor who turned his back on the twentieth century and was hostile to 'progress' (the quotation marks are his). Alternatively, he may be viewed as having been a Green writer before ecological awareness was commonplace; a poet who was radical in vision, pioneering in form and challenging in content. With every book he published, he added a further stitch to the 'Orkney tapestry' on which he worked for over forty years: stitches dark as death or bright as a Christmas star, sober as ceremony or merry and irregular.

George Mackay Brown's season was winter, his time-span from Viking to Victorian or Edwardian, his place Hamnavoe (the ancient name for Stromness). If he looked back longingly at the crepuscular certainties of lamplit cottages and spark-strewn forges, he was also the prophet of our high-tech vulnerability to destruction by nuclear flame. Without ritual, ceremony and an acknowledgement of human limitations, he suggested, our acquisitive age is doomed. As he wrote in his unusually self-revealing story, 'The Tarn and the Rosary' — an important complement to the autobiography — 'Ceremony makes everything bearable and beautiful for us. Transfigured by ceremony, the truths we could not otherwise endure come to us.'

Mackay Brown's favourite writers included Thomas Mann, E M Forster, Evelyn Waugh and J L Borges. Although he relished the work of a small number of contemporary poets (among them, the Scottish poets of his own gifted generation and younger talents such as Liz Lochhead and John Whitworth), I suspect that his choice of reading — other than historical texts like *The Orkneyinga Saga* (his *Holinshed's Chronicles*) — was mainly in the fictional realm. His own superlative fictional skills (surely essential to his survival as a writer in a gossipy town on a tiny island) are as evident in his poems as in his stories and novels; they not only allow him to adopt disguises but also to distance himself from material which would otherwise be so close in range as to blur his vision. Lairds, tinkers, monks, crofters and fishermen populate his poems; the months, seasons, days and the stations of the cross provide them with a ready-made structure and an archetypal pattern.

Anyone unfamiliar with George Mackay Brown's work ought to invest in his *Selected Poems*, even if the choices made are not entirely satisfactory. Some crucial poems are omitted; and the sequence, *Fishermen with Ploughs* (the best of the poetry volumes), becomes — through unnatural selection — fragmented and disjointed. The autobiography, too, might have been longer — it skims quickly along and never quite rises to the heights of his mentor, Edwin Muir, the fellow-Orcadian whose own *Autobiography* was a sacred text for Mackay Brown; yet, given his shyness and self-effacement, the fact that it exists at all is a cause for rejoicing. *For the Islands I Sing* ends with a mystical equivalent of chaos theory: 'Everything we do sets the whole web of creation trembling, with light or with darkness. It is an awesome thought, that a good word spoken might help a beggar in Calcutta or a burning child in Burundi; or conversely. But there is beauty and simplicity in it, sufficient to touch our finite minds. I say, once a day at least, "Saint Magnus, pray for us . . ."'

George Mackay Brown, who had dreamed of becoming a soccer reporter, gradually emerged as one of the finest writers of our time. A mild, modest, wise and inward man, he was buried on St Magnus Day, 1996.

Poetry Review (Autumn 1997)

R S Thomas: *The Poetry of Paintings*

It was to a painter, Edgar Degas, that Mallarmé addressed his remark that 'poems are made not of ideas but of words'. Yet words constitute only one of the elements (verbal, musical, visual) which form a poem. Reversing the natural order of things, some poems could be said to be made of images and some visual art to be made of words. In conceptual and installation art, it is almost true to say that the words *are* the work of art far too often; bombastic texts written to accompany trivial exhibits read like attempts to justify verbally what disappoints visually. It is as if the manifesto and not its manifestation was what finally counted.

The combined wall space of all the world's galleries would not be sufficient to accommodate the poems about paintings which appeared in the past hundred years. These range in quality from major works like W H Auden's 'Musée des Beaux Arts' (based on paintings which are themselves based on texts — the Bible and Ovid's *Metamorphoses*) to the numerous banal transcriptions of paintings in which the poet insists on laboriously spelling out what we have already gleaned for ourselves. Whereas the average poem about a painting looks suspiciously like the produce of someone whose inspiration level is at a low ebb, and whose faltering gifts are sustained through a kind of art transfusion, a poet like Auden makes major art out of major art.

Instead of a schedule of the contents of the painting, listed dutifully like a landlord's inventory (which is the best that many poems on paintings can muster), Auden in December 1938 views the Brueghels in the Musées Royaux des Beaux-Arts in Brussels with a perspective of such amplitude that it can simultaneously accommodate the medieval world captured by the painter, the menacing contemporary events unfolding beyond the gallery and the timeless body-language of humans and animals in the presence of suffering. Above all, the poem is a profound statement about necessity: just as the sun — because it 'had to' — shone undimmed by the tragedy of Icarus (the poet/dreamer), the fields must be ploughed, the flocks must be tended, the trading ships must continue their journey if life is to be maintained. The ploughman 'may' have heard the drowning man's splash and the ship's crew 'must' have seen the plunging boy but they had their own lives and livelihoods to attend to. That life will endure is the poem's consolation; that the price paid will include cruelty and indifference is its despair.

It is arguable that the development of abstract art has removed the image as the bridge linking the poet with the painter. However, an image in the sense defined by Ezra Pound — 'that which presents an intellectual and emotional complex in an instant of time' — is something which a poem can share with an abstract painting no less than a representational one. Yves Bonnefoy, in his extensive writings on art, is suspicious of the limitations imposed by the mimetic and representational aspects of the image; what he demands of art is expressed — almost mystically — in terms of 'presence'. For Bonnefoy, 'presence' means the 'mystery which transforms an instant into the eternal' and is summarized by Richard Stamelman, the editor of Bonnefoy's *The Lure and Truth of Painting*, as 'that unseizable unity within an instant of time that precedes and exceeds form, image, and representation' — a description which brings it tantalizingly close to Pound's sense of the image. Bonnefoy values painting which is analogous to poetry rather than prose and he glories in works of sublime evocation rather than slavish imitation.

Paintings need to be seen, not heard; any serious gallery visitor whose pleasure has been diminished, if not obliterated, by the non-stop recitative with which viewers insist on accompanying art works would welcome the introduction of a vow of silence as an entrance fee. Similarly, poems aspiring too literally to the state of a 'speaking picture' (Simonides' term) can undermine the paintings which they should enhance. By interposing their reductive badinage between viewer and art, such poems can be as difficult to dislodge from the mind as the TV advertisements which appropriate snatches of great classical music to sell cars or cigars.

Yves Bonnefoy's own magnificent 'Dedham, vu de Langham' ('Dedham, Seen from Langham') is both a celebration of a Constable painting and an address to the painter himself: 'I think of Constable as one of those who have gone the furthest towards the fullness, the completeness, the infinite simplicity the world offers . . . at certain moments when consciousness seems freed from language.' Some contemporary poets have collaborated directly with artists (Ted Hughes and Anthony Hecht with Leonard Baskin, Peter Porter with Arthur Boyd, Eiléan Ní Chuilleanáin with Brian Lalor, Thomas Kinsella with Louis le Brocquy); others have imagined dead painters back to life (Derek Mahon on Van Gogh, John Heath-Stubbs on George Stubbs). Illuminating manuscripts about artists have been published by poets (Charles Simic on Joseph Cornell, New York School poets on New York School painters, Zbigniew Herbert on the Dutch masters, Stephen Dobyns on Balthus). There are famous artists who have published poetry (Penguin issued a selection from Paul Klee, Hans Arp and Kurt Schwitters in the 1970s). Then, there are poets who studied art (David Jones, Mark Strand, Liz Lochhead, Peter Reading, George Szirtes) and poets who, though less formally trained, produced drawings or paintings of their own (D H Lawrence, Charles Tomlinson, Derek Walcott, Stevie Smith, Elizabeth Bishop).

The painter-poet intersection also includes major figures such as Wallace Stevens (the Matisse of poetry) and W B Yeats (who attended art college and was himself the son and brother of distinguished painters); Yeats's 'The Municipal Gallery Revisited' is a self-portrait assembled through the portraits of others ('Around me the images of thirty years'). Seamus Heaney — whose catalogue notes and opening-night speeches for painters are masterpieces in their own right — assumes some knowledge of visual art on the part of his readers when he writes in 'The Swing': 'Not Fragonard. Not Brueghel. It was more / Hans Memling's light of heaven off green grass'. However, even when poets (Craig Raine and Christopher Reid, for instance) use imagism as a form of painting through words, reading their poems is an experience quite unlike that of standing before an original canvas on which the artist's centuries-old hesitations and emphases can still be traced in a maelstrom of brushstrokes.

Dissimilar though paint and print may be, instructive though it is to put a pencil to two different uses ('You may write with a pencil, but once you come to draw with it, what a diverse end those marks serve,' as Charles Tomlinson has observed), poets feel a closer empathy with painters than with novelists. It is surely much more true of novels than of poems to say that they are made of words; the novelist for whom words are essentially the means to a narrative end will adopt a more functional approach to language than a poet like Mallarmé, who is conscious of the exact role — symbolic, syntactic, prosodic, even spatial — played by each word in the construction of a finished text. 'To paint not the thing, but the effect it produces' represented Mallarmé's ideal and his choice of a visual verb is significant. Silence, transcendence and resistance to paraphrase are the qualities which poems and paintings are most likely to have in common; and what they share is no less valid for being experienced on a spiritual or emotional level rather than an effable one. John Burnside, a poet who is a master of the everyday epiphany, has neatly side-stepped some of the problems associated with painting by metrical numbers in 'A Miracle on Market Day'. He recreates the atmosphere of a Stanley Spencer resurrection painting so convincingly that it takes a while to realize that the artist's name has never been mentioned anywhere on the page. The result is an imaginary Spencer work, an original painting in words:

> *A girl in a cotton dress*
> *is raising the dead,*
> *peeling the turf back, lifting them out of their graves*
> *and setting them on their feet with a gentle shove*
> *to start them in motion.*
> > *Some have already*
> *wandered as far as the gate,*
> *weak as kittens, blind in the common light,*
> *they stand on the pavement, blinking; unsure of*
> > *themselves*
> *they stare at the palms of their hands, find smudges of*
> > *loam,*
> *the smell of old water, the sweetness of wasp-pitted*
> > *apples . . .*

The fascination which visual art holds for R S Thomas — a man convinced that one can 'grow rich / With looking' — may be accounted for, in part, by his private life. Speaking of himself in the third person — in his autobiographical essay, 'No-One' — Thomas relates that, by the time he met his future wife, Mildred E Eldridge, she 'was a recognised artist with experience of art school in London and also of Italy. Looking at her paintings, he identified with the artistic life.' The fact that art galleries are modern places of worship — secular temples in which a unique crucifixion by an old master becomes as awesome as a medieval relic of the one true cross — presumably heightens Thomas's interest. Thomas is forever doubting and delving, searching and testing, his life a long pilgrimage among sheep-dotted hills and sea-gnawed peninsulas, with great art, music and literature as additional sustenance. For all his hesitations, though, the thread of his faith never finally snapped and the cast of his mind, like the cadence of his language, has been profoundly shaped by the King James Bible. Thomas's poems — whether about paintings or places — can be ascetic and frugal in style, yet he is no puritan: nothing human is alien to him, least of all human sensuality and love (the power of which, like that of God himself, is most keenly conveyed through its absence).

About half of the poems in Thomas's 1981 collection, *Between Here and Now*, are about paintings. The pictures which captivate Thomas tend to be of this world rather than the next and to concern temptations rather than resurrections of the flesh. Instead of Murillos and Zurbaráns, Fra Angelicos and Cranachs, instead of cloud-propelled ascensions into heaven and halo-toppling banishments to hell, the paintings represented are virtually all secular in nature — drawn from one school (the Impressionists), one gallery (the Louvre collection now in the Musée d'Orsay) and even one book (Germain Bazin's *Impressionist Paintings in the Louvre*). Each poem is accompanied by a dreary monochrome reproduction so unsatisfactory as to challenge the poet to restore its colour through words.

He brings a blush of colour to the cheeks of a young woman in a Degas portrait; but, while accepting that the painter's priority lay in 'tonal / values, the light and shade / of her cheek', he admits that — for him — the 'meaning' of the painting lies in the woman's innocence, in her resistance to the Fall. She rejected the fruit of knowledge, having 'looked upon evil / and not seen it'; under the poet's gaze, she herself becomes a latent Eve nonetheless:

> *Her young being*
> *waits to be startled*
> *by the sweetness in roughness*
> *of hands that*
> *with permitted boldness*
> *will remove her bark*
> *to show under how smooth a*
> *tree temptation can shelter.*

In the poem about Monet's 'The Bas-Breau Road', the road too is 'startled' into knowledge — not carnal, in this case, but car-induced. The road's innocence was lost to the motor-car with its speed and its conviction that destinations matter. Thomas prefers — quite literally — a world of pre-destination; his ideal road, like his ideal poem perhaps, follows its own natural direction and 'is not for getting people / anywhere, at least / not at speed.'

Ingrowing Thoughts (1985), another collection of Thomas's in which each poem is juxtaposed with a black-and-white reproduction of its companion painting (Modernist or surrealist in this instance), includes 'L'Abbaye de Chartre' in which Adam and Eve are 'waiting for the serpent / to turn into a road / to bring them temptations / of a new kind':

> *no longer*
> *the apple's indigestible*
> *seeds, but internal*
> *combustion of original sin.*

Ideas of progress also animate 'The Gare Saint-Lazare' in *Between Here and Now*; Thomas's response to Monet's painting begins at the departure platform: 'The engines / are ready to start, / but why travel / where they are aimed / at?' In the end, it is art itself which can stop undesirable progress in its tracks: an ambiguous sentiment expressed in another of his painting poems, 'Art is recuperation / from time', reads very like an article of faith. In the poem which accompanies Pissarro's 'The Louveciennes Road', the silence at the heart of great art ('without a murmur') can freeze a precious moment forever, so that the passers-by might be kin to the figures on Keats's urn in 'not bothering / to arrive; exchanging / progress without a murmur / for the leisureliness of art'.

Like the young Degas woman who saw no evil, the players in Degas' 'Musicians in the Orchestra' have had their eyes 'sealed' by the conductor 'lest they behold / on the stage's shore / the skirts' rising and falling / that turns men to swine'. Attention in 'The Dancing Class' is again deflected away from seeing — scarcely what we expect in a poem about a painting. Degas' teacher is looking 'no higher' than the dancer's feet, 'listening / for their precise fluttering':

> *And they surround him, flightless*

> *birds in taffeta*
> *plumage, picking up words*
> *gratefully, as though they were crumbs.*

'The Dancing Class' has been, in every sense, translated into words. While 'The Bathers', based on Renoir, appears at first sight to be another see-no-evil poem ('Here is flesh / not to be peeped / at'), the candour of the painter's vision raises the work to a level of artistic truth at which notions of lust or temptation are rendered irrelevant. Not only is beauty truth in this poem, but — again with echoes of 'Ode on a Grecian Urn' — the bodies 'toll / an unheard music' and will never 'under the lapping / of all this light / . . . become blurred or dim'.

R S Thomas's emphasis on temptation, even when the paintings are not overtly religious, could be cited as evidence that the priest has supplanted the poet in these poems. Yet, while he can sometimes seem out of tune with the secular temper and the gender revolutions of our age, much of what underlies his work is as timeless as it is universal: a sense of the otherness and mystery of people — their ultimate unknowability; the tensions between innocence and experience, desire and disappointment. Frequently, it is a subtle allusion or linguistic twist which brings a religious dimension to his poems and it is precisely this dimension which saves them from flatness and triteness. For instance, the sin in 'Absinthe' lies in the hint (a mere sleight of language) that the drinking couple in Degas' well-known painting may be a kind of downcast Adam and Eve, expelled from Eden. The woman — who 'couldn't resist' the temptation to spend a night at the inn — is 'repenting / for having drunk of a liquid / that made such promises / as it could not fulfil'. The very locution, 'drunk of a liquid', brings to mind the phrase in Genesis about having 'eaten of the tree' of knowledge.

A further Degas poem of Thomas's, 'Mademoiselle Dihau at the Piano', is more explicit in its allusions to Genesis — 'Almost / we could reach out a hand / for the mellow-fleshed, / sun-polished fruit / that she is'. Again, what rescues this poem from banality, from being nothing more than a verbal doodle when set against a great work of art, is Thomas's adroitness with language, the foreplay of the poem's opening ('Asking us what she shall play?') and the telling adjective chosen to describe the young pianist's forbidding eyes ('her eyes / are the seeds of a tart / apple'). Critics and journalists writing about R S Thomas seem determined to believe that he, too, is 'tart' when, in fact, his poems reveal a great deal of punning wit, playfulness and irony to temper the grim stoicism.

Most of *Ingrowing Thoughts* could scarcely be reckoned among R S Thomas's finest poetry; nonetheless, here too his meticulous attention to language is apparent. In one of the wittier poems, 'The Meeting' (based on a painting by Gustav de Smet), Thomas — having begun to impose too fanciful an interpretation on the picture — immediately checks himself:

> *I translate the encounter.*
> *But the flag at attention*
> *at the house corner prefers*
> *the original: Vive la France.*

Thomas, who is sceptical about the translation of poetry from one language to another, here tacitly acknowledges how much is lost in translation between canvas and page.

R S Thomas's painting poems are at their best as voice-afters rather than voice-overs, when written not in the heat of observation but in the reflective afterglow. Thomas's own awareness of the danger of talking a painting out of existence was expressed in a self-effacing comment to an interviewer in 1990: 'The poems are attempts to comment and to draw out extended meanings in a way which most of the painters would have found reprehensible, because painting has its own plastic and compositional values.' In the case of 'Captain Cook's Last Voyage', the poem actually improves on the rather modish surrealist sculpture by Ronald Penrose which inspired it; this is achieved through a characteristically chilling metaphor ('flesh that is the iceberg / on which we are wrecked') and by a richly desolate response to Penrose's pretentious title and to his central image — a metal globe encasing a female torso:

> *On eternity's background*
> *is the shadow*
> *of time's cage, where nautically*
> *we are becalmed*
> *listening to the echoes*
> *in the nerves' rigging*
> *of that far-off storm*
> *that is spirit blowing itself*

> *out in the emptiness at the Poles.*

Insofar as imagery and metaphor are fundamental to Thomas's poetry, he might be said to have a strongly visual imagination. Indeed, it is the power of his metaphors which has distinguished his poems from collection to collection and brought variety and memorability to what might otherwise have been thematically repetitious and formally predictable. In *Between Here and Now* one finds carved saints perched like twittering birds on the ledges of a cathedral, a domestic room transformed into a theatre, a road deliquescing into a 'looking-glass smooth' river.

R S Thomas's poems are so closely identified with 'the brown bilge of earth' or the lustreless metal of the machine that it is easy to overlook how variegated and visual his work can be. The peasant wading that 'brown bilge' may have 'colourless' eyes (just as 'the rain's / Colourlessness' saturates the eyes of another Thomas peasant); yet, while sensitive to the countryman's 'want of deference to the painter's skill', Thomas is at work in the long tradition of artists depicting the lives and locales of peasants: 'what brushwork could equal / The artistry of your dwelling on the bare hill?' He is determined to show as well as tell: 'Look at this', 'Can you picture . . .?' In the poem, 'Maes-yr-Onnen', he describes himself as 'Painting faithfully the mossed tiles and the tree'. We see a 'cloud the colour of the carnation', 'light's peculiar grace', a day with 'a blue lining / Partly of sky, partly of sea'. His love of the Impressionists surely owes something to the contrast between their dazzling outpourings of light and his own more mildewed climate.

Sometimes, an R S Thomas poem resembles a sketch for a painting ('Here are men / who live at the edges / of vast space. / Light pours on them / and they lift their faces / to be washed by it'). Occasionally, so visual is the poem that it is as if one had actually entered a painting:

> *The white house in the cool grass*
> *Membraned with shadow, the bright stretch*
> *Of stream that was its looking-glass;*
>
> *And smoke growing above the roof*
> *To a tall tree . . .*

The terms of the art versus nature debate posited by the poem,

'The Earth Does Its Best for Him', are over-simplified. The poet returns home to Lleyn, the incense of hay fumigating the memory of an airless art gallery where the paintings are 'tired / of returning the hard stare / of eyes'. These ruminations notwithstanding, Thomas is clearly a poet who is in no serious danger of siding with those who — as he observes in 'Correspondence' — file 'ignorantly . . . through a gallery / of great art'; his temporary blind spot in 'The Earth Does Its Best for Him' is a symptom not so much of philistinism as of world-weariness or perhaps city-weariness. The outward jadedness he attributes to the paintings is a simulacrum of the inward jadedness he himself feels. Normal vision is restored not only in *Between Here and Now* and *Ingrowing Thoughts*, but in a scattering of individual poems inspired by David Jones, Paul Klee, Ben Shahn and Veneziano (whose 'Annunciation' provides, for once, a religious painting as stimulus).

The most perfect match of poem and painting, a duet for cello and voice, is found in 'Woman Combing'. This sensual response to Degas' painting belies Thomas's image — among those who confuse coldness of eye with coldness of heart — as a rather cheerless and forbidding figure:

> *So the hair, too,*
> *can be played?*
>
> *She lets it down*
> *and combs a sonata*
>
> *from it: brown cello*
> *of hair, with the arm*
>
> *bowing. Painter,*
> *who with your quick*
>
> *brush, gave us this silent*
> *music, there is nothing*
>
> *that you left out.*
> *The blues and greens,*
>
> *the abandoned snowfall*
> *of her shift, the light*

> *on her soft flesh tell us*
> *from what score she performs.*

Whereas in his poem, 'Mademoiselle Dihau at the Piano', the score on the piano is interpreted as a 'notice / against trespassing' on the musician's body, the hymnodist in the poem, 'Ann Griffith', is invited by God to 'Play me . . . / on the white keys / of your body'.

The sonatas of the body, like the 'silent music' of painting, are ways of transcending language. Although a passionate supporter of Welsh, Thomas has concluded that one cannot write poetry in a language which one has mastered only in adult life; the child bonds simultaneously with his mother and his mother tongue (English, in Thomas's case). However, Thomas's inability to practise poetry in the Welsh language remained a source of sorrow to him and, in this context, one can see the special appeal of music and painting — arts which soar beyond language — for a writer of his disposition. The poem, 'Gallery', begins: 'The stillness of paintings! / Move stealthily so / as not to disturb'. God — whose 'chosen medium', silence, affects Thomas so deeply — is the ultimate creative artist. He speaks 'all languages and none, / answering our most complex / prayers with the simplicity / of a flower'. God's work is always in progress and always complete. In Him, R S Thomas — poet, priest, patriot — finds unity and fulfilment:

> *Like a painting it is set before one,*
> *But less brittle, ageless; these colours*
> *Are renewed daily with variations*
> *Of light and distance that no painter*
> *Achieves or suggests. Then there is movement,*
> *Change, as slowly the cloud bruises*
> *Are healed by sunlight, or snow caps*
> *A black mood; but gold at evening*
> *To cheer the heart. All through history*
> *The great brush has not rested,*
> *Nor the paint dried . . .*

Agenda (Autumn 1998)

Michael Hofmann

Approximately Nowhere

The sudden death in 1993 of his father, the German novelist Gert Hofmann, left Michael Hofmann not so much speechless as in mid-sentence. While his father had completed a new manuscript by the time of his death, the book of his life was decidedly unfinished — without a final resolution of the tense father/son aspects of the plot:

> *some months before, a choleric note dashed off to me*
> *cutting me off, it would once have been said,*
> *for nothing I could this time see that I'd done wrong . . .*

Death marks a fresh phase of the dialogue rather than its end, a new adjustment rather than a last judgement. As in Alastair Reid's poem, 'My Father, Dying', the 'hesitant conversation' now beginning is destined to go 'on and on and on'.

Michael Hofmann, born in Freiburg in 1957, is not only the son of a distinguished novelist but also a trusted translator of novelists such as Joseph Roth, Wolfgang Koeppen and Beat Sterchi (dedicatee of Hofmann's laconic poem, 'Pastorale', and author of *Blösch*, a masterpiece regarded as the *Ulysses* of the dairy cow). He shared the 1998 International IMPAC Dublin Literary Award for his translation of Herta Müller's novel, *The Land of Green Plums*. His own powers of characterization — themselves worthy of a novelist — have augmented his gifts for atmosphere and ambience in a series of trenchant portraits of Gert Hofmann: pointed rather than rounded, one-sided but certainly not one-dimensional. Biography has proved instructive too; Michael Hofmann's third book, the transitional collection *Corona, Corona* (1993), opened with a series of portraits of artists not unconnected with the father/son theme. Among these potted biographies is found a painter who 'slayed' his father, a father who shot his famous son, and Crassus 'whose head was severed a day later than his son's'. As if to emphasize the inescapability of the paternal motif, one of his profiled painters is called Dadd, another is a Dadaist.

Michael Hofmann's best work tends to be dense in style and tense in mood. The poet's father is viewed unsparingly yet not altogether unlovingly, however muffled the emotion may be. One suspects that it was his son's coolly detached stance, his artistic sangfroid, which caused offence to Gert Hofmann — and he *was* undoubtedly hurt by the poems — as much as the unrestricted access granted to his private peccadillos: the salami breath, the snorting, the duplicity, infidelity, forced bonhomie and patriarchy. Aiming, in his own words, to be 'nagging . . . or provoking', Michael Hofmann wanted to test the nature of the response his poems could provoke from his father. As son remarked of father on the BBC television documentary in which they circled one another warily like a pair of Achilles' heels, 'If you have the power to hurt someone, I expect it means they still love you . . . and I wanted to be assured of that.'

In another BBC programme, Michael Hofmann laid claim to 'candour' as an un-English quality he brings to poetry. His 'mania for truth' (a reaction, he has suggested, to being the son of a fiction writer) makes him concerned with understanding his father more than with exalting him in death. The *Approximately Nowhere* poems written in Gert Hofmann's memory are as devoid of sentimentality as those which gave his second collection, *Acrimony* (1986), its rancorous title; and, while they may sometimes seem as 'diamond hard' as the potatoes which his father 'bestirred himself to grow one year', they are the offshoots of an obsessiveness which is the opposite of indifference. Indeed, there is something of the inverted self-portrait about a number of the poems written over the years. In scrutinizing his father's lifestyle, and the behaviour of the other literary figures he depicts, Michael Hofmann is implicitly asking how he himself should live. *Nights in the Iron Hotel* (1983), his posed and poised debut, contained a poem to his father which ended:

> *Once there was a bureaucratic inquiry*
> *to determine where you should be registered.*
> *What was the centre of your life-interests?*
>
> *You said your family; your family said your work.*

This choice between 'perfection of the life, or of the work' remains a pressing issue three collections later in *Approximately Nowhere*.

It would be grossly unfair to Hofmann — easily among the best and most adventurous poets of his generation — to represent him as a one-theme poet. On the contrary, he has from the beginning forged a poetry capable of swallowing anything it is fed, with scarcely a discernible gulp. *Nights in the Iron Hotel* juxtaposed spark-plugs and tampons, nuclear bunkers and cave art, a girl's photograph and an aeroplane propeller. In the new book, as in its predecessors, worldly goods — the tacky, comforting and absurd — are everywhere on view: radios and Teasmaids, mattresses and condoms, 'a Spanish guitar and a Dustbuster hanging together like a yellow-grey Braque'. Hofmann's poems sometimes sweep all before them — people, places, possessions — in lists ('Zirbelstrasse' and 'Litany', for instance) which are redeemed from monotony by the intensity of the alienated memories they evoke. No one does dinginess better than Hofmann. 'Malvern Road', with its Lowellesque 'do you remember' planted in the third line, goes on to recall the street where a couple 'first set up house' together:

> the corner pub we probably never set foot in,
> the health centre padlocked and grilled like an offie,
> the prefab post office set down at an odd angle,
> the bank that closed down, the undertaker who stayed
>   open . . .

Hofmann's openings spring suddenly, his endings strike abruptly, his middles are deadpan and downbeat. His poems can survive without perceptible rhythms but not without pliant tones. In the absence of rhyme and metre, the glue which binds his poems together is manufactured from a fusion of foreign phrases, cinematic transitions, sexual tensions, volatile emotions, elliptical observations, oblique suggestions, literary allusions, disinterested self-examinations . . . The weaker poems are those which, because some of the essential ingredients are missing, are too thinly-textured to rise above anecdote or whimsy. Many of the slighter pieces in *Approximately Nowhere* are short, in one case ('My Life and Loves') amounting to a single gnomic — or, at any rate, knowing — line ('Frank Harris. And a syringe for afters'.)

Short poems present a particular challenge to Hofmann, who

has absorbed the work of Ian Hamilton (to the extent of hoarding copies of *The Visit*), Bertolt Brecht (the towering genius who could cram an epic into an epigram) and Adam Zagajewski (a specialist in brief insubstantial poems). As a restless poet — showing no more inclination to settle for one stylistic mode than for a conventional, suburban middle-age — Hofmann can be expected to worry at the short poem until he has mastered it, perhaps even devised a truly contemporary equivalent of the classical epigram. The drawback with brevity is that it denies him scope for those aggregations of detail on which the success of his poems typically depends. When brevity and scathing wit blend convincingly in the shorter poems, however, they wear a winning grin, as in the irony-packed six-liner entitled 'Ingerlund':

> *The fat boy by Buddha out of Boadicea*
> *with the pebbledash acne and half-timbered haircut,*
> *sitting on the pavement with his boots in the gutter,*
>
> *we must have made his day when we pulled over*
> *and asked him for the site of the Iron Age fort*
> *in his conservation village.*

The pebbledash and half-timber are reminders of how visual Hofmann can be. Not greatly given to metaphor or simile (though accomplished when inclined: 'my vast desk / like an aircraft carrier'), he can daub words on the page with an Expressionist palette ('a fizzy orange-purple sky') or more subdued tints. Those who remember the 'field-grey Mercedes' and the 'caramel-coloured' slugs of earlier poems will relish the similarly precise brushwork of *Approximately Nowhere*: 'liver-coloured buildings', a 'sidewalk . . . the colour of old snow', the 'ochre bodystocking pancake colour' of his father's corpse.

Instead of smoothing out the foreign component of his language with Home Counties dubbing, Hofmann brings his multi-lingualism into the English he uses. He consciously and exuberantly mixes registers, languages and idioms, letting his macaronic tongue speak for a deracinated contemporary world. His large vocabulary does not discriminate between the lingua franca of the study ('abscission', 'fauve', 'cryogenics') and street lingo ('gimme', 'puke', 'muso'); yet he never succumbs to the New Philistinism which plays down learning for the sake of modish street-cred. Books are a fundamental part of reality for writers, even more so presumably for those who happen also to be the children of writers. It is perfectly natural, therefore, for Hofmann to invoke Kafka and Kleist, Vallejo and Montale in *Approximately Nowhere*, just as names like Byron, Brooke, Horváth and Chekhov had dotted his previous collections.

'XXXX', which finds the forty-year-old Michael Hofmann grappling with a personal crisis, connects a feverish reading spell with a bookish childhood. And the poet is momentarily — not to mention unexpectedly — on the same wavelength as the novelist father whom, in *Acrimony*, he had accused of drowning out his voice ('"Why did God give me a voice", / I asked, "if you always keep the radio on?"'):

> *Most of the day I'm either lying down*
> *or asleep. I haven't read this many books*
> *this avidly since I was a boy.*
> *Nights are difficult. Sometimes I shout.*
>
> *I'm quarrelsome, charming, lustful, inconsolable, broken.*
> *I have the radio on as much as ever my father did,*
> *carrying it with me from room to room.*
> *I like its level talk.*

Thumbscrew (Autumn 1999)

Simon Armitage

Killing Time
Short and Sweet: 101 Very Short Poems (editor)

Simon Armitage likes to have it both ways. He is the streetwise poet who is at home in a BBC Radio 1 studio; but he is also the ambitious literary figure who aspires to 'nothing less' than a Nobel Prize. He is at ease with youth culture ('I didn't have a classical education of any type, so I tend to use characters from popular culture'); yet, far from stoking rebellion, he writes tenderly of his parents and looks up to literary elders like Weldon Kees, Ted Hughes and W H Auden. Asked to nominate his 'Book of the Century', he plumped not for the works of Irvine Walsh or Bret Easton Ellis but for Samuel Beckett's *Waiting for Godot*. The idea of Armitage in Beckettian exile, refusing to grant media interviews, would be about as plausible as 'Chaucer at his laptop, / auto-checking his screenplay proposal for spelling and style' or 'Shakespeare making / an arse of himself for Children in Need or *Sesame Street*', two of the scenarios conjured up in *Killing Time* (again calculated to have wide appeal, amusing a literary audience without alienating one for which Shakespeare and Chaucer may be nothing more than heavyweight names in a pub quiz).

Killing Time is the poem of the Millennium Dome, commissioned by the New Millennium Experience Company from Simon Armitage as their poet-in-residence. The stately pleasure-dome at Greenwich needed a poet as prominent as the edifice itself; old-fashioned sensitive souls who were likely to be distracted from their poetic reveries by busloads of schoolchildren from Porlock were never likely to be front-runners for the job. The notion that it would be appropriate to depart from the old millennium in a 1,000-line stretch limo, rather than an eco-friendly haiku or a streamlined sonnet, seems to have been Armitage's own. Thanks to the thrust of his long lines and the energy of his strong rhythms, his progress is relatively smooth, although bumpy rhetoric is sometimes an obstacle. The well-judged version of the poem which he broadcast on BBC Radio 3 lost nothing by discarding lines in which — merely killing time, it seems — he becomes overly ponderous:

> *Make it real again, because*
> *this is the cycle to which we are all born.*
> *We journeyed ashore*
> *to set the past free, to release the secret of time from stone,*
> *uncurl the stubborn fist of what is gone,*
> *to flood the rocks that hold the limited supply of time,*
> *to irrigate memory*
> *and float the great, revolving permanence of humankind.*

The long poem is associated with ambition in Simon Armitage's mind. In the introduction to *Short and Sweet*, his anthology of brief poems from several centuries (101 of which — Anonymous and Apollinaire to Wyatt and Yeats — convey a vast cross-section of human experience in considerably less than 1,000 lines in total), he recalls Robert Graves's suggestion that the long poem may be 'nothing more than a poet's attempt at greatness, at becoming "major"'. While, on the one hand, Armitage asserts that 'Today, it is still the short poem that stays in the mind as language, whereas longer poems tend to be remembered for their overall structure or patterning, or for the occasional quote', his other hand is busy drafting long poems and sequences. Still in thrall to the long poem, one suspects that the association of largeness of scale with magnitude of achievement is one which he is incapable of shaking off (notwithstanding the example set by Seamus Heaney and Wislawa Szymborska — both represented in *Short and Sweet* — whose Nobel Prize-sized reputations were earned through lyric-length writings).

Since the launch of his trail-blazing first collection, *Zoom!*, into the upper orbits of poetry's audience in 1989, when he was twenty-six, Armitage has written long poems and poetry sequences of mixed quality for television, radio and the printed page. The exhilarating, improvisatory title sequence of *Book of Matches* (1993) consisted of thirty short poems — semi-sonnets, mini-*Dream Songs*, virtuoso vignettes — in which globs of experience were swabbed up without any intention of pursuing a clear narrative line. That collection, his third, also included 'Reading the Banns', a light, witty and tender wedding-day poem of twelve pages (more than one kind of match featured in the book).

If 'The Whole of the Sky', the central section of *CloudCuckooLand* (1997) — which found him spying on the constellations through a Russian telescope — was the least satisfactory of his longer sequences, it did contain a small number of stellar poems, such as 'Virgo' and 'The Ram'. Among Armitage's most underestimated achievements, however, is the 512-line poem, 'Five Eleven Ninety Nine', with which his collection, *The Dead Sea Poems*, came to a blazing finish. Although published in 1995, this is very much a millennial poem: the last Guy Fawkes bonfire of the twentieth century transforms into something unexpectedly apocalyptic and life-changing ('a people waiting for a word or sign'). The 'Five Eleven Ninety Nine' bonfire was a spectacle sufficiently large in itself ('take notice of its changing shape: a cairn / becoming wigwam, then becoming dome') to have warranted his appointment as honorary poet-in-residence to the Dome without needing to establish further millennial credentials in *Killing Time*.

What will have made *Killing Time* a particularly demanding poem to write — even for someone who has versified the 150th anniversary of Rochdale's Co-operative Society and who, at the drop of a mortar-board, composed a poem for a degree-conferral ceremony — is its self-imposed length. It is one thing to write a numerically-regular poem like the brilliant but brief 'Ten Pence Story' (ten-syllable lines distributed among ten stanzas — the sort of poetry mathematics of which Peter Reading, an admirer of Armitage's work, is master), but altogether another to write 1,000 lines to a year-end deadline, not least when the aim of the poem is essentially a public one: to reflect on contemporary life and to recollect in verse some recent headline-grabbing stories. One of the saving graces of *Killing Time* is that Armitage has desisted from offering a mere review of 1999 in verse. In the section about Piccard and Jones, the round-the-world balloonists, he cleverly employs negatives as escape clauses when he wants to tick off some of the horrors of the age without pretending to be able to generate poetry from them. In the process, he makes strange bedfellows of the likes of Tracey Emin and Slobodan Milosevic:

> *Meanwhile, hot air rises.*
> *And the two men held for twenty-one days in living*
> *conditions*
> *decidedly worse*

> *than those in most high security prisons*
> *   are not the victims*
> *of some hard-line, oppressive regime, or political refugees,*
> *   or eco-warriors*
> *digging in on the side of rare toads and ancient trees,*
> *   or dumbstruck hostages,*
> *or Western tourists kidnapped by gun-toting terrorists,*
> *   or moon-eyed murderers*
> *on death row, or self-captivated Turner Prize exhibitionists,*
> *   but balloonists, actually . . .*

Having jettisoned so much heavyweight ballast, Armitage can yield to free-floating riffs in which the phrase 'We could do worse' introduces a succession of alternative modes of human behaviour: 'We could do worse / than hang around up there, thoughtful and vacant at once . . . / while wounds heal, battle-fields go to pot, weapons to rust. / Impossible of course, / but couldn't we just, couldn't we just?' Armitage does not lay claim to a politically-engaged imagination; his preference for soaring above the battlegrounds, rather than reporting from them, distinguishes his work from that of Tony Harrison, a fellow-Yorkshireman and a pioneer of television verse documentary (*Killing Time*, tarted-up as a TV documentary, was transmitted on Channel 4). In a sixtieth birthday tribute to his colleague, Armitage noted that Harrison has established 'a written version of his voice, a sort of acceptable presentation of West Yorkshire utterance that stops short of dialect poetry'.

Armitage's collections capture his own sprightly speech like a voiceprint. Determined never to sound cloth-eared, he aerates his demotic language with emphatic rhythms and catchy rhymes (often of the half or para variety), while at the same time ensuring that he does not transgress the cloth-capped — or, more likely nowadays, the baseball-capped — conventions of contemporary Yorkshire lingo. *Short and Sweet* includes Hopkins's exquisite 'Pied Beauty' ('rose-moles all in stipple upon trout that swim; / Fresh-firecoal chestnut-falls'); yet, Armitage, in his introduction, holds firmly to his conviction that 'the best literature' is 'a kind of written-down talk': 'Not talk as it might come out from between the teeth, but a sort of imagined talk.' To the intensely musical 'talk' of his poetry, Armitage brings wit (verbal and anecdotal) and grit (he can be deeply moving and poignant but is happy to leave tears, like politics, to Tony Harrison). In addition, he has a gift for sustained metaphor and the capacity to see and sound a word from all possible angles, squeezing every imaginable nuance from a phrase or — an Armitage speciality — cliché. His confidence, that brisk self-assuredness with which he faces into every poetic project, is no doubt bolstered by the fact that he belongs to the first generation of British poets in many years which does not find itself overshadowed by Northern Irish coevals.

If *Killing Time* is shadowed by any Ulster poet it is the Louis MacNeice of *Autumn Journal* (1939), another long and long-lined poem which drew spontaneously on the unfolding events of its time. Simon Armitage and Glyn Maxwell travelled to Iceland in the footsteps of MacNeice and W H Auden; their book, *Moon Country* (1996), was marketed as a follow-up to the Auden/MacNeice classic, *Letters From Iceland* (1937). But one cannot step into the same geyser twice; even MacNeice himself, in *Autumn Sequel* (1954), failed to produce a convincing successor to his own earlier masterpiece. The tension and apprehension which are characteristic of parts of *Autumn Journal* can be accounted for by the fact that so much that is personal is at stake; as T S Eliot, its original publisher, remarked, 'the imagery is all imagery of things lived through, and not merely chosen for poetic suggestiveness'. MacNeice, during the period of the Munich crisis, anxiously 'Listening to bulletins / From distant, measured voices / Arguing for peace / While the zero hour approaches', contrasts with Armitage anxiously vetting news bulletins as the deadline for his poetry commission approaches.

While he can offer a vivid and witty eye-witness account of the 1999 solar eclipse, as seen through his protective glasses, Armitage handles some of the more tragic stories with protective layers of metaphor. In the case of multiple shootings in a Colorado high school, he makes effective use of a Sixties-style substitution of flowers for guns, so that sprays of bullets become floral sprays. By doing so, by keeping the slaughter at a proper distance, he avoids appropriating the misery of others or intruding on private grief:

> *Upstairs in the school library, individuals were singled out*
> *for special attention:*
> *some were showered with blossom, others wore their blooms*
> *like brooches or medallions;*
> *even those who turned their backs or refused point-blank*

> *to accept such honours*
> *were decorated with buds, unseasonable fruits and rosettes*
> *the same as the others.*

The parallels between the bloody massacre and the gentle metaphor — emphasised here in 'point-blank', 'brooches or medallions' and 'honours' — culminate in the section's double-edged final word, 'kind'. Armitage's concluding question recalls his years working as a probation officer: 'As for the two boys, it's back to the same old debate: / is it something in the mind / that grows from birth, like a seed, or is it society / makes a person that kind?'

The penultimate section of *Killing Time* concentrates on Bosnia and Kosovo; perhaps taking a hint from Glyn Maxwell's poem, 'The Sarajevo Zoo', Armitage selects an aviary for his opening shot: 'Some aviary in the Balkans / suffered damage from a nearby blast; / eagles, buzzards, vultures and falcons / all flew the nest.' Eventually, he focuses on one creature, a lyrebird — a species noted for its habit of mimicking sounds; in this case, tellingly, 'the sound-bytes' it 'parrots' bear witness to the brutality of war:

> *boots marching on tarmac,*
> *razor wire shredding the breeze,*
> *the onward grinding of tank-tracks*
> *through deserted streets,*
>
> *orders given in a foreign tongue,*
> *the smashing of locks and latches,*
> *petrol poured from a petrol can,*
> *the striking of matches . . .*

Armitage's choice of the phrase 'sound-bytes' has a polemical resonance. One of the underlying themes of *Killing Time* is a revulsion at the exploitative behaviour of the modern news media. He makes a monkey of the media at the beginning of the poem ('fibre-optics for body hair, / a mouse for a hand, / a fax-machine derrière, / a joystick gland'), constructing a creature which thrives only on news ('The news — that's what the monkey loved, / it ate like there was no tomorrow, / had a particular taste for anything live / and a thirst for sorrow'). Attacks on the intrusive nature of the media ('That interference jamming the air') are repeated in the aviary section. Valid though these criticisms are, it is difficult to read *Killing Time* — let alone sit through its Channel 4 makeover, featuring the newscaster Jon Snow — without being reminded how much Armitage (a veteran of radio and TV as presenter, interviewee, scriptwriter and documentary maker) owes to television news footage for information and inspiration.

Astutely, Armitage guards against squandering his entire 1,000 lines on news, lest his poem should become all too literally 'news that stays news'. Wherever possible, therefore, he escapes from topical to timeless themes (such as time itself) — subjects by which he would feel stimulated even if he were not paid to write in a millennial mode. That *Killing Time*, in defiance of its unpromising origins, is by no means without merit is due to Armitage's fidelity to the grain of his imagination. Since poetry cannot be willed into existence, instant reactions to public events are usually banal in the extreme. It is scarcely surprising that the eternal comedy of the English weather ('A consignment of grey sky / treading water all week / off the coast, waiting for clearance, is given the green light / and rolls in to port') elicits a more compelling response from Armitage than a rail tragedy, about which he finds little to add to his journalistic sources. Avoiding tedium, he relieves the longer sections of the poem with snappy, stand-alone quatrains that would have qualified for inclusion in *Short and Sweet*.

Simon Armitage has referred to 'Goalkeeper with a Cigarette', his hymn to nonchalance, as a 'manifesto': 'He is what he is, does whatever suits him, / because he has no highfalutin song / to sing, no neat message for the nation / on the theme of genius or dedication'. As *Killing Time* demonstrates, Armitage sets his goals higher than this, in fact, and — while still wary of the 'highfalutin' — is not in the least inhibited about disseminating messages to the nation; he is the Poet Laureate-in-waiting. A few years ago, the *Radio Times* published a photograph of Seamus Heaney above an announcement of BBC Radio 3's 'Sunday Feature': 'Nobel Laureate Seamus Heaney reads *Station Island*, his sustained meditation on the artist's role'. Turning the page, readers discovered that Monday's Radio 1 schedule included 'John Peel . . . live in Manchester with Number One Cup in session and poetry from sex-bard Simon Armitage'.

Armitage's ability to play goalkeeper in both divisions, to two-time Radio 1 and Radio 3, to learn not only from Seamus Heaney but from John Peel (about whom he has written with reverence in his lively prose compendium, *All Points North*), could prove counterproductive if he were to settle — as he sometimes seems tempted — for ephemeral, commission-driven compromises and a kind of superior rap poetry, at the expense of the more profound challenges for which his prodigious talents have equipped him. Laudably, though, he has managed to achieve his popularity without having lapsed into pop poetry; and, as a succession of outstanding poems have proved, there is an inner life of some depth concealed beneath the laddish persona. On past form, he will continue to gamble on having it both ways: as a media poet and a literary one; as Seamus Peel and John Heaney; as a poet seeking the approbation of telly addicts and Nobel Prize academicians. Having spoken for the dying twentieth century in *Killing Time*, the odds are that the lavishly-gifted Armitage will be among the essential voices of our new century also — provided that the inner voice, and not the voice-over, prevails.

London Review of Books (27 April 2000)

Roy Fuller

Roy Fuller: Writer and Society by Neil Powell

It is the life rather than the work which the contemporary reader wants; not the parts of the life that will illuminate the work, but the parts of the work that will serve as props or clues in a dramatized version of the life: poet as drunk, poet as lecher, poet as suicide, anything except poet as poet. Even where there is a will, there is no sure way nowadays for writers to limit the posthumous fate of their personal papers. The lucrative market for literary archives ensures that, whatever the testatory wishes of an author, the most private material enters the public domain with indecent speed. 'Incautious to the point of innocence' was Alfred Corn's assessment of Philip Larkin's epistolary style. Never such innocence again . . .

A building society solicitor who lived with his lifelong spouse in a suburban bungalow, and whose poetry sales were so unspectacular that he was ultimately forced to wander from publisher to publisher like a poetry vagabond, may not seem a likely subject for a contemporary biography. Neil Powell, however, is content to foreground the work rather than the man and to sketch in the personal background delicately. Superficially at least, Roy Fuller might be regarded as a confessional writer. He produced hundreds of pages of memoirs; his novels contain heavily autobiographical episodes; and many of his poems display the qualities of a good journal. Unlike the American school of confessional writers, though, Roy Fuller has less interest in hyping up his traumas than in playing them down. Powell describes the memoirs as 'emotionally reticent' and, at one point, 'transparently evasive'; sweeping some childhood dust under the cheap carpet of a Blackpool hotel where his widowed mother made a home for herself and her two sons, Fuller wrote: 'dim period, scarcely worth trying in the least to depict'.

In 1920, when Roy Fuller was eight, his father died; the resultant decline in family fortunes took him from a mock-Tudor house with two maids and a chauffeur to a succession of dubious lodgings with unhygienic landladies and elderly fellow-residents, experiences which imprinted themselves on his character and imagination. He practised extreme care with his finances ('I am very petty-bourgeois about money'), shunned bohemianism and succumbed to 'a lifelong obsession with sartorial correctness'. But the man on the Blackheath omnibus, the 53 ('one of the few worldly things that improved rather than degenerated during my latter life'), every elegant inch a solicitor in appearance, was an odd combination of submissive and subversive. His 'great respect for rules and authority' coexisted with 'a strong nonconformity of thought, a willingness to be in a minority of one'. Fuller's Marxism, which would certainly not have isolated him in the 1930s, had still not been abandoned long after he should have known better (and despite his sense of solidarity with his fellow-men having been severely undermined by the reality of contact with the milling masses on a wartime troop ship bound for Africa).

Neil Powell does not confuse a biographer's role with a psychoanalyst's and he holds the reader's attention while directing it to where it should be: on the novels and poems. Occasionally, though, one's curiosity is raised — against one's better instincts perhaps — to a pitch where it is frustrating not to have it satisfied. Fuller's close friend, Julian Symons, is quoted as saying, 'Roy underwent an emotional crisis at the end of the 40s or in the very early 50s'. But, as with references in the book to the poet suffering 'a particularly complicated sort of middle-aged crisis' or requiring anti-depressants after 'a particularly agitated time', a vapour of mystery hangs over certain remarks.

If Powell is sometimes over-protective of Fuller, he never lets his loyalty interfere with his critical judgements and he is as honest in faulting individual works as he is persuasive in cherishing the work as a whole. He tours Fuller's books like an intern on ward duty, expertly and cheerfully diagnosing any defects he finds: the 'inhibited' novels, the 'defensive mannerisms' in the poetry, the mix of 'mischievous irony (and) solicitorial circumlocution' in the memoirs. While missing no opportunity to champion the best of the early work, Powell convincingly argues that Fuller's poetry found its true voice in his sixties. Ironic and self-mocking ('I play — I am! — the Shakespearean daft old man'), these poems are at the same time imbued with a sense of transience and evanescence, rich in last lingering looks. Even if the world he depicts in retirement is an atrophied one, no bigger than his back garden, it gains a certain universality from being bathed in the pathos of autumnal light.

Fuller's late poetry was responsive to every experience and — as one of his poems for children puts it — he needed only to go 'To shops a hundred yards or so away / For something to enrich a humdrum day', a point literally proved by poems like 'Shop Talk', 'Philosophy in Marks and Spencer' or the delightful 'Supermarket Days (and Nights)'. Contrary to Fuller's conservative image, such poems are audacious experiments in how much of the quotidian a poem can accommodate, how low-key a poem can be and still qualify as genuine poetry. Fuller considered himself a belated Thirties poet (his first book appeared in the last month of the decade) and, as well as trust in the continued relevance of traditional prosody, what he took from W H Auden was a sense 'that there was nothing that was not poetic'.

From the young war poet to the poet in old age affecting the persona of a retired colonel, Neil Powell places Roy Fuller's career into illuminating biographical and bibliographical perspectives. 'People are inclined to think that when one has made some sort of name in the world of letters publication follows as a matter of course,' Roy Fuller remarked in *Spanner and Pen*, 'Nothing could be further from the truth for a highbrow writer who has never really "caught on".' He would find it encouraging to know that a book such as this can still be written and published; if, as one hopes, Fuller does eventually 'catch on', Neil Powell will have done much to make the case for this lawyer poet's defence.

PN Review (July/August 1996)

W S Graham: *Professor of Silence*

W S Graham was among the most neglected poets of his time. According to one anecdote, his publishers (whom he would disparage as 'Fibber £ Fibber') assumed that he had died in the long silence that followed his collection, *The Nightfishing* (1955). Graham is said to have phoned Fabers with a view to refuting their assumption. Near the close of his *Collected Poems* (1979) — a book much preoccupied with communication and silence — he wrote more in irony than in anger to a dead friend:

> *Speaking to you and not*
> *Knowing if you are there*
> *Is not too difficult.*
> *My words are used to that.*

William Sydney Graham was born to his West of Ireland mother at 'five o'clock the bright nineteenth / Of November nineteen-eighteen'. In 1938, his apprenticeship as an engineer already completed, he attended Newbattle Abbey College where working people were given an opportunity to further their education. Nessie Dunsmuir, who was to become his friend, inspiration, supporter and wife, was a fellow-student; and the Orcadian poets, Edwin Muir and George Mackay Brown, would become associated with the college later.

A few years after Newbattle, W S Graham's first collection of poems, *Cage Without Grievance* (1942), was published by his patron, David Archer. It displayed some of the worst obfuscatory characteristics of its time. A Dylan Thomas accent was, no doubt, a licence to consume alcohol in the 'sodality of Soho' among painters and poets. Even the titles of Graham's poems ('As If in an Instant Parapets of Plants'; 'Say that in Lovers with Stones for Family') outdid his master's excesses. In his essay on Dylan Thomas, John Berryman listed the following as features of Thomas's verse: unusual epithets, compound words, notions of dichotomy, marine imagery. Graham seemed to seize on all of them as a job lot without allowing words the breathing space which Thomas did. Instead, he threatened to choke his poems with force-feeding:

> *Those funnels of fever (but melody to gales)*
> *Tenant the spiral answer of a scarecrow daisy.*

In Graham's first two collections, *2ND Poems* (1945) — a title literally capitalising on Nessie Dunsmuir's initials — as well as *Cage Without Grievance,* the main interest is rhythmic rather than linguistic. While some of the poems are probably better hummed than recited, they do supply valuable early evidence of Graham's abiding fondness for winding sentence structures:

> *Let nothing through love's way leave*
> *But the ringing through hawthorn disciple's name*
> *That ever by my bellstrong mouth I scold*
> *On the grindwheel gale that draws me to calm.*

Another justification for reading his precursory collections is the inkling they provide that he saw language from the start as a mysterious and refractory medium. He began by using (or, perhaps, abusing) language and ended by allowing himself to be used by it. To pass through the opening sections of the *Collected Poems* is to make a journey through the dense smog of a city before arriving within clear view of the shimmering sea; or, following Graham's own biography, it is like the journey from 'Clydeside, / Webbed in its foundries and loud blood' (page 54) to Cornwall's 'far-off simple sea' (page 210).

Reading Graham's verse from start to finish reminds me of a fascinating poem, 'Shaker Shaken', by his friend, Edwin Morgan. Taking a Shaker sound-poem of 1847, Morgan pretends to decode it until what seemed opaque and impervious becomes gradually coherent. The limpid later poems of Graham are like a translation of what has gone before; but the syntax and rhythm retain the stretchmarks of their struggle towards lucidity. The opening poem of *The White Threshold* (1949), his first Faber collection, depicts that struggle as a trek towards 'the word's crest' and its down-to-earth references to hobnail and rucksack come as a relief after so much that is rhetorical and recondite. But, despite successes like the confident 'Listen. Put on Morning' and partial successes like 'The Search by a Town', much of the book is still maddeningly convoluted, with poems scarcely communicating among themselves as stanza coldly rebuffs fellow-stanza.

Another Scottish poet, Norman MacCaig, wanted his early 'vomitorium of unrelated images' wiped from the record — and his first publications were therefore excluded from his *Collected Poems*. Graham, however, was proud to re-circulate his early work in his own *Collected Poems*. As belatedly as 1979, he was rather vaguely defending his youthful flings: 'I wouldn't like it to be easily accepted that those were boyish balloons and effervescence. No, I get a certain kick out of early poems that I don't get out of later work . . . Certain things occurred in the early poems which couldn't occur now, and make not just a random shape out of ignorance but something else.' This is even less precise, and certainly less excusable, than his defence to Edwin Morgan almost forty years before: '*Cage Without Grievance* is a first book of poems. It's all right, better than most first books, because I am potentially a greater poet than most today which does not make me very great but I am . . . The chief value is the realization that my voice is heard and the involuntary responsibility which comes down on me and makes me more hard working at my poems . . .'

Graham's hard work brought two notable advances to *The White Threshold*. The first was an increased skill in dealing with the power, awe and mystery of the sea:

> *Always the saving seadoors well*
> *Worth salt homecoming speaking up*
> *The heaving hundred weights of water,*
> *Save me down into a homecoming tiding*
> *Worth while and breath here with my smothering farers.*

Equally significant were the three letters in memory of his mother with which the collection concluded. These represented the first moves in the direction of those extraordinary poems in which Graham addresses family and friends (living and dead) and plays his own peculiar verse rhythms against the demands of colloquial language. Not that one could really describe the 'Three Letters' in *The White Threshold* as colloquial to any significant degree; but one does sense, in places at least, an abandonment of factitious language and the emergence of the poet's natural voice. A certain grandiloquence remains, nonetheless, as in these lines to his father:

> Entirely within the fires
> And winter-harried natures
> Of your each year, the still
> Foundered man is the oracle
> Tented within his early
> Friendships . . .

That is a long way from the affecting and unbridled intimacy of his dream-encounter with his father much later:

> Dad, what am I doing here?
> What is it I am doing now?
> Are you proud of me?
> Going away, I knew
> You wanted to tell me something.

The 'Seven Letters' in *The Nightfishing*, the collection which followed *The White Threshold*, could be said to mark the point at which Graham emerges as a thoroughly original poet. Glittering with sea imagery and flickering with puns and internal rhymes, the 'letters' coil down the middle of the page in short, sinewy lines. Now, for the first (and certainly not the last) time, the reader feels drawn into the poem and spoken to directly by the poet. Some of the letters seem at once addresses to a loved-one and flirtations with the reader. The opening letter, captivatingly musical, contains the lines:

> Dear you who walk
> Your solitude on these
> Words, walk their silences
> Hearing a morning say
> A welcome I have not heard
> In words I have not made.

'Letter VI' is a particularly evocative love poem:

> And as you lay fondly
> In the crushed smell of the moor
> The courageous and just sun
> Opened its door.

And there we lay halfway
Your body and my body
On the high moor . . .

Elsewhere in this sequence, there are linguistically virtuosic poems in which he retraces his younger self discovering his vocation for poetry ('Then in a welding flash / He found his poetry arm / And turned the coat of his trade') and begins to employ a metalinguistic imagery ('Here where I lie in language . . .'; 'I heard voices within / The empty lines and tenses'). What Edwin Morgan has termed Graham's 'obsessional preoccupation' with 'the endless dyings and metamorphoses of the self' is evident throughout *The Nightfishing*. He cannot forget that we are changing and dying with each passing moment ('Only / Myself I died from into / These present words that move'; 'Now he who takes my place continually anew / Speaks me thoroughly perished into another'). The repetition at the end of 'Letter II' gives mimetic emphasis to the point:

> *He dies*
> *Word by each word into*
> *Myself now at this last*
> *Word I die in. This last.*

The title poem of *The Nightfishing* is a long seven-part sequence rich in sea images and rhythms, though excelled in both qualities by other poems in the collection such as 'Letter IV'. The short poems which surround the central fishing section may seem like loose threads hanging from the mainsail of the poem but Graham himself opined, in his interview with John Haffenden, that 'The fishing section is too long and filled with the same stuff. If it was Mozart writing that as music — and I'm not speaking of the sound of the poem — he wouldn't have gone on as long as that. It's not filled with enough invention.'

Whatever its faults, it sways with the movement of the sea rather than with Graham's earlier word-drunkenness, though the journey he takes *is* partly a linguistic one. He refers to 'those words through which I move' and declares that 'Each word is but a longing / Set out to break from a difficult home. Yet in / Its meaning I am'. We also encounter a 'script of light', a 'book of storms'; and 'The steep bow heaves, hung on these words, towards / What words your lonely breath blows out to meet it'.

Dennis O'Driscoll

Some of the more reflective moments in 'The Nightfishing' threaten to destroy the illusion that an actual fishing trip is underway. While parts of it may seem to be products of desk rather than deck, Graham sought and gained the approval of a fisherman for the poem, just as Richard Murphy had done in the case of 'The Cleggan Disaster'. Graham's language, despite a rhetorical cargo which makes it quite unlike Murphy's, depicts the sea with astonishing exactness. His admiration for Pound's version of 'The Seafarer' is easily deduced:

> The brute weight
> Of the living sea wrought us, yet the boat sleeked lean
> Into it, upheld by the whole sea-brunt heaved,
> And hung on the swivelling tops. The tiller raised
> The siding tide to wrench us and took a good
> Ready hand to hold it. Yet we made a seaway
> And minded all the gear was fast, and took
> Our spell at steering. And we went keeled over
> The streaming sea.

Graham's efforts to simplify his language are nowhere more evident than in the foot-tapping ballads, 'The Broad Close' and 'Baldy Bane', with which he concludes the collection. But even simplicity of language does not quite guarantee clarity of purpose at this stage of Graham's career; and 'The Broad Close', catchy and witty though it is, is a bit rambling in places. 'Baldy Bane', while not particularly compelling either, is definitely the better ballad:

> Make yourself at home here.
>   My words you move within.
> I made them all by hand for you
>   To use as your own . . .

At the end of 'Baldy Bane', 'Silence is shouted out' and it was to be fifteen years before Graham's next book, *Malcolm Mooney's Land* (1970), appeared. What he endured in material and artistic terms in the intervening years can only be guessed at. *Malcolm Mooney's Land* is the most literal manifestation imaginable of the claim made by Joseph Brodsky in his Nobel Prize speech that literature 'addresses a man tête-à-tête, entering with him into direct relations'. Graham, a vivid and engaging inhabitant of these poems, fixes us with his ancient mariner's eye. His tone is confidential but it is muffled by the barrier of art:

> *Meanwhile surely there must be something to say,*
> *Maybe not suitable but at least happy*
> *In a sense here between us two whoever*
> *We are. Anyhow here we are and never*
> *Before have we two faced each other who face*
> *Each other now across this abstract scene*
> *Stretching between us. This is a public place*
> *Achieved against subjective odds and then*
> *Mainly an obstacle to what I mean.*

In the Poetry Book Society Bulletin for Spring 1970, Graham offered eight 'facts' and four 'observations' regarding *Malcolm Mooney's Land*. Among the 'observations' was the following: 'I am always very aware that my poem is not a telephone call. The poet only speaks one way. He hears nothing back. His words as he utters them are not conditioned by a real ear replying from the other side. That is why he has to make the poem stand stationary as an Art object. He never knows who will collide with it and maybe even use it as a different utensil from what he intended.' This brings us as close as is feasible to the essence of *Malcolm Mooney's Land*, Graham's best book and one of the twentieth century's outstanding collections. As Calvin Bedient remarked, 'The isolation almost all modern poets feel, having lost their sense of an audience, Graham has had the inspiration to theatricalize; and in so doing he has revealed more about loneliness, about the give and take of words, and about the moment, than poetry had laid bare before.' Unlike many critics who have been crassly dismissive of Graham as a navel-gazing poet, preoccupied with nothing but his own relationship with language, Bedient identifies some of the broader implications of the poetry. Graham's profound and playful exploration of human isolation brings Beckett to mind; apart from Beckett, his acknowledged mentors include Pound, Eliot, Joyce (whose fondness for puns he shares) and Marianne Moore ('her beautiful self-conscious language').

The title poem of *Malcolm Mooney's Land* charts a lonely journey through landscape and literature, through the 'printed' snow and the printed page. He writes of 'Footprint on foot / Print, word on word and each on a fool's errand'. From this first poem onwards, Graham recognizes the necessity and artificiality of art ('Why did you choose this place / For us to meet? Sit / With me between this word / And this . . . Yet not mistake this / For the real thing'). He asks us to break his isolation by communicating a response ('To answer please / Tap tap quickly along the nearest / Metal'). At the close of the remarkable title poem, we witness a triumphant metamorphosis:

> *I have made myself alone now.*
> *Outside the tent endless*
> *Drifting hummock crests.*
> *Words drifting on words.*
> *The real unabstract snow.*

That transformative moment is paralleled in 'The Dark Dialogues' when 'over the great / Gantries and cantilevers / Of love, a sky, real and / Particular is slowly / Startled into light'. In the beginning is the word but the world is eventually created by Graham also.

His aspiration is to be allowed, through words, 'A place I can think in / And think anything in, / An aside from the monstrous'. Silence is never quite subjugated, however. We see a 'northern dazzle' of it, hear a 'long blast' of it, observe the 'behaviour' of it. He holds 'The Chair of Professor of Silence', fascinated and frustrated by it at once:

> *Having to construct the silence first*
> *To speak out on I realize*
> *The silence even itself floats*
> *At my ear-side with a character*
> *I have not met before . . .*
> > *For some reason*
> *It refuses to be broken now*
> *By what I thought was worth saying.*
> *If I wait a while, if I look out*
> *At the heavy greedy rooks on the wall*
> *It will disperse. Now I construct*
> *A new silence I hope to break.*

Beyond its silences, *Malcolm Mooney's Land* has something illuminating to say about love and sex, one-arm bandits and paintings. It also contains a splendidly unorthodox elegy for the painter,

Peter Lanyon, who was killed in a gliding accident. Having lived mainly in Cornwall from the mid-Forties onwards, Graham was acquainted with many of the St Ives artists and was as much a poet among painters as were the New York School of James Schuyler, Frank O'Hara and John Ashbery. In fact, it was a painter, Nancy Wynne-Jones, who granted him the free use of the house in Madron which he and Nessie occupied. As he told an *Observer* interviewer: 'The cottage is free. We have no telephone or car, an outside toilet with jug of flowering currant. I did get an Arts Council Grant in 1975. Also I have a Civil List Pension. That works out really at not very much. When something comes up like fixing the front door or thinking of a bathroom or buying clothes or doctoring my poor boy (I mean my cat who has gone and gone out of my poetry) we have little but I am able to put the Capitals at the beginnings of my lines and cook a good steak and kidney pie . . .'

The Peter Lanyon elegy, 'The Thermal Stair', is a far superior poem to the forceful but clotted elegy for the painter Alfred Wallis, in *The White Threshold*, though 'the jasper sea' and, indeed, Wallis's name occur in both. In 'The Thermal Stair', places associated with the painter are used to plangent effect — the prehistoric Lanyon Quoit is delicately and appositely alluded to, while the name of a local tin-mine, Ding Dong, makes a tolling sound for the dead friend. Graham's final collection, *Implements in their Places* (1977), included touching elegies for two further painters. The first recalled his friend, Roger Hilton, to whom the earlier 'Hilton Abstract' was also addressed. Hilton was an excellent artist whose descent into illness, self-pity and squalor will be depressingly recalled by anyone who has read his *Night Letters*, a book which ends with Graham's elegy:

> *He switches the light on*
> *To find a cigarette*
> *And pours himself a Teachers . . .*
> *The images of his dream*
> *Are still about his face*
> *As he spits and tries not*
> *To remember where he was . . .*

It is appropriate that Graham should have written an elegy (or 'night letter') for Hilton, since they were both nocturnal creatures, Graham being laureate of the 'nightshift', 'nightwalker' and 'nightfishing'. He thinks of his native Greenock 'mostly / At night', writes a love poem 'To my Wife at Midnight', and asks in one of his letter-poems 'Are you / Awake or sound and deep / In the bolster-buried ear / Adrift?' When, in his last two books, we catch glimpses of him writing at his 'Untidy Dreadful Table' or (in 'Yours Truly') replying to one of his own verse-letters, it is night. The most haunting night-life occurs in 'The Beast in the Space':

> . . . *on this side*
> *Of the words it's late. The heavy moth*
> *Bangs on the pane. The whole house*
> *Is sleeping and I remember*
> *I am not here, only the space*
> *I sent the terrible beast across.*

The second of the elegies for painters in *Implements in their Places*, 'Dear Bryan Wynter', reaches perfect pitch in the verse-letter form. Graham's heartbreak quality has never been more discernible and his tone (ranging between the poignant and the ironic) is deftly modulated. One is reminded of the 'transparent' style favoured by certain East European poets.

Some of the poems in *Implements in their Places* continue to deal with the conundrums of language but Graham quickly sets about *using*, rather than meditating on, language. He welcomes his embarking readers aboard: 'The beginning wind slaps the canvas. / Are you ready? Are you ready?' The evolution of his style towards limpidity is complete and he can write lines as unforced and unornamented and unhampered as these:

> *Ancient of runes the stone-cut voice*
> *Stands invisible on Zennor Hill.*
> *I climbed here in a morning of mist*
> *Up over a fox's or badger's track*
> *And there is no sound but myself*
> *Breaking last year's drenched bracken.*

He assumes numerous disguises in *Implements in their Places*, 'choosing / An attitude to make a poem'. He adopts the 'attitude' of jungle-dweller, letter-writer, speech-maker and photographer in performances that again show him to be a poet of beguiling sophistication and originality and the supreme comic poet of our time. A strong whiff of menace pervades the photography poem, however; 'Ten Shots of Mister Simpson' — with its references to gassings, a chimney, an inscribed number — hints at sinister experiences. By contrast, 'Enter a Cloud', which ends with an amusing 'Thank you' speech, is that rarity — a good poem of contentment and celebration ('I would say I was a happy man,' Graham once declared).

Of the disguises adopted in the book, none is more engaging than that of the flautist and composer, Johann Joachim Quantz (1697-1773). This poem, 'Johann Joachim Quantz's Five Lessons' ('a bit off my usual beat, whatever that is') — introduced by Graham on radio as 'inspired by the prose of Quantz who wrote the definitive book on the transverse flute in the eighteenth century' — concerns art and its creation and interpretation. 'Every poem is a different way of speaking,' Graham believed, and he loved to act out this very oral poem (something of an *ars poetica*) in which Quantz, through a series of atmospheric vignettes, is heard advising, chastising and encouraging 'a young man with talent / And the rarer gift of application':

> *You are getting on.*
> *Unswell your head. One more piece of coal.*
> *Go on now but remember it must be always*
> *Easy and flowing. Light and shadow must*
> *Be varied but be varied in your mind*
> *Before you hear the eventual return sound.*

Implements in their Places is a marvellous collection, despite the over-extended title sequence. The uncollected poems written between that book and Graham's death in January 1986 suggest that its successor was shaping up to be another fine — probably even finer — collection. He had earned the Freedom of the Language and was availing fully and inventively of the privilege. 'The Alligator Girls' is charming and moving as he remembers 'An afternoon by the river with two sisters' when he 'worked in America as a young man'. In 1947, he had won the 'Atlantic Award' for poetry, as a result of which he lectured at New York University. 'The Alligator Girls', subtitled 'Remembering Crowe Ransom', alludes to Ransom's 'Vision by Sweetwater':

> *. . . would you like to bring the girls at ransom*
> *Over to have a picnic beside the sweet*

Dennis O'Driscoll

Clear water. This is the very day for it.

Inklings of approaching death surface in poems such as 'Falling into the Sea', 'The Visit' and 'The Musical Farmer'. Other uncollected poems include 'I Will Lend You Malcolm' ('Mister Mooney / Will look after you wherever you wish to go') and 'Alice Where Art Thou' (in which Graham's ability to move the reader, without succumbing to sentimentality, is once more in evidence as he recalls his first love). Poems like the partly auto-biographical 'A Page About My Country' or this nonchalantly audacious eight-liner, entitled 'The Fifth of May', defy para-phrase:

> *This morning shaving my brain to face the world*
> *I thought of Love and Life and Death and wee*
> *Meg Macintosh who sat in front of me*
> *In school in Greenock blushing at her desk.*
> *I find under the left nostril difficult,*
> *Those partisans of stiff hairs holding out*
> *In their tender glen beneath the rampart of*
> *The nose and my father's long upperlip.*

He proved himself to be a fine occasional poet also, responding with gusto to invitations to salute the sixtieth birthdays of John Heath-Stubbs and David Wright. The Wright poem is called 'An Entertainment for David Wright on his Being Sixty' — 'All good poems are entertaining,' Graham said in an interview. The enter-tainment in the case of this particular poem was very much 'live' — it is one of his most spontaneous works. He sustains irony, intimacy and wit with apparent effortlessness throughout 'a shapeless poem / Of 132 lines', pausing along the way to resume exploring the theme of the ever-dying self:

> *You realise I am older*
> *By seventy-seven lines.*
> *I am older early*
> *Up this morning grazing*
> *Mistress Muse's pastures . . .*

Among Graham's uncollected poems, one must finally mention 'A Dream of Crete', inspired by his visit to that island in 1964. In the parts of the poem which have been published, he writes of being 'busy learning / How to translate / English into English' and of trying 'to speak what I think is / My home tongue'. It is when he finally comes to speak his own language, especially from *Malcolm Mooney's Land* onwards, that W S Graham speaks to all of us. He does so with an immediacy and rapport that inspire great affection among his readers, achieving what he termed 'Intellect sung in a garment of Innocence'.

'It will be a pleasant thing to have people think I'm a wee bit good,' he told *The Observer* as his *Collected Poems* was about to appear. Although his posthumous audience is growing, the fact that he was a poet brushed by a wee bit of genius remains a better-kept secret than it ought to be.

Krino (Autumn 1988)

Michael Hamburger and Helmut Heissenbüttel: *Language Lessons*

When words take a writer beyond words, he knows that he has found poetry. Some poems aspire to the condition of silence, others to song; in a poetic playwright like Samuel Beckett, the dramatic pauses are like the white spaces around the text of a poem. Michael Hamburger has more than once invoked Hofmannsthal's distinction between 'word-scepticism' and 'word-mysticism', firmly identifying himself with the word-sceptics and (Beckett again comes to mind) surmising that his 'linguistic transplantation' may have had 'something to do with the distrust of verbal richness and euphony that became acute in my later work'.

For a 'linguistically transplanted' writer, painfully conscious that 'to write in a language that is not one's first is to be at one remove from the seeming identity of word and thing', performing the act of translation presents a salutary complement to practising the art of poetry. As a poet in his adopted English and a translator from his native German, Michael Hamburger is in a sense — like the birds of his poem, 'Migrants II' — always 'going home'. To assert that his reputation as a translator — of his monumental Hölderlin and his magisterial Celan not least — has overshadowed his work as a poet might seem merely to state the obvious. Yet it is equally accurate to claim that it is precisely because he is not only a poet, but a poet of a particular kind, that his translations are so widely respected. At the very heart of his poems is a renunciation of the egotistical and the exhibitionist, a factor which adds to his readers' confidence that his translations are *of*, not 'after', the original authors. Michael Hamburger's approach ('my unfashionable habit of trying to get under the original poet's skin') distinguishes him from those less modest poets who must 'improve' the original poem, often distorting it out of recognition and claiming it as a work of their own composition.

Michael Hamburger and Helmut Heissenbüttel

One volume of translations which certainly cannot be accused of diverting attention from Hamburger's own poems is his edition of Helmut Heissenbüttel's *Texts* (1977), a book which was virtually ignored on publication and has never taken its rightful place in the Hamburger canon. *Texts* is a captivating work, not simply because it has so few equivalents in English but also because of the delicate threads which bind the highly unorthodox writings of Heissenbüttel with the apparently more conventional poetry of Hamburger. Michael Hamburger may have written in the persona of Friedrich Hölderlin and alluded in 'Travelling' to Paul Celan; yet any influence exerted by these poets is a subtle one. Sceptical though he himself may be about language, Hamburger's work — however acute the pressure behind it — is not of the kind which splinters into the fragmentary or hardens into the lapidary.

Nonetheless, even as he remains resolutely faithful to the poets he translates ('The translations are as literal as I could make them,' he remarks in his introduction to Heissenbüttel), there is a sense in which his translations also enable him to engage in a kind of vicarious experimentalism. This is not to imply that he intrudes between reader and translated poet — something he sedulously avoids. But the process whereby the faithful translator seeks exact analogies in English for original poems in German is an intensely creative one, amounting to nothing less than an exploration of the potentialities of the English language itself. In frequently choosing to translate poets who stretch the resources of English in unprecedented ways, Hamburger is also stretching his own resources as a poet.

Having used the word 'experimentalism' rather loosely in the last paragraph, I should point out that, in a provocative review of Samuel Beckett's poetry, Michael Hamburger remarked that 'The only writers who can meaningfully be described as experimental are those primarily concerned not with expressing themselves or conveying their sense or experience of life, but with the quiddity, laws and possibilities of their medium.' By this definition, Helmut Heissenbüttel is a quintessentially experimental poet. Born in 1921 in Wilhelmshaven, he had published numerous books — including several volumes of 'text-books' — by the time of his death in 1996; the use of the general term 'texts' reflects the reluctance of his writing to remain neatly encased within the borders of any one artistic genre. As Michael Hamburger points out, 'Not only do his texts cross the frontiers between poetry, prose fiction and drama, but they are as closely bound up with developments in the visual arts and in music as with developments in literature; and his methods are inseparable from the philosophical and linguistic interests evident in everything he has written.' If such a poet shatters the expectations of his readers and makes considerable demands on them, the demands levied on the translator must be immeasurably greater.

To attempt to translate a writer who is so preoccupied with language into another language would seem foolhardy were it not for Hamburger's writerly inquisitiveness about how exactly these 'texts' are constructed and a critic's perceptiveness about their strengths and shortcomings. Having disassembled the writings at his translator's workbench, he is more impressed by Heissenbüttel's practice ('The end of Heissenbüttel's art is enlightenment; and enlightenment brought about without recourse to persuasion, appeal to emotional stock responses, or any of the traditional devices of didactic art') than by his theory. He has scant patience, understandably, with Heissenbüttel's mechanized vision of a 'general' literature which would be 'practicable by anyone who has grasped the methods'. This naive conception might seem an amusing eccentricity, a rush for alchemist's gold, a literal quest for William Carlos Williams's 'little word machine', were it not for the ugly abstractions in which Heissenbüttel's instruction manual is couched, complete with references to 'the practice of post-subjective progressive literary methods'. Furthermore, valuable though Heissenbüttel's ground-breaking work is, to replicate its methods would be simply to go over old ground.

The semi-lyrical writing which forms the first section of *Texts* is free-ranging and far-reaching, a trial-and-error sketchbook complete with sudden shifts of angle and abrupt changes of direction. Sometimes the author seems a Surrealist, at other times a Constructivist:

> *small black verticals intersect slow black horizontals*
> *rain-shaped things intersect rain-shaped things*
> *squads of walls*
> *small black sad rectangles incessantly roaming*
> *hesitant diagonals*
> *finite straight lines intersecting . . .*

'Fragment III', a further poem with a Constructivist touch ('the plain's flat disc'), makes a swerve typical of Heissenbüttel, mutating into a gloss on art and politics:

> *The voice on the radio says*
> *FREEDOM IS AN IMPOSSIBLE THING.*
> *After that*
> *String Quartet No. 4 by Arnold Schoenberg.*

Even if Derek Mahon is more Mozartian than Schoenbergian in style, Heissenbüttel's lines remind one of Mahon's 'Morning Radio', in which the architecture of London's Broadcasting House ('the art-nouveau liner') suggests a *Titanic* and BBC Radio 3 resembles a ship's orchestra. Here is how Mahon's poem unfolds after its opening stanzas:

> *Seven o'clock —*
> *News-time, and the merciful*
> *Voice of Tom Crowe*
>
> *Explains with sorrow*
> *That the world we know*
> *Is coming to an end.*
>
> *Even as he speaks*
> *We can hear furniture*
> *Creak and slide on the decks.*
>
> *But first a brief recital*
> *Of resonant names —*
> *Mozart, Schubert, Brahms.*
>
> *The sun shines,*
> *And a new day begins*
> *To the strains of a horn concerto.*

The healing and restoring power of music strikes a chord common to both poems. The emphatic capitals in the Heissenbüttel raise a hectoring voice which the quartet subverts, bringing hope (however provisional) and freedom (however illusory). But whereas Derek Mahon's word-scepticism — evident especially in his early poems, one of which depicts a hermit who is driven 'despite my scepticism, almost to the point

Dennis O'Driscoll

of speech' — has led to only a single concrete poem, numerous Heissenbüttel poems shuffle their verbal packs in a manner resembling concrete poetry.

Empirical observation forms no part of Heissenbüttel's programme, although tenuous, even poignant, connections can be traced among the apparently disconnected memories which cluster and collide in the early pages of *Texts*:

> *All these sentences.*
> *The inventory of occasions.*
> *Don't forget.*
> *Jabber of gramophone records.*
> *The memory of sound tracks on reels put away.*

Elsewhere, pre-empting his more characteristic explorations of language itself, words are tested for their veracity and duplicity. Heissenbüttel, who fought in the German army until severely wounded in 1941, was assailed (like so many of his contemporaries) by fundamental doubts about the trustworthiness of language as a conduit of truths. He sets out individual phrases, as if in a school primer, contemplating the significance of each statement and its antithesis until a wall of silence looms ('I do not talk'):

> *I go straight ahead*
> *I do not go straight ahead*
> *I declare myself in agreement*
> *I declare myself not in agreement*
> *I tell the truth*
> *I do not tell the truth*
> *I recognize*
> *I disrecognize*
> *I assert*
> *I talk*
> *I do not talk.*

One of Heissenbüttel's prose texts, 'Talking with the Doctrinaire', alludes to the pressure (exerted by our conformist, pollster-influenced world) to adopt the correct opinion among a plethora of competing ones, each separated by a simple but crucial word or phrase. And, of course, one's view on the 'correct' opinion is itself a matter of opinion:

Do you consider that your attitude is right? Do you consider that you are right to take that attitude? Don't you consider that you should take a different attitude?

By the end of 'Talking With the Doctrinaire', the speaker is so 'wrapped up in meshes of opinion and proverbs' that he must abandon language altogether and 'signal my way on'. There are parallels here with the work of W S Graham, a poet who is greatly admired by Michael Hamburger:

Can you see my As and Ys semaphore
Against the afterglow of the slaughterhouse
Roof where I stand on the black ridge
Waving my flagging arms to speak?

W S Graham, persistently troubled by the slippery nature of language, can be said — like Heissenbüttel — to have anticipated some of the preoccupations of the French deconstructionists and the American L-A-N-G-U-A-G-E poets.

'What Is The Language Using Us For?', W S Graham asks in one of those later poems described by Michael Hamburger as making 'the most extraordinary use of "laboratory" experience — the poet's struggle with the material of his art, language — in a way that is never tediously methodical but engrossing, moving and alive'. Heissenbüttel's response to Graham's question is to let language have its head and see where it leads. 'The Future of Socialism' is among the most successful of such pieces, because it avoids the tedium inherent in deliberately repetitious texts (a fault from which Heissenbüttel, for all his impressive structural skill, is by no means exempt) and creates the exhilarating illusion that the political ironies — and, more importantly, the truths — of the poem are latent in the language rather than imposed on it, that the poem presents discoveries rather than declarations as it moves from utterances like 'no one owns anything / no one exploits / no one oppresses' to 'all own everything / all exploit all / all oppress all'.

Even more mordant is 'Final Solution', which obliquely but uncompromisingly adumbrates the casualness with which debased ideas can lead to evil actions. While not exculpating language (to 'hit on the idea' involves a linguistic process, after all), Heissenbüttel takes us beyond the slippery signifiers to the suffering flesh-and-blood objects of Nazi propaganda and the victims of the 'final solution':

> *so they hit on the idea that what one is against must be*
> *something one can see touch revile humiliate spit at lock*
> *up strike down annihilate because what one can't see*
> *touch revile humiliate spit at lock up strike down annihi-*
> *late one can only speak of and what one can only speak of*
> *can change and one never quite knows what it will turn*
> *into whatever one may say against it.*

The humour pervading 'Family Politics' — a travesty of Biblical genealogies — is of a different kind to the tongue-twisting, Gertrude Stein-like variations on the theme 'Persecutors persecute the persecuted' found in 'Political Grammar'. In the latter, a potential lapse of taste is averted by the serious sub-text which alerts the reader to the dangerous proximity in language of sense and nonsense, of truth and falsehood. 'Political Grammar' also touches on the disconcerting chasm 'Between the idea / And the reality', between the word 'persecution' and the experience of persecution.

For sheer pleasure, however, the Heissenbüttel text to which readers will return is 'The Water Painter', a fascinating portrait of one whose art was writ — or, rather, painted — on water and, therefore, a study of the ephemerality of art. It is a tribute to Hamburger's unshowy integrity as a translator that the multiplicity of ethical and philosophical quandaries raised by *Texts* translate into English and that the reader can sense the full breadth of Heissenbüttel's linguistic range, from the disturbing babble of voices in 'Germany 1944' — set out in a succession of neat rectangles like war graves — to the amusingly elliptical chatter of 'Bremen Whereyou'. As Hamburger remarks of Heissenbüttel, his 'many-sided work has been an exploration and a trying-out of the behaviour of the most diverse kind of language, from that of philosophy to that of propaganda and politics, from that of idiomatic usage to that of topographical description, Romantic poetry or sentimental fiction.'

Heissenbüttel's claim that he has 'nothing to say' is accurate if we expect a poem to be subjective, even autobiographical; the fact that his work is freed of ego leaves it free to express things other than the self, among them what Michael Hamburger has classified as 'possibilities of truth, inherent in language itself, rather than in the individual consciousness and sensibility that we expect to meet in the poems, short stories, novels and plays of writers less austerely, less rigorously, experimental.' This work can strike a cold, even evasive, note; yet it can just as readily convey a fresh and revelatory sense of language as subject and object (as subject-matter in its own right and as a physical entity). The most rewarding moments arise when the mesmeric repetitions of language yield insights well beyond the scope of more orthodox poetry and refreshingly at variance with the prevalent poetic norms. That many of those insights relate to the nature of language does not diminish their importance, language being (as Samuel Johnson observed) 'the dress of thought'.

Although some of his work bears an undoubted resemblance to concrete poetry, and he studied Architecture and History of Art, it nonetheless remains essentially verbal rather than visual. Lines of near-identical text may shimmer like op-art, but there are passages elsewhere that will recall the short prose of Beckett rather than the ideograms favoured in purer forms of concrete poetry:

> . . . *peat smell in July moorland concentration camp in July many white houses in the green swallows around the tower of clouds wind-motion in the sky Zschocke democraticus on a walking-tour to encounter a castle or a ruin is always an enrichment of the day's experience a hundred and eighty-one times.*

When considering Heissenbüttel's work in his critical studies, *The Truth of Poetry* and *After the Second Flood*, Michael Hamburger has discussed it alongside that of the Austrian poet, Ernst Jandl, whose output includes poems which are variously aural, visual or verbal, ranging from sound poems to 'lyrical poems of a non-experimental kind.' Twenty years after the publication of his Heissenbüttel translations, and having for decades drawn attention to 'the distinction' of Ernst Jandl's poetry, he finally assembled a Jandl collection (*Dingfest / Thingsure*, 1997). Like Heissenbüttel — who contributed an epilogue to his 1966 collection, *Laut and Luise* — Jandl is both fascinated by words and determined to outwit them. As writers, they are linked by an openness to the untried and a wariness towards language; it is because he shares both their openness and their wariness that Michael Hamburger translates these poets with empathy and conviction.

Dennis O'Driscoll

The shortcomings of language are explored in Hamburger's own poems ('Words? Yes, words. I can't do without them. / But I hate them as lovers hate them / When it's time for bodies to speak') and one senses his kinship not alone with poets like Heissenbüttel and Jandl but also with another poet with whom he is associated, Hans Magnus Enzensberger ('the moment / when the word *happy* / is pronounced / never is the moment of happiness'). The spirit animating both Ernest Jandl's 'nothing and something' and Hamburger's 'An Inspiration' is a similarly wry one:

'nothing and something'

nothing in my head
i sit down
at the typewriter
insert a sheet
with nothing on it

with something on it
i extract the sheet
from the typewriter
and read as a text
something out of my head

'An Inspiration'

This morning I thought that perhaps
Only the unpublished poem preserves its worth,
That to publish it is to cast it
Into a rubbish dump to decompose
Together with last week's murders and Football Pools,
Stock prices, social occasions and statements of policy.
The quirk convinced me. Quickly I typed it out
And to a well-known weekly despatched these lines.

Hamburger, in the introduction to *Dingfest / Thingsure*, accepts that there is some affinity between the Jandl poems of 'the straight kind' which he finds congenial and those barbed poems of his own which he classifies as 'unpleasantries' or 'owl's pellets'. What Hamburger aims at are 'very simple words, images, situations that are somehow transparent, so that the complexity remains under the surface'. But even the surface ripples in his work can form circlings and windings which are — fleetingly at least — comparable with the language-led patterns of a writer like Heissenbüttel. One thinks of his powerful poem, 'In a Cold Season' ('Words cannot reach him in his prison of words / Whose words killed men because those men were words'), or his 'Variations':

> *I move on, closer now to the end*
> *That is no end as long as*
> *One mountain remains, one lake,*
> *One river, one forest*
> *Yet to be named, possessed,*
> *Relinquished, forgotten, left*
> *For Earth to renew. Move on*
> *To no end but of 'I', 'you'*
> *And the linking words . . .*

In the beginning was the word. But it is silence which has the last word in the kind of poetry which Michael Hamburger writes and in much of what he translates. As both poet and translator, he has succeeded, over many decades, in placing the best silences in the best order.

Agenda (Autumn 1997)

Peter Reading: *'No-God and Species Decline Stuff'*

Very little of contemporary poetry has kept pace with contemporary life. The revelations of science, the disseminations of the media, the destruction of the natural environment — those features which lend our era its distinctive and often bitter tang — are so overpowering as to drive most poets into solipsistic retreat. Peter Sirr has written of 'the blind alleys of the English empirical mode', while in a rousing essay in *Cambridge Quarterly* Jerzy Jarniewicz associated contemporary British poetry with 'empiricism and regionalism, technical accomplishment and modesty of intention, traditionalism, and imaginative moderation'. Tony Harrison is the English poet most widely associated with an exploration of social conflict and social change. Peter Reading has won recognition more slowly than Harrison, although he is equally adept at converting the scrawls of graffiti vandals into poetry and at giving voice to those who fail the 'Received Pronunciation' test and whose speech is, as Harrison puts it, 'in the hands of the Receivers'.

When Andrew Motion and Blake Morrison published their *Penguin Book of Contemporary British Poetry* in 1982, Peter Reading already had five books to his name. When Dannie Abse's *Hutchinson Book of Post-War British Poets* appeared in 1989, Reading was prolific enough to have produced six further collections. In neither anthology is a line of Reading's to be found, and one doubts whether he will have cared much either way. Although he has been published by major houses and has enjoyed regular exposure in the *Times Literary Supplement* (the deputy editor of which, Alan Jenkins, is also editor of a selection of Reading's work), he is a natural outsider. He sneers at 'Grub St reviewing its own lame valedictory bunk', a charge also pressed in a double haiku:

In last week's press, X
reviewed Y: One of the best
poets now writing.

In this week's press, Y
reviews X: One of the best
poets writing now.

Reading's outsider status is not accounted for simply by the continuing ambivalence of some critics towards his work and the indifference of many others. Educationally, too, he is unusual in having had a background in visual art rather than literature; and for a brief but 'insufferable' period he was a lecturer at Liverpool College of Art. Painters like Jim Dine, Robert Rauschenberg and Jasper Johns were at the height of their influence during Reading's studenthood and he has linked his own 'magpie' tendencies — the use of 'found' material in particular — to their example. There are glancing references in his work to many painters, including Auerbach, Ingres, Bosch, Ensor, Botticelli and Picasso, as well as to a hapless art critic who 'don't know his Arp from his Albers'. In 'Ballad', the lovers, John and Joan, would

> *. . . talk through lunchtime*
> *(of Puvis de Chavannes,*
> *Erich Heckel, Karl Schmidt-Rottluff,*
> *Maurice Denis, Mondrian,*

> *Matthew Smith, Odilon Redon,*
> *Edvard Munch, Chaim Soutine,*
> *Emil Nolde) holding hands*
> *in the college canteen.*

At a time when poets are mainly supported — either as tenured professors or as temporary residents — by third-level institutions, Peter Reading's choice of occupation for much of his writing life accentuated his detachment. Employed by an animal feed mill in rural Shropshire, he laboured at 'mauling unwieldy sacks around a warehouse' and at blending food compounds. Later, he operated the mill's weighbridge, the source of 'a plentiful supply of ready-made *dramatis personae* — ghastly, funny or just plain bonkers — from which to draw'. Another attraction of the job — one which he identified as a 'useful and enjoyable literary resource' — was the 'continually mutable demotic of lorry drivers' ordinary banter'. Some of Reading's poems ('Parallel Texts', 'Pacepacker', 'Duologues') draw directly on his experiences at the feed mill; but everywhere in his work there is evidence of a life well-endowed with demotic badinage and its concomitant malapropisms. 'Parallel Texts' makes a direct comparison between colloquial colour and newspaper black-and-white, while 'Duologues' opens with a Shropshire 'Home Burial'.

Water and Waste, an Outposts pamphlet and Reading's first publication, appeared in 1970 when he was twenty-four. It was a remarkably mature gathering of poems, most of which were included in his first full-length collection, *For the Municipality's Elderly* (1974). In these early poems, his characteristic tones (wry, ominous, sardonic, elegiac) are already discernible, as are his pithy language, his rich vocabulary. Peter Reading is the kind of poet who likes to make ironic use of archaisms ('omnibus') and circumlocutions ('Cadaverous Thespian' for Ronald Reagan) and who is uninhibited about using technical words. The opening page of *Final Demands* (1988) refers to 'drip-fed' P_2O_5 which 'fails to restore dull cotyledons / Liquinured past revivification', while the scientific process depicted in 'Ex Lab' is all the more convincing for being expressed in scientific language:

> *Dilute acetic*
> *has exposed from the matrix*
> *(limestone, Jurassic),*
> *ischium and ilium*
> *and interlocking pubis.*
>
> *These demonstrate how*
> *ornithischian hip-joints*
> *differ from those of*
> *saurischians. These bits are*
> *believed* Scelidosaurus.

Reading is therefore not so much flaunting a vocabulary (though he does occasionally succumb to the autodidact's temptation to do so) as evoking a milieu. The palaeontological, medical and astronomical experts who inhabit his poems are fully-realized creations speaking a professional patois and not some simplified poetical version of it. Similarly, natural phenomena, especially birds (Reading is an experienced ornithologist), are very precisely delineated. Reading's world is large not only because of the largeness of his linguistic resources (as Randall Jarrell said of Wallace Stevens) but because he knows — or is prepared to learn — more about the world than most poets.

What alerts the reader above all else to the presence of a unique talent is an uncompromising ferocity, an eschatological vision, an intensity and passion, of a kind rarely encountered in poetry. For many poets and readers of poetry, the primary function of the art is to celebrate. For Reading, it is a struggle to keep faith with poetry at all in an age when '*H. sap.*' is doomed and there is 'no posterity to write for'. But he persists in the Beckettian spirit of his own tellingly-named character, Viv ('have to get on with it just GOING ON is / all we can do in the present situation'). If the future 'has no future', there is not much point in fretting over the sensibilities of those who wish poetry to be relaxing and soporific 'like Ovaltine'. In his *Poetry Review* interview, Reading observed that 'art has always struck me most when it was to do with coping with things, often hard things, things that are difficult to take'. *Water and Waste* makes reference to the 'throw-away society', a 'gathering maelstrom', 'general annihilation' and responds negatively to the question 'Will there be any tangible thing to remember us by?' The final image in *For the Municipality's Elderly* is of a corrupted Eden: 'Livid fur smothers an Old Testament, / big black dormant flies tremble in Genesis'. Ten years later, facing a volley of predictable barbs, Reading defended himself in *Ukulele Music*:

> '*Life is too black as he paints it*' *and* '*Reading's nastiness sometimes*
> *seems a bit over the top*' *thinks a review — so does* he.
>
> *Too black and over the top, though, is what the Actual often happens to be, I'm afraid. He don't invent it, you know.*

The darkness which pervades *Water and Waste* (lightened by brio and wit rather than compromise) is that of a poet concerned about environmental issues long before it became fashionable. Allied to this concern is a hostility towards most nature poetry, which he finds sentimental and downright dishonest. He has denounced anthropomorphism; an untitled poem in *Diplopic* reads:

Phoney-rustic bards,
spare us your thoughts about birds,
butterflies, fish, snakes
and mammals (including us)
— biologists write more sense.
Down the lab they think
these crows, peasants, pikes, eels, swifts
are twee, ill-observed.

Bumpkins, from whose bums
you consider the sun shines,
think you're townee twits.
Like that haiku frog,
unscientific fauna
is a bore in verse.

When Reading himself finds the charms of nature irresistible, he reacts with a self-consciousness verging on embarrassment, as though he were falling into a Parnassian trap and allowing himself to be distracted from some deeper and harder truth. Again, this attitude had already established itself in 'Raspberrying' in his apprentice pamphlet:

Last sun ripens each one, through rubicund, black
then each rots. Lines are tight with late swallows,
oak rattles leaves icicle-brittle . . .

A bit neo-pastoral, one will admit,
but then something conspiring to make decay more
than the usual end of a season makes Nature
itself as anachronistic today
as a poem about it.

Yet one feels almost justified still to acknowledge
the deeper reflection of, albeit hackneyed,
the Human Condition in Nature (reduced
as she is from the nympho once over-extolled
for ad-nauseam cyclic fecundity, to
today's stripped-bare and thorny old sod half-heartedly
whorily pouting a couple of blackening nipples).

Reading's wariness concerning readymade or inflated emotions towards nature has led him to respond with a blend of helpless celebration and sceptical asides. The effect, though, is to convey the fragile sense of beauty or celebration all the more convincingly for having overwhelmed his doubts. Sometimes the celebration is wholehearted, as when honeysuckle and hay are allowed to mingle freely. More typically, he will accept with 'impotent gratitude' what 'tweely' patronizing bards have demeaned in verse. A punctuated idyll is offered as a sop to those who ask 'Doesn't he ever write about *happiness?*' His suspicion that he may be surrendering to 'mawkish platitudes' gives way to some ravishing lines:

> *Most savoured plump pork pie ever picnicked-on,*
> *gleaming, the glazed baked crust, like a varnished Strad;*
>   *relish of Meaux tang, crunch-grained; brittle,*
> *peppery, fluted columns of celery;*
>   *hot earthy radishes; crisp frilled lettuce;*
> *bottles of Bass, beck-cold, effervescent gold,*
>   *yeasty the foam. Plush cushions of whinberry,*
> *sheep-nibbled, silver-lichened, deep-pillow us . . .*

> *Paean to celebrate this: [pastoral, cliché, old hat —*
> *blush at the schmaltzy word] Love [but today it*
>   *is, though, it is this].*

If Reading's intermittent exultations provide reassurance that he is not blind to the wonders of the world, his work as a whole presents views of the world which we might prefer not to see ('Carrying on as though nothing is wrong is / what we are good at'). He is a remarkably direct writer, defying the assumption that a poet must keep at a distance — whether symbolic, metaphorical or otherwise — from his subject-matter. The idea of a 'balanced' outlook is not one to which Reading aspires; whether he adopts a persona or not, the reader is left in no doubt as to where the poet stands. He sets out to paint the world exactly as he sees it, to bring it into focus rather than to transform or transcend it. Some of the hostility engendered by his work is simply a result of the queasiness readers feel when confronted by evidence — as conclusive as it is repulsive — of the destructiveness and degradation of our species.

The bleakness of the early poems is mild compared with what will be found in C (1984) and *Perduta Gente* (1989) and the sporadically brilliant, but less consistent, *Ukulele Music* (1985). *Ukulele Music* (especially 'Going On', its second section) is notable for the way in which Reading holds *The Mirror* up to art ('this is the Mirror and not my*self*'), converting tabloid journalism into poetry, reflecting on the grim reality underlying the stories of violence and cruelty: 'hang on this isn't just *news*'. The volume's slide show of horrors ('Few atrocities / of which H. sap. *can conceive / remain unfulfilled*') includes displays of police intimidation, child abuse, castration, South African injustice, guerrilla warfare, murder and rape, muggings, slashings and mere spittings. No wonder Eliot's 'human kind / Cannot bear very much reality' (quoted by Reading in *5x5x5x5x5*) is recast as 'real kind cannot spare / very much humanity' in the collection, *Tom o'Bedlam's Beauties* (1981).

Despite his prodigious skills, Reading does not always save his characters from inhumanity of a different kind — the descent into caricature. *Diplopic* (1983), for example, opens with four skinheads — 'Three of the four are cross-eyed, all are acned'. Then we encounter a Scottish woman, all 'Hoots' and 'Toots' and 'mon' whose daughter, having run away with an African student, ends up in a cooking pot. While Reading knows how to be grim without needing to be solemn — his wit often matches his despair — his comic writing is at its least effective when it operates at comic book level. Viv in *Ukulele Music* is the source of the book's funniest moments. Yet her misspelt letters with their amusing malapropisms ('reprimanded in custardy', 'pry ministers') leave us not only with the sense that she is a caricature (that much seems intentional) but that the reader is encouraged to feel a degree of superiority towards this unlettered charlady.

Ukulele Music is merciless in its presentation of a world so absurd and so beleaguered that the shaping of words into a poem is a form of playing the ukulele while the world burns:

> *Meanwhile, I've gotten the* 5-Minute Uke Course
> *(Guaranteed Foolproof)* —
> *plinkplinka plinkplinka plonk plinkplinka plinkplinka*
> *plonk.*

Characteristically, the strains of Reading's ukulele music reverberate throughout the book. Viv condemns inner-city 'LUTE-ing'. Her husband damages a barometer by 'playing it just as a banjo . . . singing the George Formby Song', so that it now points permanently to 'Stormy'. The song about playing 'his Youker-laylie as the Ship Went down' heralds a series of voyage poems, saltily narrated but full of disasters. In one, a boat passes close to Bikini (the nuclear threat is among the book's leitmotifs), while another ends with an attempt at some musical diversion:

> *Thro the long night some sang,*
> *attempting to keep up spirits.*
> *Merciful Providence*
> *preserving some measure of wine*
> *and rum from the hold, the mate*
> *contrived then to engineer*
> *a musical instrument*
> *on which he made bold to play.*

By the close of the *Ukulele Music* sequence, Reading's virtuosity has arranged the dissonant notes of the book into a polyphonic shanty:

> *falling barometer, send down the skysail yard from aloft, sir,*
> *strum with felt pick back and forth, lightly across all four*
> *strings,*
>
> *all sail should be doubled-gasketted, stow the mainsail*
> *and crossjack,*
> *make yr pentameters taut . . .*

Ukulele Music is not all plain sailing — there are too many of the voyage poems and (on grounds of tedium, not taste) I would have preferred fewer of the tabloid pieces. Nonetheless, it is a powerful work and Reading's shock therapy is generally success-ful, pummelling hardened sensibilities until sight and feeling are restored. One is reminded of Stephen Vizinczey's assertion:

> *We cannot understand anything profoundly unless it*
> *moves or shocks us so deeply that it touches our subcon-*
> *scious; great writers are not those who tell us we shouldn't*
> *play with fire, but those who make our fingers burn.*

As the most casual acquaintance with his work will reveal, Reading does not concern himself with good taste. 'Almanac' (which reads rather like a black parody of George Mackay

Dennis O'Driscoll

Brown's cyclical poems) equates Christmas with 'surfeit of calories, / cards bought for Spastics, nuts'. The 'Going On' section of *Ukulele Music* invokes the Muse to 'Sing the Rasta. who stabbed out a / baby's eye with a Biro'. A visit to the zoo raises the charming spectre of 'a *Cercopithecus* wanking / and a baboon (with its thumb stuck up its arse) to revile'. . . It is salutary when reading his poems to recall John Updike's remarks on the subject of taste:

> *I think 'taste' is a social concept and not an artistic one. I'm willing to show good taste, if I can, in somebody else's living room, but our reading life is too short for a writer to be in any way polite. Since his words enter into another's brain in silence and intimacy, he should be as honest and explicit as we are with ourselves.*

Even when his raw material is at its most raw, Reading's finished work is fastidiously constructed. He is certainly not to be found in the ranks of those who, in Piotr Kuhivchak's words, 'give primacy to experience (and) forget that literature is a form, through which the experience may be mediated well or badly'. An ingenious technician, his range extends well beyond the predictable iambic quatrains of today's so-called 'formalists'. He is proud of his prowess in this area and will sometimes announce from his flight-deck which metre we are being piloted through. Having sung the Rasta, in the poem already quoted, he leaves technical instructions for the Muse:

> *[Halve the hexameter after three*
> *dactyls, making it 2 lines;*
> *   halve the pentameter thus —*
> *   this way it fits on the page.]*

Later in 'Going-On', when the mood turns celebratory for a moment, a prosodic gear-change is called for:

> *[This isn't elegy but*
> *   thanksgiving; therefore invert —*
> *place the pentameter first and the*
> *   hymn/hexameter after.]*

The essential concern of the poem 'Ex Lab' may be to set contemporary life in a geological time-frame; yet there is time also to draw attention to the fact that it is made up of tankas. Ultimately, prosodist and palaeontologist speak along similar lines:

> *What one enjoys most*
> *is the manipulation*
> *of these hapless things*
> *at such impartial distance*
> *to fit an imposed order.*

Reading's introduction to *Diplopic* (the volume in which 'Ex Lab' appears) for the Poetry Book Society places particular emphasis on form:

> . . . *every second view of a subject is ordered into a sonnet or sonnet-variant* . . . *As well as Elizabethans and Petrarchans there are blank pentameter 14-liners, dispersed couplet sonnets, a quasi-Meredithian (i.e. 16-liner), a 12-syllabled but 5-stressed 14-liner* . . . *Most of the stuff is formally ordered: there are blank iambics, there are trochaics, there is my own invention, a hypertanka (where the 5/7/5/7/7 formula extends to numbers of tanka stanzas per section of a five-section sequence), there is something not Sapphics proper but meant to recall them* . . .

Apart from his versatile handling of the sonnet, Reading is a seasoned practitioner of syllabic verse. An early poem, '10x10x10', is structured in ten ten-line stanzas, each line containing ten syllables. This cubist poem gives its hero the last say:

> *'One might as well invent any kind of*
> *structure (ten stanzas each of ten lines each*
> *of ten syllables might be a good one),*
> *the subject matter could be anything.'*

The idea that any fuel may fire poetry is vindicated by Reading's own achievements. So distinctive is his use of language and so abundant his technical skills that no topic can defeat his ingenuity — high-rise holiday accommodation, a nose-picking clerk, supermarket trollies in a canal, 'Reps and execs in *Plastics* and *Packaging*'.

The poem '10x10x10' and, more especially, the sequence '5' in

Dennis O'Driscoll

Fiction (1979) are the forerunners of *5x5x5x5x5* (1983) which (as its prefatory note states) 'consists of 5 sections, each section of 5 units, each unit 5 stanzas, each stanza 5 lines, each line 5 syllables'. Once Reading has made a mould, anything he pours into it will set. *5x5x5x5x5* includes a section which looks back to the conversation piece, 'Trio', in *The Prison Cell & Barrel Mystery* (1976). Both sequences recall the novel, *House Mother Normal*, by B S Johnson, another notable British innovator and experimenter. Reading's challenge in *C* was to produce '100 100-word units' relating to terminal illness. Even here — with his subjects, as it were, dying around him — he tests out various forms for resistance: a '13-line sonnet for unlucky people'; a 'bloody haiku'; an acrostic forming 'carcinomatophobia'; 'two last Spenserians'; catalectic tetrameters for a mastectomy; a hospital plan in verse . . .

Other manifestations of Reading's resourcefulness occur in his 'found' poems, his invented poets (the witty and pithy Sanraku Koshu and the ironic and erotic Kokur Niznegorsky) and his pseudo-poets (Victorian versifiers and successful entrants to *Comfy Home's* 'Poem of the Week' slot). If he has not yet made poetry from the telephone directory, he has at any rate proved his ability to draw on crossword puzzle clues and wedding-gift lists for inspiration.

Unity of theme and cross-references between characters or events bring to Reading's work something of the dimensions of the novel. As he told *Poetry Review*, 'The concision of poetry appeals to me, but the novelist's job — big-scale serious tacklings of things, as in Dickens or Smollett — is something I try in a smaller way to get into what I do.' The earliest collections share a certain unity of tone and attitude, while later volumes like *C* and *Perduta Gente* are far more consistent in subject-matter. Mistimed love and mismatched lovers recur in *The Prison Cell & Barrel Mystery:* 'fell in love / each with the other quite genuinely / — but not, regrettably, concurrently'. The spirit of Browning's 'Never the time and the place / And the loved one all together' trails a number of the poems; others yield to romantic sentiments without any of his customary protestations:

> *I have worn this jacket a decade; its first*
> *night out you deposited a dark copper*
> *hair on the shoulder which I kept*
> *in a page of La Vita Nuova where*
> *it still is . . .*

A couple of poems in *Nothing for Anyone* (1977) — the best of Reading's early books — continue to probe love and its ironies ('I have fallen in love with you / without falling out of love with my wife'). Neither this book nor its clever but less convincing successor, *Fiction*, attains the thematic unity which is in evidence from *Tom o'Bedlam's Beauties* onwards. Reading's own introduction to the latter begins:

> Tom o'Bedlam's Beauties *features lunacy. There is material about bona fide Bin-endorsed idiots as well as the more day to day mad (presidents, meths-drinkers, the Welsh). Those items not directly about insanity do imply some backdrop of irrationality . . . and those touching on the Major Issue or the Amorous fall by definition within the compass of the central theme.*

The pressure to corral Gavin Ewart (as a paragon of sanity), or people who are madly in love, into one volume which 'features lunacy' leads to strain. The quality of the poems, like their thematic pertinence, is variable and nowhere does one sense between the poet and the mentally ill an empathy of the kind that exists between him and the physically ill in *C*. Using nothing more than lists for comparison, we find that 'The Euphemisms' for madness in *Tom o'Bedlam's Beauties* ('Crackers, Potty, Loony, Bonkers, / Nutty, Screwy, Ga-Ga, Dull . . .') merely add jollity to the work, whereas the gradations of pain listed in *C* ('Flickering, Quivering, Pulsing, Throbbing, Beating, Pounding, Jumping, Flashing . . .') are appropriately piercing. In general, the density of Reading's first published poems, absent from much of *Fiction*, *Tom o'Bedlam's Beauties* and *Diplopic*, is recovered and excelled in many later books.

The double vision alluded to in *Diplopic* is not so much a disease as a double-take; each subject or character in the book is treated from two angles and in two forms. A double-take which is of singular relevance to Reading's own art is that between the poems 'War Artistes' and 'Mnemonics'. Thomas Gibb (an ancestor of the skinhead, Gibbo, elsewhere in the book) diagnoses the diplopia of the war artist by reference to the fact that 'he SEES things different to us'. Gibb's epigraph is followed by lines written from the viewpoint of the 'war artistes' themselves:

> *We are always out there*

Dennis O'Driscoll

> *with pencils raised,*
> *treacherous bastards,*
> *Double Agents*
> *not working for you*
> *but for some Secret Power.*

'Mnemonics', the companion poem, focuses on the unsentimental (easily mistaken for unfeeling) attention to technique which is the *sine qua non* of art. Like Reading in poetry, the artist masters the unflinching stare ('whitish-tallows and wax-yellows / and algal-greens of military flesh'). Graham Greene's remark that 'There is a splinter of ice in the heart of a writer' receives knowing acknowledgement as the poet ponders how best 'to dispatch' one of his characters. Reading, according to Robert Crawford, is concerned not 'with pity but with style and accuracy' — whereas the overwhelming evidence of his work shows that he concerns himself with all three.

It is 'Ex Lab', the palaeontological poem already mentioned, which is the most far-seeing poem in *Diplopic*. Fundamental questions about God, life and extinction are aired in a convincingly offhand way as he finds sermons in fossilized stones:

> *On this diagram,*
> *the Holocene or Recent*
> *(last ten thousand years)*
> *is far, far, far, far too small*
> *to register on this scale.*

The entertaining and dramatic *5x5x5x5x5*, an interim collection (though interims are notoriously brief in Reading's case), opens under the 'morose' gaze of the palaeontologist who scrutinizes the specimens 'swilling at the bar':

> *Working, as I do,*
> *with Precambrian*
> *specimens aged six*
> *hundred million years*
> *sires irreverence*
> *for the Holocene.*

5x5x5x5x5, a collaboration with the painter, David Butler, finds Reading at his most ludic. As a result of authorial intervention,

one of its cast is restored to life with a change of nationality.
There is a feebleness to the palaeontologist's cries that 'the Holocene is of scant importance' as he dies of cancer in C: 'I am dying (Carcinoma ventriculi) but what is 40 years here or there on the chronostratigraph?' He tries to insist that 'None of it *matters* (except at a purely personal level)' and what C ultimately does is to harrowingly convey a personal — rather than clinical — sense of terminal illness. C combines the intensity of the early poems with the inventiveness of Reading's subsequent work to produce not only his best book but — appropriately — one of the best poetry volumes of the last 100 years. 'C' is, of course, the Roman numeral for 100 and — as already stated — the book is made up of 100 100-word units, 'one unit per day for 100 final days'. C3, as we are reminded by one of Reading's patients (apparently the one called C, 'for reasons of delicacy'), denotes the lowest grade of physical fitness.

With further alphabetical consistency, the cancer to which Reading brings specialist attention is that affecting the colon. He takes us rather deeper than J B S Haldane's jaunty ruminations on the subject (found in Philip Larkin's *Oxford Book of Twentieth Century English Verse*):

> *My rectum is a serious loss to me,*
> *But I've a very neat colostomy,*
> *And hope, as soon as I am able,*
> *To make it keep a fixed time-table . . .*

Haldane's conclusion that 'Cancer can be rather fun' provided 'one confronts the tumour / With a sufficient sense of humour' would cut no ice in Reading's ward, where the inmates are beyond hope, beyond cure and certainly 'beyond verse'. But although their condition is beyond a joke, they are able to muster occasional outbursts of black humour:

> *It is a most terrible bore*
> *to haemorrhage, spewing-up gore,*
> *and, bubbling for breath,*
> *be blood-drowned to death.*
> *Je ne voudrais pas être mort.*

The 'big C' has never loomed so large in literature as it does in this comfortless book. From the beginning, we know to what end we are being led. On the very first page is a pub 'used by ferry-men and travellers calling for a quick drink before crossing'. The place takes on a chilling air when we learn that it is frequented by a man who likes to be known as 'Char' (pronounced 'care') or 'Mort' and whose palm is 'constantly grey from receiving pennies'. Reading packs everything imaginable on board for the Stygian journey: bed pans, large diapers, analgesics, suppositories, concentrated disinfectant, absorbent pyjamas. *C* is as attentive to the degrading peripheries of illness as to its painful centre. The special laundry services required for soiled sheets, the anxious 'unfortunates' checking their maladies in medical dictionaries, the hospital radio that blasts out nothing but BBC Radio 2, all receive due notice. Reading wrings every drop of blood and sweat and puke and shit out of experiences which we still prefer to sanitize with euphemisms. Although 'mental ease demands lies', he is determined to confront the truth rather than produce decorous poetry in the name of life-enhancement. He knows how blank a verse is in the face of terminal illness and how little a well-placed colon means to those sentenced to cancer of the colon.

C is interspersed with asides concerning the relevance of poetry to suffering. No metric, it is contended, is vindicable for 'snot, gore, filth, suppuration of the arse-gut'. Instead, most of the volume is set out as prose: 'Verse is for healthy / arty-farties. The dying / and surgeons use prose.' With this blunt style, he probes the innermost minds and bodies of patients, the responses of families and hospital staff and the commentaries of medical books and journals. Art is unmasked in the intensive-care unit, one aesthete asking 'Where is the European cultural significance of tubes stuck up the nose, into the veins, up the arse?'

As Reading brings the sick to life (and death), he articulates their fantasies and delusions. A man convinces himself that life in his bleak, litter-ridden city is coming to an end and that he is not dying alone: 'In Furnishings, Glassware, Heel-Bar, Carpeting . . . something irrevocably dying is happening.' Counterpoint of tone and juxtaposition of image are features of *C*. A bird's mute resignation before death is set against a human's regimen of drugs and artificial saliva. A beautifully-evoked breakfast on 'sun-dappled gingham' is contrasted with a patient's 'dusty handful' of compulsory bran. Even more suggestive is the placing of a specialist's pulse-taking hands alongside those of a gypsy 'affectionately' snapping a rabbit's neck.

In the end, delusions peel away like skin:

> *Suddenly, alas, the subtle grafting of a cdcdee Spenserian*
> *sestet onto an abbaabba Petrarchan octave does not*
> *matter. Vita b.; ars b. Nor does the Precambrian sub-*
> *division* Longmyndian, *ca. 600 million yrs. old, nor*
> *Holocene H.* sap *with terminal &c., nor the* conception
> *of its not mattering, nor*

The last words are: 'My wife patiently washes my faece-besmirched pyjamas, for *prosaic* love'. Never has the word 'love' had such a difficult passage and never has it earned its place in literature so convincingly.

C might well have represented Reading's own last word in poetry but, while continuing to stand as his supreme achievement, it was followed in rapid succession by four full-length books: *Ukulele Music, Stet, Final Demands* and *Perduta Gente. Final Demands*, the weakest of the four, shares some images and allusions with *C.* A child undergoing chemotherapy represents horror in the former, while (as in the latter) a blissful picnic is the touchstone for happiness. In both books there is a fantasy of curling up among Homeric leaves (leaves, incidentally, take on a variety of hues in *Final Demands*):

> *Crapulous death-fright at 3 in the morning,*
> *grim fantasizing . . .*
> *Morphean, painless, idyllic expiry, easeful, Sabaean . . .*
> *duvet and pillow-case metamorphose to sweet-smelling*
> *sered leaves,*
> *thick-fallen under two olive boles grafted, canopied tightly,*
> *such as the storm-wrecked Laertides, life-wracked,*
> *sunk in exhausted*
> *snug at the end of Book V . . .*

As those lines indicate, *Final Demands* is not without impressive writing, especially when Reading is giving personal vulnerabilities their head — the book is very much connected with his arrival at middle-age:

> *[Mostly it's other people's death sentences*
> *one has adopted, striking an attitude;*
> *suddenly, though . . .] Among a mess of*

> *skeleton, puckered skin, part-consumed flesh,*
>
> *I tug a bifurcate bone with my daughter, win, and, in*
> *secret,*
> > *wish* When I rattle my clack, may she not too
> > deeply grieve.

The death-rattle with which the book closes is that of 'barbs in a brown plastic phial'. For once, though, a Reading volume is less than the sum of its parts, because what should be vital parts (the letters and extract from a novel) seem like padding. Eric Korn, in a *TLS* review, claimed to have fostered the book by presenting Reading with a 'sheaf of Victorian family letters'. But neither the Victorian letters, nor the wartime ones addressed to Major Fashpoint-Shellingem (formerly of *Tom o'Bedlam's Beauties*) can keep us interested in the Bancroft or unsubtly-named Hurt families.

Stet (1986), like *Final Demands*, is often at its best in its personal moments — unegotistical self-portraits, snapshots from family albums, glimpses from childhood as England is losing a grip on empire. It is one of Reading's strengths that he can be personal, even confessional, without seeming trivial. The nearest he comes to confessionalism is probably the 'Trio' sequence of *The Prison Cell & Barrel Mystery* and there are blunt poems of unmistakable warmth scattered throughout his books — tributes to parents ('Post-Dated'), wife ('Sonnet'), a former teacher ('Otto Van Bumph') and, in *Stet* itself, to a bird-watching friend. There is a particularly candid poem, 'Thanksgiving', addressed to his sister-in-law who 'patiently suffered my sotted / No-God and Species Decline stuff, / and charmed me . . . entirely'.

Besides autobiographical poems, *Stet* — published two years before *Final Demands* — contains accounts of human suffering (accidentally or intentionally inflicted), ironic allusions to printing parlance licensed by the book's title ('change damaged character(s), strike out error'), some hilariously incoherent bar-room philosophy and some philosophy of a starker kind:

> *Simple complexity, dying, euphoria, nastiness, good fun —*
> *perfectly straightforward, no need to seek for variants of the*
> *theisms sired by the earliest hominid terrified shamans*
> *(cowardly greedy-weak graspings at seedy, trite consolations)* . . .

Compared with his other middle and late collections, *Stet* is a book without an agenda, except perhaps to coax a response to his further injunction — 'Muse! sing the Grotty [scant alternative]'. His prayer is never more effectively answered than in his evocation of a British Rail buffet carriage, in a poem which sinks to its occasion with perfection and obliquely signals its affection for Philip Larkin's 'The Whitsun Weddings':

> *They're queuing up to be insulted by*
> *a truculent steward who administers*
> *flabby cool BR toast at wondrous cost*
> *and steaming tea in polystyrene cups*
> *capped with thin leaky plastic lids — the car*
> *oscillates and an old unfortunate*
> *is scalded by spilt pekoe and then hurled*
> *onto the carriage floor, striking her head*
> *hard on an angle of formica counter.*
> *A cooling tower, scrap cars bashed into cubes,*
> *a preternaturally mauve canal . . .*

Perduta Gente is a book as unrelieved in its bleakness as C. Confronted with 'indescribable squalor', Reading describes his cardboard characters ('huddle of papers and rags in a cardboard / spin-drier carton'). Rather than '*not speak of them, merely observe and / silently pass by*', Reading slows down to watch a group of 'expendables' as they scoop up discarded ice-cream with 'black half-mooned fingers' in December. And he will not allow us to shrug off the Dantesque visions to which we are led 'through urinous subways':

> *And don't think it couldn't be* you:
> *grievously wounded veteran of the*
> > *Battle of Bottle,*
> *jobless, bereft of home, skint . . .*

Reading, whose poems evince a connoisseurship of wines ('fumous, a single-vintage Madeira / buttery caramel fatty, the cobwebbed bottle of Bual'), not only turns to the world — or underworld — where the dregs of humanity, the 'wino-unworthies', congregate but, consistent with his own admonition that nobody is invulnerable, imagines his alter ego in a state of 'inebriate degeneracy'. Alongside mimetic utterances ('gizzera quiddora fiftyfer fuggsay'), *Perduta Gente* creates a collage from manuscript pages of a diary, typed official documents relating to radioactivity, and newspaper cuttings ('apartments . . . £330,000 to £865,000'). With this volume, over which the ghost of Kurt Schwitters hovers, Peter Reading returns to the realm of visual art. Despite some over-the-top ironies ('dosser with Top Man carrier-bag, en- / swathed in an *FT*'), *Perduta Gente* is a grave book, a haunting dirge for the dispossessed which widens into a consideration of the 'democracy' of danger in which the nuclear threat engulfs everyone, from the 'Palace twerp' and 'propertied yuppie' to beneficiaries of tea and lice-ridden clothes in a church crypt ('feels like a / fallout-shelter'). The book is indignant, compassionate and, like much of Reading's output, deeply moral.

'But am I art?', Reading asks as the punchline of a combative poem which summarizes the contrasting reactions of reviewers to his poetry. Such questions no doubt continue to be prompted by the starkness of his verse, by the fact that a poetry of tabloid news stories or of 'found' and overheard fragments has not been sanctioned by tradition. Reading is a maverick, a poet who has explored facets of the high and low and the tensions between them: between 'the demotic and the formal in poetry', between humorous writing and serious subject-matter, between the metrics of Langland and those of the limerick, between representatives of humanity itself: 'Oafs at Blackpool, / remember, are the same species / as, say, Catullus or Eliot'.

In his effort to become art, Peter Reading could not have hoped to succeed without an exceptionally indulgent publisher. Anthony Thwaite's crucial support at Secker & Warburg led to Reading's unconventional and typographically-demanding books being published with the unusual frequency which his talents demanded. Although sometimes the books seemed to be published *too* frequently for their own good, not one is without merit and the best are undoubtedly among the best poetry of the age. If the future *does* have a future, our present time will remain preserved in Peter Reading's unvarnished verse.

In Black and Gold, edited by C C Barfoot (Rodopi 1994)

PART FIVE

Europa (North and East)

In Other Words: *Poetry in Translation*

Our poetry comes in dozens of languages — all of them English. Over the centuries, translations have tumbled from the printing presses like bricks from the Tower of Babel. Traditionally, translation has been the by-product of a classical education; Greek and Latin masterpieces were rendered into English, a practice kept alive today by C H Sisson, David Ferry, Fleur Adcock and Tony Harrison among others. And there has, of course, been the eternal presence of The Bible with its Psalms, its Song of Songs, its Books of Job and Ecclesiastes. The translators of the Authorised Version set the standard for immortal literature as well as immortal life. Not surprisingly, many of the best translations have resulted from a deep affinity between the translator and the original work. Wyatt, in his sonnet, 'Whoso list to hunt', adapts Petrarch to his personal needs. The deer in the poem is probably Anne Boleyn and Caesar is Henry VIII. The result is not unlike one of those East European poems in which Stalin or the Communist Party appears in classical disguise — according to Jerzy Jarniewicz, 'putting on a historical costume was one of the safest ways to speak critically about [the] contemporary situation: ancient Greece and Rome proved especially helpful in the writers' efforts to smuggle a critical thought without being banned'. Throughout post-war East Europe, the 'myth-kitty' (as Philip Larkin called it) continued to contain hard currency and to enjoy a high conversion rate on the black market of unofficial literature.

Translation is not just a matter of switching the words from language to language. It involves a degree of creativity comparable with original composition. The skilled translator of poetry, an *interpreter* in a far more literal sense than the official who stalks travelling Presidents and shadows EU summiteers, is not the 'taxidermist' scorned by Robert Lowell but rather a gifted surgeon who transplants the beating heart of the poem from one language to another. On the question of interpretation, Michael Hamburger has written:

> *Translation, as I understand it, is much closer to a*
> *transcription, re-arrangement or re-scoring of another*
> *composer's work, such as Bach's of works by Vivaldi.*
> *However free, such transcriptions remain interpretations*
> *of the work transcribed, and the liberties taken serve to*
> *carry it over into another convention, another age, not to*
> *break it up and appropriate some promising part.*

My own musical analogy is between the translator and the conductor. There is no definitive version of a translated poem any more than there is a definitive performance of a Haydn mass or a Bruckner symphony. Every accomplished orchestral conductor who undertakes a particular score will deepen one's understanding of the original impulse behind the music.

Instead of a multiplicity of versions of great classical poets, as in the past, the typical output now is of single volumes — many of them manifestly flat — of contemporary poets. In no previous age has the poetry of distant contemporaries been so widely known — and, indeed, the more distant the better known. Quite marginal poets in English can reel off a list of the languages into which they have been translated; and the most minor Paraguayan poets may count on their poems being rendered into Iowan English before their word processors have had time to cool.

Why *is* so much poetry in translation now available? One obvious answer takes the form of free verse. The fact that a preponderance of poetry is written without the intricacies of rhyme and metre makes translation seem less intimidating. The stark simplicity of much East European poetry, with its post-war suspicion of rhetoric and ornament, has proved especially amenable. Whatever is inevitably lost in translation, far more is to be gained from reading Feinstein's Tsvetaeva or Reid's Neruda or Hamburger's Celan than from wasting time on mediocre and imitative talents in our own language. And translation represents the only way in which verse written in minority languages — whether Irish or Finnish or Macedonian — can breach the linguistic barrier and reach a wider audience.

Reservations, however, remain. There is, for one, the pernicious influence which the neutral language of translation can have on poetry in English. The English language, already homogenized through media-speak, needs invigoration not standardization. Translations extend our awareness of what can be achieved within the bounds of poetry; but we need to be in the hands of a very adroit translator (and they are as rare as very good poets) to find ourselves viewing more than a watery midwinter shadow of the original. Among other doubts about translation, the most heretical is to wonder whether it can be meaningfully done at all. John Weightman writes of translators as if they were engaged in some kind of reverse alchemy, turning gold into dross:

> *It is one of the bitter truths of life that all poetry, whether great or less great, is untranslatable. Whereas music is universal, each good poem is ultimately shut off inside its particular language, and there is no way of appreciating its unique effect apart from knowing that language, and knowing it well.*
>
> *Of course, people will go on denying this truth, because it is so unpalatable. They will organise international poetry readings, which depend entirely on translations, and are largely non-events. Or they will spend years trying to put Baudelaire's poems into English or Shakespeare's sonnets into French, although the result is always failure as translation, even if it has some value as original creation in the second language. The scientific, linguistic fact is plain: given the irreconcilable differences between languages as regards the feel of words in the mouth and their multiple echoes in the brain, it is impossible exactly to reproduce, in another linguistic system, that strange satisfaction of the lip-muscles, the spinal chord and the diaphragm which is the test of the true poem in its native idiom.*

Weightman's attitude is an uncompromising one but it sounds a useful note of caution, nonetheless; a warning glued to the glass partition between the reader and the original text — glass which some believe to be transparent and clear but which others (Weightman included) view as smoky, shaded and opaque. Yet certain poets *do* survive translation convincingly. Miroslav Holub (himself fluent in English) was convinced that his poems worked just as well in British and American translation as in Czech, while Francis Jones's translations of Ivan Lalić were described by the poet as 'carbon copies' of his originals.

A further source of doubt for readers of poetry in translation concerns the extent to which plausible critical judgements about the work can take place. A tame or awkward poem in translation is apt to be excused on the basis that the shortcoming must lie with the translator, with his or her failure to capture the rhythm or tone of the original. As Peter Porter put it: 'It is very hard to translate poetry well. The communication is bedevilled by good will, by the desire of the reader to take the intention for the performance.' To which one can add the equal and opposite possibility — namely that the translator, especially if he or she is a good poet, may actually have improved the poem, glossed over its flaws. We may mistake the translator's talent for the author's.

What set me thinking about the problems — as well as the pleasures — presented by poetry in translation was the appearance from Penguin Books of an anthology of East European poets born after 1940. Entitled *Child of Europe*, its editor Michael March erects few signposts to direct us through the poetry of eleven countries. Instead of an introduction concentrating on the artistic, political and social backdrop, his eye too often is on the costumes, on György Petri's wide-brimmed hat and Elena Shvarts's fetching black outfit. Of Ioana Crăciunescu, March writes alliteratively but not very illuminatingly: 'I saw her big black boots in Belgrade and knew, from a distance, that she had to be a fine poet.'

As an instance of the difficulties presented by a book like this, its opening poet, György Petri, will serve as well as any. Six of his poems are included, one of which ('To be Said Over and Over Again') is the shortest poem in a volume that is so well-stocked with short poems as to be almost epigrammatic in places:

> *I glance down at my shoe and — there's the lace!*
> *This can't be gaol then, can it, in that case.*

At the risk of tying Petri's shoelaces into knots, I would like to touch on issues which even a translated poem as simple as this can raise for the non-Hungarian reader. For instance, is it too English, too Augustan, as if Alexander Pope (himself the greatest English translator) were an influence? The poem *sounds* very different when Petri himself reads it in Hungarian; and I wonder if there is metrical padding in the original to match the superfluous 'then' of the ungainly second line. As for tone, Petri's poem is undoubtedly ironic — but, to be sure about this, the reader really should know (as the anthology does not tell us) that Petri never spent time in prison — except in the sense (and this is highly pertinent) that his pre-1989 Hungary, like Hamlet's Denmark, was itself a kind of prison.

Another short poem in *Child of Europe*, 'Proverbs' by Tomaž Šlamun, is about as un-English as is conceivable:

> 1. *Tomaž Šalamun made the Party blink, tamed it,*
> *dismantled it, and reconstituted it.*
>
> 2. *Tomaž Šalamun said, Russians Get out! and they did.*
>
> 3. *Tomaž Šalamun sleeps in the forest.*

This is clearly a satire of some kind, aimed as much at the pretensions of poets as at the presumptions of politicians; to enter fully into the spirit of this poem, one would need not only to read the Slovene language or know Slovenian folk poetry and proverbs but to *be* Slovenian.

Translated verse, an essential part of any literary diet, is too peppered with preservatives to be safely recommended in large portions. It is significant that one of the most impressive contributors to March's anthology, Imre Oravecz from Hungary, writes prose poetry — which probably makes the translation process more practicable. Moreover, in its rueful ruminations on a former love affair, it shares with Wyatt's 'Whoso list to hunt' a universal and timeless subject-matter. Most importantly, Oravecz's prose poetry convinces me that it *is* poetry; and no matter how passionately it may be argued to the contrary, poetry and prose are still distinguishable — even, I would venture, in translation.

RTE Radio 1 (1991)
Poetry Ireland Review (Spring 1991)

Tomas Tranströmer

New Collected Poems, translated by Robin Fulton

Tomas Tranströmer, who was born in Stockholm in 1931, is a borderline poet. A typical poem by him will occur at the borders of sleep and waking, the conscious and the unconscious, the visible world and the otherworld. The Estonian poet, Jaan Kaplinski (whose book titles, *The Wandering Border* and *Through the Forest*, encompass some of Tranströmer's own preoccupations), has written of the Swedish poet's ability 'to reconcile and unite in his poetry many things that are considered opposites in our thinking' — Modernism and traditionalism, internationalism and rootedness, realism and surrealism. Seamus Heaney (whose *Seeing Things* and *North* would be further contenders in any Tranströmer title contest) has found in Tranströmer — or 'Tranceroamer' as he has been aptly called — a poet who cannot easily be pinned down, who is 'equidistant from surrealist kitsch and post-modernist knowingness'.

While difficulties in labelling Tranströmer suggest that he is agreeably unclassifiable, they also point to the vagueness and blandness which are characteristic of his less compelling poems. Of the many borders inhabited by his work, the frontier at which calmness of tone edges into inertness of style is the one where readers are most likely to join their author involuntarily in one of his near-sleep experiences. But Tranströmer is capable of more eye-opening poems on sleep, dreams, reveries and nightmares. The excellent 'Dream Seminar' compares the 'annihilation' of the dream world by the act of waking to 'when suspicious men / in uniforms stop the tourist — / open his camera, unwind the film / and let the daylight kill the pictures'. Another memorable image for coming to consciousness appears in the opening lines of 'Deep in Europe':

> *I a dark hull floating between two lock-gates*

rest in the hotel bed while the city around me wakens.
The silent clamour and the grey light stream in
and raise me slowly to the next level: the morning.

Tranströmer's imagistic ingenuity is one of his strengths, adding depth to some poems, lifting others to new and unexpected dimensions. 'Like', 'as if', 'as when' — images cluster around his poems like moths 'on the window pane: / small pale telegrams from the world'. New York is 'a spiral galaxy seen from the side'; unanswered letters 'pile up, like cirro-stratus clouds promising bad weather'; an excavator parked with its 'scoop against the earth' resembles 'a man who has fallen asleep at table / with his fist in front of him'. Also a poet of surprising conjunctions, Tranströmer draws together a rusting tug and a sprouting mushroom, 'sooty palm-trees / and the train whistle's flurrying / silver-white bats'; some of his most convincing poems are layered with contrasting images like successive coats of paint, each a shade different from the next, each layer altering in mood or colour those which have gone before. His most familiar poem, 'Tracks', uses this multi-layered technique in describing a train stopped at 2 a.m. 'out in the middle of the plain'. Notwithstanding its static subject, the poem travels an impressive distance in eleven lines, capturing the bleak 2 a.m. atmosphere and the comfortless associations of that forlorn hour ('As when someone has gone into an illness so deep / everything his days were becomes a few flickering points, a swarm, / cold and tiny at the horizon'). The stalled train provides a vehicle — as do cars in other Tranströmer poems — for a meditation on existential isolation and that state of habitual human 'betweenness' of which he is a tireless chronicler.

If 'Tracks' is his best-known poem, 'Baltics' — published sixteen years later, in 1974 — is Tranströmer's best, a 'truth . . . lifted out of silence'. Nothing written by him before or since 'Baltics' combines such sustained energy, such tonal range, such narrative interest. The six-part poem sets out to preserve the evanescent, to record the lives of the near-forgotten, to find a way of 'writing a long letter to the dead' (not least to his grandparents, whose intuitive traits are implicitly linked with his own artistic gifts). Tranströmer's five brief collections since 'Baltics' resume his evocation of vatic and visionary moments, unexpected epiphanies, insights which come as close to religious revelations as a secular age and a reticent temperament will permit:

Dennis O'Driscoll

> *I am an anchor that has dug itself down and holds steady*
> *the huge shadow floating up there,*
> *the great unknown which I am a part of and which is*
> > *certainly more*
> > *important than me.*

   Collected Poems is supplemented with a series of episodic childhood reminiscences in prose which are as piquant as the ethyl
acetate odour which pervaded Tranströmer's insect-collecting
youth. Much the most important short chapter is the one called
'Exorcism', revealing that 'During the winter when I was fifteen I
was afflicted by a severe form of anxiety . . . The world was a vast
hospital. I saw before me human beings deformed in body and in
soul.' Typically, Tranströmer tells his story in an unfussy, unsensational style; but, even without his admission that the sustained
anguish inflicted by this haunting was 'possibly my most important experience', one would guess, both from the content of a
number of poems and from his choice of profession (he worked
as a psychologist until 1990), how formative this visitation had
been. Painful fault lines are everywhere discernible between the
lines of Tranströmer's lonely work:

> *I close my eyes.*
> *There is a soundless world*
> *there is a crack*
> *where dead people*
> *are smuggled across the border.*

Poetry Review (Summer 1999)

Jaan Kaplinski

Through the Forest, translated from the Estonian by Hildi Hawkins

Jaan Kaplinski's new work is surprisingly wordy. Much of *The Same Sea in Us All* (1990) — an earlier book in English translation by this Estonian poet — consisted of sparse poems snowed-in by white space. Now, two books later, so luxuriantly have the words grown that even the margins of some pages seem threatened with encroachment. Alongside stronger work, *The Same Sea in Us All* contained a core of earnest, inward poems, some hermetic and opaque, others transparent and trite. The poet (echoing Chuang Tzu) may have been unsure whether his 'happy wings' belonged to 'a philosopher / or / to a butterfly' but too many poems in the collection did not advance beyond the pupa stage.

Among the successful short poems in *The Same Sea in Us All* was a philosophical one in which the wings belonged to a colony of bees:

> *All in one*
> *one in all*
> *mind in body*
> *body in mind*
> *the strange in the ordinary*
> *the ordinary in the strange*
> *a swarm of bees*
> *in an old chest*
> *in the loft*
> *of an abandoned*
> *farmhouse.*

'Through the Forest', the title prose-poem of Kaplinski's latest book in English, revisits what must be the original location of that poem, as he recalls how 'A family of bees once came to the chest — probably they were attracted by the smell of the honeycombs

Dennis O'Driscoll

. . . I drove the bees into a swarming box and brought them home.' The return to the abandoned farmhouse takes place towards the end of a half-day walk, a distinctly self-conscious foray into topographical poetry — influenced perhaps by the ambulatory French poet, Jacques Réda. Not only does Kaplinski record every minute observation but he records his recording ('If you want to be honest,' he remarks unconvincingly in another poem, 'you must write about writing').

At the outset of his forest walk, Kaplinski — with 'small black notebook and ballpoint pen' to hand — undertakes to 'stop and write' if he sees 'something significant'. Clearly nothing is without significance for him; and, by the end of his guided tour, we are virtually in a position to count every dandelion and mosquito along the way: 'I'm really writing a travel book. This time I could not go to Sweden; so I have come to this forest.' The small scale and slow progress, paced out over nineteen pages, make the walk seem like a wearyingly long one (even a Richard Long one — the English artist would surely approve of this contribution to the 'art walk' genre). Given Kaplinski's Buddhist affiliations, it may not be entirely fanciful to see aspects of a pilgrimage also in his journey, a search for the right path ('The path itself is already clearer . . . Here I can be alone. Can be myself, or someone else . . .').

Kaplinski is at his most rewarding when he adheres to a poetic middle way; the medium-length discursive poems of his second book in English, *The Wandering Border* (1992), are recollections which strike with the force of revelations. Among several poems of equivalent length and quality in *Through the Forest*, those especially worthy of mention include two (typically untitled) pieces about death and a very Northerly poem, as multi-layered as the boot tracks it describes 'under the ice and snow'. In a book which has too much to say on the subject of writing, there is the consolation of one excellent poem about writing poetry, which ends:

> *Perhaps, after all, poetry comes entirely from ignorance,*
> *is a particular sort of ignorance. And that*
> *is much harder to learn than knowing.*

Kaplinski's poems are seldom directly political and, although he served as an MP for a few years after Estonian independence, the cover of *Through the Forest* states that the book was 'written in the late 1980s . . . when Kaplinski chose not to join the world of actual borders and politics.' He is essentially a poet of epiphanies; but epiphanies cannot be faked or induced and his truest poems are those which resist any temptation to do so. At such times, he is the reincarnation of a classical Chinese poet who, having retired to the forest, creates tranquil poems of crystalline beauty.

Times Literary Supplement (18 October 1996)

Czeslaw Milosz

1 *The Optimistic Catastrophist*

The Lithuanian-born, Polish-speaking, Californian-resident poet, Czeslaw Milosz, has borne witness to some of the worst outrages of the twentieth century. Born in 1911 into a Baltic state which was subject to the rule of the Russian Czar, he saw it rapidly transformed from newly-won independence and quarrels with Poland and Germany to final absorption by the Communists into the USSR in 1940. In a chapter of *The Captive Mind* (1953), headed 'The Lesson of the Baltics', he wrote:

> *My account of the Baltic states is not derived from books or manuscripts. The first sunlight I saw, my first smell of the earth, my first tree, were the sunlight, smell, and tree of these regions; for I was born there, of Polish-speaking parents, beside a river that bore a Lithuanian name. I am familiar with the events of the past years not from the dry notes of historians; they are as vivid for me as the faces and eyes of people one knows well.*

Milosz served courageously in the Polish Resistance and later lived in exile ('the worst of all misfortunes'), teaching from 1960 onwards at the University of California at Berkeley.

Like so many of his generation, Milosz emerged from the war trusting only to what he had learned and experienced for himself. In his speech accepting the 1980 Nobel Prize for Literature, he said 'I wouldn't know how to speak about poetry in general. I must speak of poetry in its encounter with peculiar circumstances of time and place.' Criticising those poems in which Pablo Neruda had extolled the virtues of the Soviet Union, Milosz stated (in *The Captive Mind*) that he was 'inclined to believe him as long as he speaks about what he knows; I stop believing him when he starts to speak about what I know myself.' Milosz does occasionally gloat about his superior range of experiences; but, more often, he is concerned that these experiences should be put at the service of humanity. Towards the beginning of *Native Realm* (1958), his 'search for self-definition', he quite reasonably asks 'If I want to show what a man who comes from the East of Europe is like, what can I do but tell about myself?'

Milosz has compared the language situation in Lithuania, where those of landowning and noble backgrounds (including the Milosz family) spoke Polish rather than Lithuanian, with the speaking of English by Irish planters. The 'acute national hatreds', the local pride in ancient poets and kings and the culture of alcohol and Catholicism recounted in *Native Realm* will not be entirely alien to Irish readers either. Catholicism was the dominant religion of Lithuania and it left the 'most durable traces' on Milosz's mind. He once said of his poetry that 'its roots are in my childhood, in Christmas carols, in the liturgy of Marian and vesper offices, and in the Bible'. His poetry and prose bristle with allusions to devils and hell; and his obsession with good and evil is rooted in traditional, even old-fashioned, Christian belief wedded to modern experience. Here, in full, is his poem 'Proof':

> *And yet you experienced the flames of Hell.*
> *You can even say what they are like: real,*
> *Ending in sharp hooks so that they tear up flesh*
> *Piece by piece, to the bone. You walked in the street*
> *And it was going on: the lashing and bleeding.*
> *You remember, therefore you have no doubt:*
> *there is a Hell for certain.*

Milosz's novel, *The Issa Valley* (1955), is replete with Manichaean assumptions and it is not surprising to learn from *Native Realm* that his favourite heresies were 'the Gnostics, the Manichaeans, and the Albigensians. They at least did not take refuge behind some vague will of God in order to justify cruelty'. It is, however, the New Faith of Communism with which much of *Native Realm*, and all of *The Captive Mind*, are concerned. Milosz traces the route by which he and many of his most gifted friends and contemporaries were, to varying degrees, seduced by what were thought to be its clear and progressive answers. Though he did flirt with Communism, Milosz never allowed a comma of his literary output to be altered in its cause and he totally resisted Stalinism. The influence of Catholicism and the traditional hostility of his people towards the Russians were among the reasons for his wary approach. When he was obliged to declare political affiliations in 1945, he inclined towards the Left for a variety of reasons:

> My point of view can be defined negatively rather than positively: I disliked the right-wing groups, whose platform consisted chiefly of anti-Semitism. During the Nazi occupation I, like my colleagues, wrote for the clandestine publications, which were especially numerous in Poland. My experiences in those years led me to the conclusion that, after the defeat of Hitler, only men true to a socialist programme would be capable of abolishing the injustices of the past, and rebuilding the economy of the countries of Central and Eastern Europe.

Following the war, from 1946 to 1951, he served with the Polish Foreign Service. He did not want to become an émigré 'and so give up all chance of taking a hand in what was going on in my own country. The time was to come when I should be forced to admit myself defeated'. In *Native Realm* he recounts life as a Washington-based diplomat, with D P for 'Diplomatic Personnel' on his Chevrolet licence plate, when — for millions of deprived Europeans — the letters stood for 'Displaced Person'. Milosz felt hypocritical as he played out his role, a 'perverse, comic masquerade'. After four and a half years in America, he returned to Warsaw 'to see for myself Poland's Stalinist nightmare'. He arrived in France for a short stay in 1951, broke with the Polish government as soon as he could and returned only in 1981 to a hero's welcome during the heady days of Solidarity.

Within two years of his break with Warsaw, Milosz published his best-known book, *The Captive Mind* — a uniquely perceptive account of how East European writers and intellectuals were gradually induced to compromise and pay obeisance to the Party. Because it deals with those who grew up under a non-Communist regime and then adapted to the new order, the book has become — with the passage of time — of more relevance to the West as a cautionary tale than as an analysis of contemporary East European dilemmas. The attitude of the Party to literature was not least among Milosz's reasons for deserting:

In the end, I found myself driven to the point where a final choice had to be made. This was when 'socialist realism' was introduced into Poland. This is not, as some think, merely an esthetic theory to which the writer, the musician, the painter or the theatrical producer is obliged to adhere. On the contrary, it involves by implication the whole Leninist-Stalinist doctrine. If writers and painters are not forced to become members of the Party, that is because such a step is unnecessary. So long as they act in accordance with 'socialist realism', they are automatically and inescapably enrolled among the followers of Stalin. 'Socialist realism' is much more than a matter of taste, of preference for one style of painting or music rather than another. It is concerned with the beliefs which lie at the foundation of human existence. In the field of literature it forbids what has in every age been the writer's essential task — to look at the world from his own independent viewpoint, to tell the truth as he sees it, and so to keep watch and ward in the interest of society as a whole.

Elsewhere in *The Captive Mind*, he provides further critiques of socialist realism which, he argues, 'strengthens weak talents and undermines great ones'. In Milosz's view, the artist must trust his 'inner command' and this must itself be supported by 'a belief in an order of values that exists beyond the changeability of human affairs, that is by a metaphysical belief'. A sense of historical inevitability and a hankering after security and power drew intellectuals of Milosz's generation towards Communist doctrines; using specific case-studies, *The Captive Mind* charts how one compromise would lead to another until the boundary between public statements and private beliefs, between propaganda and literature, widened inexorably.

It is of no small significance that Milosz should have chosen to break with the Polish regime from Paris, a city which had close associations with his two great spiritual mentors, Simone Weil and Oscar Milosz. Weil was born in Paris in 1909 and died in England in 1943. In 1958, Czeslaw Milosz translated a selection of her work into Polish and, as his essay entitled 'The Importance of Simone Weil' enthusiastically demonstrates, she remained a source of inspiration:

Dennis O'Driscoll

> *The unique place of Simone Weil in the modern world is due to the perfect continuity of her thought. Unlike those who have to reject their past when they become Christians, she developed her ideas from before 1938 even further, introducing more order into them . . . Those ideas concerned society, history, Marxism, science.*

Czeslaw Milosz, in his 1980 Nobel Prize speech, termed Weil and Oscar Milosz 'writers in whose school I obediently studied'.

Oscar Milosz, who is not nearly as well-known in the English-speaking world as Simone Weil, worked at the Lithuanian Legation in Paris and was a noted poet in the French language. Czeslaw Milosz, his younger kinsman, became acquainted with him during a year he spent in Paris in the mid-Thirties. Oscar was an elegant, aristocratic, prophetic, independent-minded, wise man. Czeslaw characterizes him as a hermit in the desert of the city who was convinced that it was historically *'very late'* and that war was imminent; the Nobel Prize speech honoured his memory:

> *It was my good fortune to be treated nearly as a son by my relative, Oscar Milosz, a Parisian recluse and visionary . . . I learned much from him. He gave me a deeper insight into the religion of the Old and New Testaments and inculcated a need for a strict, ascetic hierarchy in all matters of mind, including everything that pertains to art, where as a major sin he considered putting the second-rate on the same level with the first-rate. Primarily, though, I listened to him as a prophet who loved people, as he says, 'with old love worn out by pity, loneliness and anger' and for that reason tried to address a warning to a crazy world rushing towards a catastrophe.*

As well as essays, critical treatises, autobiographical works and a history of Polish literature, Czeslaw Milosz's prose books include two novels. The first and (as its author would readily agree) the lesser of these, *The Seizure of Power* (1953), is set in Nazi-occupied Warsaw; the second, *The Issa Valley* (1955), is a fictionalized account of a Lithuanian childhood. Milosz's prose can seem pedestrian at times but *The Issa Valley* is a patient and sensuous delineation of the development of a young mind. In the background are village characters, bird sounds and love affairs,

hay fragrances and May altars, apiaries and herbaria. It consti-
tutes a kind of Lithuanian *Prelude*, or a Book of Genesis depicting
an Eden from which its young inhabitant will gradually be
expelled by the growth of his consciousness. Set against what we
know of the later fate of both Milosz and Lithuania, the enclosed
world of *The Issa Valley* presents a frail and humane alternative to
the rapacious future empires of Hitler and Stalin.

The Issa Valley attempts without sentimentality to recover a lost
time and place with a memory sharpened by exile. The boy's
evolving Manichaeanism and dualism and the development of
his 'scrupulous conscience' are persuasively handled. Like
Mahler's 'Third Symphony', the novel could be divided into
movements such as 'what the flowers of the meadow tell me',
'what the beasts of the forest tell me' and 'what man tells me'. *The
Issa Valley* is undoubtedly a masterpiece; but it is as a poet rather
than prose writer that Milosz's achievements stand supreme. His
attitude to poetry is neatly summarized in the final lines of the
poem '*Ars Poetica?*':

> *poems should be written rarely and reluctantly,*
> *under unbearable duress and only with the hope*
> *that good spirits, not evil ones, choose us for their*
> *   instrument.*

This emphasis on 'good spirits' as bearers of poetry is
manifested throughout his work. In an essay in *Emperor of the
Earth* (1977), he laments that 'freedom of choice is being misused
today by Western writers for the purpose of creating dehuman-
ized literature'. In *Native Realm*, he observes that 'only poetry is
optimistic in the twentieth century, through its sensual avidity, its
premonitions of change, its prophecies with many meanings.
Even if we leave no immortal works behind us, the discipline
itself is worthy of praise'.

An essay called 'The Real and the Paradigms' in *Poetry
Australia* (October 1979) gives perhaps the most forthright
account of Milosz's literary philosophy:

> *In everything I have written there is an awareness of the
> pressure exerted by the void, the absurd, the anti-
> meaning; but also there has been a protest against that
> pressure. In practical terms, this leads to a critical
> attitude towards contemporary authors and their works,*

> *with very few exceptions. I have never liked their confes-*
> *sions of despair, or the disintegration of the real world*
> *under their pens.*

The danger inherent in Milosz's 'critical attitude' is demonstrated in the same essay when he takes a literal and unsympathetic look at Philip Larkin's great poem, 'Aubade'. Milosz does have his truly Larkinesque moments when he wonders why people aren't screaming in the face of death and can perceive the world to be 'an exceptionally terrifying place'. Yet, Larkin's sombre exposition of the post-Christian psyche is excoriated by Milosz, who chides the English poet for treating 'human energy opposing death as a vain consolation' — as if this were neither a tenable nor a representative position to adopt, Larkin's way of 'look[ing] at the world from his own independent viewpoint'.

While Milosz may be dogmatic in his poetic theory, he is rarely so in the poems themselves, which often arise from sheer bewilderment. 'So Little' ends by remarking of an existence, 'now I don't know / What in all that was real', while 'Tidings' concludes, 'Or perhaps we'll say nothing of earthly civilization. / For nobody really knows what it was'. 'From the Rising of the Sun', a sometimes dauntingly difficult sequence (which many critics regard as his *magnum opus*), is peppered with questions and asks:

> *Who can tell what purpose is served by destinies*
> *And whether to have lived on earth means little*
> *Or much.*

A formidable poet, Milosz is capable of sustaining extended, multi-faceted sequences like 'From the Rising of the Sun', as well as briefer, more crystalline forms. Although he joins with distinguished English-language poets to translate his own verse, he claims that his poems 'do not translate well because of many cultural-linguistic allusions in their very texture'. He has described his poems as 'childishly naive descriptions of things'; but, unlike the work of contemporaries such as Tadeusz Różewicz, their simplicity does not have its source in suspicion towards pre-Auschwitz language. Milosz, on the contrary, has retained respect for traditional poetic forms and his poems are obsessed with time and the continuity of things across the ages. With the Polish language itself, he has something of a love-hate relationship, finding its imprecision and the deficiency of its philosophical idiom frustrating. Yet, he has remained steadfastly faithful to it in exile:

> *But who am I without you?*
> *Just a scholar in a distant country.*

His poems, even when their language is at its most simple and direct, are capable of complex thought and of communicating a deeply-felt amalgam of repose and unease. 'A Song on the End of the World' and the closing lines of 'From the Rising of the Sun' reveal an impervious bedrock of stoicism and serenity. This is work characteristic of the poet who could write of his time in Nazi-occupied Warsaw: 'My chances of survival and of seeing what came out of this cauldron were negligible. With some effort, I finally obeyed Martin Luther's advice: when asked what he would do if he knew tomorrow was going to be the end of the world, he said : "I would plant apple trees".'

'Study of Loneliness' and 'The View' are among the poems that show Milosz at his imperturbable best. The poet whose early prophetic verse earned him the label 'catastrophist' could, paradoxically, also be termed an optimist. His optimism (very different from the wishful thinking of the socialist realists) is derived from a conviction that life, however much people may abuse or debase it, is essentially praiseworthy. For Milosz, there remain eternal verities worthy of celebration and these transcend the worst human barbarities, including those which he has himself so painstakingly recorded:

> *A day so happy.*
> *Fog lifted early, I worked in the garden.*
> *Hummingbirds were stopping over honeysuckle flowers.*
> *There was no thing on earth I wanted to possess.*
> *I knew no one worth my envying him.*
> *Whatever evil I had suffered, I forgot.*
> *To think that once I was the same man did not embarrass*
> * me.*
> *In my body I felt no pain.*
> *When straightening up, I saw the blue sea and sails.*

The Crane Bag (1983)

2 *Facing the River,* translated by the author and Robert Hass

Czeslaw Milosz, who has paid verse tribute to Linnaeus and his 'classes, orders, genuses, species', prompts some critical taxonomy. If poets may roughly be classified as good, mediocre or bad, then one of the most telling sub-divisions of the good is between the clever and the wise. For every wise poet, there are numerous clever ones; but their verbal and technical pyrotechnics do not adequately answer to the deepest needs which we want poetry to satisfy.

Such was the expectation with which Czeslaw Milosz approached his art in the fiercely testing circumstances of wartime Warsaw that he could ask, 'What is poetry which does not save / Nations or people?' Fifty years later, he still keeps faith with his vocation as a poet and with the view that 'poetry below a certain awareness' is deficient. By comparison with a book like *Facing the River,* most contemporary poetry looks puny and presumptuous. Wise poets cannot be imitated the way that clever poets can: wisdom is not for the workshops; it is a gift — bestowed or earned.

Czeslaw Milosz's words have wafted from a childhood Lithuania of lakes and forests to a Californian exile among parched hills and forest fires, from a world of flax-combing and butter-churning to a land of freeways and free love: 'I reach eighty, I fly from San Francisco to Frankfurt and Rome, a passenger who once traveled three days by horse carriage from Szetejnie to Wilno.' His verse seems to come 'from the other side of time' and to speak with an otherworldly authority and calm. The fact that some of the poems in *Facing the River* record his return to Lithuania after fifty-two years heightens their haunted air:

> *I told nobody I was familiar with that neighborhood.*
> *Why should I? As if a hunter with a spear*
> *Materialized, looking for something he once knew.*
> *After many incarnations we return to the earth,*
> *Uncertain we would recognize its face.*

That Milosz, unlike many other Polish poets, maintained diplomatic relations with pre-war language should not be taken as proof that he is a conservative writer. On the contrary, as Stanislaw Barańczak has noted, 'He wants a language open to every way of speaking, every recess of vocabulary, every possible style.' *Unattainable Earth*, published in 1986, incorporated 'prose poems, prose jottings, pensées, quotations, translations and even fragments from personal letters'. His two more recent volumes, *Provinces* and *Facing the River*, continue to experiment with admixtures of prose and poetry but generally settle for a limpid, lyrical mode. Finding durable forms for the most unendurable of twentieth-century experiences, he produces a poetry which is as deeply affecting as the music of the Polish composer Henryk Górecki (who, like Milosz, knows and admires Pope John Paul II) and which is at once spiritual, traditional and contemporary in ways which will also bring John Tavener and Arvo Pärt to mind.

For the Milosz of *Facing the River*, there is no time like the past and the river he faces is decidedly not the Lethe. Like the Old Town of Warsaw, his childhood has been faithfully rebuilt layer by layer; and not just recreated but repopulated as well, with people like Kazia in her 'sailor's collar' or Zosia, the officer's wife, in her polka-dot dress:

> *However it was, whether you perished with your burning*
>   *city,*
> *Or, old, wandered in it, not recognizing the streets,*
> *I try to be everywhere with you, yet in vain.*

Astonishingly, the only access to Milosz's poetry in this part of the world was, for years, through his slim anthology, *Post-War Polish Poetry*. At that time, he was principally thought of as the author of *The Captive Mind*: 'The Captive Mind is nothing to be ashamed of. But foreigners who know only a part of what I've written have a distorted image of me.' It was the award in 1980 of the Nobel Prize which cleared a path for the novels, essays, memoirs, diaries, conversations and, of course, poems which were subsequently printed or reprinted in English. His *Collected Poems*, published in 1988, proved Milosz to be every bit as important as the poets whom he had championed as editor and translator; in Robert Hass, he was himself finally rewarded with the ideal partner for the task of finding English counterparts for the Polish originals.

Milosz's return, as a great writer, to the Lithuanian birthplace where he wrote his 'first awkward letters' completed the circle of his life and work in a manner befitting a poet with such a strong sense of destiny. His vision has always transcended his historical circumstances and he has little to say that is directly political. However, the weakest poem in the book, 'Sarajevo' — a well-meaning effort to put his views about Bosnia on the record — tells a journalistic truth rather than a poetical one; hence the need to append a literary health warning: 'Perhaps this is not a poem but at least I say what I feel.' Much the best poem, on the other hand, is 'Capri' which looks back with awe across his epoch — for some an era of privilege, for others of annihilation — asking 'What did you do with your life, what did you do?' In answering the question, profoundly and movingly, he discerns (in Edwin Muir's terms) the fable in the story: 'Early we receive a call, yet it remains incomprehensible, and only late do we discover how obedient we were.'

While a baccalaureate student, Milosz had written an essay on 'the river of time': 'I was stirred by the mystery of universal movement, where all things are linked together, are interdependent, create one another, transcend one another, where nothing conforms to rigid definitions.' *Facing the River* shows the same questing mind at work; and, as the youthful essay was awarded the highest marks, this collection of poems (published in his eighty-fourth year) deserves the highest praise. Milosz displays what John Crowe Ransom, speaking of Thomas Hardy, termed 'a metaphysical imagination, in the service of a theological passion'. Although Milosz's defiant hope sets him apart from Hardy's enshrouding gloom, both poets survived into old-age with their lyrical faculties intact. Indeed, the 'aged thrush' in one of Hardy's best-known poems is a creature of the same class, order, genus and species as Milosz, singing fervently and wisely from the shadows:

> *So little cause for carolings*
> *Of such ecstatic sound*
> *Was written on terrestrial things*
> *Afar or nigh around,*
> *That I could think there trembled through*
> *His happy good-night air*
> *Some blessed Hope, whereof he knew*
> *And I was unaware.*

Poetry Ireland Review (Autumn/Winter, 1995)

Wislawa Szymborska

View with a Grain of Sand, translated by Stanislaw Barańczak and Clare Cavanagh

Condensed wisdom is what Wislawa Szymborska offers. Her poetry combines the deepest of insights with the lightest of touches; it is detached without being impersonal, ironic without being evasive, moral but not hectoring. A slow coming she had of it. Even the Swedish Academy's Nobel citation spoke of 'a handful of slim but powerful collections of poems'; and the earliest of these seem to have been composed with her hand stretched to the far left. Magnus J Krynski and Robert A Maguire, whose translations of seventy Szymborska poems appeared in 1981, tactfully mentioned the 'officially inspired themes' of the early books, while Piotr Sommer recently alluded to 'two early [collections] she prefers to forget about'. Reviewing the American edition of *View with a Grain of Sand*, Edward Hirsch referred more specifically to poems which 'range from dogmatic denunciations of the old order to strident condemnations of Western imperialism'. Fortunately, Szymborska overcame her initial conformism to become the most independent of poets; and if her career began far less strikingly than that of her more courageous contemporary, Zbigniew Herbert, she gradually accumulated a body of work so consistently strong that it could stand comparison with his.

View with a Grain of Sand selects as its starting-point Szymborska's third collection, *Calling Out to Yeti*, published in 1957 when she was thirty-four. With each collection, her wit quickens, her gaze widens, her scepticism sharpens. Far less politically-minded than Herbert though she may be, she is nonetheless conscious of the pervasiveness of politics ('All day long, all through the night, / all affairs — yours, ours, theirs — / are political affairs.'); and the weight she attached, when the prevailing ethos was collectivist, to the fate of the individual ('my imagination . . . is bad with large numbers. / It's still taken by

Dennis O'Driscoll

particularity') is not without political implications. Her poems
are paradigms of freedom, spaces in which assumptions are
subtly challenged and orthodoxies quietly subverted. Hers is a
poetry of the self-deprecatory ordinary: her average day is so
mundane as to be forgettable ('One of those many dates / that no
longer ring a bell.'); no one in her family 'has ever died of love. /
No food for myth and nothing magisterial.' A poet of enormously
diverse subject-matter, Szymborska derives some of her 'spring-
boards for the spirit' from extensive reading of non-literary books
for review; as with Marianne Moore, the natural world is a
favourite source. An endangered sea cucumber dividing itself in
two prompts an unusual elegy ('Life on one shore, death on the
other'); another poem inspects mankind through the huge eyes of
a tarsier. Humans, to whom she denies supremacy over nature,
are viewed by Szymborska with an amalgam of bemusement and
horror; no poet could be less deceived — and yet her tone is more
often exuberant than downcast. Perhaps, like Patrick Kavanagh,
she senses that — in art at least — 'Tragedy is underdeveloped
Comedy':

> *For me the tragedy's most important act is the sixth:*
> *the raising of the dead from the stage's battlegrounds,*
> *the straightening of wigs and fancy gowns,*
> *removing knives from stricken breasts . . .*

It is not only the inexhaustible variety of Szymborska's subject-
matter (from a medieval miniature to a mathematical symbol)
and the entertaining ingenuity with which she presents it (using a
CV, a spoof critique, an overheard conversation) that are impressive but the extent to which her 'essay-poems' prove to be both
crisp and comprehensive. Although different in almost every
other respect from Czeslaw Milosz, she shares with him the
uncanny ability to see things *sub specie aeternitatis*, to simultaneously inhabit and transcend time. The translations by Barańczak
and Cavanagh take tricky puns and rhymes in their stride; and
the poems are distilled into English which — shimmering as dew,
transparent as water, potent as alcohol — honours her aspiration
that everything she writes should seem absolutely clear. There
ought to be a vodka called Szymborska.

Poetry Review (Winter 1996/1997)

Adam Zagajewski

Mysticism for Beginners, translated by Clare Cavanagh

Joseph Brodsky and Susan Sontag have penned blurbs for him. Among his translators have been Robert Hass and C K Williams. Dedicatees of his poems include Zbigniew Herbert and Derek Walcott. Faber in London and Farrar, Straus and Giroux in New York publish him. The preface to his first collection of poems in English translation, *Tremor*, was written by Czeslaw Milosz. Could the Polish poet, Adam Zagajewski, be anything less therefore than a world-class writer, a Nobel laureate-in-waiting, the kind of poet one finds alongside Seamus Heaney at international poetry conferences or who busily plies the transatlantic flight-path between a home in Europe and a university post in America?

Mysticism for Beginners is the third of Zagajewski's collections to have appeared in English; but — despite the extravagant claims ('Seldom has the muse of poetry spoken to anyone with such clarity and urgency,' was Brodsky's contention) — neither this new book nor its predecessors have presented credible evidence of a major poetic talent at work. Sometimes it seems as if untranslatability may be the problem, such are the infelicities in certain poems. This was particularly true of his second collection in English, *Canvas*, where phrases like 'skewered by their lambent gazes' and 'the Sanskrit of dusk that speaks / in a glowing tongue of joy' were overwrought and under-earned. One wonders how much clarity and urgency Henri Rousseau, the 'Douanier' whose painting of Notre Dame is reproduced on the cover of *Mysticism for Beginners*, would have found in the lines, 'the heat, like a customs officer, palpates / each thing in its skin'.

If Zagajewski, who was born in Lvov in 1945, can appear as pompous as an academic painter, his style can also be as naive as Henri Rousseau's — though to far less charming effect. The naive interrogative style of his earlier books ('Things, / do you know suffering? / Were you ever hungry, down and out? / Have you cried?') continues in the new collection: 'Where was I going? Where was the sun hiding?'; 'Houses, houses, where are you, / under what ocean, in what memory, / beneath the roof of what existence?' Ultimately, what is troubling about the work, however, is not *faux* naivety but genuine mediocrity: the parade of so-so poems on topics which others have handled more impressively — Dutch paintings, foreign cities, the journey of the Magi. The ratio of white space to words can be particularly difficult to justify in the case of the shorter, damper squibs. One example — not, alas, untypical — reads in full:

> *This day's nothingness*
> *as if from spite*
> *became a flame*
> *and scorched the lips*
> *of children and poets.*

My sense of Zagajewski is of someone with an urge to go on writing poetry but who is lost for something urgent to write about ('I drink from a small spring, / my thirst exceeds the ocean'). Czeslaw Milosz has observed that 'Zagajewski belonged to the angry "generation of 1968" and started by satirizing both in his verse and in his prose the surreal character of the totalitarian state'. Those edgy early poems of Zagajewski's were quickened into life by political frictions; unfortunately, even politics can no longer rescue his poems from infectious boredom:

> *Every Sunday I call my father.*
> *Every other week I meet with friends,*
> *thus proving my fidelity.*
> *My country freed itself from one evil. I wish*
> *another liberation would follow.*
> *Could I help in this? I don't know.*

Zagajewski's subject-matter now includes exile (he has lived in Paris since 1981), time and the duality of the world. Some of the stronger poems in this new volume touch on the exile theme — 'Refugees' (six and a half lines too long) and 'Postcards' are a little hackneyed in places, yet capable of moving the reader nonetheless: 'It was All Saints' Day / but we had nowhere to go. / Our dead don't dwell in this country'. 'Elegy' chillingly evokes

Cold War Poland; for once, Zagajewski's penchant for listing things is put to striking use:

> *It was a waiting room with brown walls,*
> *a courtroom, a clinic; a room*
> *where tables slumped under files*
> *and ashtrays choked on ashes.*
> *It was silence or loudspeakers shrieking.*
> *A waiting room where you waited*
> *a lifetime to be born.*

Exile, time, duality, Communist Poland — all of these are touched on in the title essay of Zagajewski's prose volume, *Two Cities* (1995), with a vividness, verve and poignancy that outshine anything in these poems. His achievements in poetry are few and fleeting; it is to his essays that one turns for sustained bouts of insight and pleasure.

Poetry Review (Summer 1998)

Miroslav Holub

1 *The Poet and Socialism*

Miroslav Holub, born in Pilsen in 1923, was the son of a railway lawyer and was himself at one time conscripted to work on the railways. Besides his poetry collections, he is credited with authorship of such works as *Experimental Morphology of Antibody Formation* (1958) and *Structure of the Immune System* (1979). His area of scientific expertise was outlined by another writer-scientist, Lewis Thomas, in the introduction to *Sagittal Section* (a 1980 selection of Holub's verse translated by Stuart Friebert and Dana Hábová). Dr Thomas speaks of Dr Holub having produced an extensive number of 'technical papers and monographs dealing with lymphocytes and the strange capacity of these cells to recognize and remember the most precise details of an infinite number of chemical odds and ends in the confusing environment of living tissues'.

Holub's scientific work preceded his poetry; and the influence of science on his verse goes well beyond his frequent use of scientific terms and images. A poem in *Sagittal Section* wearily recounts how its author has had to answer questions concerning the relationship between medicine and poetry 'about 892 times'. One of the 892 questioners, A Alvarez, received this answer: 'There is no deep difference between the scientific mind and the artistic mind: both include the maximal creativity with the maximal freedom. Science is both theoretic and experimental. Art is only experimental.'

Ten years later, Holub's interviewer was Jon Silkin whom he informed that 'My basic approach to reality is a scientific one, one which simplifies. Therefore, I preferred (especially in the beginning) to write extremely simple poems with one idea, on a simple language-level and with a single conclusion'. Holub went on to say that a poem should be more analytical than descriptive, yet should not create 'more obscurity in this very obscure world'. It is in the analytical and experimental approach to his poetry that the fusion of the scientific and the literary is most evident. He also told Jon Silkin that life is so 'sacred' that, in laboratory work, he feels responsible for every minute of an animal's life; if a mouse must be killed for an experiment, he spares it until the last possible second. The opening poem of the Penguin *Selected Poems* reads in full:

> *We gave a helping hand to grass —*
> *and it turned into corn.*
> *We gave a helping hand to fire —*
> *and it turned into a rocket.*
> *Hesitatingly,*
> *cautiously,*
> *we give a helping hand*
> *to people,*
> *to some people . . .*

Irony and accuracy, compassion for ordinary people and for animals, surrealism more than socialist realism, as well as amusing but trenchant similes and metaphors are among the characteristics of Holub's poems. What sets him apart from the post-1968 official Czech poets is the absence of a preconceived ideological programme. In Holub's world, 'someone laughs airily. / And therefore is'; it is 'enough that we are alive. / Are breathing. / Responsible / even for the rotation of the earth'. A poem exists simply 'against emptiness' and arises 'when there's nothing else to be done'. In the very aimlessness of poetry lies its freedom:

> *But in its aimlessness, in its desperate commitment to the word, in its primal order of birth and re-birth, a poem remains the most general guarantee that we can still do something, that we can still do something against emptiness, that we haven't given in but are giving ourselves to something.*

So subversive is Holub's vision that 'Ode to Joy', one of his finest poems, locates joy in failure. It is in failing and then trying again that we, like the scientist and the lover, will experience joy:

> *Like caryatids*
> *our lifted arms*
> *hold up time's granite load*
> *and defeated*
> *we shall always win.*

What Holub would have us do, as his delightful poem 'The Door' also suggests, is to take a chance, to risk failure in the search for revelation. He has his own anti-heroic ways of encouraging the masses . . . .

Holub's heterodox outlook is reflected too in the poems which celebrate the asking of spontaneous questions. It is not surprising that he should have written so many poems about children — one of these, 'A Boy's Head', rejoices in the capacity for singular imagination which each head represents. The poem ends by ironically suggesting that 'There is much promise / in the circumstance / that so many people have heads'. In 'A History Lesson', a class is told of kings and popes and battles and empires. It is the small boy 'who was not paying the least attention' who raises the iconoclastic question concerning war: 'And did it hurt in those days too?' Most explicitly of all, Holub rebels against the indoctrination of schoolchildren:

> *Under the classroom door*
> *trickles*
> *a thin stream of blood.*
> *For here begins*
> *the massacre*
> *of the innocents.*

There are moments, too, in Holub's verse when satirical darts spike the writing, as when he observes that 'Some mistakes are now mistakes / others are still virtues' or holds that 'A special logic must be assigned to cylinders / that pretend to be cubes. And clefts / that think they're big mountains'. Two poems in particular, 'Polonius' and 'Planning', are noteworthy for the strength and directness of their feeling. 'Polonius', of course, takes its title from *Hamlet*; an entire study could be written about the resonances of this play for East European writers. Holub has stated that he likes to keep 'the lyric I' out of his poems and to invent parables instead. In 'Polonius', the eponymous character is the obsequious functionary who 'does his duty / unswervingly. / Walls are his ears, / keyholes his eyes'. He is the party hack, the Writers' Union lackey, the bootlicker from the Ministry, the spy in the tower block; it is obvious that Holub knows him all too well:

> *He slinks up the stairs,*
> *oozes from the ceiling,*
> *floats through the door*
> *ready to give evidence,*
> *prove what is proven,*
> *stab with a needle*
> *or pin on an order.*
>
> *His poems always rhyme,*
> *his brush is dipped in honey,*
> *his music flutes*
> *from marzipan and cane.*

One can imagine the 'Polonius' of that poem as the interrogator with whom Holub is confronted in 'Interview with a Poet'. This interrogator (who, it must be said, may be regarded either as *alter ego* or as antagonist) dogmatically informs Holub that he never was, and never will be, a poet because he cannot respond to questions about his poetry and his identity as a poet with the rote replies of the Party catechism. By finally turning a question on the interrogator and asking him 'But who are you?', he challenges not only the interrogator himself but also the regime he represents.

In 'Planning', surely the most relevant of Holub's poems to socialism, those who claim to know all the answers are again answered back. A parade of future refrigerators, preserves, excavators, new-born babies, 'megawatts precise as a surgical needle', 'megatons certain as next spring' hovers in the background while the planners (who predict the future 'to three decimal points / exactly') determine each item's destiny. But sometimes, 'when all's finished and signed', the babies and excavators and so on 'pipe up / just for the heck of it, / without a reference number, / in quiet urgent voices':

> *and what about yourselves, friends,*
> *what about yourselves,*
> *to how many decimal points exactly . . .*
> *at home*

> and in the street
> and with your wife
>   and your friends,
> and morning
>   and evening,
> and on the way up
>   and on the way down,
> to how many decimal points exactly
> you yourselves, friends?

> And we should have an answer to that
> in this year's plan.

Holub's books in English translation, since the pioneering Penguin *Selected Poems* (1967), have contained flat and slight poems as well as much that lodges playfully but permanently in the memory. A book such as *Interferon, or On Theater*, consisting of poems written between 1979 and 1982, illustrates how well Holub preserved his imaginative independence (including mastery of simile) over the years. We find 'skin . . . as pink as an embryonic membrane', a woman 'obese as the seventh reincarnation of an Hawaiian guitar' and 'nature . . . as fresh as a sleepwalker's breath'. 'Collision' offers lines of exceptional verbal impact:

> The streetcar stood jammed over him
> like an icebreaker's bow; what was left
> of the car was a funny pretzel
> bitten by the dentures of a mad angel.
> Something dark was dripping onto the rails,
> and a surprisingly pale wind
> leafed through the pages of a book
> that was still warm.
> People formed in a ring and with deaf-mute
> sympathy waited for the play's
> catharsis, like black mites
> creeping from under the wings
> of a freshly-beheaded hen . . .

The Crane Bag (1983)

330

2 *Supposed to Fly*, translated by Ewald Osers

Nobody who is familiar with Miroslav Holub's original and experimental output would expect him to publish an orthodox autobiography. Indeed, nobody who is aware of Holub's lifelong determination to produce hard-centred rather than self-centred work would expect an autobiography from him in the first place. Steeped since childhood in the ancient classics, he relishes the fact that Homer, the greatest of all poets, casts 'no biographical shadow' and, 'in his blindness', neglected to behave sensationally enough to have acquired a marketable 'personality'.

Holub, who would doubtless be happy to share Homer's anonymity, once said: 'When you give a scientific lecture or make a scientific paper, there is no personal background given: no age, no numbers of girlfriends or wives or children. Nothing. So why should these be analysed in poetry?' *Supposed to Fly*, a book of reminiscences — arranged as a 'suite' of poems, short prose pieces and photographs — keeps us in the dark about numbers of wives and children, although we do catch sight of the budding scientist engaged in 'late-evening experiments' with his girl-friend. If *Supposed to Fly* is a family album, it is one full of double and triple exposures as Holub's thoughts veer off in all direc-tions. To be accurate, this is less a collection of reminiscences than a book prompted by personal experiences, the poetry and prose dipped in a bright solution of irony and imagery.

The centre of gravity — not to mention levity — of *Supposed to Fly* is Holub's birthplace, Plzeň (or Pilsen), a city famous for beer and Škodas (and, presumably, drunken drivers also). Holub's name means 'pigeon' and in this book — published in Czech in 1994 to mark the 700th anniversary of his native city — he becomes something of a homing pigeon. It was a swift rather than a pigeon which gobbled the fly at the end of Holub's most famous poem; and there is more than a dash of Jonathan Swift in Holub's pungent wit and his frequent adjustments of scale (the latter additionally influenced by a lifetime of gazing down micro-scopes).

Holub gets his facts straight by telling slant truths, by letting all kinds of parallels meet, as they do 'when we draw them by our own hand'. Yet, far from confessional though the reminiscences may be, they reveal more of the private Holub than any of his previous books: riding a toy scooter to meet his father coming from the office, winning a photograph of a local hero in a 'football chocolate competition', enduring Sunday outings with his parents on the 'privilege' train tickets allocated to railway families. Having so often in his poems provided a child's-eye view of the adult world, he proves himself equally skilled at providing adult perspectives on his childhood world.

Intellectually outstanding though he clearly is, Holub never flaunts his mental riches any more than he blinds us with science. Admittedly, he slips in the odd scientific word or phrase ('paradichlorbenzene', 'oxidative phosphorylisation'), but he does so in the same spirit in which a poet might invoke an obscure but expressive placename. It is his ready access to so many disparate areas of knowledge, and the playful intelligence and limber imagination to link them, which accounts for his improvised and ingenious use of multi-stranded metaphors: Pilseners are 'neutral as annelid worms in the land of Canaan'; rosaries have 'threaded pearl-like / molecules of antibodies to words'; a summer-house is 'the personal germ of the Tower of Babel, cut short in its evolution like the coccyx'.

Another of Holub's characteristics is his Audenesque ability to find satisfyingly epigrammatic formulas for things, defining and illuminating in one deft stroke. Spontaneous aphorisms, like the springs in Auden's limestone, 'spurt out everywhere with a chuckle' — in the prose, the poetry and even the captions to the highly dispensable black-and-white photographs intermingled with this least monochrome of texts: 'The essence of art is / that we're not much good at it'; 'every park is by definition infinite and mythical'; 'stupidity multiplies in a herd, whereas reason is divided by the number of heads, and reason thus diminishes with multitude'.

Supposed to Fly reprints some of Holub's early work, including 'Five Minutes after the Air Raid', 'A Dog in the Quarry' and 'How to Paint a Perfect Christmas', poems which have long entered the bloodstream of English-language readers. There are many new poems also; and, if not always as impressive as the meandering, mesmerizing prose (which includes fascinating accounts of wartime Pilsen), they nonetheless mark a return to his best form. On the whole, this volume is his most satisfying since the Penguin *Selected Poems* of 1967, a year when Holub recalls returning home from America to 'darkness as when a whale swallows not only the sun and the moon but also the enlightenment'.

Towards the end of the book, he muses that, had the 700th

Miroslav Holub

anniversary of Pilsen occurred a few years earlier, it would have
been celebrated with the 'installation of a red star on the tower of
St Bartholomew's church' and 'decorations for several Red Army
men who had served incognito in the US army'. But, thanks to
superlative timing, the city instead underwent a five-star face-lift
and it was Holub himself who was decorated, receiving a silver
medal as a 'Meritorious Native of Pilsen'. With the publication of
Supposed to Fly, a gold medal is surely called for.

Poetry Review (Autumn 1996)

3 *Intensive Care*, translated by David Young, Stuart Friebert, Dana
   Hábová and others
   Supposed to Fly, translated by Ewald Osers

The word 'intelligence', invoked by Seamus Heaney in an essay
on Miroslav Holub ('a poetry in which intelligence and irony
make their presence felt'), is shunned by the growing troupe of
egalitarian critics who write as if poets differed in kind rather
than quality. Intelligence complements rather than compromises
imagination — even if, as Wallace Stevens cautioned, its role in
poetry must remain a subordinate one. The surface simplicity
and clarity of many of Miroslav Holub's poems disguises their
depth. In his prose, on the other hand — and the 'prose interrup-
tions' in *Supposed to Fly* are a case in point — so nifty are the leaps
of association and so dexterous are the bounds of allusion, that
the accelerated intellectual velocity at which his playful writing
operates is unmistakable: 'In the church of the Redemptorists in
Chod Square a crib would appear before Christmas, admittedly
of plaster but richly painted, on a scale of 1:6 — assuming that
angels in real life measure 1.80 metres, adorned with conifer
branches and with an opulent background of the walls of
Jerusalem or Bethlehem.'
   Holub's poetry, as befits a scientist (he has worked as Chief
Research Immunologist at the Institute for Clinical and Experimental Medicine in Prague), is always experimental, determined
not to repeat what has already been achieved by himself or
others. Of course, as he remarks in 'Suffering' — a science poem
of almost religious intensity — 'Experiments succeed and experi-

333

ments fail, / Like everything else in this world, / in which the truth advances / like some splendid silver bulldozer / in the tumbling darkness'; and the 'Brief Reflection' and 'Syndrome' series of poems, as well as several of his puppet theatre poems and dramaticules, are less than uniformly successful.

I once heard Holub tell a group of schoolchildren that poetry is a virus transmitted by the poet. His own poetry is immediately infectious and it is appropriate that his field of scientific research should involve experiments with 'nude mice' which lack control of the immune system. *Looking for a Thymus in a Thymusless Mouse* is the title of one of his numerous scientific papers. Even rarer than a thymusless mouse is an egoless poet and Holub keeps himself out of his poems as much as possible. Not surprisingly, *Supposed to Fly* contains more self-revealing poems (such as 'Reading') than in the past; not even Holub can absent himself entirely from a book of reminiscences.

Intensive Care, offering 'selected and new poems', serves as an excellent introduction to the entire range of Holub's output; his first book in Czech was published in 1958, to be followed in less than ten years by the Penguin *Selected Poems* containing translations of poems like 'The Fly' (an immortal poem about mortality), 'Love' (evincing a scientific mind capable of taking an emotion apart and putting it together again) and 'Man Cursing the Sea' (where the man reconciles himself to the ocean by reducing it to his own proportions) which were to win him an immediate following in English.

Because his output is grouped more thematically than chronologically, readers of *Intensive Care* will be forced to engage in some research of their own to determine the order of composition of the poems. Later successes, by my reckoning, include 'Masterpiece', 'My Mother Learns Spanish' and 'Anencephaly' (subtitled 'newborn without a brain') — in which the poet gazes, awe-struck and appalled, in the direction of the 'tiny avant-garde miracle'. As the metaphors for freedom, in the post-Communist poems 'The Moth' and 'At Last', rise up like doves out of a magician's hat, we realize that Holub (the word, as previously noted, means pigeon in Czech) has been well named:

> *And then we opened the cages*
> *and ferrets ran out.*
> *Out of the skull ran brown and white*
> *spotted rats.*

Out of the heart flew
blood-soaked cuckoos . . .

Some of the poems found in *Supposed to Fly*, published in England, appear in different translations in the American-published *Intensive Care*. This may bewilder Holub himself who, echoing his own poem, 'Brief Reflection on Accuracy', once told an interviewer: 'I don't feel good about two or more translations of a single poem. It's like the man who always knew the exact time when he had just one watch, but from the moment he had two watches he never knew what time it was.' If *Supposed to Fly* keeps English time and *Intensive Care* is more American in tempo, it scarcely matters. Both books have a universal appeal and will be numbered among the works by which the times we live in will be remembered and known.

Harvard Review (Spring 1997)

Sylva Fischerová

The Tremor of Racehorses, translated by Jarmila and Ian Milner

Censorship was the principal obstacle which modern East European poets had to circumvent. In outwitting it, they evolved new forms that have become as distinctive as the sonnet or the haiku. The ironic fable was particularly favoured and seems destined to live on, like a human appendix, long after its evolutionary (or revolutionary) beginnings are forgotten. In fact, certain East European styles have already been adapted to Western use by poets as diverse as Seamus Heaney, Christopher Reid and Charles Simic.

Except for Ulster writing, Western poetry is seldom read with the alertness to political undercurrents that we bring to cold war East European poetry (which is assumed to be political unless proved otherwise). We have preferred eastern bloc poets to be not only political but dissident and have unravelled their metaphors accordingly. But political integrity is no guarantee of artistic quality and we must (as with, say, C H Sisson and Adrian Mitchell) look beyond the politics to the poetry.

Sylva Fischerová is a twentyseven-year-old poet, emerging into the limelight from the Czech literary underground. There is an abstruseness about her work which makes the unravelling of *her* metaphors rather tricky. Abstruseness in translated poetry is troubling because one is unsure whether its source lies in local cultural and linguistic nuances or is merely an instance of that universal phenomenon — obscurity masquerading as profundity. Perhaps a Czech reader nods knowingly on coming across references to 'the last fence of mechanism' or to 'tamed / ravens drinking coffee / and croaking KING KING'; or perhaps, like me, he or she must puzzle over them. The general outline of Fischerová's political verse is clear and references to 'occupation', 'foreign riders', 'cement phrases from the newspapers' and sounds of 'marching' easily draw attention to themselves. The problem with many of the poems is that they remain outlines, blurs. If Fischerová's intention was to mirror — in language and imagery — the absurdity of her times, she may have succeeded all too well. A sense of her people's indecisiveness and prevarication is more coherently communicated: 'We don't know what to do / or whether to wait, / for by waiting / we're doing something. / Or aren't we?'

Significantly, the best poems in *The Tremor of Racehorses* tend to be written in a lighter vein ('The Primer') or with greater intimacy ('From Hospital', 'The Death Mask', 'The Pripet Marshes', 'Girl with a Hasidic Candle'). These begin on a personal note ('I wake up at midnight'; 'I thought of you') and their privacies are far more powerful than her public protests. Sylva Fischerová is fortunate; the time for a more private Czech poetry has arrived and she has time and talent on her side as she nurtures her Muse on the rhythms of peace rather than those of marching boots:

> She needed so much to hear silence
> complete silence
> standing in the white fields
> and in the soundless air a deep voice
> slowly calling
> her name.

Poetry Review (Summer 1990)

Modern Hungarian Poetry

The Colonnade of Teeth, edited by George Gömöri and George Szirtes

Hungarian poetry has an image problem. In his foreword to *The Colonnade of Teeth,* an anthology of modern Hungarian poetry in English translation, Edwin Morgan acknowledges — and rebuts — the common assumption that it is uniformly afflicted with 'heaviness or overwrought solemnity'. A more expansive charge-sheet, drawn up by Morgan himself a few years ago, portrayed a poetry which (with 'obvious exceptions') 'has been thick-imaged, serious, often myth-haunted, sometimes rather ponderously "literary", seldom witty, humorous, ironical, satirical, or verbally outspoken'.

Although he is a poet with a light and ludic touch, Edwin Morgan has devoted considerable energy to Hungarian poetry, not least through his skilled translations of Sándor Weöres and Attila József — sufficient indication that he regards the 'obvious exceptions' as worthy of defence. These poets — along with others of the stature of János Pilinszky and Miklós Radnóti — are not only world-class writers but remind us that, even in an absurd century, the road to major poetry need not be paved with irony. In any event, a definite rise in the level of irony and levity in *The Colonnade of Teeth* is discernible towards the end of the book. While these later poets experienced less oppression than their elders, compromise and collusion remained dangers for the unwary and the unwise. In exchange for official publication and a state-sponsored livelihood, writers in the pseudo-liberal years of the Kádár regime were expected in effect to employ their own thought police and to privatize state censorship ('The sheepfold may have grown in size, but we are still inside the fence', György Konrád remarked in 1983).

The most impressive of the poets to have emerged in 'the post-1968 period', György Petri, chose the precarious freedom of *samizdat* rather than the 'velvet prison' of the state publishing system. A tone of defiant insolence characterizes certain Petri poems and, in Clive Wilmer's words, 'what he lost in worldly success he made up for in artistic independence and authenticity of social vision'. Petri is not by any means the sole representative of the Hungarian artist as national seismograph. The birth dates of the poets in *The Colonnade of Teeth* range from 1900 to 1954, a span broad enough to record at first-hand the shock waves of twentieth-century wars and the traumatic consequences of the 1956 anti-Communist revolution, as well as the happier tremors of 1989. The brief lives of Miklós Radnóti (aged only thirty-five when murdered in 1944 by soldiers accompanying his forced labour squad) and Attila József (who, mentally unbalanced and politically disillusioned, was thirty-two when he chose death under the wheels of a freight train in 1937) epitomize different aspects of the tragic times to which they bore reluctant but reliable witness. József's prayer, 'Come, freedom! Give birth to a new order', appeared to have been posthumously answered during the 1956 revolution when even Gyula Illyés's epoch-defining poem, 'A Sentence About Tyranny', could be exposed to public view before being pulverized by the Russian tanks and kept out of sight — though not out of mind — for the next three decades.

'A Sentence About Tyranny', stretched out over nearly fifty stanzas, passes sentence on tyranny, the way it soils everything, infiltrates everyone, leaves nothing untainted. The poem ends with tyranny pursuing its victims to the grave; but 150 pages further down this anthology's contents, Ottó Orbán seems close to the grave of tyranny itself as he reflects on the fallen statues of 'The Father of the People' ('His was the way, the truth and the life, but chiefly the death; / his world was as simple as Russian Roulette'). He concludes his poem with the long perspective of a Cavafy:

> *sooner or later the lie starts to rot in the firm-looking*
> *   binding,*
> *and chronically sneezing, time, the monumental mason,*
> *   carves on the tombstone*
> *of common memory: Xerxes; Capone; the once fearful*
> *   name of the emperor.*

It is to the consolations of private life that people turn during periods of oppression, so it is hardly surprising that *A Colonnade of Teeth* should contain intense love poems. László Nagy was a love poet married to a love poet, Margit Szécsi, the dedicatee of 'Love of the Scorching Wind' — a hectic onrush of images and emotions, described by George Gömöri as 'the passionate chronicle of love blossoming miraculously in the "wasteland" of the early 1950s'. Equally remarkable is Attila József's 'Ode', its imagery pitched somewhere between early Neruda ('the gentle / dales of your fertile / body') and a surrealist 'Song of Songs':

> *Your veins quiver like bushes,*
> *ceaselessly, bushes of roses.*
> *They move in the undying stream,*
> *for love to flourish in your face*
> *and your belly to bear its fruit.*

Although the omission of Imre Oravecz's obsessive love poetry is a loss to this otherwise generously comprehensive anthology, the book's more sensual moments include the torrid 'skin language' of László Marsall's '. . . Amores Te Salutant' and Zsuzsa Rakovszky's post-coital 'Noon'. György Petri's 'Gratitude' — which, incidentally, makes for striking comparison with John Berryman's 'Sonnet 71' — mixes public and private in a way which bypasses the injunction of Hungary's revolutionary poet, Sándor Petőfi: 'If you cannot do other than sing of your private sorrows and joys, you are not needed by the world, so put the sacred lyre aside.' One hundred and twenty years after Petőfi's death, Petri wakes beside his lover in a dingy room to the raucous clamour of some Communist celebration. Petri's contempt for 'people in collective idleness' (his adjective is a loaded one) is mitigated by his individual tenderness in a setting where every tacky detail is as telling as it is damning. A scabrous outsider, he throws an illuminating light on the mindset of someone born into Communism with a congenital independence of spirit.

The bleakness of Petri's poetry perfectly encapsulates a mood and a time. Even darker moods and harder times crystallize in the chilled landscapes of Ágnes Nemes Nagy and the mildewed vision of Attila József ('Everything is damp. Everything is heavy. / Mildew maps the countries / of misery on the walls.') Miklós Radnóti, the most heartbreaking poet in the anthology, writes, 'Of all beasts, Man is the basest! / Here, tiny babes are dashed against walls and, over there, / The church tower is a torch, the house an oven roasting / Its own people.' The idyllic and bucolic pedigree of the eclogue, employed in this and other Radnóti poems, counterpoints the savagery to which this form must now give voice. There are few joyful brushstrokes in Sándor Weöres's 'Mural of the Twentieth Century' either and the 'black nothing' is illuminated by the flames of burning human flesh. The spare presentation of unsparing images typifies the work of János Pilinszky, whose poems are almost speechless with horror:

> *I am alone. And by the time you come*
> *I shall be the only one still alive.*
> *Feathers in an empty roost.*
> *Stars instead of a sky.*

If the dominance of free verse often relieves translators of contemporary poetry from the burden of transporting metres and rhymes into another language, the Hungarian tradition does not let them off so lightly. Hugh Maxton, one of Ágnes Nemes Nagy's translators, points out that 'Hungarian rhymes very readily, rhyme is still widely practised, and the Hungarian attitude towards translation recommends fidelity to rhyme patterns and rhyme frequency'. The Hungarian-born editors of *The Colonnade of Teeth* have assembled a powerful anthology in which no challenges are shirked and no shortcuts taken. One has the illusion always of reading original poems in English; that this must ultimately remain an illusion is borne out by George Szirtes (a distinguished poet in English, as well as a translator from Hungarian) who has noted that 'English and Hungarian contain different experiences. Even the metres mean something else.' But whatever the rate of loss (as high as 80% is Szirtes's estimate in the case of Weöres), the most striking poems in the anthology — poems as diverse as Miklós Radnóti's 'À la Recherche . . .' and Ferenc Juhász's 'The Boy Changed into a Stag . . .' — represent a triumph of translation and a triumph of human tenacity in a century when Weöres's 'Angel of Disgust' so frequently hovered 'above the ruins'.

Times Literary Supplement (18 April 1997)

Vasko Popa

Collected Poems, translated by Anne Pennington and
Francis R Jones

Poberthol — Vasko Popa, Zbigniew Herbert and Miroslav Holub
— became an East European MacSpaunday soon after they first
appeared in Penguin's *Modern European Poets* series in the late
1960s. Always spoken of in one breath, they had more than a
publisher in common: they shared an outlook moulded by the
brutalities of the Second World War, a detached, concise style and
an aversion to socialist realism. Although Miroslav Holub was
the actual scientist among them, Francis R Jones (editor of this
enlarged edition of the *Collected Poems*) depicts Popa's detachment as 'scientific'; the same adjective would not be misapplied
to Zbigniew Herbert.

Over the years, however, Vasko Popa (who was born in
Yugoslavia in 1922 and died there in 1991) has become detached
in a different sense, lagging behind both Holub and Herbert in
readership and reputation. One reason for this may be the arcane
nature of certain poems, especially those of his middle period
which draw extensively on Serbian history, myth and fable.
'Much of this folk flavour is lost in the English translation, since
English literary usage is too far removed from our folk tradition
to mingle with it happily,' his principal translator, Anne
Pennington, concedes. If the poems of Popa's middle period
present his English readers with a kind of mid-book crisis, it is
not only because of their obscurity but also because of an under-
standable queasiness — in the light of recent history — engendered by poems obsessed with the battles, heroes and totems of
the Serbian past. Nonetheless, Popa's Serbian tapestry seems
sufficiently subtle and sophisticated in stitching and colouring to
resist crude diversion into a contemporary battle standard.

Francis R Jones, having acknowledged the difficulties which
Popa's 'complex symbolic universe' can present for readers in

English, takes practical steps through compendious notes to decode the symbols without demystifying them. Readers prepared to tramp behind Jones through Serbian shrines and battlefields will emerge rewarded even from middle-period Popa. 'St Sava's Spring', for instance — written, typically, in cyclical form — blends the sacred and the surreal into something as fresh as a restored fresco on a crumbling monastery wall:

> *Around his head fly bees*
> *And form a living halo*
>
> *In his red beard*
> *Strewn with lime flowers*
> *Thunder and lightning play hide-and-seek.*

From the beginning, Popa's poems were pared down to the barest essentials of language and imagery. Anyone familiar with his anthology of Serbo-Croatian folk material, *The Golden Apple* (1980), will be aware of his penchant for riddles and charms. The riddling 'List' — one of Popa's earliest and finest sequences — makes the world more vivid as well as more mysterious. His sequences can lack an explicit context while being full of implicit significance; some associate freely, others follow a definite line of enquiry. 'Far Within Us' teases out the redemptive properties of love, while the mesmerizing, mime-like cycle, 'Games', is as playful as its title intimates but extremely menacing also. 'The Nail', probably Popa's best-known poem, may be read as an anti-utopian parable:

> *Then the workmen say*
> *The pincers are no good*
> *They smash their jaws and break their arms*
> *And throw them out of the window*
>
> *After that someone else is the pincers*
> *Someone else the nail*
> *The rest are workmen.*

What makes these sequences so compelling is the sense that the ultimate riddle with which they are concerned is the riddle of life itself. The lightness, conciseness and niftiness of Popa's best work are extraordinary and he has exerted a notable influence on Ted

Hughes (whose enthusiastic introduction to Popa is reprinted in this volume); the 'Epilogue' to *Gaudete* and the sequence, 'Prometheus on his Crag', are just two examples of this transnational, trans-linguistic influence.

Popa's *Collected Poems* ends as it begins — on a high note. The final collections contain moving and direct poems, some of which draw on his first-hand experience of a wartime German concentration camp: 'We smile like conspirators / And whisper to each other / Be seeing you / We don't say when or where.' Dark though many of the poems in *Raw Flesh* (1975) may be, the mythic now coexists with the everyday and the 'bloodthirsty howl' of Popa's wolf poems (his American translator, Charles Simic, refers to the lame wolf as 'the old Serbian tribal god') is refreshingly exchanged for thirsty workers drinking their 'evening beer'. Beyond the pathos of Popa's more personal work comes a splendid closing sequence, 'The Little Box': 'her little length grows / Her little width her little emptiness'. The little box keeps on growing until it contains the whole world in miniature; the same could be said of this expanded *Collected Poems* and Popa's reputation may be expected to grow along with it.

Times Literary Supplement (8 August 1997)

Seeing Red: *The Poetry of Survival*

Good poetry and bad criticism are written on more than one level. In the case of good poems, the words will reverberate satisfyingly on several linguistic and emotional planes; with bad criticism, the sub-text is more likely to be personal — returning a favour or avenging a slight. When Daniel Weissbort's anthology, *The Poetry of Survival* (1991), was reviewed by Donald Davie in the *London Review of Books* (27 February 1992), he denounced it in the kind of language one associated with Communist commissars rather than distinguished English critics. Davie fumed and fulminated against a book containing the work of twenty-five poets from Yehuda Amichai to Natan Zach — translated by Michael Hamburger, Charles Simic, Stephen Mitchell and others — in terms which involved hurling intemperate insults: 'confidence-trick', 'con-job', 'careerists'.

Weissbort set out to gather the work of translatable poets who 'took the risk of addressing, of trying to express, what many regarded as inexpressible, incommunicable, whose early adult years coincided with the era of global conflict, and who were subsequently caught up in the Stalinist, Soviet-backed or -imported totalitarian revolutions . . .' Davie, however, accused Weissbort of nothing less than duping the public:

> *The ploy was at bottom a familiar one: since the British poetry they inherited in the Sixties required of them a longer apprenticeship than they could contemplate, and since readers wouldn't appreciate the fruits of that apprenticeship in any case, there was every reason for the careerists (who included A. Alvarez and Ted Hughes, along with Daniel Weissbort) to look for, and claim to find, a short cut. Philip Larkin's art, not to speak of Basil Bunting's or Norman MacCaig's, was too intricate for them to master. There must be a simpler way! And, brilliantly, they found that there was indeed one such*

> *simpler model on offer: in translation, poetry from the*
> *Soviet Union's satrapies in Europe. Moreover, this didn't*
> *just give them the streamlined and rudimentary poetics*
> *they were looking for: it also yielded up to them what*
> *looked like the moral high ground.*

At this point, Davie's sub-text becomes clear: that quality-crafted English verse (his own included, no doubt) has been almost put out of business by the flooding of the poetry market with cheap imports from East Europe. It would have been unsporting to have kicked the East European dissidents while they were gagged; now, as though himself a long-suffering Western dissident, Davie feels free to speak out. So determined is he to reach his sub-text quickly that he virtually forgets the actual text, failing to quote a single line from its 300 pages of poetry.

Many English poets of his generation enjoy considerable reputations, including Charles Tomlinson, Charles Causley, D J Enright, Patricia Beer, Vernon Scannell and Elizabeth Jennings, while Philip Larkin is infinitely better-known and more popular in England than any of the poets in Weissbort's anthology. There is a fair degree of self-pity and self-deception in Davie's inference that he and his less celebrated colleagues would be better off had those freeloading East European immigrants not been encouraged to dig in and grab the prime positions.

It was certainly not in search of an easy read or a lazy aesthetic that poetry enthusiasts found their way to translations of, say, Zbigniew Herbert (with his cultural and mythological erudition) or Paul Celan (a notoriously recondite poet). Besides, there was no shortage since the Sixties of English poets who could supply instant gratification, including the Liverpool Poets whom Larkin had no hesitation about anthologizing. What the best East European poets offered, on the other hand, was wisdom and vision, breadth and brio, originality and incisiveness of an order that far exceeded the achievements of most of Davie's generation, good though some of them are. Neal Acherson has commented that 'At its most extreme, the argument that a writer needs official hostility, the persecution of the censor, to develop is as absurd as the old recommendation of garrets for poets.' However, he conceded that the experience of life under dictatorships had produced a distinctive kind of literature:

*These writers know more about extremes of good and evil
than the mild, alienated Westerner, and they also know
infinitely more about the nature of compromise and irony,
of the importance and difficulty of simply behaving
decently and attempting to preserve an ethic of truth.*

Readers of the finest East European poets will immediately
recognize the kind of verse to which Acherson alludes. It has the
capacity to make parables out of anecdotes, to bypass the trivial
and the meretricious, to charge the commonplace with moral
significance, to interrogate reality with irony. But to speak of
English and East European poetry on an either/or basis is to fall
into Davie's trap. The reason I, and so many others of my generation, first read poets like Miroslav Holub, Vasko Popa and
Tadeusz Różewicz was purely for pleasure, for their lightly-borne
profundity. The height of their moral ground mattered less than
the depth of their insights.

The biographical notes in *The Poetry of Survival* point to a
vertiginous variety of personal experience that defies the notion
of the East European poet as some homogenous figure to be
classified under the *genus* 'dissident'. Those of us who admired
dissident poets before we knew they were dissident will have no
difficulty in continuing to savour their work now that the major
cause of such dissidence has been removed. There are excellent
poets in Weissbort's book who received State prizes ('First Class')
and Ministry of Culture prizes from Communist regimes, while
others suffered censorship and exile. There are poets who
endured prisoner-of-war camps and concentration camps and
others whose trials were relatively minor. While they all lived
through a common era, their survival, like their experience, was
individual and so, therefore, was their poetry. Weissbort speaks
of these poets as having insisted on 'individual values in the face
of collectivist pressures'. Yehuda Amichai offers a parable-poem
in prose on the subject:

> Once I sat on the steps by a gate at David's Tower, I placed
> my two heavy baskets at my side. A group of tourists was
> standing around their guide and for a moment I became
> their reference point. 'You see that man with the baskets?
> Just right of his head there's an arch from the Roman
> period. Just right of his head.' 'But he's moving, he's
> moving!' I said to myself: redemption will come only if

Dennis O'Driscoll

> *their guide tells them, 'You see that arch from the Roman*
> *period? It's not important: but next to it, left and down a*
> *bit, there sits a man who's bought fruit and vegetables for*
> *his family.'*

The opening poem of *The Poetry of Survival* is 'The Burning of the Books' and the opening writer — courageously because he was a Marxist, but appropriately because of the influence of his poetic genius — is Bertolt Brecht. Hatred of Hitler, rather than love of beauty, 'drives' him to his writing desk, according to 'Bad Time for Poetry'. Weissbort's book does not include Brecht's great poem, 'To Those Born Later', in which he asks 'What kind of times are they, when / A talk about trees is almost a crime / Because it implies silence about so many horrors'. But Paul Celan's defiant riposte is represented:

> *A leaf, treeless*
> *for Bertolt Brecht:*
>
> *What times are these*
> *when a conversation*
> *is almost a crime*
> *because it includes*
> *so much made explicit?*

Celan's poems are of the kind that communicate before they are understood or, rather, which communicate without ever being fully understood. They negotiate the obstacle course of language warily, avoiding the obvious and well-known routes. His is the voice of an oracle, enigmatic and vatic, drawing on incongruities ('Autumn eats its leaf out of my hand'; 'Pray, Lord, pray to us'; 'Black milk of daybreak') and addressing voids ('Blessed art thou, No One').

The grim biography of Paul Celan, whose parents died in Nazi custody, is in contrast with the privileged cosmopolitanism of Hans Magnus Enzensberger, another German-language poet. Enzensberger's early poems seem somewhat dated — rather like collages incorporating yellowing slivers of newspaper from *circa* 1960. Far superior are the extracts from his long poem, 'The Sinking of the Titanic', a bill of lading of the cargo (so much of it wasteful and absurd) borne by the Good Ship Earth:

. . . do I watch the whole human race over there,
  haphazardly
hanging on to some run-down cruise liner, fit for the
  scrapyard
and headed for self-destruction?

The Poetry of Survival includes a number of less-familiar poets (Artur Miedzyrzecki, Slavko Mihalić, Tymoteusz Karpowicz) — Jerzy Ficowski in particular is a discovery. Among the well-known names, Czeslaw Milosz (a poet greatly respected by Donald Davie) is under-represented. If Milosz is a classical poet through his 'attachment to old Polish verse', Zbigniew Herbert is a classicist in the Cavafy-like ease with which he can enter and evoke a resonant past:

I've decided to return to the emperor's court
once more I shall see if it's possible to live there
I could stay here in this remote province
under the full sweet leaves of the sycamore
and the gentle rule of sickly nepotists.

Herbert's 'Pan Cogito on Virtue' lifts irony to a visionary pitch, while the lapidary 'Pebble' is a salute to an object that is absolutely true to its own nature. His poem, 'Five Men', in a further challenge to Brecht, posits the view that, when speaking of ordinary things ('of how vodka is best / after wine you get a headache / of girls / of fruit / of life'), we are not avoiding the big issues but actually highlighting them. We are celebrating what is under threat. Like the conversation of the five doomed men in that poem, a great deal that is urgent and significant is happening beneath the unadorned surface of Herbert's verse.

While some of the Herbert translations are by Milosz, it is disappointing that none of Milosz's consummate translations of Tadeusz Różewicz are included. Różewicz plain poems scramble for meaning in a world stripped of innocence and hope. 'In the Midst of Life' and 'Warning' are primers of human respect, struggling to reach ethical and linguistic foundations that might support post-Holocaust life. They are the equivalent of a stroke patient's efforts to walk again:

man must be loved
I learnt by night by day

Dennis O'Driscoll

> *what must one love*
> *I would reply man.*

János Pilinszky, who spent time in prisoner-of-war camps, emerges very strongly from the anthology. Having written that '. . . the war has ended and the gates of the concentration camps are shut, but I believe that it is precisely this final hush which signifies the supreme reality in our midst today', it is not surprising that his poems should be so profoundly dark. Out of that darkness crawl harnessed men dragging a cart, a starved man 'gulping raw cattle-turnip', a prisoner who 'forgot to cry out / before he collapsed'.

The best poets in *The Poetry of Survival* find something eternal in the historical. Ireland's tradition of political dissent through metaphors of silken kine and radiant maidens shares something of the spirit of the East European allegory. In Britain, Donald Davie's colleagues, such as Ted Hughes, Norman MacCaig, Paul Hyland, Christopher Reid, D J Enright and Michael Hofmann, have all to some extent been influenced by contributors to *The Poetry of Survival* and one assumes that post-war East European poetry will be as unignorable a part of the literary history of the reign of Elizabeth II as certain French and Italian poets are for students of Elizabeth I's. Introducing his *New Oxford Book of Sixteenth-Century Verse*, Emrys Jones remarked that 'the decisive moment came, as contemporaries clearly recognized, with Sidney and Spenser in the late Seventies and early Eighties. What they did was at once to raise literary standards and establish new models both through the force of their own example and by putting English writers in touch with the most recent developments in Italy and France'. Reviewing *The Poetry of Survival*, Michael Hofmann wondered 'whether the possession of one language, and an innocent unbroken relationship to it, will ever again be able to make great poetry'. The political cataclysms which gave rise to *The Poetry of Survival* have passed; and the anthology is to an extent the curtain call of a singularly gifted generation.

Finally, returning to Donald Davie, it must be readily granted that much of his voluminous output of criticism is powerful and persuasive and that he is as justified in his scepticism about translation standards as he is in his enthusiasm for Milosz. But neither scepticism nor enthusiasm can excuse extremism of the ill-tempered kind he displays when faced with Weissbort's important anthology. In another outburst of arrogance, Davie promised to 'return to haunt whatever Britain may emerge in the 21st century'. All of this biliousness suggests that Davie ought to have worried less about his reputation and let posterity take care of itself. A few poets receive, during their lifetime, the recognition they deserve; rather more receive the recognition they do not deserve; and most receive no recognition, deserved or undeserved. As for haunting, our East Europeans will do that for us.

Graph (Winter 1992/Spring 1993)

EPILOGUE

EPILOGUE

Losers, Weepers: *Christian Boltanski's* 'Lost Property'

After you have seen the visiting art exhibition, there is nothing to hold on to except the memory and a few inadequate catalogue reproductions. Like the circus, it has moved elsewhere, leaving an impression on the mind like the ring of mud in a field where clowns tumbled and horses pranced.

My only tangible evidence of an installation called 'Lost Property' by Christian Boltanski, which I viewed in the summer of 1994, is a postcard I bought at the Douglas Hyde Gallery in Dublin where the work was displayed. The postcard photograph looks down from balcony level to a dimly-lit gallery floor which is densely, randomly, raggedly layered with objects of every kind. One might have chanced on the aftermath of a bomb or tornado; or the raw material — the infill — of an ecologist's nightmare.

To be left with a mere postcard, like a snapshot from a holiday. A holiday which has been sifted by the subconscious, edited by the imagination, until only the essentials — sunshine and stillness — remain in the memory. Shaded cobble. Honeyed stone.

I first came across Christian Boltanski's work at the 1977 Rosc exhibition in Dublin. His exhibit consisted of twenty-four photographs on wood, all of them prompted by childhood memories. It is lost property to me. I can locate it nowhere in my mind. I spent many hours visiting that Rosc and would not have neglected

Boltanski's contribution. But, it seems, I never felt inclined to reclaim this mental baggage; it was eventually disposed of after the memory's equivalent of the period beyond which a bus company will no longer assume responsibility for goods forgotten by passengers. The mind operates according to its own by-laws.

❧

It is only when I rediscover the 1977 Rosc catalogue among other mislaid items, property lost in my own house, that I realize the Douglas Hyde exhibition was not my first encounter with Boltanski's art. Had I been asked which work in that 1977 exhibition was concerned with childhood, I would instantly have answered 'A desk from "The Dead Class"', Tadeusz Kantor's unforgettable installation of the boy in military-style uniform at his school bench. When (like a class reunion) I caught up with that boy again twenty years later, in the art museum at Lódz — still at his wooden desk, learning the cruel history lessons of that tragic city — he seemed more dead, more doomed, more necessary, more moving than ever.

❧

Christian Boltanski (born in Paris, 1944) has cited Tadeusz Kantor (born near Cracow, 1915) as his favourite artist. Both have produced work in which childhood is evoked with vividness and portentousness. Despite his Christian name, Boltanski is the son of a Jewish father, a doctor who took refuge in a cellar during the Second World War. His mother was Catholic. In one interview, he said: 'I know nothing about Jewish culture and religion; I've almost never been to a synagogue. If I had to choose a religion, I would choose the Christian religion. I think it would suit me better because it's more universal than Judaism.' Yet, to another interviewer, he starkly declared: 'I was born a Jewish boy, and to be Jewish is something always very strange.' Boltanski is one of those artists who should be seen, not heard. Tender and touching though his work can be, some of his pronouncements — the assertion, for instance, that the fall of the Berlin Wall represents the death of hope — seem best ignored.

❧

When his art does the speaking, Boltanski subverts political ideologies through his rejection of the general, his embrace of the personal. His 1992 photographic work, 'Children of North Westminster Community School', shows rows of pupils — many of Asian background — who will soon outgrow their portraits. They are the dead classes of the future. Meanwhile, we are invited to inspect each uniformed child in turn, wondering what life has in store for him or her, as we might have looked at what purports to be the artist himself in his 'Ten Photographic Portraits of Christian Boltanski 1946-1964'. In the latter, the location is always the same; but the boy in the pictures and the vegetation in the background mature, change and will eventually be cut down. The blue strips of fluorescent light, placed on the foreheads of smiling children in Boltanski's 1994 installation entitled 'Jewish School of Grosse Hamburgerstrasse in Berlin in 1938', resemble not so much neon haloes or caste marks as the paint daubs with which foresters brand trees destined for the axe. These children have parents, brothers and sisters, friends, homes, hopes, ambitions, longings and belongings. They want to be something when they grow up. They want to grow up.

The New Yorker of 12 February 1996 published a Magnum photograph showing 'A memorial to the seventy-two people who died on a spring evening last year when a Serb shell hit a crowded square in Tuzla's old city'. The memorial in question seems to consist of little more than a crudely-framed, glass-covered, street-corner shrine containing passport-size photographs of the victims. Around the corner, in the restored calm, an anoraked man is walking to work — the dawn shift — past peeling alley-ways and shut, stale cafes. A thin braid of rainwater glistens in the gutter. The eye returns to the memorial, its photographs as ordinary as those reproduced on the cards with which we remember our own dead. As ordinary as the unsuspecting infant faces in Serge Klarsfeld's searing photographic monument to French children of the Holocaust. As ordinary as the faces of 'The Dead Swiss', snipped from the death notices in Swiss newspapers and exhibited by Christian Boltanski on towering panels and tottering metal boxes.

Dennis O'Driscoll

In choosing to commemorate the neutral Swiss, Boltanski turns his attention to anonymous domestic death and away from the genocidal horrors of recent history: 'Before, I did pieces with dead Jews, but "dead" and "Jew" go too well together, it is too obvious. There is nothing more normal than the Swiss. There is no reason for them to die, so they are more terrifying in a way. They are us.'

If the camera steals the soul, it restores it once its subject has died. The people depicted in the anniversary notices in newspapers — awkward in their Sunday-best or grinning from a holiday snapshot (the pint glass they were fondling having been tactfully cropped) — had no cause to appear in print until they died. Their death notice was the first public notice they received. Privately, they go on being loved and remembered; and every year someone cares enough to write out an 'In Memoriam' text in block capitals, to choose a suitable rhyme ('Today, tomorrow, / Our whole lives through, / We will always love / And remember you'), to sacrifice the newspaper fee from a widow's pension or the grocery money . . . By making art from memorial photo-graphs, Boltanski responds not only to the human need for ritual — our hunger to enact our grief and signal to the dead that they are cherished and cared for — but he also suggests that, unless each individual death is mourned individually, unless each person is valued on a personal scale, then humans blur into mere ciphers and the mentality which sanctions mass killings will prevail. In the post-Auschwitz world, Boltanski's art of primal memory and loss, based on the most humble materials, may be the least feigning. Even the names and dates of 'The Dead Swiss' (CLAVIEN Robert, 1913-1991, SCHULZ Liane, 1952-1991, LATTION Caroline, 1897-1991, and so on) — his altar list of the dead — become, in their context, a found poetry more minimal than even Beckett would have dared. Boltanski is the kind of artist who would draw inspiration from a telephone directory.

I retrieve the memorial cards for my own parents. In Boltanski's words, 'When the photograph is taken, the subject is not thinking that this will be his last photo. He doesn't know that he will be remembered by this image.' So it happened with my father. He was gardening on a lark filled, sweet william scented Saturday when I surprised him with the camera. Does his smile mask some inconsolable undertow, or is it his grim death a few years later (when he is fifty-seven) that retrospectively shadows his face? The photograph selected for my mother's memorial card was taken at one of those lavish feasts — rich in cholesterol and conviviality — at which siblings, cousins and in-laws noisily converged. It was St Stephen's Day. She had been allowed home from hospital to spend a last Christmas with her family. Whatever euphemistic formula her doctor had presented her with, as a Christmas gift, her unremitting pain must have delivered its own plain-speaking message. Her death from cancer, aged fifty, would occur in less than two months, on St Valentine's Day. The house near Thurles where we lived was becoming lost property to her. Starting her final journey to St Vincent's Hospital in Dublin, she looked back at the town. Shoppers and farmers. A car giving way to a Vale Oil truck. The primary schools in which, at that moment, her youngest son and daughter were seated at wooden desks just like those of 'The Dead Class'. She wept.

The lost property list from the Tramway in Glasgow which accompanied Christian Boltanski's exhibition there (preceding his Dublin show): soft toy (hairy dog), rucksack (plastic Batman), bag (velvet sequinned), hat (red beret), hockey stick ('Club' markings), shoulder bag (Royal Bank of Scotland), football shirt ('S.M.F.C'), skirt (short, black and white piping), postcards (six colour Isle of Isla), book (*Practical Chess Endings*), slipper (Dennis the Menace and Gnasher), apron (McDonald's), hairband (velvet thick green), umbrella (burgundy, telescopic) . . . The detritus strewn on the Douglas Hyde floor was like the teeming fulfilment of this list. Each of the items not only missing but missed; little losses that are like trial runs for the big ones. Advertisements I used to read in *The Tipperary Star*: Strayed. Lost. Will the person who by mistake or otherwise. Great sentimental value. Substantial reward.

As children, we were forever losing things. Gloves had to be tethered to our duffel coats, money to be safety-pinned into our pockets. But everything we hoard as adults, that we try to protect with comprehensive insurance policies and monitored house alarms and fireproof safes, will become lost property eventually too. It will die on us or we will die on it. Boltanski loves lists, loves Georges Perec's 'I Remember' text. Looking at the items scattered around the Douglas Hyde Gallery, I remembered the mounds of musty clothes sold in the open-air market in Thurles. I remembered the rags left spiked on whitethorn bushes by tinkers whose rainbow-coloured barrel-top caravans had jingled further down the long acre. I thought of a yearned-for package that gets lost in the post. I thought of landing at a destination to discover that the airport carousel has failed to dispense your luggage. I thought of the empty suitcases of Auschwitz, piled up like abandoned hopes. I thought of the grey plastic bag, scrawled *O'Driscoll, J. decd.* with smudgy felt-tip, in which my father's worldly goods were returned to me by the hospital. I thought of the pyre I made of my dead mother's clothes. The heat. The smoke. The ash.

Graph (Autumn/Winter 1998)
London Magazine (April/May 2000)